THE PRISON
AND THE HOME

THE PRISON AND THE HOME

A STUDY OF THE RELATIONSHIP BETWEEN DOMESTICITY AND PENALITY

by
Ann Aungles

The Institute of Criminology Monograph Series, No 5

Sydney
1994

Institute of Criminology Monograph Series

Series editor: John Braithwaite
                    Professor, Research School of Social Sciences
                    The Australian National University

Series co-ordinator: Elizabeth Schwaiger

Published by

The Institute of Criminology
Sydney University Law School
173–175 Phillip Street
Sydney NSW 2000
Australia
Ph: (02) 225 9239; Fax: (02) 221 5635

ISBN 0 86758 903 5

Typeset by the Institute of Criminology Publications Unit, Sydney University Law School.

Printed and bound by Robert Burton Printers, 63 Carlingford Street, Sefton NSW 2162.

Acknowledgements

I would first like to thank Julie Stubbs of the Institute of Criminology for her editorial support in the preparation of this monograph, Mark Findlay for his practical advice about the shape of the chapters and Liz Schwaiger for her expert and meticulous editing.

I was particularly lucky in the help given to me by the women working in the families of prisoners support group just outside Pentonville Prison in London, the Relaties van Gedetineerden centre in Amsterdam and in the family support centre at the Long Bay complex of prisons in Sydney. Sheila Scott was especially helpful in enabling me to make the initial contacts with the visitors to men imprisoned in New South Wales gaols. In addition Sue Smith and Joan James in England, Norman Bishop and Birgitta Gorannson in Goteborg, Birgit Altahr-Cederberg in Slottgatan and Fay Nash and Heather Deane in New South Wales were generous in the help they gave me in gaining access to unpublished material. My thanks too to Bill Steineke and to Laila Edholm for the translations of the Dutch and the Swedish material.

My colleagues, at the University of Wollongong, have listened patiently to the several rewritings of various chapters. Rebecca Albury has been a listener, commentator and source of fresh ideas. David Shaw and Nicole Rankin have provide invaluable technical help. I am grateful, too, to Sheila Shaver and Anne Edwards for their editing advice and critical comments.

The pleasant task remains of acknowledging the help of Andrew Jakubowicz and Stan Aungles, for the academic criticism and the moral support they both provided for the duration of the research.

Finally and most importantly I owe a special debt to the thirty-seven women and the men who gave their time and experience when they were already so over-committed in their work of caring for men imprisoned in New South Wales gaols. Their caring and tolerance was priceless. It is to Cheryl Matthews that I am particularly indebted. Her generosity in sharing her extensive knowledge, and her warmth and skill, have been central features of this research.

AA
January 1994

Contents

CONTENTS

1

INTRODUCTION

THE HOME AND THE PRISON

The central objective of this study is to investigate the relationship between the domestic sphere "the home", and the legal-penal sphere "the prison" as two institutional orders whose intersection constructs specific modes of social control. It is argued that the social control of corporate capitalist society occurs in its most condensed form in this social space: between "the home" and "the prison". This interpretation of social control is set within a context of the historically changing intersections between the penal and the domestic spheres with the four major forms of this relationship comprising:

1   "the family in the prison",
2   "the family outside of the prison" with the clear segregation of the two spheres of social control,
3   "the family outside but entering the prison" as the boundaries between the two spheres become more permeable in the reformative discourses of imprisonment,
4   "the prison in the home" as the domestic sphere becomes the site of penal control.

These patterns of association between the home and the prison are interpreted in this study not only as historical orderings but as moments in penality with the current interdependence between the two sites of social control constructed as a "layering" of those four sets of relationships. The social space between home and prison then currently comprises a complex, contradictory maze of policies and practices.

The corollary of this argument is that it is the people in the population "families of prisoners" who bear the greatest burdens of this contradiction.

PEOPLE WITH FAMILY OBLIGATIONS TO PRISONERS

This account includes an examination of the experiences of a specific group of people, mainly women, who are drawn into the legal-penal system through their family obligations to men who have been sentenced to imprisonment.

There have been several studies of "families of prisoners".[1] However, most of these texts or articles are prefaced with the claim that "families of prisoners" are an under-researched group. This paradox highlights one of the central concerns of this study — the contradiction between the significance yet the invisibility of this population. Because the people who have a family obligation to care for prisoners have to do the work of maintaining family contact with their imprisoned sons or partners in the "impossible middle ground" between the home and the prison, one particularly important aspect of this experience is the social invisibility of the forms of exploitation and domination that they experience. Their experiences are constructed in the social space that occupies the intersection between that symbolically most rational realm — the legal-penal sphere, and that symbolically most emotional or *a*rational realm — the family. The mainstream discourses of penality resolve the contra-dictions that develop from this intersection between such incompatible areas of social life by masking the significance of domesticity within the legal-penal domain. These processes of marginalisation add to the economic, psychological and political costs of belonging to the population "families of prisoners".

THEORETICAL ISSUES

The investigation of the relationship between these two contradictory sites brings together questions posed in three areas of investigation of social life — feminist criminology, feminist materialist analyses of "caring work" and the radical critique of penality.

The feminist challenge to criminology has focused attention on the invisibility of women in the literature on crime and on the ways in which women's experiences as prisoners, as professionals in the legal-penal sphere, or as victims of crime have been distorted in the mainstream male literature on crime and punishment. This approach then develops into a broader critique focusing on the masculinity of crime and criminology as well as the masking of the gendered nature of deviance and control.[2] However, this concern with the gendered nature of both crime and criminology does not address the associated but separate structural issue — the significance of the family in the discourses and practices of crime and punishment.

Yeatman[3] argues that questions about the interdependence between the domestic and the public spheres, the false assumption of the self-sustaining nature of public life and the consequent masking of the significance of domesticity, comprise the main feminist challenge to social analysis. Yeatman's point here is that feminist theory fails to remedy the invisibility of the domestic domain because its focus remains on the dualistic concern with gendered personalities. This argument is pertinent to the analysis of penality where the feminist focus has been on the differential treatment of women and men either as prisoners, as victims of crime or as crime professionals. The aim of this monograph is to redirect that focus, to make problematic the mutual interdependence of "the home" and "the prison", and in doing this to make problematic too the experiences of those people who are becoming increasingly important in the policies and practices of the legal-penal sphere, the people in the population "families of prisoners".

The feminist materialist analyses of the relationship between the state, the economy and the family provide significant conceptual tools for this approach. This group of scholars have questioned the taken for granted assumptions about the naturalness of family life. In several studies of public policies and public institutions these researchers have demonstrated that "the family" is socially constructed in the discourses of public life. This family discourse is used to establish who should care, when and for how long for children, for the aged and for other adult dependents. At the core of this research is the analysis of the complexity of the way that the term "care" is employed in policy discourses to ensure but at the same time to devalue the carers' provision of unpaid services.

As this study of the work of caring for imprisoned men draws extensively on the feminist materialist analysis of the social construction of "caring work", the several aspects of that analysis of the term "care" are:

1   caring is *contradictory*. It has both material and emotional aspects. It is about both labouring and loving. Materially, caring ensures life and physical wellbeing for the individual being cared for and in this provision it also creates an infrastructure of support that relieves the state of major economic responsibilities. This provision of labour then creates the contradiction of caring: "for children and men economic dependency is the cost of being cared for, for women economic dependency is the cost of caring";[4]

2   family relationships within liberal capitalism have been constructed as dependent relationships to ensure the continued provision of care. Caring then emerges out of particular positions of powerlessness as well as furthering the conditions of poverty and dependency that reinforce that powerlessness;[5]

3   caring labour is *invisible or marginal*. The conflation of the terms "caring about" (its emotional element) and "caring for" (its material aspect) serves to mask the significant material aspects of the labours of loving in the discourses of social policy makers. A further process of masking centres around the conflations involved in the use of the term "community". As Finch and Groves[6] argue, there is a double equation in the public policy discourses where "in practice community care equals care by the family, and in practice care by the family equals care by women;[7]

4   caring work is *ideologically* constructed. Public sphere discourses construct "caring" as a "natural" form of labour.[8] The conflation of the terms "natural" and "normal" then imposes further burdens on the carer. The image of caring as unproblematic means that the actual difficulties of the reversal of gender and generational roles makes the work a difficult social process. Furthermore the

premise of "normality" makes the carers feel guilty about the extra problems they are facing;

5   caring labour is *undefined*. The unbounded nature of caring work stems from the immediate nature of the dependency of the young, the ill or the dying as well as from the way that the work comes to be defined in the external political economic climate. This unspecifiable aspect of domestic labour then places major demands on the carer who has to make cohesive what is essentially fragmentary. Moreover this uncertainty imposes extra economic costs on the carer in undermining the possibility for long term career planning;[9]

6   "caring" labour is *socially isolating*. It is labour that "tightens the bonds that tie the carer to the lonely and narrow sphere of home".[10] This privatised nature of the work compounds the risk of *political quietism* about the extent of the exploitation of the labour of caring. The basic step towards redefining inequality and exploitation as a public problem rather than a private difficulty, the recognition of the commonality of the exploitation, is made more difficult when the physical space and the emotional discourses within which the work of caring operates is the confined particularistic life of the family ...

7   ... nevertheless, "caring is also *politically ambiguous*. The commitment to care, the force of concern based on family relations of loving, can lead too to political action to defend the interests of family dependants;[11]

8   the skills of caring work are complex and extensive and are acquired through practice. Nevertheless caring as tacit knowledge is undervalued or even denied in public discourses employing the Cartesian separation of emotion and intellect.

This focus on the "nexus between care and dependence" has become a useful analytic tool in the current feminist materialist investigations of the relationship between the family and the state. From being a taken-for-granted aspect of everyday life, "caring" has become a term that has generated major theoretical and empirical studies of the embeddedness of masculinism in the policies and practices of the welfare state, and in both orthodox and radical academic accounts of public policy.

Hilary Graham[12] has shown how the separation of the two worlds of home and work, and its attendant separation of "breadwinners" and "dependants", has led to the two components of caring — love and labour — being dismantled and reconstructed in the separate disciplinary domains of economics, psychology and social policy. Nevertheless, she argues, it is the conflation of those two terms that creates the conditions of caring work. It is the tensions between labouring and loving, between the material and the emotional aspects of care, that create the conditions of the domestic work of caring for dependants.

One of the major concerns of this study is that there is a further conflation that needs to be made problematic. The distinction made by Graham between the emotional and the material aspects of caring work masks the third dimension of the relations of power in the constitution of domestic life. The material aspect of care needs to be further demarcated into its economic and political components. In this distinction caring is about labouring, loving *and controlling*. The constitution of the carer and of caring work is founded on the economic, cultural *and political* structures of the social relations of capitalism.

This distinction has particular relevance to questions about the caring labour of people with family obligations to prisoners. The radical critique of punishment and control characterises penality as the sphere in which the relations of the wider world are played out in a particularly condensed form.[13] From this perspective then "the prison" is the site in which the gendered nature of social life is most masked, the social space in which the individual is defined most specifically in terms of rationality rather than affectivity. The prisoner is a legally constituted individual specifically redefined in the narrowest terms of rational individualism in the legal sphere of the courts and then sentenced to a life in a social space that specifically excludes the domestic. It is at the same time the social space that is the most masculine but where that masculinity is most specifically denied. The totality of social existence is lived in a sphere in which rationality is most clearly differentiated from affectivity in the language of liberal pluralism or, in the reconceptualisation taken from feminist materialism, where state power is most openly divested of its domestic components of loving.

This concept that the penal sphere condenses the social relations of the broader society has two aspects. Firstly, that punishment is the symbolic and the concrete representation of the relations of force and authority of the broader society. Secondly, that punishment does not merely echo the cultural and structural processes of the wider society. The form that punishment takes becomes a text which shapes the meaning of the image of the social state.[14] The policies and practices of punishment project an image that partially constitutes societal relations of power and authority.

These aspects of our knowledge of the relations of power within the penal sphere, although they change to transmit and transmute the different forms of authority relations of the successive forms of capitalism, are nevertheless often so fundamental that they remain "unvoiced". Radical critiques of penality then concern the study of both the manifest and the unvoiced rules of authority as they occur in the sphere of punishment and control.

Garland draws on the Foucaultian analysis to emphasise that penality forms subjectivities. Modern punishment is geared to "making up people" with the prison as a key site in the modern programme of individualisation. What this approach sidesteps, however, is the significance of the domestic sphere. In liberal capitalism the family is constituted as the central site of the reproductin of personality. Garland further argues that penality constructs the "normal" relations of social life. The feminist challenge then to this radical critique of penality is to pose the questions from Yeatman and from feminist materialism about the relationship between the state, the family and the economy but to focus those questions on the relationship between the public and the domestic in the specific site of punishment and control — to examine the interdependence between "the prison" and "the home".

This examination of the significance of the family in the condensed sphere of penality concerns questions about the shifting boundaries between public, civil and domestic life, the permeability of these boundaries, the way that the official visions of the separation of the different realms mask the experiences of the people caught up in the actual contradictions and porosities of legal penal systems. These broad questions lead to the specific propositions of this monograph:

MAJOR PROPOSITIONS

1   that domesticity is incorporated into the system of punishment and control in Australia through the nexus between caring and dependence that characterises the relationship between the state and the family in other areas of public policy;

2   that this incorporation involves a mutual interdependence yet a mutual incompatibility between the penal and the domestic spheres;

3   that this contradiction is resolved by the marginalisation or the formal invisibility of this incorporation of the family into the punishment system;

4   that these two processes — the incorporation of the family into the penal realm, and the marginalisation of that process, place major burdens on those individual people who have a family obligation to prisoners anad to prisoners' children;

5   that it is women rather than men who are most at risk of taking on the double burden of marginalised care for prisoners;

6   that the domestic work of caring that is incorporated into the system of punishment in this invisible intersection of the domestic and legal-penal realms is three-dimensional, having economic, emotional and political components: the domestic work of caring for people drawn into the penal realm is about labouring, loving and controlling;

7   that the nexus between caring and dependency that is character-istic of the social relations of public, private and domestic life in the wider society takes on a particularly condensed form in the realm of penality;

8   that the incorporation of "the family" into the realm of penality through this nexus of caring and dependency takes different forms in different periods of the development of the political economy;

9   that the basic contradictions between philosophies, practices and policies between the public, private and domestic spheres are made more complex and contradictory with the shifts in philosophies, policies and practices in the realms both of "the family" and of "punishment". These shifts reflect and modify the changing social relations of the wider society. Moreover, these changes are not necessarily sequential but, rather, are layered onto previous sets of policies and practices.

OUTLINE OF CHAPTERS TWO TO NINE

Chapter two reviews the critical literature on the social construction of the two spheres — "the home" and "the prison". This historical account charts the changes as the construction of two sites of morality, the state and the family, within the context of the development of liberal capitalism and its successive forms, and on the constitution of those two sites as inherently unequal spheres of social relations. These changes are described as being associated with the development of the concept of the freedom of the individual. Individual legal subjectivity was a consequence of the necessity to establish and guarantee the conditions of exchange at the earliest stage of capitalist economic development, the securing of the rights of individual bourgeoisie to be free of political or kinship commitments in the process of accumulating capital for the business of exchange or trade. Law as an autonomous social institution guaranteeing this economic freedom of exchange was the development of a specific form of government, the development of the capitalist state. The rational legal power of the state in liberalism, according to these accounts, depended upon its operating upon the impersonal, universalistic principles which were dereived from the common morality of the society. In the powerful discourses of liberalism and protestantism, domestic morality based on love and altruism came to be defined as ranking lower than the morality of public life. In the legal-penal sphere, punishment systems became increasingly clearly segregated from family life in the classic era of liberal capitalism.

The segregation of the family from public life raises an especially significant issue of naming. In the descriptions of the historical development of the prison and the home in Chapter two the term "familial political economy" is used in preference to the term "political economy". Although this is a clumsier term, it is preferred here as it is the relationship between the domestic, the public and the private spheres, or between the family, the polity and the economy, which is the central focus of this study.

Chapter three reviews the specific literatures, policies and practices that constitute the population "families of prisoners" and, in a critique of those literatures, outlines the four major ways in which the family is incorporated into the penal sphere. In this chapter the three questions posed by Yeatman become even more significant. The social processes of the mutual dependence of domestic and public life yet the marginalisation of that relationship are played out in a particularly intense form in the social space between the home and the prison. Yeatman's questions are used to catalogue and to bring to the surface the many ways in which the people who do the work of maintaining family contact with imprisoned men are caught up in the contradictions of the penal sphere. They become defined as potential criminal associates of the men inside but also as the source of the prisoners' eventual reformation. At the same time the practices of punishment and control based on the specificity of punishment emphasise the individuality of the prisoner and marginalise the effects of imprisonment on the family "doing time" outside the prison gates.

This theme is continued in chapter four which specifically examines the way that the social sciences have been incorprated into the realm of punishment either as techno-reformist techniques of control or as a basis for criticism of the hidden punishment of families of prisoners. Yeatman has also argued that the social sciences, even though they seemingly have access to the appropriate tools for the analysis of domestic life, have failed to contest the taken for grantedness of "the family".[15] In the dominant discourses of classical sociology "the family" is conflated with "the community". The feminist materialist analyses of various policies and practices within the Welfare State have shown how this social scientific trick of fusing domesticity into the abstract sociality of the term "the community" then becomes part of the political practice of the exploitation of the people providing the family work of caring for the aged and the invalid. In this chapter the questions raised within this perspective are used to evaluate the current expansion of programmes of community corrections. Special attention is focused on the most intensive form of this conflation of "community" and "family" in the penal sphere — the introduction of home inprisonment programmes based on electronic surveillance.

In chapters five to eight there is a move from the general analysis of penal policies to an account of the experiences of 38 people who provided the work of caring for imprisoned men[16] in New South Wales in the late 1980s. Chapter five details the material and emotional aspects of the work of maintaining family contact with imprisoned men. The false assumption of the self-sustaining nature of the penal realm is examined through an account of the penal discourses, policies and practices of the New South Wales Corrective Services Department in the 1970s and 1980s and through the experiences of the people who were partners of parents of men in prison. This chapter includes the description of the specific problems of caring work that occur from the contradictions of the way that the population "families of prisoners" is constituted in the discourses of punishment and control.

Chapter six details the complex contradictions of the way in which power, morality and rationality come to be constructed in the work of caring for the children of the prisoners. The parenthood of men in prison is a particularly condensed example of the invisibility of domesticity in the penal realm. Few penal systems provide sufficient resources to enable imprisoned fathers to experience their individuality as men who are also fathers. In this chapter the argument is made that the tensions created by the official invisibility of prisoners' fatherhood are borne by the extra demands made on the emotional and material work of the outside carers of those imprisoned men and their children.

Chapter seven outlines the several ways in which people with sons or partners in prison are caught up, through their commitment to the labour of loving, in the processes of control and punishment. The work of caring for prisoners involves punishment for the people doing the work of caring but that caring work is also incorporated, in a variety of ways, into the punishment and control of the prisoner. The experiences of the 38 carers in New South Wales are interspersed in chapters six and seven with the material from two other studies of partners of imprisoned men, Sue Smith's[17] discussion of her own experiences in the English penal system and Judith Jones' unpublished study[18] of the experiences of wives of men imprisoned in Victoria in the early 1980s. The caring/controlling work of each of these groups of people is experienced within the contradictions of the reformative and segregative moments of imprisonment. This chapter details the tensions between the contradictory moments of penality that make the work of caring/controlling for imprisoned men a particularly stressful form of emotional labour. The issue of why it is women who are controlled to be the controllers and the particular resonance of this question for people in the population "families of prisoners" is addressed in this chapter.

The issue of agency that the emphasis upon control raises is addressed in chapters five to seven through the accounts of the carers' concerns for the rights of their imprisoned partners and sons and the carers' challenges to prison authorities in defence of these rights.

This aspect of caring is a feature of the work outlined in chapter eight, which describes the labour of caring when the site of control is shifted to the domestic sphere. There are a range of "community" based forms of punishment and control and the insights from the feminist materialist critique of the double equation between "community" and "family" and between "family" and women's unpaid labour are drawn on in this overview of the accounts of people whose partners or sons are serving some form of post-imprisonment community based sentence. The condensed form of the contradiction between caring and controlling when home is the site of punishment is outlined together with an examination of current shifts in penal policy and practice which are likely to intensify the exploitation of the unpaid work of caring of families of prisoners. New South Wales penal policies of the 1970s and 1980s are especially interesting as the state introduced a form of home based imprisonment prior to the spread of intensive surveillance based on electric monitoring that was introduced in the United States in the mid 1980s. Foucault has called the modern penal system a "carceral continuum" with punishment, discipline and surveillance being extended over a range of sites. Garland adapts this image to his model of modern penality as a continuum from segregation to correction to normalising moments of penality. The real life experiences of the people who share the tensions of family based controls are rarely recorded. The argument is made here that the academic invisibility of this particularly intense intersection of "the home" and "the prison" is further evidence supporting Yeatman's contention about the marginalisation of the significance of domesticity.

Chapter nine is an epilogue in which the major propositions provide a perspective for reviewing the changes in penality and domesticity in the period between 1988 when the data was collected and the current time of writing, 1992. This chapter includes a review of the impact of the penal policies introduced in the New Right, Liberal state administration in New South Wales, and the "family policies" introduced by the Labour administration through the Department of Social Security at the Federal level of government.

In the conclusion (chapter ten) the argument is made that the exploitation and punishment of people in the population "families of prisoners" is likely to be a continuing and increasing aspect of social life in the contemporary structure of the productive and reproductive relations of corporate consumer capitalism. The contradictions of social life in this form of familial political economy are increasing. Consequently one of the major characteristics of the penal sphere is that it is expanding: in an increasingly criminogenic society, more people are becoming caught up in ever widening processes of punishment and control. The legal-penal sphere, "the prison" then is likely to become even more dependent upon the domestic sphere, "the home". The chapter and the book then ends with the argument that the study of the intersection between "the home" and "the prison" should become an increasingly significant focus for two critical schools of social analysis — the feminist analysis of the relationship between the family, the state and the economy and of critical studies of the sphere of punishment and control.

NOTES

1   Fifty-seven texts that address the issue of "the prisoner's family" are listed separately in the bibliography. This literature is reviewed in chapter four.

2   Among others: Heidensohn, F, *Women and Crime* (1985); Carlen, P, *Women's Imprisonment* 1983; Hatty, S, *Women in the Prison System* (1984); Naffine, N, *Female Crime: the Construction of Women in Criminology* (1987).

3   Yeatman, A, "Women, Domestic Life and Sociology" in Pateman, C and Grosz, E (eds), *Feminist Challenges: Social and Political Theory* (1986).

4   Graham, H, "Providers, Negotiators and Mediators: Women as the Hidden Carers" ch 2 in Lewin, E and Oleson, V (eds), *Women, Health and Healing* (1985) at 24.

5   Graham, H, "Caring: a Labour of Love" ch 1 in Finch, J and Groves, D, *A Labour of Love: Women, Work and Caring* (1983) at 25–30.

6   Finch and Groves, ibid.

7   Id at 494.

8   Ungerson, C, *Policy is Personal: Sex, Gender and Informal Care* (1987) at 116–117.

9   Above n5 at 26; Watson, E and Mears, E, *Women in the Middle: caregivers with a double burden of care* (1988) at 138.

10 Above n5 at 26.

11 Rowbotham, S, *Hidden from History* (1973) at 24–28; Stone, J, "Brazen Hussies and God's Police" (1982) 89/1 *Hecate*; Allen, M, Hutchinson, M and MacKinnon, A, *Fresh Evidence, New Witnesses: Finding Women's History* (1989) at 218–220.

12 Above n5.

13 Garland, D, "Towards a Sociological Analysis of Penality", ch1 in Garland, D and Young, P (eds) *The Power to Punish* (1983) at 21.

14 Garland, D, *Punishment and Modern Society: a Study in Social Theory* (1991) at 265–266.

15 Above n3 at 159–165.

16 This study focuses on the work of caring for male prisoners because men comprise the majority of prison populations. The work of maintaining contact with prisoners then is predominantly the work of people, usually women, who visit men in gaol. Moreover prison is a different experience for women prisoners. Women in gaol face problems which Dobash et al describe as immense (Dobash et al, *The Imprisonment of Women* (1986) at 213). The experiences of people who do the work of maintaining family contact with women in prison needs to be considered as a separate and even more complex issue.

17 Smith, S, "Neglect as Control: Prisoners' Wives", paper presented to the 14th Annual Conference of the European Group for the Study of Deviance and Social Control, September 1986; Smith, S, "House Arrest: the Pain of Prisoners' Wives" (1986) 21 *New Soc* at 11–13.

18 Jones, J, "Prisoners and their Families", unpublished PhD thesis, Melbourne: Monash University Department of Anthropology and Sociology, 1983.

2

THE SOCIAL CONSTRUCTION OF DOMESTICITY AND PENALITY

INTRODUCTION

The impact of liberal capitalism on the construction of "the home" and of "the prison" as separate institutions, is considered in this chapter through a review of literature on family life and on the constitution of penality.

The development of liberal capitalism, through the mercantilist, industrial laissez faire, corporate welfare, and advanced corporate forms of familial political economy, has been underpinned by the "new" or "modern" configuration of power, morality and rationality in productive and reproductive life. However, the central contradictions and tensions that develop within each phase of capitalism result in different forms of intersection between the sphere of production and the two major sites of reproduction, the home and the prison.

In the literature on both domesticity and penality there are a number of different perspectives through which changes have been plotted. Liberal studies of the development of both domesticity and penality generally chart these changes as a relatively smooth process of improvement from a pre-modern social system characterised by the diffuse interrelationship of family, economy and polity to the "modern" form of society in which there is an increased specialisation of the major spheres and an increased rationalisation in the ways in which each sphere, and subsystems within each sphere, function. The progressive character of this increased specialisation of systems is manifested in the greater efficiency and humanity of modern life and of the modern form of penality.[1] Although the family becomes the repository of the values that are in polar opposition to the specialised rationality of the wider world, its segregation contributes to the smooth functioning of that world. Thus its development is also part of this progressive transition from pre-modern to modern life.[2]

Critical studies of the history of social control in relation to penality and domesticity contest both the progressivism and the unilinearism of the liberal approaches. The critical studies of penality can broadly be summarised as approaches theoretically concerned with the link between relations of production and relations of reproduction. However within this broad framework there are several alternative approaches:[3]

1   analyses that connect specific forms of punishment directly to the state of the labour market;[4]

2   studies that focus on the congruence between disciplinary styles of management in the economic and penal realms in which the punishment system is seen as generating, reinforcing or complementing the reproduction of social relations of production through the development of parallel although not necessarily replicate forms of surveillance and control;[5]

3   a focus on the extension of areas of surveillance and control to realms of social life other than those operating in the purely penal sphere. The works of Foucault on madness, health, and sexuality are central studies in this approach.[6] There are however several other major investigations of this more diffuse way in which control is manifested.[7]

In these two latter sets of writings it is the increasing *rationalisation* of social life as it is mediated through the sphere of punishment and control that is the central characteristic of the analysis of the development of the penal realm.[8]

A materialist feminist account of social control, however, should insist on the interdependence between the "rational" and the "arational" spheres of social life. It is through the interdependence of penality and domesticity that changes in either sphere should be charted. The review of the two literatures in this chapter then outlines the parallel constructions of the two spheres of social control as the two major sites of the reproduction of social relations of capitalism through its several phases. The underlying themes of the chapter are:

1   that with the increasing rationalisation of social control in the public sphere there has been a parallel process of the constitution of the domestic sphere in terms of its arationality;

2   that these two processes are interdependent but mutually incompatible; that this contradiction is resolved by the masking of the significance of the interdependence between the two realms of social life.

PERIODISATION

The changes were a gradual and uneven process, uneven across class and uneven in terms of the specific society and nation state in which the developments occurred, and in New South Wales did not absolutely replicate the forms taken by the reconfiguration in England. The constitution of social life in the colony was contingent on the very particular relationship between a penal colony and its "mother" country which then had a major effect upon the internal relationship between penality and domestic life in the new colony, particularly in the period up to the mid nineteenth century. These factors make the categorisation of specific eras in the separate but interdependent constitutions of the penal and the domestic realms an indeterminate process. It is not possible to draw absolute time boundaries between each phase. However this chapter will follow the historical model suggested by Garland's[9] discussion of the variety of models of penal change and of Tilly and Scott's[10] description of the shifts in the forms of the family economies of labouring families.

FROM FEUDALISM TO LIBERAL CAPITALISM:
THE PERIOD OF MERCANTILISM (16th – 18th Century)

The three hundred or so year period prior to industrialisation was the establishment phase of the social relations of primitive accumulation. Within this era a new form of domesticity emerged within the households of the bourgeoisie.

The distinct dichotomies between domestic and public sphere values have been common to most societies.[11] However, the most complete division of the two spheres occurred amongst the families of the upper and middle classes of the new bourgeois liberal society of Northern Europe and North America during those 200 years.[12]

There were two cultural arenas in which these changes were articulated — the political philosophy of liberalism and the religious edicts of Protestantism. Although the Protestant restructuring of power and morality within the family (and through the family to wider society) was initially formulated as the transfer of spiritual power from the church to the father with the "proper wife" acting as an obedient and junior spiritual partner, this spiritual partnership was not long lasting. Roberta Hamilton argues that with the separation of the domestic and the economic aspects of the family, "the marriage was left with only one spiritual partner, the woman. That was no longer a partnership."[13]

The lives of the majority of labouring classes were still experienced in the family labour economies of the rural economy. In the urban centres the family life of craftsmen and skilled labourers reflected the family economies of the agricultural labourers with men and women both involved in productive work but largely within the home and with much of the domestic labour of reproduction the shared responsibility of a number of members of the family.

In these family labour economies, although there was a division of labour within the household, this was based on the *form* of productive activity rather than a distinction between productive and non-productive work. Married women were able to combine their domestic and productive labour, "the organisation of production in this period permitted them to integrate their activity, to merge wage work, production for household consumption, and reproduction."[14]

Nevertheless, with the enclosure movements from the 16th century onwards there was a new and increasingly numerous class — the labourers dispossessed by the appropriation of land in the shift towards an increasingly capitalist form of agricultural production.[15] It was this class that was most precariously linked to the economy. The "free" labourers whose labour was only periodically in demand were in the most precarious economic situation in this period. The increase in home based manufacturing restructured the dependent relationship for labouring families. In the putting out system a wife became an economic asset rather than a liability. Men were likely to remarry quickly on the death of a spouse. However, men were reluctant to marry older women or would marry widows only with the proviso that children be relinquished to the care of the parish.[16] Women without access even to a husband's occasional earnings were in the most precarious position of all. The only exchange of labour they were able to make was in the most marginal sectors of the economy, in petty trading that needed little or no capital, or in the below subsistence wages of seamstress, lacemaking or cleaning.

The families of labourers whose labour was defined as unskilled and who lacked even the meagre capital necessary for any business other than the forms of petty trading that merged into begging, became the focus of the new concern with social control and the new definitions of behaviour as criminal from the 16th to the late 18th century.[17]

There were three distinguishing characteristics of penality in the 16th and early 17th century societies of Northern Europe: (1) the intersection of household and state in the mangement of penal control; (2) a central concern with control of the dispossessed labouring classes; and (3) an ambivalence about the nature of punishment and control.

Firstly, in the intersection of household and state, the principle of familial economic responsibility was a significant aspect of penality in this period of the establishment of capital labour relations. The state worked with and through the hierarchical structures of power in allowing husbands, fathers, employers and masters to have wives, children, apprentices and servants confined.[18] As Hamilton indicates the paradox of the centrality of familism and individualism was bound up with penal policies and practices from the very beginning of liberal capitalism.[19] Women's wages were only half those of men so, without access to income other than their waged labour, marriage became a liability for many men. It was for this reason that the Poor Laws included men's economic responsibility for their families. Men were forced to marry pregnant women by the parish constables, sometimes being brought to the church in chains.[20] Women and men could also be punished by being whipped through the streets for failure to support their children.[21]

Second, the control of class relations through punishment in this period was effected on both the workers at the margins of the political economy, the wandering poor, and on labourers who were more embedded in the rigid structures of social life. The control of the floating population of dispossessed male, female and child labourers, however, was not so easily managed through this system of patriarchal community surveillance. The universalistic character of the labour market in class relations acted as a kind of decentralised panopticon, ensuring that labourers were aware of the lowest limits at which they could bargain.[22]

These impoverished but "free" labourers in the cities also constituted a double sided political threat to the liberal bourgeoisie. They constituted a continual potential for direct political action.[23] Moreover, less directly but equally political, was the threat posed by the potential for individual criminal behaviour, especially those offences against property. The shift towards systematic punishment and control directed towards the behaviour of the offender rather than symbolic punishment effected on the body of the offender was therefore an uneven process of change. Throughout the seventeenth and eighteenth centuries the number of crimes, especially of crimes involving property, for which the punishment was death, increased to 200.[24]

Children and women as well as men were at risk of receiving these extreme penalties. The familial political economic relations of this era of ascending capitalism meant that young single women from the labouring class were particularly at risk of the sentence of capital punishment. In the urban forms of the family labour economy in this period between feudal and industrial capitalism, single children were likely to leave home to balance resources and for single women this primarily meant entering an alternative patriarchal household, but as domestic servants rather than as daughters.[25]

This aspect of the familial–political–economic configuration of mercantilism had dreadful consequences for those at the bottom of the gender class power structure when in 1713 theft from a dwelling house, a law mainly directed at domestic servants, became a capital offence.[26] Women who did not hang for petty thefts from households nevertheless were at risk of gross forms of physical punishment. Dobash et al cite the case of a Dutch woman in the seventeenth century who, on separate occasions, was mock-hung eight times, branded five times, and had both her ears cut off by the hangman for stealing minor articles of clothing.[27]

The seventeenth century in England was a period of intense conflict securing the basic tenets of liberalism that reshaped the configuration of the familial-political economy. In the liberal form of commodity production both products and people appear in the process of exchange as abstractions, as objects embodying universalistic legal-rational character-istics free of particularistic traditional-political or emotional-familial components. That is, in the free market men have rights of possession over the property/commodity they exchange including their own labour as a commodity. Picciotto points out that this most basic aspect of the fetishisation of social relations under liberal capitalism is this separation of economy from polity as "the capitalist state emerged to establish and guaranteed exchange as the mediation of production and consumption."[28] Thus the law comes to be defined as the abstract, universalist protector of the individual rights of the free property owner and the universalism of the law is the sole guarantor of the legal subject as property owner. Attacks then on the property of the legal subject are attacks on the very personhood of the legal subject and on the basic principles of liberalism from which the political economy is constituted. With this universalist signification of property, theft even of minor items attacks the central principle upon which the free capitalist relations of exchange are based, the right of property ownership, and the legal subjectivity of the property owner. The security of liberalism was continuously defended against "the enemy within" in the urban and rural households and properties of the bourgeoisie where the civil war against King Charles in the 1640s was refought against housemaids, chambermaids, footmen and labourer-poachers over the next two hundred or so years.

Domestic servants posed another kind of threat, particularly towards the end of the eighteenth century, with the increasing sanctification of the role of the bourgeois mother. The separation of labour and loving in bourgeois households with the woman as loving wife and mother meant that the servants increasingly became the domestic labourers in — but not of — the household, threatening both the legal subjectivity of the father by the theft of his handkerchiefs, clothing or wine[29] and the potential legal subjectivity of his children by their corrupting influences on the purity and health of this significantly new generation of ruling class children, the inheritors of property defined within the social relations of protestant liberal capitalism.[30] This redefinition of domestic labour impinged on the lives of a significant number of working class women.

Daughters were more likely than sons to be young single children who were sent out of the household to work to balance the family's resources in the labouring and small scale craft households.[31] As those young women usually went to work as live-in domestic servants, they thus became subject to the potentially criminalising familial-political economy of the master servant relationship within the household of their employer.

The third distinguishing characteristic of penality was the ambivalence about the nature of the punishment for the new crimes of vagrancy and begging that had been created by the dispossessions. In the same decade in England — the 1570s — two Acts were passed in an attempt to control the dispossessed labourers: the Act enforcing the whipping and imprisonment or death for vagabonds and the Act to set up the building of the Houses of Correction, the Bridewells.[32] From 1576 to 1590 twenty-one were created through a range of English counties.[33] Control of dispossessed labour was thus attempted through forms of penalty described by Foucault as significantly separate discourses. Punishment in the Houses of Correction was directed to the reform of labour through systematic control, by incarceration, and aimed at reforming the soul through the body. Alternatively there were the public physical punishments of the body. The latter punishment was a major threat to the dispossessed. Well over a hundred thousand were hanged during the Tudor regime.[34] Labouring class women were subject to the risk of suffering gross theatrical forms of torture if they threatened the "natural" order of domination. One serving girl in eighteenth century France, had her hand severed and burned, her chest, then head, cleaved, and, after she was killed by strangulation, her head was severed and exhibited on a pole twenty feet high.[35]

Nevertheless, in parallel with this strand of "pre-modern" punishment were the attempts to impose new forms of control. From Thomas Cromwell and Coornhert in the 16th century to Cesare Beccaria and Bentham in the late 18th century, emphasis was upon the rationality or regularisation of punishment.[36] The state became increasingly significant both as a regulator of relations between employer and labour with the introduction of laws on wage limits, periods of employment, and as the regulator of property relations in the creation of a range of new forms of crime and of penal laws.[37] Idleness, vagrancy, destitution, failure to support dependents, appropriation of minor items of property, all became punishable by incarceration in the new houses of correction which had specific and systematic rules governing the behaviour of inmates. The major aim was to make use of the labour of inmates rather than lose it through the irrational and wasteful symbolic punishment of execution and torture.[38]

In 1617 transportation was introduced as a major form of punishment. The liberal concern with both thriftiness and rationality was neatly manifested in a punishment which secured, at one stroke, symbolic punishment to the offender, removal of her or his politically threatening and socially corrupting influence, useful employment of their labour, defence of the realm in a period of fierce foreign competition, and a significant supplement to the golden triangle of trade of labour, primary products and manufactured goods between Europe, Africa and the Americas.[39]

There was however a discrepancy between the rationality of this form of punishment within the penal realm and the irrationality of penal methods in the sphere of surveillance. The ascending classes' concern about individual crimes and political control outside of their households with the increasing disparities between poverty and wealth in the cities posed a problem for the liberals. Freedom from the restrictive practices of traditional community life and from the polity was basic to the principle of rational entrepreneurship. This meant that in the relatively disorganised life of the cities in the early 18th century, the state was comparatively weak with little organisational control over the policing of the behaviour of threatening classes, in contrast to the established hierarchies of control over labour in the fifteenth and sixteenth centuries and prior to increasing control through the social sphere and direct government policing in the 19th century. The solution to this policing vacuum in the city in the seventeenth century was to enforce state control of criminality through thief-takers, agents who were on both sides of the law.[40] In the country, policing agents were more directly associated with the propertied classes as overseers, gamekeepers and local constables.[41] There was an inherent instability of this form of surveillance and control through mercenary intermediaries.[42] In the case of the thief takers the mercenary aspects of their role reinforced the symbolism of greed and amorality they were employed to control. In the case of overseers and gamekeepers their relatively explicit connection with the agricultural capitalists undermined the principle of universalism of law.[43] In neither case was there either an administrative basis for widespread control nor a moral basis for the symbolic superiority of the ruling class. Similarly the sentences which focused on the ghastly corporal or capital punishment of both men and women offenders were increasingly irrelevant to the exponential growth in the problem of control, brought about by the social upheaval triggered by the transfer of relations of production from an agricultural village based society to an industrial urban setting. Over the final third of the eighteenth century, the increasing levels of capital investment in production meant that there was pressure on the state to deliver a more stable civil population and labour force with a set of moral dispositions centering on quietism and orderliness.[44] The earlier penal philosophies, which emphasised the reform of the offender and promised a form of control that would bring about an internalisation of the mores of a respectable citizen and a "good worker", increasingly dominated the discourses of control towards the end of the eighteenth century.

LAISSEZ FAIRE AND INDUSTRIAL CAPITALISM: (1780s – 1880s)

It was the individuality of the bourgeois property owner that was established through the reconstruction of the penal and domestic spheres in the period representing the early establishment of capitalism. With the almost universal[45] extension of the commoditisation of labour in this next era of industrial capitalism it was the individualisation of the labouring classes that took a central place in the reconstitution of penality and domesticity.[46] The objectification of labour was parallelled by an object-ification of both crime and the criminal.[47] The restructuring of the domestic sphere in working class life was accomplished as a result of several factors. Tilly and Scott identify the emergence of the family wage economy as the dominant response of women and men in the labouring class, in this stage of capitalism.[48] The enclosure movement created waged workers long before industrialisation, but it was with industrialisation that control within factories emerged, physically separating productive labour from repro- ductive work in the domestic sphere, with the father and children leaving the home to go out to work and earning wages based upon their individual labour.

. The differentiation between the family and the individual wage was, for several reasons, still not clearly marked. Firstly, the father acted as a subcontractor, employing and supervising in the factory his own daughters and sons. Patriarchal control was incorporated into the earliest forms of factory control up until the 1820s.[49] Secondly, the wages of the children, especially those of the daughters, were based on the convention that they were dependent upon their fathers: their wage was based on their ascribed status within the family. Thirdly, the income of both fathers and children were defined as belonging to the common fund of the family.

The division of labour between men and married women in this new family structure — the working class family — that emerged in industrial capitalism, was more clearly differentiated than in the family labour economies of the putting out system in the pre-industrial era of manufacturing. In most families for much of the time, married women remained within the domestic sphere, taking on the role of manager of the household's resources, and the bearing and rearing of children.[50] However, in emergencies this segregation of husband and wife into productive and domestic workers was not so distinct. In economic crises wives of manual workers did supplement the family's income, although their major defining role was as housewife and mother. For many families of manual workers in insecure employment, economic emergencies were a frequent aspect of their lives.[51] However, the new wage earning capacities of children meant that children were increasingly likely to stay at home until they were married, thus increasing the importance of the domestic role of married women.[52]

The dual role of performing both domestic and productive labour was made more difficult for married women in an economy in which, increasingly, waged labour was located in the public sphere. The tension was reduced in part, for many, by bringing their productive work into the domestic sphere; for example by doing outwork, taking in lodgers, or taking washing and ironing.[53] However this resolution created a further major tension for women who were attempting to combine productive and domestic labour. This dual obligation undermined their bargaining power and the income that married women earned in this stage was likely to be much less than that of their daughters in factory work and significantly lower than the male wage.

The reconstitution of working class domestic life however was not only a consequence of the response of working class wives and husbands. The early 18th century intermediaries of the state, the thief-takers, who mediated the state control of the labouring class were replaced in the next era of the change in systems of control of reproduction of relations of labour by two new policing agents. Firstly, there was an increased formalisation of policing with the development of a state controlled police force and secondly there was an extension of informal policing with the development of a new sphere of civil life, the social, that linked the two dominant sites of social control of the individual: the state and the family.

In this era discourse about how these controls were to be effected revolved around four problems in relation to the control of labour: how to provide for the indigent without discouraging the poor from engaging in waged labour, how to develop a sense of orderliness and regularity, the work ethic suitable for disciplined labour in the factory and how to develop a parallel ethic of political quietism in the face of the explicit political economic forms of exploitation and appropriation in this period and, fourthly, how to create a social climate in which the familial-political economic relations of work become acceptable not only to the workers but in the reflections of the ruling class to themselves as members of a civil society. Various sectors of the ruling class joined the debates, and intervened in the domestic and the penal sectors of social life in this era of vigorous discourses of control. There were two major consequences of the impact of a full scale market economy on the reconfiguration of power, morality and rationality: the increasing rationalisation of social control with both policing and responsibility for imprisonment being shifted from the private to the public sphere,[54] and secondly, what Donzelot has characterised as the development of the social.[55] The contradiction between the centrality of the principle of laissez faire and concern with the reconstitution of the individual personality of the labouring classes and control over the political volatility of the working class as a whole was resolved by this development of a sphere between the public and private realms. This was the era in which religious, scientific, philanthropic and political economic elites felt entitled through their superior moral and intellectual qualities, legitimated by the protestant liberal ethic relating prosperity and property ownership to spiritual grace and political entitlement, to decide on the resolution of the great problems (from the perspective of the bourgeoisie) of control of labour and social life: how to make workers work, how to make them work methodically and how to resolve the imposition of the coercive techniques necessary to effect these controls with the principle of laissez faire. The great problems for the majority, the labourers alienated from the means of production, were how to survive in a familial-political economy which, at the same time, proscribed all means of material survival other than waged work yet provided that waged work only unevenly and periodically.

Melossi and Foucault, although from different perspectives, identify the key issue in all these grand discourses as the problem of the establishment of order.[56] It is important to emphasise that the disorder derived not only from the rate of change, although the social disorder inherent in a society that shifted from a predominantly agricultural family labour economy to an urban industrial family waged economy in just fifty years was immense, but also in the privileging of the sphere of public life in which order and "disorder" were most delicately balanced. The problem with a purely narrow economistic interpretation of this process is that the central principle upon which the familial-political economy rested in this era was the principle of the primacy of the natural realm of economic relations, that the hidden hand of the market should be free of the "unnatural" intervention of the polity. However the social costs to labour of the free play of market relations were associated with social and political conditions that called for strong political intervention. The key contradiction was in the need to enforce order in the period of class relations that both engendered disorder but was the "most allergic to rioting than any other economic system"[57] whilst maintaining the principle of a minimal regulatory role of the polity.

State intervention in penality and domesticity coincided with the interests of the rise of two specific powerful lobby groups. Authority in the social sphere was legitimated in the first half of this period by philanthropic religious rationality. Over the nineteenth century this seemingly oxymoronic basis of the configuration of power, morality and rationality was resolved as intervention in the social sphere was increasingly legitimated by the appeal to authority based on scientific rationality. In the first half of this period it was the work of the religious and philanthropic groups whose authority to influence the reconstitution of domesticity and penality rested on their assumption of their own moral superiority as members of the property owning and employing classes sanctioned by the principles of Protestantism and classical liberal theory. It was women in particular whose intervention was influential in the social sphere in this era. The same morality which excluded them from the public life of the political and economic spheres in the pre-industrial period of the 18th century was the basis on which their influence in the sphere, between the public and the private realms — the social — was legitimated. Their moral position in their own family life was the platform from which they launched vigorous campaigns to effect changes amongst the working classes in both domestic and penal spheres.

It was notable that one particular group of ruling class women was especially vigorous in the moral campaigning of the social sphere. The women in the Evangelical sects, especially those in the Quaker movement, engaged in reform movements in the spheres of education, health, slavery, poverty, and penality.[58]

Morality in the home became associated with a specific form of denial of self-interest that distinguished domestic morality from moral authority in the public sphere of the polity: moral authority within the home was sanctioned because it was limited to the home. Women's moral authority stemmed from the particular nature of domestic relationships and their deliberate denial of an interest in universal forms of authority. However, the moral boundaries between universalist and particularist authority in Quakerism were not so rigid. This increased standing of women in Quakerism, in relation to the authority of women in the dominant forms of Protestantism, was perhaps the reason why this particular sect of ruling class women became the bridgehead for the establishment of this extension of ruling class women's morality into the social sphere.

The Evangelical revival placed morality and the affections above intellect and opened its doors socially to women. Religious sensibility and social pity stood much higher in the minds of women like Hannah More than abstract, frequently arid theology. It was through Evangelism that the conditions for the reproduction of productive life were specifically tied to a set of discourses connecting penality and domesticity — as alternative points of a continuum of proscribed to prescribed relationships — that was to become the major aspect of the relations of reproduction in the following century.

There were three main themes in the various discourses of penal transformation. The conservative reformers emphasised the punitive, degrading aspects of prison, the utilitarianism of Bentham focused on the impersonal systematisation of useful labour and the Evangelical movement which was concerned with regularising prison life through the personal relations between reformer, prisoner parents and their children.[59] Systematic reform was the principal theme uniting the three discourses — degradation, economic productivity and personal rehabilitation — but the dominance of one or other of these three discourses varied with the immediate contingencies of the wider familial-political economy. Melossi points out that, in the period 1840 to 1865, the emphasis of penality shifted towards the punitive or terrorising corner of the triangle of punishment, reform, and economic productivity within the prison.[60] In this period the principle of "less eligibility" dominated the constitution of penality in laissez-faire capitalism. The move away from reform to repression with the establishment of laissez-faire industrialism, Melossi and Pavarini argue, was a response to the explicitly class nature of the extreme growth in pauperism and criminality with the accompanying extremely low standard of living and the immense industrial reserve army. The contradiction between the bourgeoisie and aristocracy that had been a primary influence on the development of the penal legal realm in the period of primitive accumulation became secondary to the contradiction between bourgeoisie and proletariat in this era of established industrial capitalism.

This shift to repression over reform was further complicated by the need to absorb the prisoners previously sent to the penal colonies, with the accompanying move away from transportation in the mid-century.[61]

In this period of the "great confinement" approximately 1,000 per 100,000 people, or in absolute terms nearly 200,000 people, were imprisoned in Britain in one year. In England and Wales a quarter of these were women but in Scotland, in 1849, nearly 40 per cent were women.[62] Both men and women were subject to terrorising forms of imprisonment. However in the separate women's prisons introduced in this period the emphasis was more on the combination of humiliation and degradation combined with useful labour. Terror was important but as the punishment of last resort, allotted to the most recalcitrant prisoners in a vertically organised classificatory system that placed prisoners on a scale from incorrigibility to reformability.[63]

The internal and inter-sphere contradictions in the constitution of domesticity and penality were echoed in very specific forms in New South

Wales throughout the nineteenth century. However, the laissez-faire period of capitalist development was preceded by an era closer to the domestic economic and penal relations of the mercantile capitalism that was just coming to an end in Northern Europe.

EARLY SETTLEMENT OF NEW SOUTH WALES
(1788 – mid 19th Century)

In the period 1780s to the mid-nineteenth century there were three key differences in the familial political economies of Northern Europe and New South Wales. Social life in New South Wales was characterised by :

1   the explicit nature of state control of economic conditions of exchange of labour and capital;
2   the reproduction of labour based primarily in the penal sphere in the system of transportation rather than in the domestic sphere;
3   the imbalance of the sexes, and the agricultural rather than the industrial basis of the political economy.

The political economy of Australia was much more clearly an "artificial" creation of "natural" economic and domestic relations.[64]

The explicit use of force by the state and the private sector was the distinctive feature of political economic life in the early settlement of the colony.[65] The policing, sentencing and penal administration of political economic relations in the sphere of production were mainly conducted through agents directly representing the interests of the private sphere. Initially the city merchants employed their own constables and the large landholders controlled rural policing through their control of the magistracy in the major country centres.[66] In threats to civil order this form of policing was supplemented by the military. This combination of private and military policing that suited the "plantation capitalism" of the pastoral landholders was the point of struggle as the balance of political economic power shifted more towards the interests of the mercantile capitalists in the cities towards the middle decades of the nineteenth century.

Policing in the social sphere was the moral realm of ruling class women and men. As in Europe in this period the moral sphere of ruling class women extended to include the space between the private and the public realms, the social sphere. Their domestic and class position, sanctified by religious rationality — especially Evangelicalism — gave this class the authority to act as the new intermediaries or policing agents of the state, intervening in the construction of domesticity amongst the labouring classes.[67]

However, it seems likely that domesticity was not a major concern of the ruling class in this period in spite of the plethora of moralistic discourse on the immorality of unmarried convict women. The reproduction of the labour force did not primarily depend on domesticity but on penality. Women were part of the formation of the penal society but they were not

24

transported or encouraged to come as "free" settlers in large enough numbers to constitute a balance to the masculinity of the colony nor to provide a substantial domestic basis for the reproduction of labour either in terms of a new generation or in the day-to-day regeneration of a domesticated labour force.

One of the major reasons for their transportation mirrored that for which they were castigated: to provide for the maintenance of hetero-sexuality in the colony at a cheaper cost than that necessary to support a family system of monogamous heterosexuality.

Ambiguity about domesticity in the colony was the major character-istic of the discourse surrounding marriage and morality. There was major dissonance between the articulated views of the ruling class, of the construction of domesticity of the lower classes, and the actual experiences of the children, men and women in the convict and working class families in the period of early settlement. The majority of children were brought up in stable, regular families,[68] but these families were not formalised by a marriage contract: two out of three of the children in New South Wales in 1806 were illegitimate.[69] Cohabitation rather than marriage was, at least in part, the result of decisions by the ruling class themselves. Nevertheless the conflation of marriage with morality meant that there were assumptions by the ruling class that all of these children of convict parents were exposed to the "polluting culture" of their parents.

Alford[70] points to the contradictory attitudes in the literature of the period, in that crime was blamed both on the absence and presence of women. It stemmed, according to the contemporary moralists, both from the sex imbalance in the colony and from the incitement to crime by the morally inferior women. Single convict women were caught in a downward spiral created by the signification of femininity and morality. Their initial sentence condemned them to transportation to a labour colony that provided them with little economic support. They were not granted land and they did not have access to the range of work available to the male convicts.[71] The allocation system left them open to sexual exploit-ation by the settlers. They could not then avoid the moral disapprobation conferred on prostitution and on non-legal cohabitation. Marriage in the early settlement tended to be between free women and convict men but not between free men and convict women. As Alford[72] points out, this indicates that once women lost the label of morality they were much less able to have it restored to them than were men. Morality was so embedded a signifier of femininity that its loss, once detached, was likely to be permanent.

The dynamic of the impact of the familial-political economy on the variations in the lives of people is related to a second incongruity between ruling class perceptions of domesticity of labouring class people and the actual experiences of day-to-day life in those families. The dual circumstances of the convict background of most of the families and the high levels of cohabitation and illegitimacy led to expectations and false perceptions of a high crime rate in the colony in the eyes of the ruling class. Yet the levels of criminality, measured by official records, in the early settlement period of New South Wales were lower than those in British society in the same period.[73] One specific source of crime that had a greater impact in the "mother country" than in the penal colony was directly related to the comparably worse economic conditions of life for labouring class families in Britain. Young single women born into the early labouring class families in the colony were much more likely to stay at home prior to marriage, working in either the urban or rural family labour economies of New South Wales, than were their contemporaries in the "mother" country.[74] For the young women, born in the colony, working in their family labour economies of farms, trade, or business there was no necessity to go out to balance the resources of the family as there was in British society. Robinson[75] argues that this meant that they were unfamiliar with poverty and destitution and were less exposed to the risks of "having to stray from the paths of virtue" as had their mothers. It means too that they were less likely to be caught up in the circle of destitution and criminalisation through the sequence of seasonal factory work, domestic service, pregnancy, prostitution and petty theft that their mothers had been exposed to and that continued to circumscribe the lives of their contemporaries in cities in France and Britain.[76] In the two cases where young women born in the colony who were brought up in stable convict families were convicted of crime, they were assigned to their own parents.[77]

Of the the young women born in the colony to the convict and free families of the transported culture, it was usually only those who were defined as orphans who became domestic servants. Only twelve per cent of native born single non-koori women were in that group.[78] It was children who were separated from family life in New South Wales then who were likely to enter the cycle of domestic service and criminalisation. In 1789 a fourteen year old servant girl was sentenced to thirty lashes for "insolence" in the household of one of the chaplains of the colony.[79] Although this girl was a convict, not a "born free" servant, it was her particular familial-political-economic relationship within the household that put her at risk of punishment. Moreover it was the particularly penal intersection of work and domesticity that created the risk that children would enter the cycle of employment and criminalisation. In families in which, due to the assignment, death or desertion of their partner, one parent was left with the care of the children, both fathers or mothers were forced to work with employers who made the conditions of that work such that it was impossible for them to retain custody of a child. Not even married couples were necessarily allowed to live together and economically support each other if the man's labour was useful to the government or his employer. It was the particularly gendered constitution of "free" labour that meant that it was likely to be men who deserted families rather than women as it was they who were able to get work on the ships that took them back to Britain. That option was not open to women who had served their time.[80]

There seems then to have been a direct inversion of the intention of the ruling class. The upbringing provided by the "polluting" convict families seems less likely to have placed children at risk of criminality than that provided by the ruling class. However, this particular aspect of the constitution of domesticity had contradictory consequences for women for, whilst the first generation of women born in the settlement were more sheltered from exposure to the risk of criminality, they were also not "free" in terms of economic independence. Women's economic dependence on men was a major aspect of the constitution of domesticity in this period. There was little demand for women's labour other than below subsistence waged work in domestic service or their castigated sexual labour. Land grants were only in exceptional cases allocated to women. Even propertied women were denied access to this key form of means of production in the developing agricultural political economy of the penal colony.[81] For convict and free women this meant they were forced to depend on men for support or, after the 1820s, to take refuge in the female factories. It was married women who were widowed who constituted the major proportion of women cited as successful in business in New South Wales in this period.

In summary, this initial period of white settlement in the colony was characterised by forms of domesticity and penality closer to those constituted within the familial-political economy of mercantile capitalism from the sixteenth to the end of the eighteenth century in Northern Europe. Children were reared within family labour economies in which the productive and reproductive labour of men, women and children was not clearly separated. Penality was based on public, corporal or capital punishments or else on a system of transportation within transportation. In this specific period of the triangulation of penality, domesticity and productivity the dominant relationship was between the penal and the political economic spheres. The reproduction of productive relations was tied to penality more than to domesticity.

The penal sphere extended into the constitution of domesticity through the establishment of the female factories for women and charity schools for children both of which reinforced the normality of domestic life as a form of familial-economic relations characterised by children's and women's economic dependence on men. Destitution was conflated with pollution for women as either sexual partners or as parents.

There were both continuities and discontinuities in this triangulation of domesticity, penality and productivity in the next era of the familial-political economy in New South Wales — the period of laissez-faire mercantile capitalism from the 1840s to the 1880s.

27

MID 19TH CENTURY CAPITALISM IN NEW SOUTH WALES

Although the Australian familial-political economy in the mid-nineteenth century was based on mercantile capitalism, the social relations of production were closer to those characterising industrial production. The constitution of domesticity and penality was also more in line with the parallel relations constructed within laissez-faire capitalism in Northern Europe. By the 1840s through a series of contestations and negotiations between the pastoralist and the urban bourgeoisie sections of the ruling class, the conscripted labour of convicts was largely replaced by the waged work of "free labourers". This rationalisation of the relations of production fitted laissez-faire principles of a social order predicated on a capitalist mode of production and exchange. The "free" market was reflected in the "free" conditions of civil society. The systems of policing and punishment shifted from the overtly class dominated and paramilitary forms of control to the more independent and democratic form of control involving a change to a system based on a centralised bureaucratically organised civil police force and a sentencing and penal system nominally founded on the formal impersonal rule of law. O'Malley[82] argues that this move to a legal-rational form of control developed in relation to the problems of civil disorder in an urban industrial form of capitalist society.

Imprisonment as the deprivation of liberty became the major mode of punishment. There was a significant decline in capital punishment between 1835 and 1850.[83] This transformation of penality reflected both the centrality of "free" labour and an "equality" of punishment in a more systematic technical rational form of penality, "abstract labour time in capitalist production reappears in the existence of a sanction whose unit of measurement — time — is abstractly, universally and equally applicable to all individuals."[84] However the reproduction of the conditions of waged labour was associated too with a shift in the importance of the relationship between domesticity and production. The dominance of waged labour relations of production was closely parallelled by the energetic constitution of a universal domestication of working class life, especially through the intervention of ruling class women working through the social sphere. Shiploads of families of convicted and emancipated men, and of single women sent to create new families, were delivered to the ports of the colony over the decades 1830s to 1850s. The increased abstraction and rationality of economic and political life was parallelled by a major concern to increase labourers' access to the affective, personal relations of domestic life. Civil society depended on the conjunction of abstraction and affectivity, not the negation of the latter by the former.

The specific relationship between caring, dependence and control was explicitly spelt out in this period of the wholesale construction of domesticity in the colony. Caroline Chisholm, one of the main social sphere architects of the political-economic relationships of family life, argued that the rate payable for female labour should be proportional on a lower scale than that paid to men ... high wages tempt many girls to keep single while it encourages indolent and lazy men to depend more and more on their wives' industry than upon their own exertions, thus partly reversing the design of nature.[85]

Nevertheless, the transported wives were expected to be able to maintain themselves as servants, needlewomen, dairy maids or laundresses at the same time as they provided the moral labour of providing a powerful influence over even the "worst" of the convict men.[86]

Summers[87] details the several discursive practices through which in Caroline Chisholm's telling phrase, working class women became "God's police" as spouses and mothers of labouring men and their families. The responsibility for the reproduction of the next generation of labour was transferred from the penal sphere to the family labour of women in the domestic sphere.

The work of Donzelot[88] and Foucault[89] indicate that the labour of caring, controlling and reproduction in urban capitalism was effected not simply through the relations of domesticity and penality but through the several practical and physical reorderings of space and time through which the two spheres were reconstructed. Discourses on sexuality, education, housing space, hygiene and health effected the systematic ordering of family life and the relations between husbands and wives and parents and children.

These reorderings of space were policed through the continual imposition of "moral order" by ruling class women in the social sphere. In New South Wales, they also came under the direct surveillance of the formal police force. The shift towards hegemonic forms of policing in laissez-faire capitalism meant that the police force had to be seen as representing all sections of society, identified not just as law enforcers but as agents of the "community".[90] The pattern of change in policing and surveillance in Australia in this period followed the processes of rationalisation identified by Spitzer in the earlier period in Northern Europe. Initial policing in the colony was the responsibility of a police force explicitly identified with the squattocracy. By the mid-nineteenth century policing was organised in a bureaucratic impersonal structure closer to the ideal of the rule of law of a capitalist state. As part of this broader hegemonic role, the police force in New South Wales in the late 1850s was responsible for reporting on the condition of the working class. These reports reflected the earlier conflation of destitution with moral pollution, especially in the case of young women and their families. However there were also several reports based on close inspections of working class homes in terms of hygiene and of the relationship between domestic space and sexuality, in which family life was defined in a

29

pathological discourse. These concerns with pathology were articulated in terms combining medical and moral discourses rather than the more religiously based descriptions of parental pollution in the earlier ruling class condemnations of convict family life.[91]

One particular form of State intervention in the construction of domesticity was especially effective in narrowing the physical space in which women could operate. The *Contagious Diseases Acts* enabled police to apprehend any woman in the street to force her to undergo a medical examination. Whilst the British Act was confined to garrison towns and naval stations the Queensland Act, for example, applied to the general civil population.[92] The acts were vigorously debated on the grounds of the invasion of the civil liberties of the women, and the fact that they applied exclusively to women, but they stayed in force over the next twenty years.

One of the major consequences of these Acts and of the various State commissioned reports on the conditions of working class life was to pathologise and even to potentially criminalise the public behaviour of all working class women.

If the criminalisation of labouring life in the sixteenth and seventeenth centuries was about securing the property rights of the bourgeois and consequently the new form of class relations of liberal capitalism, the criminalisation of working class life in the latter decades of the nineteenth century was oriented to the imposition of clear boundaries between private and public spheres and confining working class existence out of the arena of the public realm. In this, the legislation was one of several strands in the constitution of the next form of dominant family — the family consumer economy.

Families were also increasingly privatised in terms of the breaks with wider family networks. The first few generations of family wage and family labour economies in New South Wales were internally sustained by the extended networks of kinship that developed within the first few generations of family life.[93] Similarly extended kin networks were important for the "free" labourers in the extensive immigrations of the mid-nineteenth century.[94] Families provided emergency accommodation, material support and occupational contacts for a wide range of relatives in the expansion of the familial-political economy of Australian capitalism. The domestic labour of women in working class families provided an intricate web of infrastructural support for the expanding economy as increasingly domestic labour within the family came to be the responsibility of the wife and mother in this period. However towards the end of this period the family consumer economies were characterised more by the "pure" domestic relationships between wife and husband and mother and child.

The disciplinary orderings of time and space were also a major feature of penality in this period of mercantile capitalism in New South Wales. In this period of classic capitalist relations, Australian prisons were built on the same principles of panopticon surveillance and control as those in

Europe and America.[95] The administrative and disciplinary classificatory processes produced detailed knowledge about the individual prisoner and the prisoner's activities were planned in what O'Malley[96] describes as a careful and refined patterning of space and time.

In summary, although the family labour economy form of domesticity continued in the several small businesses and farms that supported family life for many people throughout the century, families increasingly depended primarily on the waged labour of men and children and the specialised domestic labour of the wife and mother, in the classic period of class relations in New South Wales which lasted for the relatively short period from the mid-nineteenth century to the 1880s. However, Australian women's domestic labour, even in family wage economies, was particularly extensive and intensive, and likely to involve the productive work of providing vegetables and poultry, clothes and furniture, in the elaborate domestic economy of an "urban peasantry" that characterised working class life in nineteenth century Australian cities.[97] Nevertheless destitution was a feature of waged relations of production for the people in working class life Australia as it was in Northern Europe. The structured uncertainty of waged labour periodically exposed families to the risk of impoverishment and destitution when wages were the principal source of income. Moreover the separation of women and children from their own access to sources of subsistence put families headed by women especially at risk of impoverishment and institutionalisation through the death or desertion of men, or through spinsterhood if women were unable to secure through marriage their "natural" unpaid domestic employment as wife.[98]

The middle years of the nineteenth century were also a period of rapid shift in the constitution of the legal penal sphere. Forms of punishment and control as forced labour in the community combined with irregular public symbolic punishments to the body that suited the plantation capitalist of early settlement gave way to a greater emphasis upon the hegemonic policing and punishment suited to urban capitalism — the legal-rational, centrally administered, bureaucratically organised, precise control of convicted people within the prison. This reconfiguration of power, morality and rationality placed far more emphasis on the hegemonic control of productive relations through a major restructuring of both domesticity and penality. Both the family and the prison became sites for the reproduction of the conditions for productive life.

Onto this classic relationship between political economy, family and the legal penal realm of laissez-faire capitalism was layered the next patterning of social control and the reconstitution of domesticity and penality in the stage of corporate welfare capitalism.

WELFARE CAPITALISM
(late 19th & early 20th Century)

Lisa Peattie and Martin Rein[99] distinguish the three spheres of liberalism as the economic, the familial and the political, with the former two representing the "natural" axis and, initially, in the period from the late eighteenth to the late nineteenth century, the intervention of the polity representing an "unnatural" control in laissez-faire terms. Throughout the 19th century two specific areas of expertise developed, deriving from claims to knowledge of the laws of the natural in the economic and the familial realms. By the end of the nineteenth century the state entered into a far more interventionist mode of control. The opposition between the polity and the two natural spheres of the social and the economic was reconstituted from a "natural/unnatural" to a "natural/artificial" dichotomy. The more legitimate characterisation of the polity as "artificial" rather than "unnatural" underpinned a new era of direct state intervention through scientifically legitimated policy analysts and administrators who are "able to conceive themselves as students of the laws of the natural ... which must be described, generalised, and applied in the field of ... policy."[100]

Foucault[101] locates this development of the sciences of "natural" laws of human behaviour in the disciplinary techniques of surveillance, documentation, differentiation and observation that characterised control in the panopticon penitentiaries. By the end of the nineteenth century, the earlier individuation of the criminal progressed to a much more detailed and prescriptive set of scientifically legitimated state interventions in the family and the individuation of the working class in general.

The increased interventions in family and economic spheres brought a major expansion in public service employment in the 1880s. However, this expansion of state intervention also coincided with and was part of the complexity of shifts in other sections of the familial-political economy. The early nineteenth century shift to a wage based family economy for working class people led to the "revolution of rising expectations" of working class families and the development of the third stage of the family economy: the family consumer economy.[102] This was compounded by several factors: the experience of the "long boom" of the 1860–1890s when men's wages rose enabling wives and some daughters to concentrate on domestic work and give up the arduous double shift of paid and unpaid work,[103] the increase in responsibilities of child care with the emphasis on the importance of childhood and the introduction of universal compulsory education. This latter feature was both part of, and a factor in, the constitution of childhood for working class children that meant that they no longer brought income into the home but became an economic and domestic responsibility until their mid-teens.

The family consumer economy, developing towards the end of the nineteenth century, differed from the family wage economy, in terms of the increasing emphasis on the father's role as the major productive worker in the family, and the much clearer segregation of working class women into their domestic role within the home, caring for their families. Although by this time women had fewer children, paradoxically this demographic change increased the mothers' domestic role, because with the decline of both the birth rate and the infant mortality rate, those children who were born had an increasing amount of time and money spent on them.

The move to control the size of the family was not an easy transition for working class women. Birth control was not a universal aspect of the lives of working class women. Judith Allen estimates that the percentage of women experiencing dangerous back yard abortions was approximately 30 per cent in this period.[104]

By the early decades of the twentieth century the separation out of the two realms of productive and domestic life had become the "normal" form of family structure for working class men and women. This does not mean that all or even most working class families were able to fit this form throughout their lives. It does mean that in both public policies and in peoples' own conceptions of family life this family structure became defined as the normal style of family relations.[105]

This was not only a consequence of the voluntary withdrawal of working class women into the domestic sphere. There were both pro-scriptive and prescriptive forms of control over working class women which reinforced the constitution of domesticity in the form of the classic nuclear family. Those working class homes which did not provide a clean and regular family life were in danger of losing their children to the state.[106] The development of the range of experts in the laws of the natural relations of social life meant that this voluntary withdrawal was continually reinforced by processes of "normalisation" which defined woman's domestic work as her ability to make the home so attractive that it would result in husband and children being drawn away from the public to the domestic "haven".[107]

The "normality" of the family was reinforced by a network of surveillance and control as the family became the central focus of the gaze of a range of "new professionals" in health, medicine, education and welfare.[108]

In a society centred on the insecurity of "free" waged labour in a political economy characterised by the booms and depressions of capital labour relations, the tension between the cultural prescriptions and the structural limitations on the separation of productive and domestic life created major costs for working class family life. For several women the exigencies of life in the 1920s and 1930s meant that they were not able to depend on their husbands as "breadwinners".[109]

Both Donzelot's and Kereen Reiger's work indicates that women actively worked with doctors, nurses and "psy" experts in the construction of a family increasingly turned in on itself, excluding servants from domestic relations in the case of the ruling class, excluding lodgers, wives' mothers, and all but the immediate two generation family from the home life of working class families in order to secure the exclusion of working class men and children from the public life of the streets and the pubs.

Moreover the exigencies of working class life meant that the "family wage" decision by Higgins in 1912 was an achievement for those working class families which conformed to the "normal" pattern of breadwinning husband and economically dependent wife and children. This decision, however, was economically punitive for families which did not conform to this pattern. Households in which working class women had to support themselves or where they bore the economic responsibility for their dependants, whether the dependants were children, aged parents, invalid or unemployed husbands, were all penalised for their, usually involuntary, deviance from the normal. Moreover within the "normal" families the family wage did nothing to guarantee that the resources would be distributed evenly within the household.[110] Indeed the constitution of the husband as sole breadwinner could then be interpreted, by both police and husbands, as condoning the father/husband's greater economic and political power within the household with all the risks of domestic violence[111] and within household impoverishment[112] that such inequality brings with it.

In those families where women's productive labour was still important, the continuing family labour economies of farms and small businesses, the wife's productive contribution to the economy was effectively masked by the negation of that work with the disappearance of unpaid labour as a Census category in the 1890s.[113]

Single women's paid work anticipated their later married dependency, providing employers with below subsistence labour in factories and offices in the period between the 1880s and the second world war.

The development of state provision of education, welfare, communication and health services from the 1880s led to an expansion of occupations in the public sector. This was parallelled by a strong campaign to prohibit the employment of women in the newly extensive public bureaucracies with the language in which these campaigns were set being one of pseudo-science about the "natural" distinction between the biological, domestic role of women and the cultural, public sphere of male life.[114] Women, through Public Service Association campaigns, vigorously, although unsuccessfully, opposed their segregation and exclusion from economic independence.[115]

The construction of gender relations in the public sphere was not an uncontested development. It was through the multiplicity of knowledge experts in the reconstitution of domestic relations that the control of the state expanded into social life in this era. This development was parallelled by the changes occurring in the legal-penal sphere. Garland characterises this transformation as a positivist shift in penality that involved a move away from the centrality of the principle of the individual to the idea of a constituted personality. It was the move "from a philosophy of freedom to a psychology of human behaviour and its determinants."[116] Both domesticity and penality then were reconstructed by this move towards a commitment that the social sciences, the sciences of human nature, could be effective in the constitution and the reconstitution of the human personality.

The penal realm reflected the oppositional relationships of the market place, with the competition between capital and labour presided over by the State.[117] With the shift to corporate capitalism control was based on consensus rather than the more destabilising conflict basis of market relationships. The moral authority of legal rationality was replaced — or rather substantially reinforced — by the authority of scientific rationality in both the economic and the penal spheres. This resulted in a more organic relationship between actors in the two realms with an emphasis on neutrality and facilitation rather than on the more distant juridical means of solving disputes.

O'Malley[118] traces the shift to scientific authority not only in sentencing procedures but also in the policies and practices of punishment and policing. This was an era of the drastic reshaping of the penal realm. Garton[119] outlines the developments in New South Wales which parallelled the changes in punishment and control delineated by Garland, Donzelot and Rothman in Europe. He summarises the key aspects of the changes in the penal realm as: the decline of the prison in terms of numbers of people imprisoned, the increase in different forms of punishment with the increase in fines and probation, the removal from prison of people other than "hardened criminals", the growth of other areas of penality, the multiplicity of sites of regulation, the shift in the legitimations for regulation from rational-legal to a more positivistic scientific knowledge and, finally, the shift from a repressive regulatory system to one that incorporated both repressive and coercive or voluntary elements.

Garland[120] describes these changes as a shift from a system of control based on a vertically organised form of classification within one major site, the prison, to one in which the differentiation between those under control was ordered along a horizontal axis in several sites. He points out that there is now a social-penal complex in which there is a general mechanism of promotion and demotion. The three sectors in this complex are those directed towards "normalising", "corrective" and finally to "segregative" procedures. So domesticity becomes connected to penality along this line of possible transfers.

In this era there is a decline in the numbers of people in prison in Australia.[121] Paradoxically, however, in this remodelling of the functions of confinement prison as a last resort enters into the lives of a much wider section of the general population. Family relationships in the home, especially mother-child relationships, became the starting point of a network of control and surveillance that, through a system of filtering agencies, ends at the "coercive state-run terminus".[122]

Garton[123] details the major changes from the 1880s, when the imprisonment rate in New South Wales was 1,400 per hundred thousand, to the 1930s when the rate was down to approximately 50 per hundred thousand. However, the numbers of people under some form of social regulation increased in this period. The changes in penality were many sided. Imprisonment became more systematic, and by the 1930s only "genuine criminals" were in gaol. All other categories — women, children, the inebriate, the "lunatics", the vagrant, petty and first time offenders — were in the control of a multiplicity of other regulatory institutions. Prison became exclusively the site of control of adult, "sane" males. This process of masculinisation of crime and imprisonment took place over a remarkably short period. In the 1870s the male:female ratio of imprisonment was roughly 3:1 and by the 1920s it was 40:1.[124]

One of the key processes in this increasing differentiation of deviance is that prisons came to be the space in which only those whose criminality could be defined in terms of their rational choice of criminal behaviour were confined. The experts in the hidden laws of the arational came to dominate the regulation and control of the other categories of social behaviour that had to be controlled: psychiatry, probation and social workers, child care experts. And it was predominantly medical expertise that became the new legitimating force underpinning penality.

Regulation increasingly incorporated the voluntary action of the person under surveillance, especially in the case of women mental patients, but also voluntary appeals from neighbours or family. Of the three themes of liberal reform of penality through regularisation of control at the end of the eighteenth century, it was the Evangelical platform that most clearly emphasised the co-operation between the prisoner and the controller.[125] With the shift away from competitive towards consensus relations in both the economic and the penal spheres, this inheritance from the Evangelical penal architects became a keystone of the new structures of penal control.

There is a key difference here between Garton and Matthews in the interpretation of the changes. Garton[126] attributes the voluntary aspect of regulation to the shift to a more therapeutic culture. Matthews' analysis[127] indicates a much more complex pattern involved in this alliance between expert regulators and client deviants. She points up the difference between people's expectations of the forms of help they would get from the regulators and their eventual embroilment. Matthews also emphasises the imbalance of power in the alliances: "by and large, medicine took the credit for whatever was deemed progressive and successful. Women took the blame for individual failure." Moreover, Matthews' work indicates the structural rather than the purely cultural reason why people, particularly women, formed alliances with the regulators. She shows how being a "good woman" was potentially an impossible experience for many women caught up in the conflicting demands of being housewife, mother, migrant, daughter. For women, experiencing the contradictory impossibility of being a "good woman", there was little chance of escape other than through this alliance. Men could more easily escape the contradiction inherent in the impossible situation of being a "good provider", when there was no employment, by "deserting" the family. As Hamilton's[128] work indicates, historically this has been an option for men since the 16th century. For a complexity of reasons, women could not escape the contradictions of femininity so easily: they did not have as much experience of the public world, they had few public labour market counters of exchange, the ties of caring were much more embedded in the constitution of the feminine personality, and the public world was, and is, a much more physically dangerous place for women with no economic resources. Therefore the only escape from being a "good woman" in the prison of the home for some of the women in Matthews' account was to become a "good patient" in the mental hospital.[129]

Contradiction is a central theme in these accounts of the restructuring of domestic and penal life. The multiplicity of experts of family relations and the conflicts between them meant that to be a "good woman" was an impossibility in "a gender order that was 'ever changing and inconsistent' ... the path was a maze".[130] Similarly the penal sphere was a disputed site in this period. The psychiatrists were never able to establish their power knowledge base in the sphere as firmly as they would have liked.[131] Weatherburn's[132] characterisation of the contemporary New South Wales penal system as Byzantine has its roots partly in this pre-World War II period with the disputes between the "soft" concerns of the "psy" experts and the "hard" regulatory emphases of prison administrators whose legitimacy lay in their practical experience as career bureaucrats within the prison system.

Underlying these disputes between the two sets of penal "experts" are the contradictions stemming from tensions in the political economy. In periods of high unemployment imprisonment rates increase.[133] The economic exigencies of administering prison populations in periods of economic recession and depression have consistently underpinned the more hegemonic reconstructions of penality. From the late eighteenth century to the present penal crisis of the 1980s, prison overcrowding and the concomitant brutalising of prison life has been a marked feature of the history of penality in Western societies.

In summary, this period can be seen as a key era in the establishment of the home and the prison as the two dominant symbolic and material sites of social control. There were significant changes, firstly in the separate constitution of each of the two sites and, secondly, in the relationship between them.

It was in the era between 1880 and the second world war that domestic love, in both forms, became feminised across all classes. The family became located, in physical, social and psychological space, as the domain of the woman. At the other end of the continuum of social control, prison became fully masculinised but this masculinity of the prison, by its very singularity, became masked. Both semantically and epistemologically, and across all classes, "man" became conflated with "human" and "male prisoners" became "prisoners". At the beginning of the period the academic discourses of crime, criminality and imprisonment differentiated between the male and female aspects of their subject.[134] By the end of the period, criminological discourses including the functional, interactionist and the critical sociological analyses of crime and penality were all conducted within the false universalism that masked the most significant aspect of the subject under analysis, its masculinity.

These two sites of social control, the home and the prison, were clearly demarcated by the rigid epistemological boundaries of gender. Nevertheless, they were also connected by the continuum of "normalising", "corrective" and "segregative" procedures that now constituted the much broader penal sphere. This penetration of the penal sphere into social life, connecting the family and the prison through a process of transfers from "hard" to "soft" controls, was established in this era particularly through the constitution of the child as a potentially delinquent subject.[135] It was the mother-child relationship which was central to the reconstruction of penality as a penal welfare complex. It was in the next transformation after the second world war that this pattern of the feminised home linked to a masculinised prison through a series of normalising, corrective and segregating agencies came to be applied on a larger scale to adult deviance. There were, however, also major shifts in the gender-class relations of the labour market in this next period of consumer capitalism against which the relationship between the home and the prison need to be set.

FROM CONSUMER CAPITALISM TO THE RETREAT FROM WELFARE: (1950s – 1980s)

Tilly and Scott[136] differentiate between two forms of family consumer economies; the first lasting from the turn of the twentieth century to the beginning of the second world war and characterised as the classic nuclear family — two generational, a small number of children and with the father as sole or primary breadwinner and the mother's labour characterised by her withdrawal from productive work even in the home. With the primacy of the woman's purely domestic labour of the constitution of the individual personality of her children and husband, domestic labour becomes, unequivocably, the labour of "care".

The contradictions between this ideal for working class women (and for many middle class women) in periods of economic downturn, do not so much repudiate the validity of this characterisation as demonstrate how powerful an ideology it was, particularly in compounding the severity of the various economic crises for several families during this period up to the second world war. Nevertheless Matthews[137] identifies factors in this era that were to become the basis for a widespread questioning of this ideology of gender. The basic contradiction of the artificial construction of supposedly natural familial relations made explicit the plasticity of the constitution of gendered personalities and domesticity. This questioning, however, was associated with a range of other changes in the construction of family life that Tilly and Scott describe as the development of a second form of family consumer economy.

The second form is a modification of the classic form of the first few decades of the twentieth century. By the 1950s, the central economic problems shifted from the sphere of production to the crisis of consumption and realisation. There were increasing pressures on families to consume more material goods. The priority over concerns with consumption and distribution was associated with the development of a complex set of changes in the public sphere including the expansion of the tertiary sector, especially of routine white-collar work, the shift in the labour market from full time and long term to part time and casual employment, the decrease in the length of the male working day, and the increasing costs to individual families of the lengthening of the period of children's economic dependence as the school leaving age rose to 16. These changes, together with the continuing effects of the expansion of occupations in the social sphere, had major effects on domesticity. The single most important effect was that increasingly mothers went out to paid work to increase the material wellbeing of their families. Young single women were much more likely both to want and to be able to get work that was more than a stop gap measure between leaving school and withdrawing back into the home on marriage. These changes were not uncontested. Some, like the opening up of jobs and careers to women and the 35 hour working week for full time workers, resulted from severe class and gender based battles. Nor are these changes necessarily to be interpreted as successes for either the working class in general nor for women as a group. The number of hours people spend in work, including male and female, paid and unpaid labour in the domestic and public spheres, now totals substantially more than did those in the period of dominance of the classic nuclear family.[138] This restructuring of the relationship between domestic and political economic spheres means that there has been an effective shift of surplus value to capital.

Matthews[139] identifies the major ideological discourse pervading this period as the shift to permissive consumerism. The influence of this political economic culture on the construction of domesticity is complex. Familism became the central target of massive advertising projects centred on guilt and inadequacy. "Normal" family life was constituted around high levels of commodity consumption and economic and financial institutions were created, locking family life into engulfing credit systems. However, the wider diffusion of the permissive ethic sustaining consumerism made a major impact in terms of liberalising of attitudes and policies in the sphere of family life. Homosexuality was decriminalised in this period. Divorce became more accessible, abortion was made legal and unmarried mothers became eligible for supporting parents benefits. There were major contradictions for women, especially working class women, when the ethic of permissive sexuality became located in a political economy sustaining both familism and a continuing structured inequality of access to the labour market in terms of both class and gender. Single parenthood became and remains associated with the risk of impoverishment in Australia because the familial work of caring is still constructed in terms of economic dependence.[140]

There are several other particular tensions in the present period between the extension of women's labour into waged work in the public sphere and the continuing demands for caring work constructed as unpaid labour in the domestic sphere. Moreover, there are several aspects of the contemporary form of familial-political economy that exacerbate the contradictions between the two spheres. These include: the retreat since the early 1970s, of the state from its earlier commitment to welfare,[141] the related but separate question of deinstitutionalisation,[142] the increased significance of education and the prolonged economic dependence of children, the development of sets of professional/semi-professional hierarchies in various welfare and medical spheres,[143] the impact of improved health and medical techniques in terms of the extended dependence of several groups of people whose access to resources lies outside of the wage capital relationship,[144] and the displacement of increasing sectors of the population from waged labour with the expansion of capitalism.[145]

The neo-right versions of liberal capitalism reduce state intervention on two fronts, shifting costly state supports for the reproduction of non-productive life to the community and the family at the same time as they shift the profit-making sectors of state intervention to the private entrepreneurial sphere.[146] The increased participation of women in the waged labour market seems likely to make little impact on women's greater propensity to take on unpaid caring work. Women's subordinate position in the labour market means that men are still less likely than women to forego their capacity for wage earning to become the unpaid carers of dependent kin.[147]

The constitution of domesticity in this period, then, is overshadowed by the demographic and political economic shifts involving an ideology of community based care that potentially puts women at risk of a lifelong obligation to unpaid caring work. The central contradiction of the current shifts in the relationship between the two sphere lies in the paradox that it is the economic rationalism of the neo-liberalist political administrations that is the most likely to be dependent upon the hidden contracts between men and women and between employers and workers, that commit women to unpaid caring labour.[148]

The dominance of the ideology of community based care in the social sphere was concurrent with the "take off" in community forms of penal control. The establishment of community based penality occurred in the early twentieth century, but it was not until sixty years later that community based punishments dominated, in numerical terms, the range of penal options for adults. Garland summarises the combination of factors that affected penality in the 1970s as:

1   a major disenchantment with "treatment" and "professionalism" that amounted to a collapse in the belief in rehabilitation;
2   the growth of prisoner organisations and conflict within prisons; and
3   the fiscal crisis resulting from the transnational restructuring of the political economies.

"Nothing works", the two words summarising the comprehensive review of penal practices by Martinson in 1974, became the significant phrase in penal discourses in this period of disillusionment with "treatment".[149] Nevertheless, this combination of factors resulted in a reinforcement rather than dissolution of community based controls. Numbers under some form of community control kept increasing whilst the numbers imprisoned behind institutional walls fluctuated sufficiently for prison administrators to occasionally point to "successful" attempts to keep offenders out of prison.[150] However, by the mid 1980s prison overcrowding was the major concern of penal administrators in the USA, northern Europe and Australia.[151]

The introduction of community controls in the penal sphere seemed have direct parallels with the deinstitutionalisation occurring in the social policy field.[152] However, community controls serve to extend, diffuse and strengthen the principle of incarceration in the punishment system.[153] There has not been any major closure of existing prison structures. Prison remains as the central point of the penal sphere. The addition of lesser community controls increases rather than decreases the importance of prison in the penal sphere.[154] Moreover, as prison becomes the site of control of the offenders who have become defined as the "hard cases"[155] the practices and strategies for control within prison become more militaristic. New South Wales has introduced riot squads, tactical response groups and dog detection units in this era of "retreat from welfare".[156]

Nevertheless, although the fiscal argument is not a sufficient one, the explosion of community based controls does have an important economic aspect: a much wider range of the population can be controlled using fewer resources than would be necessary if imprisonment were the sole form of punishment.[157]

This new construction of penality as comprising a partnership between the "hard" prison and the "soft" community styles of punishment parallels the hard/soft style of control and surveillance in policing and O'Malley[158] points to the similar blurring of boundaries between criminal and civil law. This extensive pattern of hard/soft procedures seems to indicate that there is something more penetrating occurring in the realm of control than simply a concern to limit state expenditures.

Cohen[159] argues for the existence of four processes which profoundly change the nature of penality in this era. First, community controls involve an expansion of state intervention as more people are being caught up in the net of State control and surveillance. Secondly, the filtering processes become narrower, catching not only more but a wider range of people for smaller offences, thus state intervention becomes more penetrating. Thirdly, the incorporation of formerly non-penal community institutions means that these formerly familial or social groups are transformed, taking on the characteristics of controlling organisations. Finally, these transformations serve to mask the extent of the widening, and the increased penetration, of state control and surveillance.

Both O'Malley and Spitzer argue that the increasingly intensive levels of investment in capitalist production are associated with more organic forms of control of social life. State intervention is increasingly about pacification rather than adjudication. It moves away from the narrow regulation of market contracts to the more proscriptive interventions of promoting smooth social relations and defusing social conflicts.

However, O'Malley rejects the left functionalist analysis that this delineation of increased state intervention seems to imply. He argues, like Garton, that there is a contradictory character to state intervention and the blurring of boundaries between state, social and family life. State intervention can be both liberating and repressive: "For many purposes, the state emerges as the only readily available, potentially effective countervailing force to a large array of repressive interests and arrangements."[160]

SUMMARY

In conclusion, Garland[161] argues for penality to be seen as the specific institutional site through which political, ideological, economic, legal, gender and social relations operate. Penality, he argues, is "the over determined site" in which the social relations of the wider familial-political economy are both reflected and mediated. Both the penal and the domestic spheres are constituted as the sites in which the relations of capitalism are reproduced. However, the specific forms of gender-class relations within penality and domesticity vary with the particular crises that characterise each phase of the historical development of capitalist relations.

In the earliest era of class relations, the phase of primitive accumulation from the 16th to the late 18th century, the principal crisis was in the sphere of exchange. It was the establishment of the constitution of the individual liberal bourgeois capitalist in terms of his legal subjectivity as property owner that was the major point of tension in the familial-political economy. The "invention" of crime, the punishment by segregation (particularly by transportation) in the field of penality and the segregation of the domestic sphere in the families of the bourgeoisie were the major consequences of tensions arising from this phase in the establishment of the gender-class relations of liberal capitalism.

The 19th century crisis, in the next phase of the familial-political economy, was located in the sphere of production and the focus shifted from the individuality of the bourgeoisie to the individualisation of the labourer and the control of the dispossessed labouring class. The constitution of the family life of the labouring classes as a key site of control, reinforcing the "dull economic compulsion" upon the bread-winning father, parallelled a development of the centrality of imprisonment as the major form of punishment depriving the labourer of his freedom to exchange his labour at the same time as his labour became the primary resource for the labouring class family. Both the home and the prison became "sites of moral order" but with morality in the former stemming from the *arational* relations of family life and in the latter from the *rationality* of the regulated and systematic patterns of punishment and control.

The third and most recent crisis of capitalism, in the latter half of the 20th century, developing out of the tensions in the sphere of the realisation of value, concerns not the constitution of the personality of the bourgeois nor the personality of the labourer, but the personality of the consumer and the management of the relations of consumption. Both domesticity and penality are reconstituted within the complex sets of tensions that characterise this latest phase of the gender-class relations of the familial-political economy. The two sites are also much more manifestly connected through the various dimensions of repression and coercion that characterise the complexities of social control in this era in which the earlier tensions of the relations of exchange and production are not so much replaced by as mingled with those of consumption.

The configurations of power, morality and rationality take complex and contradictory forms in the several reshapings of the intersections between family, state and economy as the tensions of each era are layered onto those of the earlier period.

A key element in this hegemonic interpretation of the way that the penal and domestic spheres are constituted and reconstituted in relation to the social relations of the wider society, is the way that both the home and the prison become sites of the resolution of tensions arising from two major processes of dispossession: the dispossession of the peasantry from the land in the establishment of the bourgeoisie as property owner and the second and recurring process of dispossession of the labourer from waged labour. Whilst this latter process occurs periodically in the recurring cycles of capitalist production and the concomitant swings in the labour market, there is also a more general push towards unemployment and under-employment in "first world" familial-political economies, with the internationalisation of the labour market in the transnational corporate phase of capitalism and the various fiscal crises of the nation states of "the first world".

Garton points to the significance of the masculinisation of prison and its consequences for women in terms of their increased risk of becoming the subjects of psychiatrically based care and control. However, there is another population, predominantly women, that is constituted by this masculinisation of prison populations. This population has a singular characteristic — its invisibility. It is the construction of this marginalised population of "families of prisoners" that is addressed in the next two chapters.

NOTES

1   Durkheim, E, *The Division of Labour in Society*, 1893, transl 1960; Parsons, T, "The Law and Social Control", in Evans, W (ed), *Law and Society* (1962).

2   Parsons, T and Bales, R, *Family Socialization and Interaction* (1955); Goode, W, *The Family* (1964); Parsons, T, *Societies: Evolutionary and Comparative Perspectives* (1966).

3   These categorisations are based on but do not re-present the reviews by David Garland (*Punishment and Welfare* (1986)), A Edwards (*Regulation and Repression* (1988)) and Stephen Garton ("The State, Labour Markets and Incarceration: a Critique", in Findlay, M and Hogg, R (eds), *Understanding Crime and Criminology* (1988)).

4   Rusche, G and Kirchheimer, O, *Punishment and Social Structure* (1939); Quinney, R, "Crime and development of Capitalism", in Quinney, R, *Class, State and Crime: On the Theory and Practice of Criminal Justice* (1979); Braithwaite, J, "The Political Economy of Punishment" in Buckley, K and Wheelwright, E (eds), *Political Economy of Australian Capitalism* (1980); Jankovic, I, "Labour Market and Imprisonment" (1977) 8 *Crime & Soc Just* 17–33.

5   Foucault, M, *Discipline and Punish* (1977); Melossi, D and Pavarini, M, *The Prison and the Factory System: Origins of the Penitentiary System* (1981); Ignatieff, M, "State, Civil Society and Total Institutions: a critique of recent social histories of punishment" in Cohen, S and Scull, A (eds), *Social Control and the State* (1983).

6   Edwards, above n3.

7   Donzelot, J, *The Policing of Families: Welfare versus the State* (1979); Garton, S, " 'Bad or Mad': Developments in Incarceration in New South Wales 1900–40" in Sydney Labour History Group (ed), *What Rough Beast? The State and Social Order in Australian History* (1983); Cohen, S, *Visions of Social Control* (1985); Garland, above n3. The other authors working within this perspective are cited throughout this chapter.

8   Spitzer, S, "The Rationalization of Crime Control in Capitalist Society" (1979) 3 *Contemporary Crises* 187–206; O'Malley, P, *Law, Capitalism and Democracy* (1983).

9   Garland, D, *Punishment and Welfare* (1985) at 4–5.

10   Tilly, L and Scott, J, *Women, Work and Family* (1978).

11   Rosalda, M, "Women, Culture and Society: a Theoretical Overview" in Lamphere, L and Rosalda, M (eds), *Women, Culture and Society* (1974).

12   Cott, N, *Bonds of Womanhood* (1977); Stone, L, *The Family — Sex and Marriage in England* 1500–1800 (1979).

13   Hamilton, R, *The Liberation of Women* (1978) at 102.

14   Above n10 at 59.

15   ... although the dispossession had been occurring since the Statute of Merton legislated for the first enclosures in the 13th century.

16   Above n10 at 51.

17   Spitzer, above n8; Dobash, R, Dobash, R E and Gutteridge, S, *The Imprisonment of Women* (1986) at ch1.

18   Dobash et al, above n17 at 23.

19   Above n13 at 41.

20   Id at 40.

21   Dobash et al, above n17 at 23.

22   Lea, J, "Discipline and Capitalist Development" in Fine, B et al (eds), *Capitalism and the Rule of Law: from Deviancy Theory to Marxism* (1979) at 79–80.

23   Annette, J, "Bentham's Fear of Hobgoblins: Law, Political Economy and Social Discipline", in Fine et al, above n22.

24   Dobash et al, above n17 at 29.

25   '... in Ealing in 1599 almost three quarters of female children (between the ages of fifteen and nineteen) seem to be living away from their parents, most often as servants.' Above n10 at 35.

26   Dobash et al, above n17 at 29.

27   Id at 17.

28   Picciotto, S, "The Theory of the State, Class Struggle and the Rule of Law", in Fine et al, above n22 at 171.

29   Dobash, above n17 at 28–29.

30   Aries, P, *Centuries of Childhood* (1973); Donzelot, above n7 at 11–17; above n10 at 58.

31   Above n10 at 33.

32   This version of an ambivalence in the state's approach to punishment conflicts with Rusche & Kirchheimer, above n4.

33   Dobash et al, above n17 at 23.

34   O'Malley, above n8 at 151, citing Rusche & Kirchheimer, above n4.

35   Dobash et al, above n17 at 16.

36   Id at 23.

37   Id at 27.

38   Id at 22.

39 Transportation as a major system of punishment then is better explained within the Rusche and Kirchheimer's labour market thesis, rather than the Foucaultian emphasis on the symbolic importance of public and physical punishment to the body in premodern penality. Rusche & Kirchheimer (1966) cited in Garton, above n3 at 311–313.

40 Spitzer, above n8 at 193.

41 Dobash et al, above n17 at 27.

42 Above n40 at 193.

43 ... although the rule of law was evidenced on occasion by the odd infrequent case of the sentencing of a landlord.

44 Above n40 at 193–196.

45 'Universal' in terms of male labour in the public sphere.

46 However, Garland argues that the key shift from individualism to individualisation occurs with the next transformation at the end of the the nineteenth century. His argument is examined later.

47 Smart, B, *Michel Foucault* (1985) at 84.

48 Above n10 at ch4.

49 Id at 113.

50 Id at 123–136.

51 Alford, K, *Production or Reproduction? An Economic History of Women in Australia 1788–1850* (1984) at ch8; above n10 at 123–136; above n50; Holley, J, "The Two Family Economies of Industrialism: Factory Workers in Victorian Scotland" (1981) 6/1 *J Fam Hist* 57–69.

52 See pp 42 above.

53 Bythell, D, *Sweated Labour: Outwork in Nineteenth Century Britain* (1978); Burman, S (ed), *Fit Work for Women* (1979).

54 Spitzer, S and Scull, A, "Social Control in Historical Perspective: From Private to Public Responses to Crime" in Greenberg, D (ed), *Corrections and Punishment* (1977) at 276–7.

55 Donzelot, above n7 at 88–9.

56 Melossi, D, "Institutions of Social Control and Capitalist Organisation of Work", ch6 in Fine et al, above n22; Foucault, above n5.

57 Polyani, K, *The Great Transformation* (1944) at 1186, cited in Spitzer & Scull, above n54 at 277.

58 Dobash et al, above n17 at 41. It is also worth noting that Fry was influenced by the penal reformers of North American Quakerism. Thus the penal changes in New South Wales and Tasmania in the early to mid nineteenth century can be linked to the influence of the moral vigour of the particular combination of morality, power and rationality developing in North American industrialism in the early nineteenth century.

59 Dobash et al, above n17 at 36.

60 Melossi, D and Pavarini, M, *The Prison and the Factory System: Origins of the Penitentiary System* (1981) at 46–47.

61 Dobash et al, above n17 at 60.

62 Id at 62.

63 Id at 64.

64   Marx, K, *Capital* (vol 1) 1887 repr 1974 at ch31.

65   Connell, R and Irving, T, *Class Structure in Australian History: Documents, Narrative and Argument* (1980) at ch2.

66   O'Malley, above n8 at 52–53.

67   Windschuttle, E, "Women and the Origins of Colonial Philanthropy" in Kennedy, R (ed), *Australian Welfare History* (1982) at 12.

68   Robinson, P, *The Hatch and Brood of Time: a study of the first generation of native born white Australian 1788–1828* (1985).

69   Above n67 at 17.

70   Alford, above n50 at 22.

71   Id at ch4; Robinson, P, *Women of Botany Bay: a reinterpretation of the role of women in the origins of Australian society* (1988) at ch9.

72   Above n70 at 66.

73   Above n70 at 22; Robinson, above n71 at 153–171.

74   Above n68 at 150; above n10 at 35.

75   Above n68 at 150.

76   Of the 2.7 million employed women in Britain 2 million were in domestic service in the mid nineteenth century. Beddoe 1983 at 112 cited in Dobash et al, above n17 at 226; above n68 at 151.

77   Above n68 at 151.

78   Ibid.

79   Robinson, above n71 at 45.

80   Above n70.

81   Id at 75–76.

82   O'Malley, above n8 at 56.

83   Id at 153.

84   Id at 152.

85   Cited by Alford, above n70 at 207.

86   Daniels, K (ed), *So Much Hard Work: Women and Prostitution in Australian History* (1984) at 39.

87   Summers, A, *Damned Whores and God's Police* (1985).

88   Donzelot, above n7 at 16–17.

89   Foucault, above n5 at 143–157.

90   O'Malley, above n8 at 56–58.

91   Detective Inspector Harrison (1859) reproduced in Kingston, B, *My Wife, Daughter and Poor Mary Ann* (1975) at 167–173 and Dr Read (1875) reproduced in Connell and Irving, above n65 at 159 & 160.

92   Daniels, K, Murnane, M and Picot, A, *Women in Australia: an Annotated Guide to Records* (1977) at 21.

93   Above n68.

94   Grimshaw, P and Willett, G, "Women's History and Family History: an exploration of colonial family structure" in Grieve, N and Grimshaw, P (eds), *Australian Women: Feminist Perspectives* (1981) at 134–155.

95   Grabosky, P, *Sydney in Ferment: Dissent and Official Reaction 1788–1973* (1977).

96   O'Malley, above n8 at 154.

97   Above n94 at 146.

98   Above n70 at 218–9.

99   Peattie, L and Rein, M, *Women's Claims: a Study in Political Economy* (1983) at 6–8.

100   Id at 7.

101   Foucault, above n5 at 29.

102   Cass, B and Radi, H, "Family Fertility and the Labour Market", in Grieve & Grimshaw, above n94.

103   Sinclair, W, "Women at Work in Melbourne and Adelaide since 1871" (1981) *Dec Economic Record* 344–353.

104   Allen, J, *Sex and Secrets: Crimes Involving Australian Women Since 1880* (1990) at 96–105.

105   In a set of interviews with sixty women, 30 from Adelaide and 30 from the Illawarra, married between 1905 and 1929, all interpreted their position as married women, as a commitment to full time unpaid work within the domestic sphere. (Aungles, A, "Family Economics in Transition: Adelaide Women in the Depression", unpublished MA thesis, Flinders University, Adelaide, 1982.)

106   Barbalet, M, *Far From a Low Gutter Girl. The Forgotten World of State Wards: South Australia 1887–1940* (1983).

107   Donzelot, above n7 at 82–95.

108   Matthews, J, *Good and Mad Women* (1984) at 176.

109   Aungles, above n105; Aungles, A, "Illawarra Women in the 1930s Depression", unpublished MSoc thesis, University of Wollongong, New South Wales, 1984.

110   Oren, L, "The Welfare of Women in Labouring Families 1860–1950" (1974) 1/3–4 *Fem Stud* 107–25; Pahl, J, "Patterns of Money Management with Marriage" (1980) 9/3 *J Soc Pol* 313–335.

111   Bryson, L, Mugford, J, Mugford, S and Weiser Easteal, P, "Social Justice, Public Perceptions and Spouse Assault in Australia" (1989) 16/3 *Soc Just* 103–124.

112   Above n110.

113   Deacon, D, "Political arithmetic: the nineteenth century census and the construction of dependent women". Unpublished paper, Canberra 1982. Cited by Matthews, above n108 at 58.

114   Taperell, K, Fox, C and Roberts, M, *Sexism in the Public Service: the Employment of Women in the Australian Government Administration* (1975) at 8–16; Matthews, above n108 at 58–63.

115   Deacon, D, "The Employment of Women in the Commonwealth Public Service: the creation and reproduction of a dual labour market" (1982) 41/3 *Aust J Public Admin* 232–250.

116   Above n9 at 91.

117   O'Malley, above n8 at ch9.

118   Id at ch4.

119   Garton, above n3 at 319–323.

120   Garland, above n3 at 234.

121 Garton, above n3 at 320; Mukherjee 1981 at 98.

122 Garland, above n3 at 234.

123 Garton, above n3 at 230.

124 Braithwaite, above n4 at 202–204.

125 Dobash et al, above n17 at 54–56.

126 Garton, above n3 at 324.

127 Above n108 at 176.

128 Above n13 at 93.

129 Above n108, part III.

130 Id at 27–28.

131 Garton, S, "The Melancholy Years: Psychiatry in New South Wales, 1900–1940", in Kennedy, R (ed), *Australian Welfare History* (1982) at 144.

132 Weatherburn, D, "Reducing the New South Wales Prison Population: sentencing reform and early release" (1986) 10 *Crim LJ* 121–138 at 137.

133 Braithwaite, above n4; Jankovic, I, "Labour Market and Imprisonment" (1977) 8 *Crime & Soc Just* 17–33; Box, S, *Power, Crime and Mystification* (1983).

134 Heidensohn, F, *Women and Crime* (1985) at ch6.

135 Garland, above n3 at ch4 & ch8; above n106; Donzelot, above n7; above n131; Garton, above n3.

136 Above n10 at ch8.

137 Above n108 at ch5.

138 Hartmann, H, "The Family as the Locus of Gender, Class and Political Struggle: the example of housework" (1981) 6/2 *Signs* 366–394.

139 Above n108 at 89–91.

140 Gilding, M, *The Making and Breaking of the Australian Family* (1991).

141 Graycar, A (ed), *Retreat from the Welfare State: Australian Social Policy in the 1980s* (1983).

142 Scull, A, *Decarceration: Community Treatment and the Deviant — a Radical View* (1977).

143 Hearn, J, "Patriarchy, Professionalism and the Semi-Professions" in Ungerson, C (ed), *Women and Social Policy* (1985).

144 Moroney, R M, *The Family and the State: Considerations for Social Policy* (1976); Finch, J and Groves, D, "By Women for Women: caring for the frail enderly" (1982) 5/5 *Women's Studies International Forum* 427–438.

145 Walker, in Finch, J and Groves, D (eds), *A Labour of Love: Women, Work and Caring* (1983).

146 Finch & Groves, above n145; Williams, F, *Social Policy: a Critical Introduction* (1989).

147 Ungerson, C, *Policy is Personal: Sex, Geder and Informal Care* (1987) at 13.

148 Gowler, D and Legge, K, "Hidden and Open Contracts in Work and Marriage" in Rapoport, R, Rapoport R N and Bumstead, J (eds), *Working Couples* (1978).

149 Lobban, A, "Whose Gaols? Whose Goals?" in Vernon, J (ed), *Developments in Correctional Policy: More Prisons?* (1987) at 37; Cohen, above n7 at 179–181; Mott, J, "Social Research on Adult Prisons and Prisoners in England and Wales" (1984) 18 *Res B*, London: Home Office Research & Planning Unit; details this move away from rehabilitation discourses over the period 1966 to 1977 in England and Wales.

150 New South Wales Department of Corrective Services, *Annual Reports* 1975–1986.

151 Ibid.

152 Above n142.

153 Hudson, B, "The Rising Use of Imprisonment: the impact of decarceration policies" (1984) 2 *Crit Soc Pol* (Winter) at 46–58.

154 This point is also made in the comprehensive review of changes in penality in Australia by Chan & Zdenkowski: Chan, J and Zdenkowski, G, "Just Alternatives — Parts I & II" (1986) 19/2-3 *ANZ J Crim*.

155 Sinclair, P, "Alternatives to Gaol: solving some problems, creating some new ones" (1974) 15/2 *Health in NSW*; above n153.

156 New South Wales Department of Corrective Services, *Annual Reports* 1982, 1983, 1984.

157 O'Malley, above n8 at 160.

158 Id at 164–6.

159 Cohen, above n7.

160 O'Malley, above n8 at 177.

161 Garland, D and Young, P (eds), *The Power to Punish* (1983) at 21.

3

THE HOME AND THE PRISON:
FOUR MODES OF INCORPORATION

We must go back in time to trace the sources of the contradictions and
forward in time to see the policy arena as a site in which these contradictions
work themselves out.[1]

In chapter two Garton's[2] question was posed: "what populations are
constructed by the discourse of power and control as it occurs in the realm
of penality?" The feminist materialist perspective however, indicates that
the tensions between patriarchal and capitalist forms of domination lead to
a further set of questions: what populations are masked or marginalised in
these discourses? what are the economic, social and personal costs of the
contradictions of the interdependences yet incompatibilities between the
domestic and penal spheres? which sectors of the population are most at
risk of bearing those costs?

In this chapter it will be argued that the domestic and legal-penal
realms are interdependent but that several mechanisms exist which mask
the ways in which this interdependence is experienced. These parallel
processes of interdependence, privileging, masking and marginalisation
vary as the tensions between and within the spheres of state, family and
economy are reconstituted in each phase in the development of the
familial-political economy from the sixteenth to the late twentieth century.

In this chapter, the specific caring work of women who comprise the
population "families of prisoners", is examined in an outline of four major
phases in the interdependence between the domestic and the penal spheres
at the various stages of development of the familial-political economy.
Both spheres are interpreted here as both physical places and as sets of
values about relationships. Thus the charting of the changes in the
intersections of the two spheres is both a topology of spaces and a typology
of discourses.

In one of the most comprehensive reviews of the metatheories and
practices of penality, Cohen uses the Foucaultian criteria of exclusion/
inclusion to summarise the major stages in the changing styles of
punishment policies and practices:[3] from punishment out in the "open"
community, to punishment as invisible incarceration "inside" the walls of
the prison, and in the final transformation, to punishment as both
confinement in the closed institution and out in the community. However
in this third phase punishment in the community is not so publicly visible.
The blurring of the boundaries between punishment and welfare diffuses
and masks the extent of the penetration of the legal-penal sphere into the
wider society.[4]

51

These criteria of exclusion and inclusion are used here to specify four ways in which the family is incorporated into penal strategies. The feminist critique of theories of social change points up the potential biases in adopting the periodisation of non-feminist literature.[5] This chapter, which focuses on the interdependence of home and prison, indicates one major realignment in the conventional charting of the key points of transformation of social control. In brief the four major modes of the incorporation of the family into the penal sphere are: the home *within* the prison; the home *outside* the prison; the home *outside but allowed into* the prison; and finally the prison within the home.

In addition to the spatial metaphor adapted from Cohen's categorisation, the differences in the four modes of incorporation are also about changes in the relations of production and reproduction. They are shifts in the ways in which the nexus between care and dependence is constituted in the various phases.

Thus the changes are also shifts in the relationship between "punishment" and "providence". This modification of Cohen's chart then introduces a significant change in the *periodisation* of social control. The focus on the interdependence between home and prison marks the mid 1980s as a period of significant transformation in the discourses of surveillance and punishment.

Figure I on the next page charts these changes, in the topology of spaces and in the typology of discourses, that have been constructed around the relationship between "the home" and "the prison" in the period up to and including this latest transformation.

These forms of incorporation are not mutually exclusive. Punishment practices in Cohen's words are formed of "deposits " of various ideologies and style.[6] The site of punishment has been described by Weatherburn, in his description of the Corrective Services Department in New South Wales, as having become a place characterised as a Byzantine maze of policies and practices difficult for controllers and controlled alike to negotiate.[7] However, when the interdependence between the family and the legal-penal sphere is delineated, the maze is shown to be even more complex than Weatherburn indicates. The evidence of women who have to negotiate the triple complexities of the legal-penal, the family-welfare spheres, and the intersections between those two social domains, is outlined in chapters five to eight.[8] The various forms in which the domestic labour of caring is embedded into the various systems of punishment are outlined below.

1 The home in the prison

Home site of 'family labour
economy' within prison

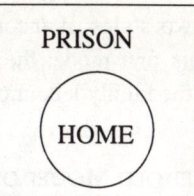

2 The home and the prison separated by clear boundaries

Home 'invisible' in
penal discourses

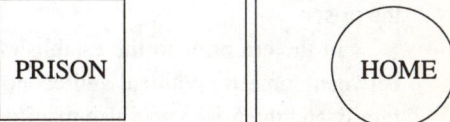

3 More permeable boundaries between prison and home

Home 'prime treatment
agency' in penal discourses

4 The prison in the home

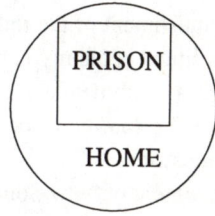

Home 'naturally related community
resource' in penal discourses

FIGURE I: Four Modes of Intersection Between Home and Prison

I   THE FAMILY IN THE PRISON

There are two styles of incorporation of family life into prison life that comprise this first mode: the household model of power relations within prison, and the family labour colony.

1   THE HOUSEHOLD MODEL OF POWER RELATIONS WITHIN PRISON

As discussed in chapter two, prior to the nineteenth century regularisation of prison life from the 1820s on, prisoners were generally either people awaiting sentence of transportation or physical punishment, or they were debtors.[9] They were, therefore, not subject to coercive routines but ran the internal procedures within the prison themselves, "according to an oral and common law tradition of rights, privileges and immunities" that reflected a household pattern of authority and control within the prison.[10] Prisoners were called a "family" and the gaoler and his actual family all resided in the prison.

In the era prior to the establishment of explicitly drawn distinctions between domestic political and economic spheres, the fusion between the family and the prison was also manifested in the way that the father-master outside of the prison had the authority to use imprisonment to exert control over the members of his household.[11] The familial-political economic power of the home then merged into the penal sphere through this patriarchal authority to have servants, wife, children or apprentices confined. The prison was an element in the constitution of the domestic sphere but the authority pattern of the household in turn permeated prison life.

2   THE FAMILY LABOUR COLONY

The family within the prison is also a feature of penality when punishment is enforced labour and transportation and the site of control becomes the labour colony. In this form of incorporation of the family into the penal system the punishment of the individual is manifestly shared by the family. Where the political economy is based on family labour and the demand for labour is high, punishment can be incarceration in a labour camp or labour colony where the family work together either in agriculture or in small scale craft industries.

The settlement of New South Wales has some of the characteristics of this pattern. Lieutenant Shapcote of the Neptune, a ship in the second fleet taking convicts to the penal colony of NSW received these instruction from W H Grenville, who replaced Lord Sydney at the Home Department:

> as it is probable that some of the male convicts put on board the ships ... may
> be desirous that their wives should accompany them, it has been thought
> advisable that so many of them shall be allowed to emboard, as can be

conveniently accommodated. If the number of convicts who may apply to you ... should not be sufficient ... you will in such case acquaint the rest of the convicts that women who may have cohabited with them will also be received on board.[12]

Although this form of incorporation of the family into the prison as labour colony ended with the shift in laissez-faire capitalist societies in the middle period of the nineteenth century in North America, northern Europe and Australia, there are currently family labour prison settlements in Guatemala, Mexico and the Philippines, Jordan, and three Indian states — Maharashtra, Rajasthan, and Uttar Pradesh.[13]

These examples of family based imprisonment are not some relics of a pre-industrial penal system. The largest of the family penal colonies was established in Mexico on the Isles des Marias only in 1971. It was introduced on the basis of being a humane alternative to the pre 1970s use of the prison island as a terrorising "last resort" of a prison within a prison. By 1981 the island held 1,500 prisoners and 2,000 family members.[14] Moreover the Mexican Federal Department of Co-ordinated Services for Crime Prevention and Social Rehabilitation opened two other family penal colonies in the early 1980s.[15] In the 1970s penal crisis in North America "correctional" professionals in both the USA and Canada were casting a variety of nets in their search for a solution to the tensions inherent in prison control in an era of post-authoritarianism.[16] These included calls for a return to the labour penal colony. Specifically, in 1984 there was an argument from the social sciences for the establishment of penal labour colonies within the US.[17] The argument in this case centred principally on economic rationality. Domestic penal labour colonies, it was argued, would be a cost effective punishment making use of the labour of prisoners and providing them with training in labour skills whilst ensuring that the cost of the support for their dependants was not borne by the State.

... prisoners could be transferred to one or more domestic penal colonies to be built by the convicts. Such facilities could be modeled after the Civilian Conservation corporations camps created during the depression. Such labor colonies are cheap to construct, idleness is eliminated, and prisoners would be compensated and pay taxes, support their dependents, make restitution, and learn skills. The prisoner could thus be 'banished' and society would have its 'pound of flesh' while reducing violence, escapes, and recidivism[18]

It is not clear here whether the family would be a part of the penal community. However, the American Correctional Association specifically lauded the system of family imprisonment represented by the Isles des Marias family labour colony.

The Isles des Marias Penal Colony — the largest and most unique penal colony in the world — is a community that provides a less expensive, more civilized alternative to traditional incarceration while preserving and promoting mental health and the family unit ... the results of this study may point to new opportunities for facility design, policies, and procedures for correction in the United States and Canada.[19]

The family labour colony was presented by the nine member team of ACA professionals as a penal reform that would serve several uses. It was seen as being more effective in terms of containment and prison management,

> despite the large population of inmates and their dependents, ... the large proportion of offenders convicted of violent crimes, ... and the relatively small number of staff, ... there is apparently very little violence or behavioral infractions.[20]

more effective as a "normalising" experience thus reforming the prisoner through his

> daily contact with fellow workers and neighbouring families (that) encourages prisoner to adopt a socially viable pattern of life — a lesson in socialization ... it is expected that ex-convicts will have adopted normal standards of behaviour, having acquired a taste for a 'better life'.[21]

but this normalising process is specifically located within the prisoner's assumption of authority within the family :

> the system ... allows the criminal to acquire an element of self-respect as well as an opportunity to assume the responsibilities customarily associated with household heads[22]

The family labour prison would thus provide the most rational mixture of segregation, punishment, reform and useful labour.

To date however there is no example of the family labour colony appearing as a reforming alternative within the systems of penality in the advanced corporate consumer capitalist societies of the "first world". However, these appeals to transforming punishment by a system of containment that combines domesticity and penality and thus effects a cheap and effective system of control with a promise of reform through "normalisation" re-emerge in a number of different forms of incorporation of the family into the penal sphere. However before the description of this re-emergence of diffused control through the manifest insertion of domesticity into the penal sphere, it is important to outline the classic form of relationship between domesticity and penality — the family outside prison.

II   HOME AND PRISON AS SEPARATE SPHERES

The prison and the home became two of the key sites of social control but in a very specific form in the era of the great upheaval from the 1780s to the 1840s. Bentham's description of the panopticon prison and its effect on the people incarcerated within it and on social morality evidences his concern with this ideological nature of penality. He advocated the continuous inspection of the prison by members of the public:

> and what would they see? — a set of person deprived of liberty which they had misused — compelled to engage in labour, which was formerly their

aversion — and restrained from riot and intemperance, in which they formerly delighted ... What scene could be more instructive to the great proportion of spectators? what a source of conversation, of allusion, of *domestic*[24] instruction.[25]

The misuse of liberty is directly related here to idleness, political threat and personal and social hedonism. The systematic reordering of prison life is directly related in Bentham's principles with the implications for domesticity. The home of the working class labourers was to be reconstituted, through the example of prison life, as that site where the rationally ordered material and social relations of productive life were to be reproduced.

In the classical model of imprisonment centering on the specificity of punishment there is a clear separation between the individual offender shut away in prison and the family "free" outside — the central paradigm of punishment in liberal capitalism. The offender's punishment is to lose his "freedom" to exchange his[26] labour for a family wage. In an economy that centres on the man as the primary or sole breadwinner, the family's incorporation into the punishment system is manifested in their impoverishment outside prison. In the 1840s economic depression in New South Wales, one of the groups of unemployed who were specifically denied relief were women whose husbands were imprisoned.[27] The policy of control by neglect then put the family experiencing the shadow punishment at risk of imprisonment themselves. In 1867 the three children of Mrs W, whose husband was in gaol, were arrested by the police for begging and being neglected children and sent to an industrial school.[28]

Chapter two describes the dual pushes away from large scale institutionalisation of children in the last decades of the nineteenth century: first, the retreat from costly State interventions as a consequence of the 1890s economic depression and secondly, the reconstitution of family life of labouring classes as the site of the control of husbands and children. By the end of the century the shift towards emphasising families' economic responsibilities for destitute or neglected children meant that children of prisoners were less likely to be taken away from mothers. Although there was still some degree of institutionalisation, prisoners' families were likely to be able to have the same access to the meagre resources dispensed by charities as other groups of destitute people. Of the twenty-five families on the visiting list of Mrs Hughes, a Victorian dispenser of charity aid, were three women with large families and imprisoned husbands.[29] However these families, in common with the other groups on her list, were subject to strict controls over their moral behaviour.

Penal policy reconstructed the family as a dependent relationship between men and women through the principle of deterrence. This mode of incorporation through imprisonment continues to be the dominant symbolic form of punishment. Financial distress is the major problem cited by families of prisoners in the several reports from 1926 to date.[30] Even those studies dominated by a psychological therapeutic framework point to economic difficulties as the major problem experienced by families outside.[31]

This parallel punishment of the family outside *is* effective in adding to the punishment of the prisoner. Two of the family crisis studies found that the men inside were "fraught with guilt" over the women's financial hardship.[32] With the shift to welfare capitalism the loss of the primary breadwinner does not push the family into absolute destitution as it did in the mid-nineteenth century but the relative loss of accumulated goods, mortgaged homes, cars partly paid, and the continuing impact of the break in credit payments is likely to mean that imprisonment imposes a severe economic penality on the whole family both during imprisonment and for years after the prisoner leaves gaol.[33] In addition the families of prisoners are unique in that they are the one group of single parent families whose loss of a primary breadwinner is enforced by the state, when to be a member of a female headed single parent family is to be at risk of the relative destitution of being below the poverty line.[34] Prisoners' partners become the the widows of the "civil dead".

There is a central contradiction in the imposition of imprisonment as the classical punishment of liberal capitalism. Sue Smith has pointed up the significance of this contradiction by citing the classic liberal penal philosopher Beccaria on the necessity for the separation of the family from the punishment of the individual:

> confiscations put a price on the head of the weak, cause the innocent to suffer the punishments of the guilty ... what spectacle can be sadder than that of a family dragged into infamy and misery by the crimes of its head which the submission ordained by the law would hinder the family from preventing even if it had the means to do so.[35]

Smith then contrasts this argument for specificity with the actual punishments experienced by English families of prisoners in the 1980s.[36] Both Smith and Hounslow et al, in a survey of families of prisoners in New South Wales,[37] have pointed out that the contradiction between the philosophy of specificity and the shared but invisible punishment of the family outside prison is not the result of an unfortunate, unconsidered oversight in penal policy. Smith argues that the shared punishment of the family and the invisibility of that punishment are rather the direct result of penal legal practices:

> their persistent omission from penal and welfare policy is informative and indicative of a process too concerted to be accidental indifference ... the neglect of prisoners' families forms a particularly punitive element in a wider network of social control policies, both of women and of men through women, and further, that it is a deliberate strategy aimed also at reinforcing the principle of deterrence.[38]

Hounslow et al in a similar argument say that the invisibility of information about children of prisoners which adds to the punishment of those children

> ... is not accidental. It is both convenient and necessary, because those who uphold the prevailing legal and penal ideology simply cannot afford to consider what happens to prisoners' kids. Any recognition of their plight strikes at the very notions of 'justice', 'innocent' and 'guilt' upon which this ideology is founded.[39]

Smith also makes the point that the recent new right emphasis on law and order reinforces the invisibility of families outside. If prison issues incorporate policies about the welfare of the prisoner as a family man this undermines the central image of the prisoner as a dangerous offender isolated from and threatening to society.

> ... it would be political suicide to build up one picture of crime and criminals to the voting public, instilling fear and prejudice, and presenting a law and order platform, and then contravene it by aiding prisoners' families.[40]

In this way then the specific case of families of prisoners reflects and reinforces in a particularly condensed form the social relations of the wider society.

The three key aspects of the relationship between public and domestic spheres in general social life are reproduced in a condensed form in the case of the relationship between domesticity and penality in its classic liberal form. The interdependence between the public and domestic spheres is exemplified in the central punishment in classic legal rational liberalism restricting the individual's freedom to exchange his labour for wages, which is not just a punishment on the individual but on his family. It developed at just that moment in the constitution of domesticity when the family's dependence on the waged work of the father became the primary source of income. The punishment of the family was part of the punishment of the individual. The families' dependence on the male breadwinner was an important feature of the "dull economic compulsion" to sell his labour that was essential to the reproduction of the social relations of liberal capitalism. The punishment of destitution to the family when there was no male breadwinner then was and remains a key element in the interdependence between the public and the domestic spheres.

The second element in the constitution of domesticity in the legal rationality of liberalism is the privileging of the individual over the family and the public sphere over the domestic. It is the punishment and control of the individual criminal that dominates the penal discourses of legal rational liberalism. The destitution of the family outside prison becomes merged with the several impoverishments experienced by other categories of female headed families. In the classic legal-rational era of penality there was almost no literature in the penal realm on the shared punishment of families of prisoners. It was not until the positivistic therapeutic gaze fell upon families of prisoners in the late 1950s that the punishment of the family outside became even marginally visible. Most reviews of literature of families of prisoners start with the 1959 study by Norman Fenton.[41] Even in this literature the punishment of the families was a contingent rather than a central feature of the discourse. Moreover, as de Connick[42] points out in an overview of the literature on families of prisoners up to 1982, although various ameliorations to the situation of families were suggested, what is most noticeable about the studies is the fact that almost none of their recommendations were ever implemented. Similarly, of the recommendations concerning families of prisoners in the New South Wales reports that include a discussion of their situation, the Nagle Report, the Children of Imprisoned Parents Report, the Department of Corrective Services Report on the effects of marital separation and the Women in Prison Task Force Report, only eight have been implemented.[43] Valerie Bauhofer[44] makes the same point about her attempts to make the hidden punishment of children visible to the Department of Corrective Services in New York in 1987:

> ... there is ... a very real, not so subtle resistance to 'outsiders' to bring about change (in the penal system). For years I have been trying, without success, to forge institutional connections between the Department of Correctional Services and child advocacy organizations. My most recent effort, negotiated at the state and regional level, to introduce Head Start's very successful 'Exploring Parenting' curriculum to inmate fathers at state prisons with the help of Head Start personnel was dismissed by the DOCS Commissioner.[45]

Thus the third aspect of the constitution of domesticity in liberal familial-political economies, the masking of the interdependence of public and domestic spheres, follows on from the privileging of public over domestic and individual over family.

Since the late 1970s there have been a number of critical reports based on feminist and class analyses of the shared and marginalised punishments of the family outside.[46] Nevertheless these stand as isolated studies. They have not been incorporated into any of the three potentially relevant critical literatures: the socialist feminist critiques of the relationship between the state, the family and the economy, the Marxist or radical critiques of penality nor the feminist critiques of penality and criminology. There has been no collection of the various studies in an anthology that indicates the commonalities as well as the specific variations across several societies of the hidden labour, hidden costs and hidden punishment of families outside of prison.[47] This isolated nature of the criticisms of the hidden punishment of families of prisoners both from each other and from other more mainstream criticisms of the relations of patriarchal capitalism means that the second stage of critical analysis, that of public systematisation, is not reached. The only publics the studies reach are those with a specific interest in families of prisoners or else the spasmodic and thus apolitical attention of a wider public. The condensed invisibility of families of prisoners then is maintained in spite of these embryonic criticisms. The dominant form of the relationship between domesticity and penality is still that of classic liberalism — the individual prisoner inside prison manifestly punished by his restricted access to waged labour and the destitution of the family outside prison whose shadow punishment is marginalised and largely invisible to the public gaze.

The invisibility of the relationship between domestic and penal spheres is described here as condensed because it remains marginal to so many discourses: the official and the radical and materialist literatures and practices in the penal sphere, the official and the socialist feminist critiques of welfare practices and the feminist concern with women and the state and with women and crime. Of the current literatures in these areas it is only in the two texts on social control by Stan Cohen[48] and Anne Edwards[49] that the issue of the family in relation to sentencing and punishment is incorporated into any wider discussions of the social relationships in the broader familial-political economy, and in these two only marginally.

The recent critical work cited above and the evidence discussed in chapters five to eight indicates that the masked punishment of the family outside of prison remains the major form of the incorporation of the family into the penal sphere. However there are other ideological deposits layered onto this basic form. The next layer of policy that makes the experiences of families of prisoners complex, contradictory and ambiguous is associated with the positivist shift from the 1880s to prison as a place for rehabilitation and treatment by experts. In this era of imprisonment as treatment, the family outside is allowed to enter prison although the extent to which the boundaries between home and prison become permeable varies with the specific balance between treatment, segregation or terror that constitutes punishment in any one state.

III PERMEABLE BOUNDARIES BETWEEN PRISON AND HOME

With the shift from a philosophy of "freedom" to a psychology of "personality" and the idea of the reformability of the offender, the ground is laid for the family to be brought into the penal sphere as part of therapeutic-rehabilitative programmes. This can take a variety of forms: conjugal visiting, co-ed or co-correctional prisons, and family visiting. The first two forms are considered here. Family visiting is discussed in chapters five to eight and in the overview of the way that the social sciences have constructed the population "families of prisoners" in chapter four.

CONJUGAL VISITING: THE FAMILY AS A "MITIGATING COUNTERFORCE"[50]

Heidensohn[51] has made the point that in the process of change from the earliest to the latest of the social scientific theories of criminality, the theorists of deviant behaviour over this century have shifted from defining criminals as pathological and abnormal to seeing criminality as normal and even admirable. The ways that families of prisoners are seen and acted upon however does not parallel this path from disapprobation to hero-worship. When criminality is defined as pathological women, through their family relationships with men, become an explicit part of the problem of criminality. When deviance is defined in more positive terms as defiant and heroic, women disappear or are depicted only in terms of their sexuality. W H Whyte, author of *Street Corner Society*, comments on his own methodological bias:

> I had done no systematic work upon the family. On the one hand, it seemed inconceivable that one could write a study of Cornerville without discussing the family; yet at the same time, I was at a loss as to how to proceed in tying family studies into ... the book. I must confess also that for quite unscientific reason I have always found politics, rackets and gangs more interesting than the basic unit of human society.[52]

The strongly individualistic character of the Chicago School "heroic" paradigms of criminality thus reflects the biases of the way punishment is constituted in liberal rationalism in the maskings of the interdependence between domesticity and penalty. Unsurprisingly, then, the heroic individualism of the Chicago School also fits the neo-liberal programmes of conjugal visiting. If women are visible only in terms of men's sexuality it would follow that the penal policies deriving from the neo-liberal version of the "back to a just deserts" philosophy of incarceration bring the family into the prison through this narrow focus on the sexuality of the prisoner and his partner.

In the neo-liberalism of the era of permissive consumerism, conjugal visiting programmes reflected in a condensed form tensions inherent in the restructuring of the domestic sphere in the narrow terms of the reconstitution of women as sexual objects and subjects. The narrow form of liberalism within a commodity culture served to define women as "other" and to increase rather than reduce their marginality as people.

However the conjugal visits programme was also used as an attempt to reclaim power back to the prison administration away from prisoner control. Women here are being used to domesticise sexuality in prisons to combat not simply homosexuality, but the prisoner power structures built up on homosexual violence. The masculinity of prison, although its most obvious aspect from the 1880s on, was largely masked by the privileging of "the individual" in legal rational discourses. The semantic and political economic conflation of "man" with "human" allowed the masculinity of prison populations to be obfuscated by its very obviousness.

The explosion of prison violence especially when it was manifested in the collective actions against prison administrations in the international prison crises in the 1970s redirected penal discourses to the volatility of all male imprisonment. There was a series of academic papers, neo-liberal reformist arguments and some penal policy changes centering on the restitution of conjugal rights of prisoners both in the United States and in Northern Europe, throughout the 1970s.[53]

In Lockwood's 1982 study of sexual aggression in an all male prison, specific parallels were drawn between forms of sexual harassment in the "free world", in which men ogle, make remarks and proposition women as well as forcibly rape them, to the forms of sexual aggression within prison. Lockwood pointed out the way in which domesticity, in terms of power , is reconstituted within the prison when women are not present, arguing that "in this sense male prisons, where sexual aggressors look upon targets as being feminine, mirror a condition prevalent throughout many subcultures within our society."[54]

Lockwood's proposed reform was in terms of a vague liberal feminist argument for eliminating the values permitting men to sexually harass women. However restoring "normal" sexual relations inside prison by bringing women into prisons for conjugal visits was one of the solutions introduced in New York as well as in several other prisons.

Goetting[55] estimated that in 1982 seven states in the USA allowed conjugal visits, five of the states implementing the programmes in the fifteen years between 1967 and 1982. In Dickinson's survey of 68 adult male prisons in the USA in 1981, 18 per cent included conjugal visits as part of their penal programmes, an increase from 6 per cent in 1971.[56]

The Budget cuts of the Reagan "retreat from welfare" period were associated with the end of this penal policy innovation. By 1983 the defence of existing conjugal visiting schemes was more likely to be in terms of prison control rather than prisoner reform or prisoner rights. The Family Reunion Programme in the New York State Department of Correctional Services was described in 1983 as being effective because

(the) program services can have a positive impact on inmate discipline, especially in those cases where good disciplinary records are directly related to participation in programs that are meaningful to the offenders ... this finding may be seen to be especially noteworthy since nearly all of the (36) cases had prior histories of numerous, as well as serious, disciplinary infractions[57]

Most of the conjugal visiting policies incorporate the home into the prison through a regulated pattern of punishment, control or reward. However, the penal policies of Costa Rica have the most systematic version of this policy of progressivism. The relationship between the prison and the home is plotted through a programme associating punishment and reward with a minutely detailed balance between control in the institution or the home:[58]

1   Maximum Security Closed inmates are allowed no conjugal visit;
2   Maximum Security Open prisoners are allowed one two hour conjugal visit every three weeks;
3   Medium Security Closed inmates are allowed one two hour conjugal visit every fifteen days;
4   Medium Security Open inmates are allowed a three hour visit every fifteen days;
5   Minimum Security prisoners are allowed one conjugal visit from 5.30 pm to 7.00 am every fifteen days;

6   Limited Confidence inmates live at home every week from
     Saturday at 1.00 pm until Sunday at 6.00 pm;
7   Widened and Complete Confidence categories ... sleep at home
     every night of the week except Saturday.[59]

These specifically allocated rewards, of carefully plotted increases of
time with the family, incorporate the domestic into the penal sphere with
Benthamesque precision and zeal. With this programme which blends the
diffuse care of the family with the precise control of the stopwatch, Costa
Rica has attracted the reputation of being "known as one of the most
penologically advanced countries in the Western Hemisphere."[60]
     What is obscured in this description is the interdependence between
penal and domestic realms in terms of the masked expectations of the
extraordinary malleability of the women outside of prison and their
willingness to use their resources of time and emotional skill in fitting in to
the demands of these precise schedules of prison control. The prison
extends into the lives of the families outside imposing major areas of
unfreedom over the woman's time and control over her own material
resources, yet the "naturalness" of the woman's family obligation to
support the prisoner masks this domestic labour so effectively it becomes
invisible in most of the articles that advocate conjugal visiting programmes
and that define the "progressiveness" of the Costa Rican penal system. It is
women's work as sexual labourers, securing the sexual rights of the
prisoner as well as the civilisation of the prison, that is the masked
exploitation in these liberal discourses of the late 1960s and 1970s.
Moreover what is even more marginalised in these approaches is the range
of other practical domestic labours that are taken for granted in the policies
of conjugal visiting. There is little acknowledgement in any of the texts
cited above, of the infrastructure of housework that is necessary for
conjugal visits — negotiating time away from paid work, organising
contraception, rescheduling the household budget to be able to afford the
work of visiting over a two or three day period, arranging for children to be
cared for, or if the children are included in the visit, all the practical
preparation that is the inevitable corollary of taking children away on a
"holiday", as well as the emotional work of preparing them for the visit
and working through the after effects of a stay behind prison walls.

CO-ED PRISONS

There is an an alternative version of this mode of incorporation of the
family into punishment systems through the domestication of sexuality and
the civilising of masculinity. In co-ed experiments the family is
reconstituted within the prison, not by bringing the family into the prison
but by using women prisoners to feminise the latter stages of
imprisonment.
     The four reasons for their introduction are:

1   the dehumanising effects of masculine prisons;
2   the inability to relate to females of young male offenders if they
     spend their youth primarily in all male prisons (ie, the paradox of
     the demasculinisation of young men in an all male prison);
3   the wider implications of this failure in gender socialisation for
     young male offenders' future productive contribution to social
     life;
4   the subversion of programmes of reform/rehabilitation in the all
     male culture of orthodox imprisonment.[61]

The early evaluations of these schemes indicate that co-ed prisons produce a classically gendered division of labour.[62] Domesticity, manifestly drawn into the "over-determined site" of penality through co-correctional programmes, reflects and reconstructs the unequal gender relations of the wider familial-political economy.

There are both emotional and material ways in which the reconstituted familial relationships within the prison replicated the gendered division of domestic labour in the outside world. Ten States in the USA had introduced co-ed prisons by 1980. In each State the imprisonment in a co-ed prison was the "reward" achieved by male prisoners only at the end of their progress through the prison system.[63]

Co-ed prisons have been reported as reinforcing women's dependency on men, undermining their self-reliance and increasing their insecurity.[64] There is greater pressure on women to define themselves in terms of their physical attractiveness and sexuality.[65] In addition, with the shift to co-correctional programmes men take over the few "best jobs" or dominate the sporting, educational or training programmes.[66]

One major feature of the reconstitution of the home within the prison through co-ed programmes is the narrow construction of family life. The family is constituted only in terms of adult male-female relations with sexuality as the most visible discourse surrounding the introduction and evaluation of the programmes. Although male prisoners have a choice whether or not to enter a co-ed prison, in some instances co-correctional imprisonment is the only option for women prisoners.[67] The co-ed prisons do not address the key problem for women in prison — their responsibility for their children outside.[68]

Flynn specifically sets this attempt at reform through domesticising the sexuality of prison life against the tensions between a continuing commitment to liberal values of reform and the rise, from the mid 1970s on, of the new orthodoxy which contests that principle. This new orthodoxy is manifested in the development of the "back to law and order" programmes that lead to an increase in imprisonment rates and the reconstitution of penality as the sphere of harsh punishment rather than reform. The tensions between these two "liberalisms" — one centering on the thesis that the individual is constituted in terms of his free rational choice, and the other on his potential psychological and social reformability — draws domesticity more manifestly into the penal sphere. It is specifically the "normal" nuclear family reconstituted within the prison through which the male prisoner is expected to regain or achieve the proper balance between the masculinity of desire (in Elshtain's terms) and the masculinity of moral responsibility. The seemingly supra-rational sphere of the all masculine prison that characterised prison life from the 1880s to the 1950s is explicitly recognised as leading to an uncontrollable amorality that threatens to shift the power away from the legally constituted authority of the state. The partnership between the powerful morality of the state and the powerless morality of the domestic sphere is explicitly manifest in this microcosm of the contradiction of social life as played out in the over-determined site of the prison through both conjugal visits programmes and the co-ed experiments.

It is notable that one group of women in the co-ed experiments are defined as not as likely to be contributing to the smooth running of the programmes. These women are the black women prisoners in the co-ed programmes. Lambiotte indicates that the black women prisoners were much less likely to adopt the normal domesticised couple relationships of co-ed prison life. Black women were defined as more deviant because they were more assertive and more organised.

It is not some essential femininity, then, on which the configuration and reconfigurations of power, morality and rationality in the various phases of the familial-political economy are based, but the specific form of femininity as it is constituted within the domestic relations of care and dependence of the classic nuclear family of liberal and corporate welfare capitalism. Family patterns in which interdependencies between women constitute the significant relationship of family life are much more likely to be defined as deviant in relation to the "normal" constitution of masculinity.

This specifically defined "familism" is also a significant feature of the most manifest incorporation of domesticity into penal life in the fourth intersection of the home and the prison — the family as the site of imprisonment.

IV THE PRISON IN THE HOME:
THE FAMILY AS A "NATURALLY RELATED COMMUNITY RESOURCE"

Whilst in this era of positivism the boundaries between home and prison became more permeable with programmes that drew the domestic sphere into the prison, the ground was also set for the fourth mode of incorporating the domestic sphere into the realm of penality. This was the form in which the family domain becomes the site of containment through a variety of sanctions: probation, community service orders, after-care and parole and, in its most invasive form, home detention.

In an almost classic case of what Yeatman calls the submerging of the family into the "abstract sociality" of public life, within this form the family becomes defined as a "naturally related community resource"[69]

Cohen[70] argues that it is in the era of community based control, that the Foucaultian description of modern penality as comprising a series of sites of the microphysics of power, with the punitive city becoming the place of " hundreds of tiny theatres of punishment", is most fully realised. In his overview of the exponential increase in community based controls from the 1970s on, he shows how several areas of social life are reconstituted as sites of social control, including examples of family based community controls along with those based in schools, work places and a range of other formal and informal organisations. However, in defining the family as merely one of the several sites of control in the punitive city, Cohen's description underestimates the way that the quest for community in penal policies falls back upon the same classic conflation that comprises what Finch and Groves[71] have called the "double equation" of community care: "in practice community care equals care by the family, and in practice care by the family equals care by women."

The domestication of control is intertwined with its commodification. Although Cohen[72] indicates the way in which forms of privatisation in the penal/welfare sphere have included the exploitation of the unpaid labour of volunteers, it is "familism" that is being used to legitimate the dual and intersecting processes of privatisation and deinstitutionalisation in the most "attractive" form.

In its most fully worked out version, prison enters the home because the home literally becomes the prison. However, symbolically prison enters the home even in minor forms of home based control. These forms of punishment introduce new layers of potential criminality — the new crimes of breaking the conditions of the home based containment. The normal social behaviours of driving a car, having a drink or being late for appointments are redefined as criminal for offenders living at home and imprisonment is the potential end punishment. Home then is not only the site of the prison but it becomes criminogenic as the site of a set of potential new crimes which can only be committed as a result of the introduction of home based containment.

In addition these criminogenic aspects of community based controls contribute through various professional "feed back loops" to a potential increase, rather than a decrease, in the numbers of people sentenced to institutional imprisonment.

The pervasiveness, diffuseness, elaboration and dispersal of penality through this proliferation of forms of community control brings about a new reconstruction of the intersection between "the prison" and "the home".

Current public discussions about the introduction of home imprisonment in Australia have been greatly influenced by Cohen's thesis of "net widening".[73] The implication of "net widening" for the intersection of domesticity and penality needs to be emphasised here. The supply side thesis — the capacity-driven argument — about imprisonment rates, that the imprisonment rate increases according to the number of prison places available, has not yet been seriously considered in relation to home imprisonment.[74] The Victorian programme of increasing community based alternatives to imprisonment has recently stemmed and even reduced the imprisonment rate in that state.[75] Nevertheless, the Queensland Comptroller General of Prisons[76] has pointed out that governments are passing more laws that have imprisonment as a breach penalty, increasing sentence penalities for many breaches and that magistrates and judges are increasing sentence lengths. Home imprisonment will release more prison places so, if all homes *can* be a prison, there is no logistical reason why increasing numbers of offenders would not be processed through institutional prisons into home imprisonment.

The issues of domesticity and power when home is the prison are rarely addressed in detail. Amanda George[77] has pointed to the problems that continual surveillance constrains the family as well as the prisoner and that family or friends who share the house will be both co-prisoners and warders. Malcolm Feiner argues that families who fear violence from a prisoner are put into an untenable position. If they object to a prisoner being released into the home they may experience subsequent vengeful behaviour.[78]

However, by combining the critical frameworks of the radical critiques of penality and the feminist materialist critiques of public policy, it becomes clear that there are several other issues that need to be raised about the exponential increase of this major new[79] mode of incorporation of the family into the realm of punishment and control.

Chapter five raises a question concerning the inversion of family roles in the care of adult dependents, and the state's exploitation of the image of caring as "normal" that then masks the problems of the tensions stemming from this extension of the usual forms of domestic labour. The South Australian scheme initially asked the home "resident" to sign a contract agreeing to accommodate the prisoner, to assist and encourage the prisoner to be of good behaviour, to abide by the conditions of the Home Detention order and to contact the Supervisor without delay on any matters of concern involving the prisoner's Home Detention conditions. Domestic labour here is being extended far beyond the "normal" forms of care. Moreover the feminist critique also indicates that caring labour is particularly open to exploitation because it comprises the elements of "coping". The characteristics of a willingness to adapt to, and internalise responsibility for, crises created by others can clearly be seen to be an especially useful and "taken for granted" component of adapting to the use of own's own home as a prison for a son or a husband. The complex skills that comprise caring labour, that in public life are accorded professional status, and that can bring an entitlement to a semi-professional, or even a professional salary, can become a very useful and free infrastructural support in the conversion of the home into a prison.

The contradictions of supporting and controlling that are obvious problems of home imprisonment for women, have been a contentious part of probation and parole work since its inception. There has been a suggestion from the probation service that this could be solved for workers in New South Wales in a home imprisonment programme by using a private security guard to do the controlling work of random surveillance, freeing the probation workers to take on the "soft" aspects of support and advocacy.[80] What is noticeably missing from this suggestion is an understanding of the extra stresses imposed on the other carer/controller whose services are being drawn on unpaid — the wife or parent in the home.

The surveillance of the prisoner in the home must inevitably be control and punishment shared by both the prisoner and his wife or parent. In most schemes the random calls can be programmed to take place at any time in the twenty four hours. The stress of waiting for a call that determines whether the prisoner is returned to an institutional prison becomes a minute by minute experience of anxiety. It is difficult to imagine that this form of control would not exacerbate the tensions already inherent in home imprisonment.

The intersection between domestic, penal and productive life is reworked in some home imprisonment schemes through the requirement that the prisoner in the home acquire waged employment within a specified period of time otherwise he has to return to institutionalised imprisonment. The New Jersey scheme that a New South Wales judge is advocating has this employment clause.[81]

Graham's work on the shift to deinstitutionalisation in other areas of social policy indicates that mediating and negotiating with bureaucratic representatives, from a position of powerlessness, is a component of the domestic labour of caring for aged or invalid dependants. The ways in which normal aspects of family life become criminogenic with the insertion of the prison into the home include failure to get a job, going out (even into the back yard) without supervision, driving a car, and having a drink, and indicate that the mediating and negotiating skills of the domestic labour of caring are likely to become an increasingly important feature of the interdependence of family, prison and productive life.

Underlying these controlling and emotional aspects of the caring work of women in Home Imprisonment programmes is the major material factor of costs of imprisonment. This considerable caring work could save the state up to $20,000 in every household for healthy prisoners, considerably more for prisoners at present in prison hospitals. The recommendations made by the Attorney General of the Australian Capital Territory that eight out of ten of ACT offenders should be transferred from New South Wales prisons to electronically monitored imprisonment in their own homes, have been made in order to save approximately $600,000 in payments to NSW over three years.[82] In this proposition the ACT seem to be at risk of implementing the situation envisaged by Terry Dorsey:

If the sole motive for programs such as Home Detention is the reduction of numbers and costs ... drastic surgery to original designs will be inevitable ... we could ... be accused, with some justification, of creating a myriad of 'three bedroomed' prisons spread throughout suburbia.[83]

The current contradictions faced by political and administrative decision-makers by the issue of prison overcrowding and prisoners health, are currently making Home Imprisonment, in Fox's words, "a wonderfully attractive package".[84]

Home detention potentially brings the feminist materialist issues usually submerged in punishment and control policies closer to the surface of both public and academic awareness. The examination of the discourses, policies and operations surrounding this shift of punishment into the domestic domain promises to make visible some of the so far masked and marginalised aspects of complex ways of incorporating domesticity, constituted as the site of powerlessness, morality and arationality, into the penal realm. To disentangle forms of this multiplicity of power relations in contemporary penality means recognising the *central* significance of the nexus between caring and dependency.

The evidence from recent feminist analyses of sentencing decisions becomes increasingly significant with the introduction and expansion of intensive surveillance programmes of penal control. With home imprisonment as a "front end" option magistrates become significant gate keepers of the incorporation of the domestic sphere into the legal penal realm.[85] Eaton's[86] analysis of mitigation pleas and decisions made in a magistrates court in England shows how sentencing judgements enforce the social control partnership between the family and the penal realms. Family status plays a major part in magistrates' decisions about the site of imprisonment for both men and women offenders. She shows how in these decisions, it is the dominant model of the family that is reinforced, as a family characterised by the conventional gendered division of labour with women responsible for the child care and expressive work and men for the instrumental role of economic responsibility.[87] Families other than the conventional man-woman unit were not acceptable as alternative sites for control.

All of these "family arguments" rest on the definition of a specific family form. It is the "normal" family that is the basis for the promise of redemption of the offender. Her summary of the way this operates in the negotiations between defendant, defending lawyers and magistrates is that "Defendants offend because their circumstances are abnormal. Defendants will reform because their circumstances will in future be normal".[88] A conventional family man is also the man whose "self" is constructed, and defended, by the woman for whom he is expected to provide. The judgement's being made about the women on probation were based on their competence in maintaining a home. The evaluations of the men, however, "were an opportunity for meeting the woman who was significant in (his) life".

Eaton's work indicates that in penal policy as in other forms of social policy that draw on the unpaid domestic work of caring, dependency has different consequences for men and women. It seems likely that economically dependent men will be more at risk of committal to institutionalised imprisonment and that it will be those men who will fit the role of provident breadwinner who will become the subject and the object of the unpaid caring and controlling work of their spouses or parents in the home-as-prison. This reconfiguration of caring and dependence then comes full circle. The reconstruction of domesticity and penality almost exactly parallels the constitution of domestic life in the penal settlement of New South Wales in the period of transportation. The major difference lies in the family's dispossession from the means of production. Caring and dependence take different forms in the relationships between state, the economy and the family labour economies of the households of the late 18th century settlement, and the irregularities of attachment and detachment from waged labour in the family consumer economies of the late twentieth century.

SUMMARY

The moral sphere of the home has been incorporated into the wider moral public sphere of penality in a number of complex forms. There is however a fundamental tension in the intersection of the two spheres that stems from their separate bases of morality: the particularistic relationships of family life in the former stand in direct contradiction to the universalistic principles of legal rationality or scientific rationality in the latter. This contradiction of the interdependence yet incompatibility of the two spheres of moral reproduction is most simply resolved in the classic form of the interdependence between home and prison — the segregation of the *supra-rational* masculine prison and the *supra-arational* emotional world of the family. The essential irrationality of the extension of punishment to families of prisoners in a legal judicial system that is based on the specificity of punishment is neatly masked by the elegant solution of the neglect of the parallel punishment to the family. Even in the penal era in which the home is connected to the prison along a continuum of segregation, correction, and normalisation, the shadowy nature of the punishment of the prisoners' families is maintained by the tactic of focusing the spotlight of social scientific interest upon the personality and relational skills, or lack of them, of the women outside.

However the resolution of segregation and neglect and redirected attention produces new contradictions. The very masculinity of prison life produces tensions that sends some reformers back into the "pre-rational" era to examine proto-capitalist forms of punishment that more manifestly incorporate the family into the prison.

However, the cost of bringing family life into prison, whether through conjugal visit schemes, co-correctional programmes or family counselling

71

courses, makes this mode economically unattractive in the era of "retreat from welfare" and of economic rationalism. The family inside the prison is only cost effective in political economies in which family labour economies are still viable.

The more technologically advanced resolution, and one that particularly suits the era of consumerism and fiscal crisis, is the inversion of the spatial relationship, the new topology of penal life that brings the prison into the home, the "wonderfully attractive" programme of home imprisonment.

Nevertheless the several contradictions within the legal-penal system itself means that there is no cohesive, coherent, penal policy. The processes of sentencing and punishment in most western industrialised societies are characterised by their Byzantine confusion of layered policies and practices with the co-existence of various forms of incorporation of the home into the prison.

NOTES

1   Cohen, S, *Visions of Social Control* (1985) at 100.

2   Garton, S, "The State, Labour Markets and Incarceration: a Critique" in Findlay, M and Hogg, R (eds), *Understanding Crime and Criminology* (1988) at 322.

3   Above n1 at 17–19.

4   Id at 19.

5   Kelly-Gadol, J, "The Social Relation of the Sexes: methodological implications of women's history", ch2 in Harding, S, *Feminism and Methodology: Social Science Issues* (1987).

6   Above n1, ch3.

7   Weatherburn, D, "Reducing the New South Wales Prison Population: sentencing reform and early release" (1986) 10 *Crim LJ* at 137.

8   This is included too in several of the texts on families of prisoners detailed in the bibliography.

9   Ignatieff, M, "State, Civil Society and Total Institutions: a critique of recent social histories of punishment" in Cohen, S and Scull, A (eds), *Social Control and the State* (1983) at 81.

10   Ibid.

11   Dobash, R, Dobash, R E and Gutteridge, S, *The Imprisonment of Women* (1986) at 23.

12   Robinson, P, *The Hatch and Brood of Time: a study of the first generation of native born white Australian 1788–1828* (1985) at 33.

13   Goetting, A, "Conjugal Association in Prison: a world view" (1982) 14/3 *Crim Just Abstr* 406–416.

14   Worrall, J, "ACA Study Team Visits Unique Mexican Penal Colony" (1982) 44/6 *Corrections Today* at 74; above n13 at 408–415.

15   Worrall, above n14 at 75.

16   Above n9 at 78.

17   Murton, T, "The Penal Colony: Relic or Reform" (1984) 12/1 *Free Inquiry in Creative Sociology* 20–24.

18   Id at 23.

19   Worrall, above n14 at 74.

20   Id at 75.

21   Ibid.

22   Ibid.

23   In addition to health, education and child welfare.

24   My emphasis.

25   Cited in Dobash et al, above n11 at 40.

26   Note, 'his' is used deliberately here. Criminality becomes masculinised with the advent of mature industrial capitalism with a decline in sentenced female offenders from 40 per cent in some parties of the United Kingdom to less than 5 per cent of offenders from the early 1800s to the late 19th century (see chapter two at 54 & 80).

27   Alford, K, *Production or Reproduction? An Economic History of Women in Australia 1788–1850* (1984) at 218.

28   Daniels, K, Murnane, M and Picot, A, *Women in Australia: an Annotated Guide to Records* (1977).

29   Swain, M, "Mrs Hughes and the Deserving Poor" in Lake, M and Kelly, F (eds), *Double Time* (1985) at 129–130.

30   These reports are listed separately in the bibliography.

31   Although there are too many to cite here, the major Australian report in this vein by Nancy Anderson exemplifies this point: Anderson, N, *Prisoners' Families: Reports I & II* (1965).

32   Morris, P, *Prisoners and their Families* (1965); Anderson, above n31.

33   Jones, J, "Prisoners and their Families", unpublished PhD thesis, Melbourne: Monash University, Department of Anthropology and Sociology, 1983, at ch5.

34   Cass, B and O'Loughlin, M, "The Needs of Single Parents" *Australian Society* 1 Jan 1984 at 20–22.

35   Smith, S, "Neglect as Control: prisoners' wives", paper presented to the XIVth Annual Conference of the European Group for the Study of Deviance and Social Control, September 1986, at 2.

36   Id at 2–6.

37   Hounslow, B, Stephenson, A, Stewart, J and Crancher, J, *Children of Imprisoned Parents* (1982), at 1.

38   Above n35 at 7.

39   Above n37 at 1.

40   Above n35 at 9.

41   All of these are themselves contained within the families of prisoners texts. See bibliography for list.

42   de Connick, G, "Actualities bibliographiques: La famille de detenu: de la suspicion de la idealization" (1982) 6/1 *Deviance et Societé*.

43   Nagle, J F, *Report of the Royal Commission into New South Wales Prisons* (1978); Hounslow et al, above n37; Kemp, B, *The Impact of Enforced Separation on Prisoners' Wives* (1981); Kemp, B, Cheron, M, McClelland, M and Cooney, G, *The Effects of Separation on Marital Relationships of Prisoners and their Wives* (1982); New South Wales Task Force on Women in Prison, *New South Wales Task Force Report on Women in Prison* (1985). The gap between the reports' recommendations and the actual consequences are discussed in greater detail in chapters five to eight.

44   Bauhofer, V, "Prison Parenting: challenge for children's advocates" (1987) Jan/Feb *Children Today* at 16.

45   Ibid.

46   Crosthwaite, A, "Voluntary Work with Families of Prisoners" (1972) 16/3 *Int J Offend Ther & Compar Crim* 29–37; Johns, C, "The Hidden Costs of the Personal and Emotional Deprivation of Prisoners anad their Families", paper presented at Resurgents Group Seminar, Parramatta Gaol, 14 November 1979; Hounslow et al, above n37; Jones, above n33; Matthews, J, *Good and Mad Women* (1984); Smith, above n35; Bauhofer, above n44; Deane, H, *The Social Effects of Imprisonment on Male Prisoners and their Families* (1988); Fishman, S, *Women at the Wall* (1991); Light, R. *Prisoners' Families* (1991); Shaw, R, *Children of Imprisoned Fathers* (1987).

47   Although Light (above n46) is a collection of several British articles.

48   Above n1.

49   Edwards, A, *Regulation and Repression* (1988) at 136–137.

50   Nacci, P and Kane, T, "Inmate Sexual Aggression: some evolving propositions, empirical findings and mitigating counter forces" (1984) 9/1–2 J *Offend Couns, Serv & Rehab* at 1.

51   Heidensohn, F, *Women and Crime* (1985).

52   Cited in Heidensohn, id at 131.

53   Amongst others: Hopper, C, *Sex in Prison: the Mississippi Experiment with Conjugal Visiting* (1969); Schneller, D, "Prisoners' Families: a study of some social and psychological effects of incarceration on the families of negro prisoners" (1975) 12/4 *Criminology* 402–412; Burnstein, J, *Conjugal Visits in Prison* (1977); Lockwood, D, "Maintaining Manhood. Prison violence precipitated by aggressive sexual overtures", paper presented at the annual meetings of the Academy of Criminal Justice Sciences, New Orleans (1978), *Prison Sexual Violence* (1980), "The Contribution of Sexual Harassment to Stress and Coping in Confinement" in Parisi N (ed), *Coping with Imprisonment* (1982); Goetting, A, "Conjugal Association in Prison: a world view" (1982) 14/3 *Crim Just Abstr* 406–416,, "Conjugal Association Practices in Prisons of the American Nations" (1984) 6/3 *Altern Lifest* 155–175; Swinnen, E, "Sexuality and Imprisonment: forced celibacy in prison" (1983) 28/1 *Tijdschrift-voor-Sociale-Wetenschappen* 36-57; Nacci & Kane, above n50.

54   Lockwood, D, "The Contribution of Sexual Harassment to Stress and Coping in Confinement" in Parisi N (ed), *Coping with Imprisonment* (1982).

55 Goetting, A, "Conjugal Association in Prison: a world view" (1982) 14/3 *Crim Just Abstr* at 407.

56 Dickinson, G, "Changes in Communication Policies" (1984) 46/2 *Corrections Today* at 59.

57 Howser, J, Grossmann, J and MacDonald, D, "The Impact of Family Reunion Program on Institutional Discipline" (1983) 8/1–2 *J Offend Couns, Serv & Rehab* 27–37.

58 Goetting, A, "Conjugal Association Practices in Prisons of the American Nations" (1984) 6/3 *Altern Lifest* at 160.

59 Adapted from Goetting, ibid.

60 Ibid.

61 Flynn, E, 'Foreword' in Smykla, J (ed), *Co-ed Prison* (1980).

62 Smykla, above n61.

63 However for women prisoners in some states the co-ed prison was the only option.

64 Crawford, J, "Two Losers Don't Make a Winner: the case against the co-correctional institution", in Smykla, above n61 at 265.

65 Lambiotte, J, "Sex Role Differentiation in a Co-correctional Setting" in Smykla, above n61 at 227.

66 Id at 262–270.

67 Above n64 at 262–270.

68 Above n61 at 11 & 12.

69 This is one of the several examples of the 'controltalk' cited by Cohen (above n1 at 273–281), in his description of the way 'technobabble' becomes part of the hidden politics of the social science technologies.

70 Above n1 at 26.

71 Finch, J and Groves, D (eds), *A Labour of Love: Women, Work and Caring* (1983) at 224.

72 Above n1 at 66.

73 At Australian Institute of Criminology conference: "Developments in Correctional Policy: More Prisons", Canberra 1987; Sydney University Institute of Criminology seminar: "Punishment Outside of Prison", Sydney, 1988, Australian Bicentennial International Congress on Corrective Services, Sydney, 24–28 January 1988.

74 Although George refers to a comment about it from the Victorian Office of Corrections: see George, A, "Privatising Prisons" (1988) Sept *Australian Society* at 32–33.

75 Kidson, B, "Controlling Prison Crowding — the Victorian Approach: practical aspects of Victorian approach" in Vernon, J (ed), *Developments in Correctional Policy: More Prisons?* (1987).

76 Lobban, A, "Whose Gaols? Whose Goals?" in Vernon, ibid.

77 George, above n74.

78 Cited in the Australian Law Reform Commission's Discussion Paper No 30: "Sentencing Penalties" (1987).

79   New only in terms of punishment strategies in liberal industrial capitalism. The BI Home Escort Sales publicity pamphlets point out that home imprisonment dates back to forms of control enforced in biblical times.

80   Robertson, M, "Expanding the Scope of Community Corrections to Meet Prison Population Pressures" in *Diversionary Programmes Workshop*, Proceedings 10–11 September 1986.

81   Cooper, H, "Punishment Outside Gaol: a Court Perspective" (1988) 77 *Proceedings of the Institute of Criminology* at 11–26.

82   B Collaery, Attorney General and Minister for Welfare and Community Services, Australian Capital Territory (1990) reported in Morris, J, "New jail replaces 'unfit' Quamby" *Canberra Times* 14 Apr 1990 at 1.

83   Dorey, T, "Queensland Home Detention Program", unpublished paper presented to Australian Bicentennial International Congress on Corrective Services, Sydney, 1988.

84   Fox, R, "Dr Schwizgebel's Machine Revisited: Electronic Monitoring of Offenders" (1987) 20 *ANZ J Crim* 132–147.

85   See Eaton, E, *Justice for Women? Family, Court and Social Control* (1986) at 29.

86   Ibid.

87   Id at 94.

88   Id at 54.

4

THE SOCIAL SCIENCES AND
THE HOME AND THE PRISON

The swings in penal administration are mediated through academic legitimations, with specific social scientific discourses within positivism tending to "fit" more or less closely with any one of a number of different political and bureaucratic discourses.

Broadly speaking, six major theories of criminality are part of the discourses underpinning the third and fourth modes of the incorporation of the family into the prison. The ways in which families of prisoners are conceptualised and acted upon are filtered through the symbolisations of family and criminality within each of these theories. They are, broadly, (a) bio-anthropological and bio-psychological; (b) psycho-dynamic; (c) subcultural; (d) structural, (e) radical, and (f) neo-classical, social science literatures on criminality.

BIO-ANTHROPOLOGICAL THEORIES

This earliest form of positivistic criminology opposed the major discourse of punishment of the classical laissez-faire era, the discourse of rational free choice. Criminality was not the rational choice of a free and calculating intellect but the result of predetermined, inherited, organically based characteristics of the offender. Criminals came from a subculture within society that was characterised by its genetic inferiority. It was the work of criminal anthropologists then to measure, classify and segregate the individuals in that subculture. Although Lombroso's work has been the subject of derisive criticism since 1913,[1] the genetic basis of moral inferiority has never been completely absent as an explanatory model in criminology. It was part of the influential eugenics movement that dominated discourses about both the family and punishment in the US, Northern Europe and Australia well into the 1950s.[2]

Karier points to the staying power of the myths of the Jukes and the Kallikaks, two 18th century American families each supposedly responsible by their profligate breeding, and the uncontrolled breeding of their later generations, for "hundreds of the lowest types of human beings" that are supposedly the pool for criminality in America.[3] There are three aspects of the paradigm of genetic inferiority that add to the mythical power of the Martin Kallikak story: the sexuality of the criminal's mother or partner, her intellectual inferiority and her moral inferiority are all interwoven strands in this paradigm of the genetic/social production of a criminal underclass. Although the genetic argument has been used to segregate the domestic and penal spheres, to set up definite boundaries between the home and the prison, these themes also re-emerge in the positivisitic discourses which bring the family into the prison.

Rock has argued that to examine the work of the early positivists is like resurrecting corpses.[4] However, although the crude Lombrosian thesis of genetically based criminality lost plausibility by the 1920s, the general thesis of inherited criminogenic characteristics has been periodically revived in increasingly sophisticated forms. The influence of body types upon criminality was the central focus in Sheldon's work and was a feature of the Gluecks' investigation into delinquency in the 1950s.[5] Chromosone imbalances, glandular dysfunctions and left hemisphere dysfunctions have been the most recent variations of Lombrosian positivism.[6]

The most manifest and dramatic consequences for families of criminals were the sterilisation programmes that resulted from these discourses. Twenty-one states in the US practised eugenical sterilisation. About 10 per cent of the population were identified as carrying "the bad seed" of feeblemindedness. Between 1907 and 1928 in the US sterilisation laws were passed and over 8,500 people were "eugenically controlled", 6,200 of them in California.[7] The crimes which qualified offenders for sterilisation were murder, prostitution, car theft and chicken stealing.[8] In some cases imprisonment was offered as the alternative to sterilisation; both of these penal policies then are incorporating a strongly eugenic function: prison serves as a place of segregation preventing the prisoner from creating his own family and passing on his "bad seed".

However there are more indirect consequences for families of prisoners. It was feeblemindedness that was associated with the atavistic degeneracy of the criminal. Terman argued that as the feebleminded were incapable of moral judgement they could therefore be viewed as potential criminals.[9] This association between intellect and criminality is part of the current socio-biological explanation in Wilson and Herrnstein's work.[10] However, if feeblemindedness leads to criminality, criminality is the indicator of inherited feeblemindedness. Both the parents and siblings and the wife and children of criminals then are categorised as socially inferior and potentially socially polluting. Families of prisoners come to be defined as part of a socially, intellectually, and morally inferior subculture, a class separated from normal society and sharing the criminogenic characteristics of the prisoner. The implicit conceptualisation of women with family obligations to prisoners within this perspective then is that they are both causes of and potential accessories in further deviance within and outside of the prison.

Although bio-anthropological theory has been overlaid by several alternative and opposing theories of criminality, there are two reasons for insisting on its significance for interpreting the symbiosis between the home and the prison.

First, this conceptualisation is embedded in several of the discursive practices within the penal sphere. The architectural layout of visiting areas, the bureaucratic procedures associated with visiting and letter writing, the routine day to day relationships between mothers and children visiting prison and the reactions of police and prison officers — the flesh and blood representatives of the the legal-penal sphere who are the mediators of penal practices and policies for most of the women who are caught up as families of prisoners into the penal realm. Chapters five to eight indicate the extent to which these conceptualisations of women and children as members of an inferior class remain part of the complex and contradictory discursive practices of penalty.

Second, as Cohen points out, criminal anthropology "lingers on and occasionally flickers up brightly enough to create a brief sensation."[11]

Nassi and Abramowitz point to the way that domestic violence, drunkenness and persistent and serious traffic crimes have been associated with "episodic dyscontrol".[12] They cite the work of Mark and Ervin as being especially influential in constituting this behaviour in the marginalising terms of pathological brain behaviour.[13] Both materialist and feminist concerns then are mystified in the definition of these contemporary crimes as functions of individual, biologically based pathologies.

With the rise of neo-classical economic policy and "the retreat from welfare" in Australia, the US and northern Europe since the 1970s, the particular attraction of a biological explanation of criminal behaviour that relocates the focus of law and order back to the inherent constitutional characteristics of the offender fits well with the hegemony of the New Right. The biological or constitutional model, although now overlayered by, is not replaced by the successive models of criminality. It remains as one of the several competing discourses within which penal policy and practices are administered.[14] The genetic theory of criminality is part of the wider discourse of the genetic theory of personality and intelligence. It has great political power of persuasion particularly for policies of the New Right, as it fits the Darwinian, functional stratification thesis justifying class, gender and racial inequalities and domination on the basis of a scientifically legitimated biological inequality.[15] Genetic explanations linking criminality with low intelligence are currently entering into the general discourse of criminality in recent texts.[16]

SUBCULTURAL THEORY

Criminality in this model still resides in the personality of the offender, but with a cultural rather than a genetically determined base creating the potential for delinquency. The two theoretical strands are not completely distinguishable. Lombroso extended the constitutional theory of criminality to include a discussion of the influences of a criminogenic subculture.[17] Criminality stems from the different subcultural values of the population defined as being "hard core lower-class" in subcultural theory, variously estimated in literature by authors such as Miller[18] and Banfield[19] as being in the range from 10 to 60 per cent.[20] Gwyn Nettler summarises Miller's and Banfield's "class oriented theses" in which the values of hasty hedonism, cunning and toughness of the criminogenic lower class are contrasted with the middle class values described as those that emphasise ambition, the ability to postpone gratification, control of aggression, and respect for property.[21] In this paradigm the family is manifestly at fault in producing criminality. It is specifically the households headed by women without economic support from their spouses in which these criminogenic values are fostered.[22] The greater propensity to crime is a result of the lesser "ego strength" of the criminal. The failure of the family to adequately socialise the child is one of the key factors in producing crime. For example, in Spinley's[23] account inconsistent and inadequate family control that fails to pass on adequate moral lessons results in an absence of shame in the children of lower class families. The inadequate family, in terms of its nonconformity to the classic, nuclear family model of bread-winning father and dependent and caring-controlling mother, is essentially the amoral family, the cause of criminality.

The biological theories of the first layer of criminological positivism were spun into a more complex skein of discourses in which criminality, intelligence and demographic policies were all pulled together into a broader thesis which legitimated the political economic status quo in the first decades of the century. These subcultural theories were woven into a wider web of discourses linking criminality, mother headed households, a "culture of poverty" and welfare policies, in the immediate post world war II societies of western industrialism. The fears which are being tapped in these successive stages shift from the threat of atavism to the threat inherent in a welfare economy which enables women to maintain households without men.

DIFFERENTIAL ASSOCIATION THEORY

In Sutherland's influential theory of differential association, the prime cause of criminal behaviour is the learning of a set of subcultural values which provides both attitudes to, and the skills for, criminal behaviour. In this variation of subcultural theory, however, it is the delinquent peers who are the significant socialisers.[24] Nevertheless, it is the family's failure to attach the delinquent to conventional family life that is the predisposing factor: "these two processes (isolation and socialization failure) are important because they increase the probability that a child will come into intimate contact with delinquents and will be attracted by delinquent behaviour".[25]

PSYCHODYNAMIC AND SOCIAL PSYCHOLOGY MODELS

Very close to the sociological subcultural theories of the 1950s and 1960s, although without attempting to resort to the latter's functional structural explanations, is the much more individualistic paradigm in social psychology that defines violence and aggression as natural. The work of Eron in the 1970s is cited by Nettler as being a major influence in this school.[26] Criminality in this model is the result of failure to provide adequate nurturing to control this natural propensity to criminogenic behaviour.[27] In this theoretical stance the domestic labour of caring is clearly linked to the function of control. Moral conformity is integrally tied to "the familial skills of adequate nurturing that includes both appreciating the child and training him to acknowledge the rights of others".[28]

When partners of prisoners are explicitly included in the psychiatric model of criminality they have been described as having "the same psychopathology as the felons."[29] It is worth noting that this conclusion comes from a study with the title: "A Psychiatric Study of Wives of Convicted Felons, An Example of Assortative Mating" and that one of its conclusions was that the psychopathology of the family was likely to be an enduring characteristic. Thus there is not a clear divide between the constitutional and the psychopathological models of criminality.

These 1970s theories of criminal behaviour are also clearly linked to the earlier psychodynamic control theories that identify the issue of criminality primarily as a defect in the control structure of the psyche of the individual offender. The family is again manifestly the cause of criminality in this model as it is the infantile and childhood experiences that fail to provide a proper balance between harshness and nurture, thus exposing the child to the eventual risk of becoming deviant.

In this "psy" discourse, in which in Donzelot's words the family becomes the site of both centrifugal and centripetal forces, the family is pathogenic if it fails either to contain or to free the individual. The family, to be successful, has to maintain the delicate balance between being inadequately socialising or over-restrictive. Failure to maintain this balance leads to risks of the child succumbing to one of three kinds of deviance (according to the particular form of imbalanced socialisation he receives): deviance as neuroticism through "over-socialisation", deviance as aggression through inadequate socialisation, or deviance as a form of socialised criminality. This latter offender does internalise the appropriate balance of freedom and inhibition but his early socialisation leads to his inability to extend this balanced sociality to a group larger than his immediate "in group".[31] The "amoral familism" of the domestic sphere is the value that limits the boundaries of the deviant's responsibility to the extended criminogenic family of the peer group.

This concept from Banfield of "amoral familism"[32] links the deviance literature to the political literature on subcultures. Deviance here is created by a culture other than that of the "normal" or mainstream. Like the genetic and the individualist psychology of deviance, explanations incorporating the subcultural theories, particularly those locating the basis for differences in cultural values in ethnicity, place the responsibility for criminality outside of normal social life. Criminals are "enemies within" who can be identified by scientifically rational experts because of the essentially arational characteristics of the criminal. They are either feebleminded, part of an earlier pre-universalistic (therefore pre-rational) culture, or they have not been exposed to the proper balance between freedom and nurture and so are not socialised sufficiently to give up their arational pattern of egocentric behaviour. In each case criminality is mediated through the family and in each case the problem of criminality is defined as the family's failure to socialise the deviant out of a primitive amorality and arationality. To become a moral citizen is the process of becoming a rational citizen capable of understanding, and willing to be part of, the universalistic principles of liberal rational society.

However, the family has a dual and contradictory part in these discourses. It becomes the site of both the blame for, but also the possible reformation of, the resocialised morally upright reformed prisoner. Although the family is to blame it also becomes the "prime treatment agency" in these master stories of deviance and control.

It is in the mainstream positivistic therapeutic writings that the family is most definitively categorised in "scientific" terms, as a necessary but inadequate moral adjunct of the penal system. In this literature, family visits are no help in reducing recidivism unless the social science experts intervene. Norman Holt and Donald Miller 's influential paper argues that "unless supplemented by family counseling these visits may be of no help to any necessary family readjustments after the inmates release".[33]

This assumption of the necessity for the family to be reconstituted by the help of social science experts is the basis for the second and "stronger" version of the family as "prime treatment agency". In the most fully worked out versions of this therapeutic model of domesticity and incarceration the family spends time in prison with the prisoner and the counsellors, towards the end of the sentence, working through family therapy or family counselling programmes.

One programme in Philadelphia in the United States brings the prisoner's partner into the prison once a week in the three months before his release to work with the prisoner in a psychodynamically oriented programme of counselling.[34] The legitimation for the programmes are that the caring work of the woman in the home prevents further criminality:

> It is hypothesised that when someone feels needed, loved and respected by his/her important others he/she is less likely to commit the kinds of antisocial acts which bring him/her to the attention of the criminal justice system.[35]

It is specifically the domestic emotional labour and relational skill of the women which is defined as being crucial to the prisoners reform in these discourses, a major determinant of the accord which a married releasee achieves when he resumed life with his wife was her avoidance of behaviour which could impair his sense of independence.[36]

Glaser in his study of family relationships cites the parolees' own phrases about how the "normal" wife should behave on the man's release:

'by being encouraging and not nagging — not mentioning anything about it (his record) and not feeling sorry for me' ... 'she don't say nothing about the past or nothing like that ... she makes me feel like I've never been away from home' ... 'Love, faith, by never nagging me ... doesn't question where I'm going when I leave in the morning'[37]

In 1964 a group of clinical psychiatrists initiated a families counselling programme in San Quentin prison.[38] This was an extension of the Increased Correctional Effectiveness ("ICE") programme, in which prisoners lived on a "ranch" just outside the main prison walls and worked during the day in prison industries. The group counselling programme that was part of this scheme for "increased correctional effectiveness" included three forms of groups: groups of prisoners and counsellors meeting every other day, weekly meetings of husband-wife groups, and monthly meetings when the wives had the additional work of bringing their children to the group counselling sessions. The finely detailed control over time allotted to these specific programmes extended to the way the psychiatrists ordered the style of family interaction:

originally, the children met first as a group separate from the parents, and then in a total family group. This proved unwise ... (then) we had the total family group meet first for 30 to 40 minutes, followed by meetings of three separate small groups, husbands and wives, children over nine, and children under nine. The children's groups were divided at their own request. These small groups met simultaneously for 30 to 40 minutes, and this was followed by a visiting period during which all the families met together, with the correctional officer present.[39]

Although the psychiatrists acknowledged the several economic and social burdens that the women faced, these were not factors that were addressed in the sessions described in the literature. The women were defined very much more in terms of their deficiencies as wives of the prisoners and as ineffective mothers of the potentially delinquent children. The women were described as both morally, sexually and socially inadequate. The myth of the Kallikaks can be seen as a clear bridge between the biological positivism of genetic inadequacy and this later psychiatric constitution of wives of prisoners as socially and psychologically deficient. In their relationships with the husband the wives' sexuality fitted what called be called the psychiatric version of "the three bears syndrome". Their sexuality was a problem in need of therapeutic counselling, either because it was insufficient ("some whose husbands are in prison for sexual offences, recognize their own frigidity and ambivalence ...") or because it was over-abundant ("... some are promiscuous, unstable women with histories of delinquency").[41]

The duality of this sexual inferiority was associated with the women's parallel intellectual inability to balance the fine line between an over-abundance or an insufficiency of love for their children:

> many fear being hurt by their children, whom they unconsciously wish to hurt or reject. This often results in extraordinary moralistic, rigid, punitive and domineering behaviour on the mothers' part. Some love their children so much they cannot bear to hurt them or disillusion them.

The women were also not conforming to the familial ideal of powerless morality by conducting their family relationships in terms of subsuming their own interests in the interests of the developing personality of their child: "sometimes the mother uses the child's dependent needs to assuage her own deprivation of affection. This tends to create a 'pawn-child' closely tied to the mother and isolated from peers."[42]

This construction of the behaviour as the deviant selfishness of the mother is interpreted as likely to produce a deviant personality in the prisoner's child: "like the mother the child becomes preoccupied with himself, driven to selfishness, and afraid of close relationships with other people".[43] However, with the aid of the superior rational morality of the psychiatrists, the family problems, the penal problem of recidivism and the women's problems, all potentially were solved as:

> the family counselling program ... helped to strengthen family ties and work out many difficulties and misunderstandings prior to the husband's parole. Such programmes might help prevent recidivisim of prisoners and improve the lot of the prisoner's wife.

The women who were reluctant to do the work of bringing their children to the prison for these sessions were subjected to some pressure: "those who were frightened or suspicious were soon convinced by other couples that 'family counselling' required that children be present."[44]

This project was explicitly tied to the shift in the sphere of penality towards extending punishment and control out into the community through work furlough and parole programmes.[45] The family was manifestly being brought into the prison to extend the control over the prisoner's behaviour within the prison[46] but more importantly to extend the moral grip of the scientific rationalists over the family outside to constitute it as the "natural" site of the moral reform of the prisoner in the community.[47] Nevertheless, within Wilmer et al's paradigm, although the family is constituted as the "natural" site of moral control, the complexities of prison life and the potentially deviant psychopathology of the prisoner's family makes essential the continuing intervention by a hierarchically ordered set of scientific experts:

> because of the complexity of family groups in prison treatment programmes we believe it imperative that such programmes be undertaken only by experienced group therapists, with the consultation of a participating psychiatrist.[48]

In both cases of control, within and outside the prison the "natural" family alone is not a sufficient guarantee of commitment to moral values. Moreover, this control through the powerful rational morality of the behavioural scientists was explicitly defined as constituting control over the prisoner and the wife and children in the "outside" world:

> we feel that family group treatment in the prison should, ideally, be supplemented by group treatment of the entire family after the prisoner is released on parole. This would make possible further observation, understanding, and assistance of the 'real life family' for which the prison programme is preparation ...

The constitution of penality as an intersection of physical, epistemological and moral control in these social science discourses is illustrated in the recommendation that "in subsequent studies there should be long term follow up as well as concurrent observations and information from schools and social agencies".

Ten years later, William Sack, Jack Seidler and Susan Thomas[49] were making the same argument for greater behavioural science intervention in the lives of families of prisoners. Although their focus was on reducing the potentially delinquent behaviour of prisoners' children they also constituted the family as the moral site of the prisoner's redemption:

> our findings suggest that the prisoner's failure to live up to society's laws often follows his failure to fulfil his family role. Yet the stated desire of the imprisoned fathers in our study to be better parents could prove a strong motivating factor in their rehabilitation.

The most far-reaching current example of family therapy programmes is the one run by the Swedish Prison and Probations Service at Gruvberget Village in the north of Sweden. In this programme both the partners and children of prisoners live in the prison village at Gruvberget for two or three weeks towards the end of the prison sentence. The programme is oriented, as is the programme in Philadelphia, to restructuring and rein-forcing family relations through a series of psychologically oriented group counselling sessions. However, the focus in the Swedish programme is closer to that in San Quentin in being oriented much more towards the parent-child relationship. From the beginning of the course in 1978 to 1986, 115 families of prisoners had been through the course including 152 children and 203 adults. In six of the families both parents were prisoners visiting Gruvberget with their children.[50]

Although there have also been family counselling sessions involving parenthood in Canada, Denmark,[51] in San Quentin, and in prisons in Kansas and Idaho in the United States,[52] male prisoners as parents are generally an almost invisible population in mainstream penal discourses.[53] The scientific rationality of the medicalised control conflicts with economic rationality, which privileges the control of prison budgets, and judicial rationality, which continues to constitute prisoners (as it did in the liberal individualism of competitive capitalism) as individuals free of all ascriptive social attributes. However, parenthood is the major issue in the political technology of the penal discourses when the social science gaze falls upon women prisoners. The generally *a*gendered nature of the reformist school which conflates the terms "prisoner" and "male" is inverted once children become the key concern. Male prisoners disappear and the term "prisoner" is conflated with "woman".[54] The official discourses too reflect this bias. There are no official records in Australia detailing the numbers of children of male prisoners.[55] The series of articles, about bonding and absence of prisoner parents, detailed discussions about the age at which children can remain in prison with their parent after their birth, and the comparative benefits of parent and babies units or release on license schemes for prisoner parents of young children, are almost exclusively about women prisoners.[56]

There are two invisible populations in this process of distortion. These two populations are: the male prisoners as parents and the women carers of all prisoners' children. The invisibility of the first population is highlighted by the title of an American text, *Mothers in Prison*.[57] Whilst there are some journal articles and a few prison programmes incorporating children of male prisoners, the male prisoner constituted as a parent is not the focus of these discourses (as is the woman prisoner) in the majority of the writings on children of imprisoned mothers. *Fathers in Prison* is a non-title in the orthodox criminological, social work and critical literature on the effects of imprisonment, because the prisoners' fatherhood is virtually never a civil status that is at issue.[58] The relative absence of a parallel discourse about children of male parents is predicated on the invisible domestic labour of the mother or mother substitute of his child.

The masculinity of the prison is a denial of the man's parenthood but that deprivation can only operate because of the extensive domestic labour of the women carers of prisoners' children. In the reformist phase of penality the man's civil status as parent is denied as part of his punishment yet it is also encouraged as part of his reformation, as the bridge back to normality. The tension between these contradictory aspects of men's imprisonment is resolved through the exploitation of women's domestic labour of maintaining contact between prisoner and child but also through the denial of the importance of that labour. Without the network of women's labour that underpins penal policies the balance between punishment and reform in terms of the prisoner's loss and retrieval of parenthood would not be maintained. The balance would shift towards the terrorising end of the scale in terms of the absolute deprivation of the prisoner's right to maintain contact with his children and the image of imprisonment as a humane and just punishment would be more difficult to maintain. The seemingly "natural" work of women in enabling men prisoners to maintain their civil status as parents is only made visible by being reflected in the mirror of the severe loss of parenthood experienced by women prisoners who do not have a parallel network of domestic labour to support them. In one of the few articles that addresses the issue of men in prison as absent parents, Linda Koban compared the different effect of incarceration on the families of men and women. She found that men have the advantage of an established support system for the child they leave outside; men's children are more often living with the other parent; more men than women have frequent contact with their children; fewer men have problems getting through to their children; men can depend on the child's mother to bring the children for a visit; men's children are less often separated from their siblings; and men are not usually incarcerated as far from their home communities.[59] Similarly, Sack et al, regardless of whether the prisoner was the mother or father, found that it was the mother who was most often called upon to perform the difficult task of explaining the imprisonment to the children.[60]

When prison programmes do address the issue of parenthood the concern is usually manifested only towards the end of the period of imprisonment, not in the traumatic periods of arrest, early sentencing and classification, and the long term period covering the main body of the sentence. Moreover, the programmes are oriented towards evaluating the "normality/abnormality" of the mother. In the small scale pilot programme on parental counselling in Idaho, the wives of the prisoners in the programme, after carrying out the extensive domestic labour of caring for the prisoners' children throughout the several earlier traumatic phases of arrest and punishment, had to allow an observer into their home to record their "parenting skills", prior to an eight week training programme in the prison attended by both the prisoner and the mother and children. The period of "at home" observation involved the prisoner's wife in being intensively measured and scored according to a "Behavioural Observation" form on which was recorded the number of times the children complied with the mothers' commands and the types of control behaviour she exhibited. The observer

> scored a wide range of behaviors including such positive responses as approval, attention and positive physical responses and such negative responses of children and parents as crying, disapproval, destructiveness, humiliation, yelling and hitting.[61]

The women also were involved in "... writing self-reports, completion of an "Adjectives Check list" on each of the children, measurement of interpersonal communication skills of parents by means of a pre-test/post-test in the parent training class ...".[62]

CONSTITUTION OF FAMILY AS "THE CAUSE" AND "THE BRIDGE": TECHNO-REFORMIST LITERATURE ON FAMILIES OF PRISONERS

It is in this mode of incorporation of the family into the legal-penal sphere that the mainstream positivist literature on families of prisoners developed. Of the several texts or journal articles on the experiences of families of prisoners the dominant theme has been one of techno-reformism. In this approach the family of the prisoner is defined as a "family in crisis" or as a "disorganised family" but it is "the family's" response or adjustment rather than imprisonment as the source of the crisis that is defined as problematic.[63] Moreover "the family" in these studies is conflated with "the wife". As the various authors of the techno-reformist studies develop their thesis it becomes the response of the wife to her prisoner husband (or, more rarely, their children) that is under scrutiny, and it is her domestic labour of responding appropriately that has to be judged and managed.

The techno-reformist literature extends from the 1930s[64] to the 1980s: in a 1981 report on the problems faced by prisoners' wives, Daniels continues to use the model of the family "... as a major untapped resource in a rehabilitative correctional system".[65] In 1983 Robert Marsh was basing his argument for greater resources for group counselling in prison on the claim that the family "... provides a stable environment for the released offender and ultimately reduces recidivism".[66] However it was in the period from the 1950s to the late 1970s that this approach dominated the literature on families of prisoners. The first of the major texts in the field was the work by Norman Fenton in 1959.[67]

Fenton specifically directed attention to the family as "the therapeutic agent". In Fenton's work most of the key elements of the approach in the later texts are laid out: the family is designated as the social unit most likely to prevent recidivism. But the family on its own is unlikely to achieve the right balance in the post-imprisonment relationship. It is necessary therefore to intervene scientifically in the relationship between the prisoner and his family and reconstruct it in terms of the appropriate balance in the relationship. He advocated a course on family counselling for custodial staff in the Californian Department of Corrections and a programme of group psychotherapy for family members of prisoners due for parole.

One important refinement added to the literature following from Fenton's work, and one that eventually became the focus of this approach, was the importance of diagnosis. The writers very quickly took on the role of scientific researcher into the domestic relationship prior to and necessary for counselling. The literature thus shifted towards a "blaming" discourse, defining several forms of domestic relationships, indicating the appropriate and normal form and, by definition, categorising all others as "family disorganisation".

One description, summarised in chapter two, of the development of the modern form of penality was that it comprised three sub-spheres: the normalising, the correctional and the segregative.[68] Scientific rationality in the social space of the overlapping spheres of domesticity and penality combines all three forms: families of prisoners experience the imposition of the *normalising* procedures of the social sciences specifically in terms of their domestic function of *correcting* the damages to the self-esteem of prisoners that are the result, in turn, of the State imposed punishment-by-*segregation* of the man from his family. In Kaslow's words counselling works:

by exploring feelings of all members about the imprisonment and the reason for it. Guilt, recrimination, desire to escape from the relationship should be handled ... is there space in the family for the ex-offender and, if so, how does the role he now will be expected to play differ from that he lived before imprisonment?[69]

With this shift, Reuben Hill's work on the "family in crisis" became the basic paradigm within which the literature developed.[70] One of the most marked features of the "family crisis" literature is the increasingly positivisitic character of the literature. "Families in crisis" are constituted in terms of highly schematic patterns of family relationships. Variables are constructed from these models and are calculated in increasingly statistically sophisticated terms. The path from nominal to more sophisticated forms of categorisation and analysis can be charted by marking the changes from the work by Norman Fenton in 1959 to Pauline Morris's study in Britain in 1965 and the studies in the United States by Stanley Brodsky in 1971, William Perry in 1974 and David Struckhoff in 1977.[71]

Morris' work on 588 women who were married to prisoners in British prisons in the 1960s[72] is one of the most influential texts in the literature. It was comprehensive both in terms of the numbers of women who were interviewed and the forms of research employed. The detailed information on impoverishment, social isolation, problems of information and the amount of work involved in maintaining the family outside of prison gives vivid and graphic evidence of the hidden punishment and hidden labour involved for women who are partners of imprisoned men. Most of this evidence comes from the detailed informal responses recorded in which the women speak for themselves about their experiences. However it is on the quantitative and analytic measurements of family disorganisation and family adjustment that Morris centred her findings, using a variety of statistical techniques to estimate factors associated with the levels of family adjustment.

Morris also developed a categorisation of prisoners' families according to the various patterns of dominant/submissive or nurturant/ receptive relations between the two partners. From these patterns six possible kinds of family relations were described: "dependent wife-dominant husband, mothering wife-dependent husband, dominant wife-passive husband, immature wife-immature husband, mature wife-dominant husband, mature wife-mature husband."[73]

After categorising the women into one of these nominal types, Morris used a case study approach to analyse the "families' adjustment to the crisis". Her work nicely exemplified Foucault's description of the rational management procedures of analytic discourse and the ways that social science can become a technology of control through confession.[74] However it was in the American studies that the proliferation of the schema for deciphering and interpreting this confessed material blossomed.

Nine years after the publication of Morris' work, Perry used the same categories but called the family forms — "Daddies and Dolls, Mothers and Sons, Bitches and Nice Guys, Masters and Servants, both dominant-hawks or both nurturant-doves".[75] This naming more explicitly placed the blame for "inadequate" family relations on the women: dolls, mothers, bitches and servants having different connotations to the terms used for the men — daddies, sons, nice guys and masters. Moreover the family crisis paradigm here clearly incorporates the "psy" assumptions that the responsibility for the adjustment to the crisis is a natural part of the domestic labour of the women. Perry's judgements of the women in his sample is that few of them measured up to the ideal of an assertive purposeful wife but were too passive and intimidated by their husbands to be able to perform the expected labour of influencing or modifying the husband's social behaviour.[76] Perry, himself a professional Classification and Parole Programme Administrator, argues that these (abnormal) women then needed the professional skills of a better resourced team of parole agents to achieve the normal and natural skills necessary for a properly rhythmic relationship with their paroled husbands.[77]

The three major texts, following Morris' work in this literature, used increasingly sophisticated, more intensive and more statistically based analytic techniques to decipher the confessions. Foucault's thesis that knowledge insidiously objectifies those on whom it is applied and that surveillance, classification ordering and coding are not simply aids to control and discipline but are themselves woven into the very form of power itself, is strongly echoed in Stanley Brodsky's description of his methodological approach and his analysis: "the study called for photocopying mail written and received, tape recording visits of the prisoner, and personal interviews".[78] Such close surveillance of the prisoner and his family created "a distressing and persistent feeling of being an unwanted eavesdropper"[79] and then became the subject of intensive scrutiny:

> ... the measure of personal pronoun frequency used (ppr) was personal pronouns per 100 words ... means and standard deviations for 1p were calculated ... the last two time segments sampled for letters to siblings produced very high 1p rates of 10.3 and 11.0 per cent respectively ... and intercorrelations were performed between 1p frequency and length of confinement ... none were significant at the 0.05 level.[80]

David Struckhoff applied even more sophisticated forms of analysis to measure prisoners' wives' attitudes. He carefully distanced his work from the less sophisticated scientific analyses of the preceding studies, none of which, he argued, had a " cohesive schema of the variables."[81]

The Foucaultian thesis that the normalising power of political technologies succeeds when they are only partially successful because when there is failure this is construed as further proof to reinforce and extend the power of experts[82] is clearly manifested in the reformist families of prisoners literature. Pauline Morris, after testing 13 factors, that is aspects of the women's lives, for their relevance to "adjustment" found that "unfortunately none of these factors was related to the adjustment score with the exception of family size ..." and she concludes her analysis of what factors are associated with the prisoners wives' ability to adjust by suggesting

> by testing separately two areas of adjustment we have been able to isolate certain factors which are relevant to this process, and we feel that this points to the desirability of testing each area individually had the resources of the research been available ... Furthermore it confirms the view that our method of constructing an overall index of adjustment was not satisfactory and greater refinement is necessary.[83]

Nine years later Struckhoff emphasises the importance of scientific rationality in the problem of reconstructing prisoners' families as sites of moral redemption. Although he clearly contrasts his own more sophisticated research techniques with the earlier literature in the field and argues that his work exemplifies clarity in its definitions of "adjustment", "family" and in the more scientifically sophisticated eight variable schema that he uses as a model to test for disorganisation and adjustment, he nevertheless continues the success-through-failure technique in his conclusion by arguing that

> the failure of the data to support six hypotheses derived from the literature indicates that the conceptualisation of adjustment to separation has not been sufficiently concise and that greater clarity in the future will be achieved through either more reconceptualisation or additional identification of specific problems of adjustment.[84]

Even though his questioning was so invasive of the women's lives that "... three wives broke down and cried, (and) others seemed upset but didn't cry", he argues for future researchers to include more specific and concise questions about the problems of "adjustment".[85]

Hence the reformist technicist studies became ends in themselves, seeking to catch the most private and delicate aspects of prisoner family relationships in sophisticated networks of analysis. The family, that is the woman, properly controlled to behave normally by a network of well resourced professional experts, is constructed as a basic resource for reform. Reform is predicated upon intensive surveillance, personal confessions and intricate analysis. In the majority of the studies there is no questioning of penality and none of familism.

More recently, however, the potential for a feminist analysis in Morris's approach has been realised in Judith Jones' study of 35 women, married to long term male prisoners in Melbourne.[86] Whilst Jones is critical of the masculinist biases in the mainstream family crisis studies she argues that, to understand the position of women caught up in the hidden punishment of being wives of prisoners, it is appropriate to develop a typology of prisoners' families based on a questionnaire covering details of the personal relations of the wife and the prisoner prior to sentencing. The form of family relationship prior to imprisonment she argues, mediates the form of hidden punishment experienced by the women outside. Jones uses a taxonomy of family forms as an indicator of the power relationships between husband and wife. This categorisation is then used to estimate the level of independence women are likely to achieve whilst their husbands are imprisoned, and the extent to which their family relationship with the prisoner becomes a source of his ability to manipulate and control the wife outside.[87] Her work is one of the few recent critical studies that set the position of women who have a family obligation to care for prisoners in a broader structural framework that incorporates a class and/or a gender analysis of the women's hidden punishment and labour.

In this period the sexuality of women partners of imprisoned men became a key feature of the literature on families of prisoners. In Donald Schneller's reworking of the families in crisis perspective[88] three of the fifteen questions in the "family change scale" that he administered to wives of prisoners intruded into their personal lives in terms of their subjective sexuality and desire. His 15 question scale covered the following:

13   Sexual satisfaction of wife (as reflected in desire for husband)

14   Sexual satisfaction of wife (as reflected in desire for other men)

15   Sexual satisfaction of wife (as reflected in desired frequency of conjugal visits — hypothetical question)[89]

In Schneller's work the conjugal visits programme is defined as the answer to the women's problems of frustrated sexuality.

A third approach, politically positioned between the psychologically oriented techno-reformist and the critical class and/or feminist discourses, has regularly re-emerged in the literature, from the 1930s to the present.[90] This is the social administrative reformist literature. This school advocates funding for practical advice and material help to "families of prisoners" in order that the family relationship with the prisoner is maintained, both to enable the prisoner to survive prison, and primarily to help the family's role in the prisoner's rehabilitation after his release. This approach does not constitute the woman in the home as psychologically deficient. Rather, it focuses on both immediate and long term effects of imprisonment as causing the problems faced by "the family" outside. However, those problems are not defined in the literature as being politically unacceptable. The women is constituted as the unwitting victim of a series of unfortunate but necessary events. Although the problem of the contradictory position of families of prisoners is made explicit in these discussions, the solutions that this school offers is a mixture of

(1)   limited changes in penal programmes with an emphasis on greater practical and material support for the family during the imprisonment and the after-care phase, and

(2) professional intervention, based on the skills of "family crisis management", to enable the woman to "cope" with the emotional, financial and child management problems that she faces at each stage of the punishment, from arrest, through the chronic period of incarceration to the stage of pre-release and release.

> *Intervention should focus on continuing to help the family to understand the prison program and the inmates' reactive behaviours* ... the family unit should be assisted to become stable and self-sufficient. The (professional) worker can provide support in times of personal crisis, encourage family members to talk to each other when they experience frustrations and loneliness, assess and encourage areas of mutual satisfaction and to do things together, teach them to utilize community resources, to help them develop and pursue outside interests and hobbies. Emotions must be understood, but adaptive behaviours should be encouraged and emphasized.[91]

The woman's labour becomes a more manifestly recognised aspect of penality in these social administrative reformist discourses, and in some cases professional intervention includes encouraging self-help groups of "(families) in association with others in similar situations". Nevertheless both "the family" and "imprisonment" are constituted as unproblematic. The self-help groups function within the overall "family in crisis" programmes that are based on the belief that the families "... are strengthened to become a major source of support in furthering the rehabilitation of the offender".[92]

It is in the more recent critical literature that the term "families of prisoners" has been made problematic. Since the early 1980s there has been a growing body of work using this perspective. What is particulary notable about this social science literature is that several of the authors are people with practical experience of the labour of caring for prisoners. These writers include Judy Jones, a voluntary worker in the Victorian prison system, Betty Hounslow, a member of the Prisoners Action Group in New South Wales, Carole Johns, a prisoners' wife in New South Wales, Heather Deane,[93] a one time member of the probation service in New Zealand, Laura Fishman and Valerie Bauhoefer battling the prison authorities in New York, Alice Crosthwaite working with the South London Wives Group in England, Roger Shaw, Eva Lloyd, Roger Light and Sue Smith, a prisoner's wife in Britain.

The title of the article by Kathleen McDermott and Roy King, "Prison Rule 102: Stand by Your Man", exemplifies the way that this most recent group of social science writings approaches the issue. McDermott and King contend that even though there are 101 official Prison Rules governing the work of the Prison Service in England, the unwritten "Rule 102" is the rule without which the service could not reach its objectives. That rule does not have the status of law, but is nevertheless "sanctioned with all the pressures that the penal system can command at virtually every stage of the penal process".[94]

All the authors in this most recent set of writings detail the ways that specific penal systems in either Europe, the US or Australasia incorporate the unpaid labour of people in the population "families of prisoners" into the administration of a legal-penal system that comprises segregative, corrective and normalising moments of control.

SUMMARY

The social sciences have been a significant component of penal discourses since the early part of this century. Underpinning the various theories or social science approaches to criminality and "the criminal personality" are assumptions, sometimes manifest, sometimes obscure, about the family of the offender. The way that the family becomes incorporated into the various programmes of therapy, rehabilitation, terror or surveillance changes with the different degrees of importance that any one state places on the competing discourses within which punishment is being addressed. In chapter two it was noted that, in general, the major transformation since the development of positivism has been the change in the mid twentieth century, away from the unquestioned professional dominance of positivism and the centrality of the closed institution as the site of control and surveillance, to the contradictory combination of a rhetoric of deinstitutionalisation and deprofessionalisation. In this era punishments have retained and extended both institutional control and professional expertise but with a parallel range of controls developing that increasingly extended, widened, dispersed and made more intensive surveillance and control within the community. As Cohen points out, this has led to the paradoxical situation that the era of deprofessionalisation and suspicion of the theorising of social science experts has led to an intensification rather than a decline in the influence of theories of criminality.[95]

One of the major questions posed by Foucault about the emergence of positivism and the analysis of the "present moment" of rationality as the spirit of modern culture was of the emergence of humans as both objects and subjects of knowledge. Foucault's question was not only about how this duality emerged but at what cost: "This is my question: at what price can subjects speak the truth about themselves?".[96] The cost however is not borne only by the individual who is both object and subject of power as knowledge. In the dual conflation in which women's experiences of social life are subsumed firstly into those of the individual and secondly into the abstract sociality of the community, the costs of knowing oneself as a sentenced offender are borne too by those people — particularly women — who are obligated through their family relationship to care for the individual who is constructed as an "offender". Through this family obligation as the mother, the spouse, the "moll" or the mother of the child of the individual prisoner women are pulled into the several scientific discourses. They, too, become both objects and subjects of the rationality of the social sciences in the several often competing theories of criminality.

Currently these objectifying literatures have been paralled by a range of studies that have made penal policies rather than "families of prisoners" the objects of their analysis. Indeed it has often been people in the population "families of prisoners" who have been the scholars in this more critical penological literature. This academic refocus from families to penal adminstrations has been accompanied by a political interest in the ways that carers and children of imprisoned men and women are incorporated in the criminal justice system. The following three chapters detail the the way that the family obligation to care was exploited and incorporated into the system of penal control in the New South Wales prison system in the late 1980s.

NOTES

1   Cohen, A, *Deviance and Control* (1966) at 50; Heidensohn, F, *Women and Crime* (1985).

2   Karier, C, "Testing for Order and Control in the Corporate Liberal State" in Dale, R, Esland, G and MacDonald, M (eds), *Schooling and Capitalism: a Sociological Reader* (1976).

3   Karier cites Dugdale, R, *The Jukes: a Study in Crime, Pauperism, Disease and Heredity* (1910); Goddard, H, *The Kallicack Family* (1912), and gives special attention to Garret, H, *General Psychology* (1961) at 56. See also Darlington, C D, *The Little Universe of Man* (1978) for the way this myth has survived.

4   Cited in Heidensohn, above n1 at 122.

5   Cohen, above n1 at 52.

6   Nassi, A and Abramowitz, S, "From Phrenology to Psychosurgery and Back Again: Biological Studies of Criminality" (1976) 46/4 *Amer J Orthopsychiat* 591–607.

7   Above n2.

8   Id at 131.

9   Cited in Karier, id at 132.

10   Wilson, J Q and Herrnstein, R, *Crime and Human Nature* (1988).

11   Above n1 at 50.

12   Above n6 at 602–603.

13   Id at 602–604.

14   Eysenck, H and Gudjonsson, G, *The Causes and Cures of Criminality* (1989).

15   Ibid.

16   Cf Mednick, A, Gabrielli, W and Hutchings, B, "Genetic Influences in Criminal Convictions: Evidence from an Adoption Cohort" (1984) *Science* 25 May 1984 at 891–894; Wilson & Herrnstein (above n10) and the bio-psychology of Hans Eysenck (above n14).

17   Heidensohn, above n1 at 112–113.

18   Miller, W, "Lower Class Culture as a Generating Milieu of Gang Delinquency" (1958) 14/3 *J Soc Iss* 5–19.

19   Banfield, E, *The Moral Basis of a Backward Society* (1958).

20   Cited in Nettler, G, *Explaining Crime* (1974) at 142–144.

21   Id at 144.

22   Id at 143.

23   Spinley, cited in Nettler, above n20 at 145.

24   Sutherland, E and Cressey, D, *Criminology* (1966).

25   Id at 227.

26   Nettler, above n20 at 172.

27   Ibid.

28   Ibid.

29   Guss, S, Goodwin, D and Game, B, "Psychiatric Study of Wives of Convicted Felons: an Example of Assortative Mating (1970) 126 *Amer J Psychiat* 115–118.

30   Donzelot, J, *The Policing of Families: Welfare versus the State* (1979) at 228.

31   Jenkins, R, "Psychiatric Interpretations and Considerations of Treatment" in Hewlett and Johnson (eds), *Fundamental Patterns of Maladjustment* [nd], cited in Cohen, above n1 at 55.

32   Above n19.

33   Holt, N and Miller, D, "Explorations in Inmate–Family Relationships", California Dept of Corrections *Research Report 46* (1972) at 40.

34   Kaslow, F, "Marital or Family Therapy for Prisoners and their Spouses or Families" (1978) 58/1 *Prison J* 53–59.

35   Id at 59.

36   Glaser, D, *The Effectiveness of a Prison and Parole System* (1969) at 253.

37   Id at 253–255.

38   Wilmer, H, Marks, I and Pogue, E, "Group Treatment of Prisoners and their Families" (1966) 50 *Mental Hygiene* 380–389.

39   Id at 380–381.

40   Id at 382.

41   This 'flanking attack' on women as the cause of men's immorality, either in terms of the women's overabundance or lack of sexuality, re-echoes the late 18th century scapegoating and denigration of women in relation to the problems of social control in the early days of the New South Wales colony (see ch2 at 60).

42   Above n38 at 382.

43   Ibid.

44   Id at 385.

45   Id at 389.

46   Id at 397.

47   'The total family group both inside and outside prison is the natural therapeutic step in the resocialisation of the total family.' Id at 388.

48   Id at 389.

49   Sack, W, Seidler, J and Thomas, S, "The Children of Imprisoned Parents: a Psychosocial Exploration" (1976) 46/4 *Amer J Orthopsychiat* 618–627.

50   Altahr-Cederberg, B, "Current Course for Inmates and their Families at Gruvberget", personal communication (1986).

51   Marsh, R, "Services for Families: a Model Project to Provide Services for Families of Prisoners" (1983) 27/2 *Int J Offender Ther & Comp Crim* at 162; Schiff, S, "The Preschool in Prison Project: OMEP Canada", unpublished paper, Canada, 1986.

52   Marsh, above n51.

53   And the courses that do run are not usually part of any long term programme.

54   Among others: *Yale Law Journal*, anon, 1978; McGowan, B, and Blumethal, K, *Why Punish the Children? A Study of Children of Women Prisoners* (1978); Hatty, S, "Maternal Infant Incarceration: sociological and psychological perspectives", in Hatty, S (ed), *Women in the Prison System* (1984) 115–162; Gaudin, J, "Social Work Roles and Tasks with Incarcerated Mothers" *Social Casework* 12 Nov 1984, 279-286; Baunach, P, *Mothers in Prison* (1985); Boudoris, J, *Prisons and Kids* (1985).

55   Hounslow, B, Stephenson, A, Stewart, J and Crancher, J, *Children of Imprisoned Parents* (1982) at 1, and personal communication with NSW Department of Corrective Services Research Department (1988).

56   The work in the United States by Sack (1976) and Sack et al (1976) on the impact of imprisonment on children of both men and women prisoners, is the notable exception here. (Sack, W, "Children of Imprisoned Fathers" (1977) 40/2 *Psychiat* 163–174; Sack, Seidler and Thomas, above n49; discussed in greater detail in chapter six.)

57   Baunach, above n54.

58   With the exception of Shaw, R, *Children of Imprisoned Fathers* (1991).

59   Koban, L, "Parents in Prison" (1983) 5 *Res in L, Dev & Soc Contr* 171–183.

60   Sack et al, above n49.

61   Marsh, R, "Services for Families: a model project to provide services for families of prisoners" (1983) 27/2 *Int J Offend Ther & Comp Crim* at 160–1.

62   Id at 157.

63   This bias in the family crisis approach has also been pointed out by de Connick (de Conninck, G, "Actualities bibliographiques: La famille de detenu: de la suspicion de la idealization" (1982) 6/1 *Deviance et Societé*) and Jones (Jones, J, "Prisoners and their Families", unpublished PhD thesis, Melbourne: Monash University, Dept Anthropology & Sociology (1983)).

64   Ernst Mowrer (1932), cited in Struckhoff, D, "Adjustment of Prisoners' Wives to Separation", PhD thesis, S Illinois University (1977).

65   Daniels, S W, "The Needs of Prisoners' Wives: a challenge for the Mental Health Profession" (1981) 17/4 *Community Mental Health J*.

66   Marsh, above n51 at 162.

67 Fenton, N, *The Prisoner's Family* (1959).

68 Garland, D, *Punishment and Welfare* (1985) at ch1.

69 Above n34 at 58.

70 Hill, R, *Families Under Stress* (1949).

71 Above n67; Morris, P, *Prisoners and their Families* (1965); Brodsky, S, *Families and Friends of Men in Prison* (1975); Perry, W, "Marital Relations of Prison Parolees", PhD Thesis, School of Human Behavior, United States International University, San Diego (1974); Struckhoff, above n64.

72 Morris, above n71.

73 Id at 144–206.

74 Foucault, M, *Discipline and Punish* (1977) at 66–67.

75 Perry, above n71.

76 Id at 88–93.

77 Id at 98.

78 Brodsky, above n71 at 119.

79 Id at 126.

80 Above n78 at 178.

81 Struckhoff, above n64 at 6.

82 Above n74 at 268–272.

83 Morris, above n71 at 227.

84 Struckhoff, above n64 at 6–7.

85 Id at 103.

86 Jones, above n63.

87 Id at ch4.

88 Schneller, D, "Prisoners' Families: a Study of some Social and Psychological Effects of Incarceration on the Families of Negro Prisoners" (1975) 12/4 *Criminol* 402–412; *The Prisoner's Family: a Study of the Effects of Imprisonment on the Families of Prisoners* (1978).

89 Id at 406.

90 The first major study in Australia, of 55 families in the early 1960s in Victoria, reported in Nancy Anderson's work (Anderson, N, *Prisoners' Families: Reports I & II* (1965)), is a good example of this approach. In her conclusion, Anderson herself points to the problems with this perspective: 'it seems useful but lacking when it deals with the ... multi-problem and lower class families.' (at 39).

91 My emphasis. Cobean, S, and Power, P, "The Role of the Family in the Rehabilitation of the Offender" (1978) 22 *Int J Offend Ther & Comp Criminol* at 38.

92 Fishman, S and Alissi, A, "Strengthening Families as Natural Support Systems for Offenders" (1979) 43/3 *Fed Prob* at 21.

93 Deane, H, *The Social Effects of Imprisonment on Male Prisoners and their Families* (1988).

94   McDermott, K and King, R, "Prison Rule 102: Stand by Your Man",
      unpublished paper, Bangor Wales: Centre for Social Policy Research &
      Development [nd] at 1.

95   Cohen, S, *Visions of Social Control* (1985) at 17.

96   Cited in Merquior, J, *Foucault* (1985) at 17.

5

LABOURING, LOVING AND CONTROLLING:
CARING FOR IMPRISONED MEN
IN NEW SOUTH WALES

The next three chapters investigate the complexities of the work of 38 women in New South Wales who, through their family obligation to care, provided an extensive infrastructure of support to the legal-penal system in the late 1980s. This chapter details the economic and the emotional aspects of this caring work.

The first section of this chapter outlines the specific conditions through which the caring work of people in the population "families of prisoners" operated in New South Wales through a summary of the policies and practices of penality as they developed in the state in the 1970s and 1980s.

THE CONTEXT OF CARING:
IMPRISONMENT IN NEW SOUTH WALES IN THE 1980s

> (we should be) directing our gaze to the brightly lit official stage where decisions are made before proceeding gradually to the semi-darkness of the places where these decisions are carried out.[1]

In chapters two and four, the 1970s were described an an era in which penality in Western societies was characterised by three major features: the profound crisis of the 1970s manifested in prisoner struggles and organisation; the collapse in the belief of rehabilitation; and the acute fiscal and discipline problems of prison administration. The New South Wales experience reflects this general picture although with its own specific features and with something of a "culture lag". There were a series of prisoner rebellions in New South Wales prisons in the 1970s. The formation of several prisoner groups and the high level of prisoner action drew attention to a range of destructive and inhumane conditions, and to a sustained period of institutionalised violence that had been a sustained feature of New South Wales gaols since the late 1950s.[2] These struggles eventually led to the Royal Commission into New South Wales Prisons in 1976 which handed down over 200 recommendations for prison reform.

The next few years were characterised by struggles between liberal and conservative factions within prison administration over the extent to which these proposed reforms should be implemented.[3] The problems of prison discipline following on from the Nagle Report included an extensive programme of strikes by prison officers over the attempts at prison reform by the newly appointed Chairman of the Corrective Services

Commission, Dr Tony Vinson, who resigned after two and half years. Most of the prison officers involved in the systematic violence against prisoners were allowed to continue in the service. Some were promoted to senior positions.[4]

During the late 1970s and the early 1980s New South Wales prisons were the sites of both softer and harder penal practices and policies. Some of the recommendations of the Nagle Report were implemented. Katingal, the heavily criticised high security unit, described as "an electronic zoo", and the older "Victorian zoo" — the Observation Unit of the Malabar complex — were closed down. Greater emphasis was placed on day release, work release and early release programmes and communication with families outside was made more open. A therapeutically oriented Special Care Unit, organised around shared decision-making, was established.[5] Transsexual prisoners were accorded official recognition of their right to maintain their identities as women.[6] Women prison staff including welfare workers, education officers as well as prison officers were appointed to positions in men's prisons.

These moves were specifically away from the constitution of prison as the site of a clearly segregated masculinity. The establishment of the Special Care Unit was an effort to reconstitute violent prisoners as men who would be participants in the management of their own penal status but at the same time it has been described as a move to "domesticise" control within prison. "The facilities of the wing are designed to give the impression of communal domesticity, rather than the spartan sense of security in a traditional Long Bay wing."[7]

To add to this move to a more consensual basis of control through the domestication of this section of prison life, prison officers were also included in the democratisation of decision-making. Their job was no longer the purely custodial one of "opening and closing gates" but was extended to include helping to plan the therapeutic programmes and assisting in their implementation. Notably one of the new innovations for the unit was the introduction of female prison officers because

in order to 'normalize' the milieu, it was seen to be desirable to introduce female officers in this environment ... it is generally assumed that the presence of females 'cleans-up' the gaol jargon, that inmates care more about their appearances and hygiene, and that women have a calming influence on the dynamics ... women's presence in gaol is restoring some basis(sic) social 'niceties' in this relatively cold and barren world.[8]

In addition, one of the other main innovations was to be the provision of private visiting facilities allowing prisoners access to family life within the prison.[9]

The purpose of this new, more democratic and more domesticised unit within the prison was to treat prisoners who had been psychologically damaged by traumas caused "from both outside and within the prison walls."[10]

The domesticised Special Care Unit then performs various functions: its manifest goal is the reconstitution of personalities whose destruction was caused by the penal system itself. It also contains its own inherent soft forms of control as prisoners who reject the conditions of their "rebirth" into the adolescent stage of contained "freedom with responsibility" are rejected and pushed out of the domesticised democracy of the unit back into the exclusively masculine "infantilising" power relations of normal prison discipline. This special group of prisoners is reconstituted too as subjects who participate in the conditions of their own subjection in therapeutic programmes of group discussion. Tony Vinson, who oversaw the introduction of the unit, describes the other explicit function of the Special Care Unit. It was to become the training ground for the new humane managers of men in prison. "A quite explicit aim was to gradually staff through the various roles in the unit so that they could acquire the skills in handling human problems."[11]

It is unsurprising that part of Tony Vinson's vision of the way that New South Wales prison management would operate also included the restructuring of prisons as sites which would more nearly replicate the competitive structure of the labour market with prisoners competing for jobs advertised in gaol, the services and amenities within prison being paid for out of prison wages, a minimum level of service provision for all, but so minimal as to "induce effort" and the building of new factories within prison walls.[12]

Here Tony Vinson was enthusiastically supporting ideas initially proposed by Gerry Hay, a senior prisoner executive at Bathurst. The domestication of penal life was also proceeding at this prison. The large impersonal cell blocks of the maximum security section of Bathurst Gaol which had been destroyed by prisoner actions in 1974 was replaced by "unit management houses" in 1982. In this new architectural design prisoners lived in smaller units where both the physical space and the penal relationships were based on a "family" form of control with eight to twelve prisoners cooking and eating in "their" unit under the supervision of two Prison Officers. The appointment of a woman as Deputy Supervisor of the gaol reinforced the familism of this "normalising" of penal life.[13] Both prisoners and prison staff were initially enthusiastic about this change. However by 1986, the evaluations of the Bathurst Management Plan were less positive.[14]

This liberal constitution of prison life manifestly reintroduces domesticity into penal control, with control managed through more horizontal, humanely oriented, dually gendered structures and with prison officers working closely in consensual agreement with fully participating prisoner-workers and willingly exchanging their labour for unequal rewards for their supposedly voluntarily unequal "efforts". It constitutes prison life as a paternalistic family structure perpetually reconstituting a stream of willing adolescents, forever achieving the balance between freedom and responsibility that will allow them eventually to be mature enough to enter the wider world as co-operative workers freely participating in a competitive and unequal labour market. Even the lads' sexual partners are allowed into the family home on occasion to enable them to achieve the correct balance between freedom and responsibility. Penality, productivity and domesticity are interwoven here in a schema that echoes the sentiments underlying the Quaker reforms of the beginning of the nineteenth century.[15]

However another set of discourses was becoming increasingly dominant in this era. It was specifically the prison leisure activity of drug consumption that was becoming the focal point of the discourses constituting penality in New South Wales in the mid 1980s. In a political economic culture constituting "freedom" as consumption and leisure, it was not surprising that drugs became endemic to the economies of New South Wales prisons when prisoners

> can't go to the beach, have a beer, go to the bush, swim, go shopping or do much of anything that isn't heavily restricted and all under the shadow of a prison officer in a tower with a rifle ... the result is that drugs appear a far more attractive form of recreation pleasure or escape, than they might outside. There are simply not many alternatives.[16]

Drugs entered into both the soft and hard discourses of prison life in the 1980s. In the soft control of the technologies of the group therapy sessions of the Special Care Unit, confessions about self-will and control over drug taking became part of the soul searching for self-identification:

> Daily group sessions are an essential part of the therapy at the Special Care Unit, for it is here that inmates get an opportunity to see themselves as others see them during sessions, members of the group help each other to face and recognise reasons for the inability to cope in gaol or the community. For instance, one prisoner says "I want to give up drugs", to which another responds "Then how come you asked me yesterday where you could get hold of drugs?"[17]

In prison life outside of the domesticated democracy of the Unit, the 1980s were also a period when militaristically oriented emergency units were established in the New South Wales gaols, with responsibilities for the control of prisoner disturbances.[18] In 1981–82 there were seventeen occasions when the units were called out[19] and in that year the Malabar emergency unit was amalgamated with a drug detector dog unit.[20] Drug detector dogs are used in the routine searches for drugs in prison that the Department proudly describes as being "... like a commando raid, (that) combines surprise with thoroughness. The dogs can detect drugs and alcohol even when these are ingeniously hidden."[21]

For prisoners managing to live day to day in the gaols this drug legitimated shift to an increased militarism involving investigations of "ingenious hiding places" means that power can be manifested in gross exploitations of control through invasions of the private possessions, spaces and even the bodies of prisoners.[22]

Drug taking complements sexuality in the late twentieth century discourses that constitute this particular form of consumption as pathological through the powerful language of "addiction". It is this construction of drug taking as the current manifestation of a lack of will over the body that legitimates the extensive State intervention over the body of the individual, even during the liberalising era of consumerism. As with sexuality in the Victorian and Freudian discourses, drug taking not only legitimates this State intervention as the physical and emotional coercion of prisoners, it also also becomes the basis for a detailed network of information collection agencies compiling dossiers on the physiological and social condition and the rehabilitative potential of prisoners. The Drug and Alcohol Court Assessment Programme (DACAP) is a post-conviction, pre-sentencing programme which assessed 496 prisoners in 1986–87. Its aims were to:

- provide sentencing authorities with accurate assessments of the nature and dependency of referred clients;
- recommend appropriate intervention;
- provide an indication where possible of the likelihood of the offender co-operating with such intervention;
- educate substance abusers as to their behaviour and encourage them to take appropriate action.[23]

The shift to a more drug dominated prison life legitimated the shift to militaristic forms of control. An alternative view of the problem of control within the New South Wales prison system was given in a submission from the Corrective Services Teachers Association to the Muir Inquiry into the Central Industrial Prison.[24] This analysis of the problem of prison violence indicated that prisoner violence was encouraged within the CIP and incorporated into the system of control.

> All too often violent but 'on side' prisoners are used by the system to keep order by heavying their fellow prisoners. Regrettably this method has greater favour than making improvements to management practices.[25]

The militarisation of prison life then can be interpreted as becoming self-perpetuating. The militaristic use of prisoners as "foot soldiers" engenders a system of prisoner to prisoner violence that can then be used to legitimate even further militarised tactics of control. In the New South Wales prisons in January 1988 a further militarised group within the already formed Special Response Unit group was formed. This was the Immediate Action Group (IAT) that was to "provide a well co-ordinated team of highly trained Prison Officers to respond to incidents of prisoner disturbances occurring within prison establishments."[26]

The Labour administration of prisons thus was characterised by its use of a "soft/hard" strategy of social control with militarisation and domestication occurring in parallel. The domestication of prison life in the early 1980s also included the two studies into the impact of imprisonment on family life, one published by the Department of Corrective Services and the other by the Ministry of Youth and Community Services.

The Department of Corrective Services report on the family life of long term prisoners was framed within the "family crisis" model of the earlier UK and USA researchers of the 1960s and 1970s.[27] The research was explicitly introduced as an examination of the way domesticity could be used to reduce the level of recidivism:

> (the) devastating effects on the prisoner and his family relationships ... can be the experience which locks the person into a criminal career. Maintaining close contact with the family during incarceration and re-entering a satisfactory role in the family on release appears to prevent many of these effects.[28]

The factors identified as contributing to the maintenance of family relationships and "neutralising the institutionalisation process" of prison life included the extent to which wives adopted a "functional or a dysfunctional" method of "coping" with the stresses of the impact of imprisonment. The study drew on the psychological classificatory schemes of McCubbin's Family Coping Inventory focusing on women's personal and social relationship behaviours. The research categorised women into whether they were "distant" or "close" in their relationship with the prisoner. The preliminary report which was based on the review of literature of the family crisis studies of separation included the recommendation

> that the Marriage Guidance Council should be requested to introduce counselling services into at least one major gaol in New South Wales, and to assist in training departmental officers in appropriate skills.[29]

One strand of policy-making then was manifestly attempting to insert domesticity into penal life through reconstituting prison officers as workers skilled in the "psy" work of policing family life, using the techniques of drawing the family into the prison towards the normalising end of the punishment in programmes of family counselling similar to those, described in chapter three, in the USA and Sweden. However, although the reformist technology of the family crisis model dominated the research methodology and most of the recommendations were oriented to opening up the prison by making it economically and practically easier for families to visit, one of the recommendations was to increase cooperation between women in the "(e)ncouragement for formation of self-help groups among prisoners' wives".[30]

The focus of the second report prepared by Hounslow et al for the Ministry of Youth and Community Services was directed more towards the political powerlessness of the outside carers of prisoners' children.[31] This report emphasised the extent of the work involved in the responsibility for the care of children of prisoners, and the hidden punishment and economic distress of the women performing this work. Like the Kemp and Cheron report, the report by Hounslow et al recommended the funding for a self-help group of outside carers. However they explicitly tied this recommendation to the lack of a political voice of the outside carers. The emphasis was very much more on the empowerment of families than on the domestication of prison life.

These reports had a minor effect. In 1983 a Children of Prisoners Support Group was funded by both the Corrective Services and the Family and Community Services Departments. However it was funded on the basis of co-ordinating the work of volunteers in line with the Corrective Services report's recommendations. The marriage counselling recommendations were not taken up. A Youth and Community Worker was allocated full time responsibility to foster understanding amongst Welfare Workers of the plight of, and the resources available for, children of prisoners.[32] The funding for a permanent Community Worker to coordinate the more political aspect of the group, the self support group of outside carers of prisoners children, was channelled through the CEP scheme. The conditions for this funding downgraded the importance of this aspect of the groups' work. The conditions of CEP funding were for the employment of a relatively inexperienced worker and funding was specifically limited to the provision of a salary for only one year. By the late 1980s the work of the group was eventually narrowed down to supplementing the work of the outside carers by providing a child escort service for prisoner parents with limited outside family support, and the staging of gala days in prisons when children could spend the day with their prisoner parents in a more normal setting than the usual restrictive conditions of maximum security visiting. However this latter work depended on the goodwill of individual prison superintendents. Few of the superintendents of maximum security prisons were willing to open up their gaols for this limited domestication of prison life. Notably it was around the parenthood of women prisoners that the group's work eventually predominantly revolved.

The ad hoc and limited nature of the "family-oriented" reforms was also demonstrated in the provision of Family Support Centres. Just prior to the publication of the two family-of-prisoner reports, the Civil Rehabilitation Committee had been successful in persuading the Department to provide a Family Support Centre for visitors to the prisons in the Long Bay complex. The Centre provided basic practical support for visitors: free child care for partners when they wanted to visit the prisoner alone, shelter during the break in visits, clean toilets, a changing room, cups of tea and coffee, an information base and most importantly a place where women could get together to exchange information and support between themselves. The recommendation of the Children of Imprisoned Parents Report that all other prisons should provide this elementary support for visitors was not taken up.

The tensions between the reformist and the punitive aspects of control in the New South Wales penal system were further complicated in this period by the introduction of the Early Release scheme. This undermined the domestication of prison life by putting to an end the Day Release II (Home Release) scheme and limiting the numbers released on the Day Release I programme.[33] The resignation, arrest and imprisonment of the Minister for Corrective Services for taking bribes for early releases was also accompanied by the end of the Early Release programme, but by the mid eighties the climate of penal life in New South Wales had swung so far back to the punitive end of the scale that the home release programme was not reintroduced.

In the 1986 to 1988 period the penal system was characterised by major tensions between hard line punitive-controlling and softer reformative policies and practices. The latter were also controlling but less manifestly so. The prisons were being run by a range of state officials whose attitudes similarly reflected the complexities of the contradictory philosophies of penality as they were being worked out in the day to day constitution of prison life. A 1987 report into the opinions of New South Wales prisoners, specialist staff and prison officers about the definitions of prisoners in general as being either "mad", "bad" or "normal", found that whilst most prisoners chose the description "normal", prison officers chose the "bad" definition with the choice of specialist staff falling somewhere between the other two.[34] Whilst this study depended on responses gathered at only one particular time, Vinson's reflections on his two years in the Commission clearly evidence the contradictory sets of ideas about criminality that New South Wales prison officers held: prisoners were alternatively defined as genetically or naturally criminal, a potentially threatening group of violent men needing to be brutally contained, deviants in need of therapeutic reform or as essentially ordinary people whom the prison officers are required to contain as humanely as possible.[35] This depiction of prison staff locked into a contradictory set of attitudes parallels the picture of prison guards and their culture portrayed in several other accounts of prison life in western style familial-political economies.[36] However, this cultural focus presents too static a picture of prison officers' attitudes. Terence Willet argues that guards are at the "synaptic point" of power in the hierarchy of prison authority.[37] They are at the last point in the chain of power where policy has to be converted into action. The social dynamics of prison life then mean that they, as well as the prisoners, experience in a condensed form the contradictions that derive from the multiple discourses of containment, punishment, rehabilitation or humane control. Similarly Kelsey Kauffman found that during the period 1971 to 1980 the contradiction between the official goals of the Massachusetts prison system and the futility of achieving those goals was experienced as devastating by the prison officers in that system.[38] The frustrations and experiences of the inherent hypocrisies of penal life, which form the context within which prison officers work, has led to an increasingly militant yet conservative unionism in Britain and in North American prisons.

> Surmounting all the evidence is an impression of frustration with their inability to 'change things' in a system that seemed to them beyond anyone's control, and the most appropriate concept that comes to mind to describe this is inertia: a condition in which there is an in-built resistance to change.[39]

Thomas Mathiesen also demonstrated the similarity of reactions of prisoners and prison guards and their common vulnerability in the face of the contradictions of prison constituted as the site of punishment, containment and therapy.[40] Both Mathiesen and Willet argue that the incongruity of these expectations as it is experienced by staff at the bottom of the hierarchy of power leads prison guards to a constant need to defend their status. David Grant's overview of the changes in prison life in New South Wales from the 1960s to the 1980s defines the issue of prison security primarily from this perspective. He describes it as a downward spiral of mistrust and disaffection on the part of the prison officers as a consequence of the shift beginning in 1968, from constituting prisoners as bodies to be controlled, to individuals able to be rehabilitated, then to "near citizens" with rights to be defended.[41] At the same time, he points out, prison officers did not experience a parallel redefinition of their role,

> Little was done to develop a model of prisoner management which recognised the needs and rights of prisoners and therefore required and provided additional skills to Prison Officers.[42]

Grant's account sets this dynamic up as a result of an internal problem of poor prison management rather than as a more deep seated contradiction of a layering of incompatible expectations that reflected and reinforced the contradictions of the familial-political economy of the outside world. Nevertheless this dynamic of prison life, of increasing expectations of prisoners and of the relative neglect of the impact of the liberalising changes on prison officers, meant that for prison officers concessions to prisoners were almost inevitably interpreted as excessive. The hierarchical authority structure of prison combined with the contradictory nature of discourses underpinning penality then created a powerful dynamic constantly reconstituting prison custodial staff as reactionary, resisting especially those changes that increase prisoners' control. The papers presented in 1975 to the seminar on "the conflict of security and rehabilitation in the 1970s" on the ambiguities of prison life indicate that the same resentments were being felt in other Australian prisons:

> the prison officer felt he was excluded from the treatments programme. There have been indications that he resents the intrusion of specialist, and is critical of the introduction of additional programmes of treatment. The feeling was strong that some treatment programmes interfered with discipline and the otherwise smooth operation of the prison.[43]

This tension continued into the 1980s. The depictions of prison struggles in both Vinson's and Anderson's accounts of the years following the Nagle Report demonstrate that the New South Wales experience follows closely the dynamics of imprisonment in Europe and America.

There are other structures within which prison life is experienced that reinforce the constitution of relations within prison towards the brutalising end of the range of controlling techniques. The social psychological studies of controlling relationships indicate the brutalising effects of those relationships on the controllers, especially within the condensed relationships of power as they operate within prison.[44] Several prisoner autobiographies attest to the brutalising and infantilising effects of prison on both prisoners and controllers.[45] David Greenberg's summary of the critical sociology of imprisonment studies indicates that the prison officers' socially shared, "common sense" categorisations of prison life effectively constitute prison as a "lawless agency".[46] In addition, the political critique of penality by George Zdenkowski and David Brown pinpoints three dimensions of prison life central to the maintenance of unequal brutalising relations: secrecy, suppression of alternative prisoner based organisation and arbitrary authority.[47] Their descriptions of prison life in the 1980s and Tim Anderson's account of his imprisonment from 1978 to 1985,[48] indicate that these three were endemic in the New South Wales prison system.

Although the period following the publication of the Nagle report in 1976[49] did see the introduction of a number of prison practices that were both more humane and that served to open up prisons to the wider society, some of these reforms were beginning to be wound back in the early 1980s and by the late 1980s the political economic climate meant that both political parties were shifting towards a "law and order" stance in relation to policing and penal policies.[50] Imprisonment rates rose until by 1987 the New South Wales prison levels were at 110 per cent capacity.[51] The concern with prisoners' rights or with humanising prison life, evident in the penal discourses of the early eighties, was translated into the more immediate and pragmatic concerns rising out of the issue of prison overcrowding, "increased stress and management problems, boredom and frustration stemming from the lack of useful activities, sexual and other assault, violence and intimidation, and dramatically increased drug use".[52]

In summary in the period of the early to mid 1980s there were three major discourses through which prison life was constantly being negotiated and renegotiated:

1   *conservativism:* The prisoner was constituted as a threatening "enemy within" and a legitimate target for the violence of the state;

2   *therapeutic liberalism:* The prisoner was constituted as a pathological member of society who was nevertheless capable of being reformed and reattached to social life through exposure to a judicious balance of the two major spheres of control — the universalistic impersonal patriarchal control of penality and the particularistic emotional attachments of domestic life;

3   *radical liberalism:* The prisoner was constituted as a member of civil society whose human rights should be protected through opening up the prison to "the community".

These three discourses impinged on the actual day to day life of the individual prisoner differently at different moments of his prison experience. The penal sphere is constituted as a site of transformation, with prisoners undergoing a metamorphosis from threatening enemy to fully restored citizen. In the late 1980s there were 23 prisons in New South Wales, 7 maximum security, 9 medium and 7 minimum security. The conditions, including visiting conditions, were either more punitive or more orientated towards "normalisation" at either end of this range (although the rehabilitative practices can also be used as forms of punitive control). In the earliest stages of imprisonment, especially in the experiences of containment in police cells prior to being charged, but also in the earlier post-sentencing period prior to being classified, the prisoner is much more likely to be exposed to the punitive *segregating* practices of penality. After this early stage penality shifts towards to the reformist corrective practices of medium security imprisonment and, finally, in the pre-release *normalising* period prison operates manifestly in conjunction with the family to reconstitute the prisoner as an unthreatening mature citizen capable of being released back into public life. At the back end of the prison programme there are a variety of semi-imprisonment practices that connect the home and the prison. Parole was introduced in 1951 and by 1986 the ratio of prisoners and parolees was approximately 2:1.[53] There are also after care probation orders, as well as the programmes in which imprisoned men are given periodic releases into the community through work release, weekend and day release programmes and periodic detention.[54]

However, layered onto this "career" version of imprisonment as different moments in the process of the re-emergence of the prisoner as "a useful member of society", are the variations caused by the shifts in the wider political economy and in the political balances within the penal sphere. After the brief reformist post-Nagle era, both Labour and Liberal parties responded to pressures from within the prison system, and from the wider sphere of political economic life, to move to a more punitive position in the areas of both policing and imprisonment.[55] As the rate of imprisonment increased, prisons became overcrowded and, at the segregating moment of imprisonment, the maximum security gaols increasingly came to house prisoners who were classified as B or C prisoners, that is as prisoners who should have been experiencing the more corrective or normalising stages of imprisonment.[56]

It is within these complex and contradictory conditions that women outside continued the work of caring, principally by maintaining contact with prisoners inside.

This specific form of caring work is described here as comprising six aspects:[57]

1   Material aspects of caring work: economic contribution to the state and to the physical wellbeing of prisoners;
2   Material aspects of caring work: economic costs to women;

3   Material aspects of caring work: economic costs to women, in providing money to the prisoner;
4   Material aspect of caring work: costs to women, their time;
5   Caring as mediating and negotiating work;
6   The double burden of caring: contradictions of caring for prisoners and their children.

1   MATERIAL ASPECTS OF THE LABOUR OF CARING FOR IMPRISONED MEN: ECONOMIC CONTRIBUTION TO THE STATE AND THE PHYSICAL WELLBEING OF THE PRISONER

The feminist materialist analyses of the nexus between caring and dependence indicate that there are major materialist aspects involved in the work of caring. These include firstly, the material contributions that the private labour of tending makes to the individuals being cared for: it is something women do for others, to keep them alive. "It is a labour that ensures life as much as an emotion which expresses love."[58] Secondly, caring labour makes a major economic contribution to various sectors of the public sphere.[59] The central contradiction of productive life lies in the inability of the political economy of the public sphere to provide adequate support for those who fall outside of the wage relationship — children, the aged and the invalid — in a society that is nevertheless based upon the professedly civil and humane values of liberal capitalism. Domesticity, as the coping work of caring or mothering, then can be seen as absorbing the inherent stresses and tensions of the contradictions of a wage based economy.

Thirdly, and paradoxically, this economic contribution results in material costs to the people providing that labour, the carers.[60] This contradiction is resolved through the devaluation and marginalisation of the work of caring through the discourses of "love" and of "natural" family obligations. It is this emotional aspect of caring that makes it significantly different from other forms of labour. Ungerson points out that "caring for" has a totally different meaning to "caring about".[61] Nevertheless the conflation of the two terms elegantly mystifies the extensive physical and intellectual labour of caring as well as its significant material contribution to the political economy. There are clear parallels in this material dimension of the work of caring, between the care of other adult dependents and the work of caring for adults made dependent by imprisonment.

Domesticity, as the sphere of social life centred around the constitution of the personality, imposes significant demands on the tending labour of outside carers of imprisoned men. If the experience of his imprisonment is defined as so threatening that the personality, health or life of the man inside is endangered, the responsibility for providing care is a manifestly important domestic task.

The importance for the health and wellbeing of prisoners of maintaining contact with the family outside is both an evident yet an invisible part of the discourses surrounding the policies and practices of imprisonment. Prison is the paradigmatic form of total institution that operates through a series of rituals designed to dehumanise its inmates.[62] Even in a well run maximum security prison that conforms to legal requirements for the care of its inmates, the personality of the prisoner is under threat: life is lived totally within enclosed walls designed to exclude the wider society, prisoners are stripped of the symbols that represent and reflect their "selves" in the outside world, the physical needs of prisoners are provided for by bureaucratic forms of organisation designed to handle large blocks of people. However, the history of prison administration in New South Wales indicates that even minimum standards of custodial care are not continually maintained.[63]

In the decade immediately preceding the years covered by the interviews prisoners in New South Wales had been subjected to brutalising forms of ritualistic degradation. Even after the Nagle Commission and the appointment of a liberal Chairman to oversee the reforms of the prison system, Tony Vinson, at that time the Chairman of the Corrective Services Commission, describes this example of a routine used at meal times during prison officer strikes: "the cell doors were opened one at a time, but not before a burly police officer asked me to step aside so that he could 'get a good swing action' with his baseball bat ..."[64]

Prison visiting then exemplifies the duality of caring work, its combination of emotional and material dimensions. The importance of visiting in relieving the tensions inherent in imprisonment has major material consequences in terms of economic costs and savings to the state. This is evidenced in the costs to the state when visiting becomes too marginal an aspect of prison life. One of the most graphic illustrations of the materiality of the domestic labour of visiting is the burning down of Bathurst Prison in 1974. The grossly inadequate visiting conditions were one of the major factors precipitating the riots in both 1970 and 1974 resulting in the extensive material costs of the refurbishing of the gaol.[65] Insufficient visits have continued to be one of the basic reasons for political activity by prisoners in New South Wales well into the late 1980s.[66] The materiality of visiting is also evidenced in the the Department of Corrective Services research into the reasons for prison escapes.[67] Worries and inadequate information about the family particularly in periods of family crisis are major factors precipitating prison escapes and their consequent costs in police and prison administration and in the eventual extensions of the prisoner's punishment.

Visiting and maintaining family contact is incorporated into the punishment system to relieve the tensions and stresses of the masculinity of total institutionalisation and to reduce the costs that those stresses incur. This is formally recognised within the Department of Corrective Services in New South Wales in its response to the Nagle Report's recommendations about improving the frequency and the conditions of visits.[68] Moreover, the state operates both prescriptively and proscriptively to ensure that the work of maintaining family contact is performed. Women who fail to do this unpaid, costly and laborious work have been formally and publicly upbraided by representatives of the legal-penal sphere. In his judgement on the causes of death of a prisoner, the coroner Mr P Heaney, indicted the refusal of the man's wife to do that work:

> For Beverley Smith[69] not to take or arrange for the children to be taken to visit their father, was both insensitive and cruel, despite her motives.[70]

There are two other principles of penal life underpinning this prescription to families outside to do the work of maintaining contact. Justice Nagle argued that maximising visits to prisoners would guard against the conditions of secrecy and isolation that enabled the prisoner officer brutalities in Grafton and Bathurst to continue for so long.[71] Caring work is incorporated then as a control upon the prison guards in a defence of the liberal principle of prison as punishment not for punishment. The review of literature in chapter two indicated that punishment as bodily violence was nominally replaced by administratively based forms of "punishment by surveillance and control" with the expansion of the administrative power of capitalism. However, there is a constant tension between this liberal rationalism and the actual day to day control and continual confinement of young able bodied men in a political economic culture that privileges masculinity expressed as physical power. Sometimes the tension is resolved by encouraging brutality but maintaining secrecy. In the more liberal periods there is an attempt to contain brutality by opening up the boundaries between prison and public life. These occasional swings back to openness then serve to legitimate the continued use of imprisonment even during the more frequent periods of secretive brutality. The tensions arising out of the contradictions of the wider society thus lead to frequent reworkings (and an increasing complexity) of the rules and regulations constraining visitors. For people with the family obligation to care for prisoners, the discourse of imprisonment is comprised of a variety of contradictory sets of rules. This complexity is derived not only from differences in administrative rules between gaols but also from the frequent minor shifts about times and conditions of visiting as they apply in any one prison.

Secondly, both the Nagle Report and the 1982 Department of Corrective Services Research Publication on the effects of separation on prisoners and their families are state recognitions of the reformist thesis that the work of maintaining contact with the prisoner contributes to the professed goal of rehabilitation.

> ... total separation from family and close friends evokes in a prisoner tension, resentment and a sense of complete alienation from the community. These are all contrary to rehabilitation gaols (sic).[72]

> ... continuing family contact is important in neutralising the institutionalisation process for prisoners. Furthermore, pre-release anxiety may also

decrease with the certain knowledge that a supporting family will be waiting.[73]

"Rehabilitation" in some current prison discourses is modified now so that it is concerned more with redressing the deterioration that occurs as a result of imprisonment than with the restructuring of a deviant personality supposedly damaged by genetic or subcultural defects.

Fears about the effects of imprisonment on the physical and emotional health and on the life of the partner or son inside prison were a major concern for the outside carers and one of the key reasons for their visits. For some women it was the effects of prisonisation that was upmost in their concern about the prisoner. In this case the work of maintaining contact is clearly related to what Yeatman describes as the defining aspect of domesticity — the constitution of the personality:

Olive: Son in CIP

If I miss one Wednesday, he phones up. He's real family. If he didn't get a visit I think he would die. He'd give up. He really would give up ... When he came out last time he came out as 18 in his mind. He blanked his mind out. He'd stayed 18 all the time he'd been inside. He went around all the time with 18 year olds (he was 21 at that time). It did worry me at the time. We talked all the time I think it's important for them I think what they need, I think if you keep in contact with them and you let them know what everyone's doing and what's going on, because they don't know what's going on, I think then they know what to expect when they get out.

Ten of the women directly expressed their concern for the way in which prison life threatened the physical health, even the lives, of their partners or sons:

Janet: Partner has been in Goulburn and Malabar. Now in CIP

He was an epileptic. I was terrified for fear that something would happen. I have had sleepless nights. It's affecting me now.

Esther: Partner has been in Cessnock, Silverwater. Now in CIP. Has served 6 months of this sentence

I don't like seeing him only once a week. He's sick, he's depressed and he needs me more than I need him and they're only allowing us one visit a week. He's in hospital at the moment and I think it's unfair that I didn't get a visit a week.

Women's fears for the health of men inside are rational. Men in prison are at risk. Prison death rates are higher than community death rates especially for prisoners in the 20–34 age groups. Death by suicide is five times more likely to occur in prison and the rate for death by homicide is three times higher than in the outside community.[74] Moreover, despite popular myth, suicides are more likely to occur amongst prisoners who have made previous suicide attempts or have a history of self-inflicted injury.[75] Although the early weeks of imprisonment is the period when prisoners are most at risk of death by suicide, several years into a sentence is also an "at risk" time for death to occur in prison.

The examples of riots and revolt, and the prisoner organisations, in the New South Wales prisons in the 1970s and early 1980s demonstrate the occasionally high levels of solidarity that can develop in gaol. On several occasions in spite of heavy physical penalties prisoners have continued to work together to improve, from the inside, the general conditions of prison life. However Judy Jones, in a review of the "prison culture" literature, and from her own interviews with prisoners about their relationships within prison and with their families, argues that the routine experience of prison culture does not provide sufficient informal support for emotional life. The prison culture of mateship, she argues, provides insufficient alternative support because other prisoners are disliked, because there are few shared interests, and because there is manipulation by the prison administration to inhibit cohesiveness between groups of prisoners.[76] Anderson's account of his own prison experience in New South Wales between 1978–85 shows how prison administrators undermine prisoner organisations in several ways, by shanghaiing members, placing prisoners in segregation, and on occasion by instigating attacks on "trouble makers" by other prisoners.[77]

Anderson's descriptions of prison life do not understate the level of dissension between prisoners. He describes the hierarchies of power and violence that structure prisoner populations especially as they operate through the drug trade run by both prisoners and prison officers.[78] However his account clearly outlines the same contradictions of prison life evidenced in Boyle's descriptions of imprisonment in Britain.[79] The institutionalised violence of the State as experienced directly in the day to day life of gaol foments both violence and solidarity between prisoners.

Nevertheless both accounts also highlight Jones' argument about the importance of the family outside in sustaining identity. Prison as the site of institutionalised violence can engender solidarity but also violence, hostility or a guarded indifference between inmates. The pervasiveness of the threat of violence and the conflictual nature of prison relationships means that self-preservation inside prison involves not engaging in self-disclosure with others inside.[80] This essentially familial aspect of the constitution and preservation of self is in contradiction to the experience of day to day life in prison. Although in the New South Wales system the Special Care Unit was specifically introduced to provide this more domesticised form of containment, the general structure of imprisonment denies prisoners access to relationships basic to sustaining a sense of self. Ernie Hinton was a prisoner in the New South Wales gaols during the 1980s. His description of the dehumanising effects of the routines of imprisonment and being cut off from the particularistic relationships of family life confirms Jones' point:

> Can you imagine what it's like ... you sit in your cell after seven hours of freedom ... of frustrations and anger accumulated during the day. There's no one to love, no woman to share your sexual needs with, no kids to hug and say goodnight to ... and in your mind you know that the next day and the next day will merely be carbon copies of the same days, unless of course it is

broken by the drama of a a hanging or a fight, or waiting for a visit or a letter, or even your name called over the intercom — at least in this sense you know you still exist ... that system which is YOUR system reduces we, the prisoner, a human being, to the status of an animal, who thus reverts to animal instinct in its crudest manifestation ... REVENGE.[81]

Prison increases men's emotional dependence upon families outside. However, as Jones emphasises, this dependence has inherent contradictions. Imprisonment increases the importance of such masculine values as emotional toughness and power at the same time as prisoners become increasingly emotionally dependent upon the women outside.[82]

Jones argues that the experience of imprisonment leads prisoners, in their relationship with their families outside, to define their own comfort as being central not only to themselves but to others and that this "selfishness" is translated into an obsession with their relationship with their wife or girlfriend. Wives and girlfriends are not only the focus of an intense need for attachment, they are seen as the people whose *duty* it is to provide emotional nurturance.[83] In prison life there is a condensation of the unequal family relationships of the outside world, which are predicated upon the unconditional love of the selfless woman for the husband, or of the mother for the son. Several analyses of the day to day care of aged dependents shows how the nexus of care and dependency exposes the carer to the only form of control that the dependent cared for person can exert — emotional blackmail.[84] This control is a feature too of the caring work of women with family obligations to imprisoned men in New South Wales:

Claire: Partner in CIP

about the second month it's 'me, me, me' until I pointed out ... and Len would be one of the most unselfish person on earth — at two months I felt 'everything's going out, nothing's coming back' especially if the man doesn't use letters or phone calls. Prison really does bring out the chauvinistic in them.

Dulcie

You've got to keep your front up. It's so bloody hard. I never cry. My husband said 'If you're going to cry, get out'.

Bettina

You have to look good. It's important. You have to look good. If you go out there looking drab, they start on you. I've sat there and he's picked and picked on me. I'd got soaking wet coming out here. He'd say 'I rang last night and you weren't there', I thought 'this is it'. I walked out of that place. Of course, I got a foul letter — yet if we didn't turn up it would break them in pieces.

This example of the importance of visiting also emphasises the other material aspect of the work of visiting. It involves women in providing extensive labour. The usual connotations of "visiting" are that it is a marginal, usually pleasurable part of social life. This image has to be reprocessed in the case of the work of prison visiting. It involves women in extensive time and labour and, even though the visit might only be for an hour, the work involved in preparing for, travelling to, then waiting for the visit dominates the day to day life of women outside.

2 MATERIAL ASPECTS OF CARING: ECONOMIC COSTS TO WOMEN

The 1982 Department of Corrective Services report into the effects of family separation showed that visiting imposed major costs on women outside. The majority of wives experienced physical or financial difficulties in travelling to gaols.[85] The 1982 report made recommendations about allaying these costs. However the thrust of those recommendations was to transfer the costs from the family not to the state but to volunteer workers who should provide child care, help with transport and increase the wives' access to information about the gaol system.[86] In the same year a separate research report was issued by the Family and Children's Service Agency.[87] This used a different perspective, emphasising the right of prisoners to maintain contact with their children as an end in itself rather than using family contact as a means to supplement the smooth running of the gaols and the rehabilitation of prisoners. Nevertheless, this report also showed that being the outside carer of prisoners' children involved major costs and that the expense of maintaining contact with the prisoner was the greatest additional cost imposed on the family outside.[88] The recom- mendations of this report also pinpointed the role that non-government groups could play in providing material assistance. However in this case the recommendations were that community groups autonomous to the Department should be funded by both Corrective Services and the (then) Youth and Community Services Departments to provide transport, information and accommodation and social and political support for the families outside.[89]

Some of the recommendations of these reports were put into effect. A free bus service — weekly to the Long Bay complex and once a fortnight to Cessnock, Silverwater and Goulburn prisons — was introduced funded partly by the Department of Corrective Services and partly by the unpaid labour of volunteer bus drivers organised through the semi-autonomous Civil Rehabilitation Service.[90] In addition, by 1987 the New South Wales Corrective Services was providing some direct financial and practical help for visiting, but this was not extensive. With a prison population of over 4,000 on any one day, or of more than 14,000 over the whole year, only seventeen families were recorded as having been given financial assistance for accommodation and supplementary costs of visiting country prisons, whilst only 45 families were recorded as having received economic assistance for travel to country prisons.[91]

Unsurprisingly then the interviews with women visiting prison between 1986 and 1988 indicated that the costs in terms of their time, labour and direct financial expenses were still major aspects of the work of visiting. Some of the visits especially to Cessnock, Silverwater and Goulburn were made cheaper by the provision of the bus or the pensioner concessions on public transport. Nevertheless, visits to other country gaols or to the metropolitan gaols by families living outside inner Sydney or in the Western suburbs of Sydney were still major costs to women visiting prisons.

Agnes: Son in Cessnock prison

Q: Have you ever worked out how much it costs you? No I daren't. I put all my dollar pieces to one side, collect them up, then use that. I've got $50 now to put aside for him for his things.

Fay

My fiance and my son are in prison (two different prisons). *How many visits do you make a week?* Once to each jail ... all by public transport. I travel 400 miles every week I get one pass, the rest comes from my pension ... it costs about $42 a week ... because I have to take my child who has epileptic fits.

Beth

I've been up to Cessnock, stayed overnight, took Tracy up with me. It cost us $100 just to stay overnight, with food and everything else.

Although as single parents travel costs can be reduced by the concessions allowed to pensioners, these concessions are lost for women who have long journeys.

Barbara

I get up at 4 (am) then I catch the train to Penrith. Then I catch the train in from there. I get in about quarter to seven to Central then I hang around there than I catch the bus about 25 past seven. I come out here, because I'm catching the early bus I don't get the concession, so I'm paying full fares

The FACSA report pointed out that taxi fares from train stations to gaols sited in remote parts of towns were major liabilities for visitors and this is still a cost for women. But this added complication to visiting is only part of the complex expenses of visiting. Visiting a man in gaol takes up the whole day for families without their own transport, so the cost of meals or cups of coffee or tea are extra expenses. In addition the policy of having a continuum of punishment, with some prisons being more lenient in the conditions of imprisonment and visiting than others, means that parents or partners of prisoners can be involved in the expense of paying for the privileges extended to the rewarded prisoners.

3 MATERIAL ASPECTS OF CARING: ECONOMIC COSTS TO WOMEN OF
   PROVIDING MONEY FOR THE PRISONER

In chapter two it was argued that the major shift in the constitution of the personality of the individual citizen in the post world war II era of corporate consumer capitalism was towards the seemingly liberalising readjustment away from thriftiness as a central core value and towards consumerism. The liberal encouragement to define oneself through one's ability to be free to buy and to consume worked through into penal policies and practices and in 1964 New South Wales prisoners were first allowed to use private cash as well as prison earnings to buy goods. The range of goods available for purchase within prisons increased and by 1976 prisoners were allowed to buy television sets.[92] This parallelled the rehabilitative policies of encouraging interests in hobbies and crafts so that in addition prisoners were allowed to buy hobby equipment that in some cases involved the purchase of expensive equipment, for example of fish tanks and exotic fish.

Having cash to buy goods with then becomes an important part of living in prison. The obvious contradiction between this seemingly liberal policy and the fact that prisoners have very restricted access to cash by the very conditions of their imprisonment is resolved often only by the increased impoverishment of the family outside.

Tricia: Partner has been in a variety of prisons. Now in Goulburn

(it's expensive) bus fares, buying a lunch and taking him some money in, he has to be able to buy tobacco. I think it cost me about $15 to $20 a week. The bus fare only cost me 60c, but it's all the extras every week.

In some cases families outside are both bringing money in for the prisoner to buy goods and having the responsibility to buy goods outside that are going to be acceptable in terms of the precise (although mysterious) rules of prison.

Julie

Buying all underwear and socks and things like that ... he's got piles of clothing back home but he had to have all new. It's regulation. I couldn't touch any of that ... all brand new. What my husband was doing before I realised that they didn't supply (underwear) was taking them off at night and washing them through in the shower, wringing them out and putting them straight back on.

Margery: Son in remand prison

He's asked for sunglasses, I had to get him the cheapest. I bought him two tee-shirts $3.99 each, because he was hot, another pair of shorts. Tiger brand, green. They were about $10 and I got a pair of stubbies for him, green stubbies. They were on special about $3.99. I shopped around to get the cheapest.

The complex regulations about taking goods result in some prohibitive expenditures for women whose sons or partners move from prison to prison or for those who have been returned to prison after an escape or second offence:

Gwen

When Terry was in here last time, I bought him a brand new one (TV). Like, I put the money in his property and he bought one. He brought it home and now he's back in there again. I've got to buy another one. I said 'Why can't he bring it back here again, why have I got to buy another one? Where am I going to get $99 to buy another one?' Stereos, cassettes, $99 for television, little shitty cassette player cost something like $80. They won't let you bring

119

it in. You can buy it a lot cheaper from outside but you're not allowed to ... It cost me about $200 altogether for things like that last time he was in.

The expansion of the drug market in gaols has the potential for placing major pressures on women concerned about the wellbeing of men inside prison. The enforcement of debt-collection in this market that operates outside the usual legal constraints means that the buyers are at grave risk of gross physical coercion:

On a number of occasions I've been a bystander to this sort of thing. On one occasion I came out of a shower at Parramatta to see a young boy getting stood over and bashed for his watch, by a couple of junkies. On another, while in the gym, I wondered for a couple of seconds why two people well known to me were taking a pulley bar outside until I realised it was to collect a debt.[93]

There was no attempt during the interviews to question women on this issue which is obviously potentially incriminating for them and for the man inside. Nevertheless three women spoke about the pressures that the prison drug market had imposed on either them or their friends:

Margery: Son in remand prison in Long Bay complex

I've given him $5 today he said for soap and shampoo. I'm frightened he might be saving up and getting marijuana smoke. I don't know. He asks me money for ... I said "I can't afford it, today. *How do you feel about that?* with this child, that's what he is, I feel the guilt I feel such a guilt. I feel a lot of responsibility. I find it very hard and he knows this (laughing). He's a manipulator. He knows how I feel ... but I'm really trying to be tough.

Lauren

When he was looking for money (for drugs in prison) I wouldn't put money in his pocket for that ... I felt terrible. I felt like I wasn't trusting him but I thought it better not trusting ... I just didn't want the temptation for him.

In addition to travelling costs and the expense of providing the commodities that enable the penal service to present itself as a liberal and humane system, the greater openness of the post Nagle prison system involves women in the sometimes prohibitive expense of telephone calls:

Pauline: Son in Cessnock

We take reverse charge calls (from Cessnock to Sydney) two days a week.

Gwen

He rings me up now and again, that's good but I couldn't handle that last time. (he was in prison) Like he went to Cooma and that's a long way to go, every fortnight. I'd wait then I'd get the cheque and go and visit him. And in between there'd be phone calls. Well the phone bill ended up being $380 and I just had to put an end to it. I didn't know it was going to be that high, because half the time I thought he was paying for it and in actual fact he wasn't, so they cut the phone off and I'm still paying that, so I said to him if you go anywhere but in the city you just can't ring me because I just can't afford it. I really can't.

It is evident from these experiences that there is a duality of pressures upon women to provide this costly subsidy to the legal penal sphere. The pressures derive, firstly, from the penal sphere, especially from the post Nagle shift to greater openness between prison and community to safeguard prisoner's rights. The second set of pressures come from the immediate family obligation to care. The "naturalness" of family provision of basic necessities like meals, underwear or socks, and telephone calls, enables men in prison, and through them the prison administration, to expect that the transfer of the costs to their parents or partners will be borne uncomplainingly by the people in those families. However family gift giving, particularly as it operates in the family clothing economy, is not a reciprocal process. In the gift relationships of the wider society, women give husbands and sons a much wider variety of clothes as presents than vice versa.[94] Moreover women are more likely to buy men's clothes on an everyday basis so that this transfer of resources becomes defined as a "much more mundane event" than gift-giving from men to women.[95] Significantly, it is in the mother-to-son relationship that gift-giving is so notably asymmetric, that the finding is "... to put it bluntly, mothers give, sons receive."[96]

It is from these taken-for-granted expectations about the mundanity of the transfer of resources through the family gift economy, that prisoners are able to exert pressures on the women outside. This then means that the state is able to maintain the liberal humane face of providing conditions in which men are reasonably comfortably clothed and have access to some of the standard accessories of modern life. Tim Anderson's account of the impact of TV on prison life also shows how prisoners' possessions can become a potential leverage in the control of prisoners. When a prisoner is accused of a breach of rules the privilege of watching his own TV is one of the amenities that is taken away from him. In addition when there are more political or collective confrontations between prisoners and prison officers one very effective revenge tactic is the official rampage, the violent search of prisoners' cells, in which colour televisions are smashed.[97] It is the increasing openness of prison to the consumerism of the wider society that then exposes women to the risks that are inherent in the contradictory moralities of home and prison. The denial of access to family life means that a major escape or "haven" from the pressures of the singularly "heartless" world of the prison is through the consumption of the major leisure commodities of marijuana or heroin.

4 MATERIAL ASPECTS OF CARING: WOMEN'S TIME

In addition to the financial costs visiting imposes major constraints on women's time. A one-hour visit can involve women in a complete day's expenditure of time and labour. Even with access to the CRC bus the journeys are extraordinarily costly in terms of women's time and labour. Many of the women come from the Western suburbs, a journey that takes two hours by bus. However twelve of the forty women spoke of journeys that were much more time consuming:

Elizabeth

I do 170 miles down and 170 miles back in one day and it's just for twice a week, and I have another 13 months to go ... I get up at 4 o'clock in the morning and I leave home at quarter to six. I get a bus to Lithgow then I get the train to Sydney the bus from Sydney out here (to Long Bay). Then I repeat the process coming home. I get home at 11.30 at night.

Olive

Coming by train and bus is an all day job from Casula. Caught the train at quarter to eight getting home not until 6 o'clock — it's a whole day gone.

Moreover visiting also involves spending frustrating periods of time waiting for the prisoner to be called to the visit.

Brenda: Partner in MTC. Sons in primary and secondary schools

the visiting hours are very short. Visiting starts at half past eight. I have to put the kids off to school then catch the train and then I might miss the bus so I might not get there until half past ten. Visiting finishes at half past eleven (but) they're very slow in the visiting part like when they call the prisoners out. It takes them about an hour or half an hour. Once I sat there for a whole two hours. He was round the other section. They kept phoning every time. I kept asking where was my husband. They said 'you'll just have to wait'. The third time I asked them they found out on the computer after I'd been waiting there for two hours. They could have checked up straight away. Some of the guards treat you like nothing.

Hilda

Look what happened today. I left home at 6.30 this morning to get there and I won't get home until 8.30 this evening — 14 hours and we're supposed to have a 3 hour visit. We have to get there at 11.30 but it always takes them half an hour to do the paper work. Why don't they do it before we come? Why do we have to wait that half hour. Then today, after all that journey up, 6.30 to 11.30 we had to wait an hour. I said to them 'have you murdered my son and buried him somewhere or something?'

These delays in allowing women to see prisoners as soon as they arrive at the gaol can be due to bureaucratic processes. Katherine Ferguson argues that client delay is a normal part of all organisations set up to provide welfare services for powerless clients because of the record keeping burdens of the bureaucracy.[98] However these delays can also be due to a distancing from the clients that develop from the systematic constraints of the bureaucratic service providers work.[99] In prison life both of these features of the bureaucratic discourse are evident. Women reported that the delays were experienced as an arrogance towards them: that their time was of no account. The delays can also be interpreted as a general demonstration of the arbitrary power of prison officers over the prisoners or as due to a direct control of a specific prisoner when undermining the visit becomes a punishment deliberately meted out to him. The humiliating aspect of this total control on women's time is illustrated in Claire's description of the way that making a decision to go to the lavatory can undermine the woman's chance of having an unharassed visit.

Claire

I had a three hour wait — it was boring, I was tense, on edge, has he been called? If I go to the loo you might miss your call ... the atmosphere is total aggression. In the CIP it's aggression.

On some occasions the same variety of manifestations of penal power means that the time that women spend in travelling is completely wasted. If prison officers go on strike, if the prisoner gets other visitors who use up his allocation of visiting time, if prisoners get shanghaied or lifted,[100] sent to hospital, or put into solitary confinement, women have made extensive expenditures of money, time and labour for nothing. Often the various restrictions on visiting are relayed back to women by phone calls from the prison and wasted visits are avoided but this is not always the case.

Fay

I went all the way up to Maitland. They were on strike. I sat there and they say 'you might not be able to go in, they're on strike'. I sat there and sat there. At 25 past 12 they said 'No, you can't come in'. I said 'I've just missed the train back'. I had to wait 2 1/2 hours for a train back to Sydney. An elderly lady about 80 she was crying. She had to go all the way back to Sydney. It's just as though they say 'stiff shit' after all that time and all that money and that was my pension week.

Rebecca

At Parramatta a friend of his turned up to visit from Armidale. They told me I could see him Saturday instead, then when I went they said 'Who told you that?'

5   CARING AS MEDIATING AND NEGOTIATING WORK

Although visiting is the central aspect of the work of caring for prisoners, caring for dependents also usually includes the work of mediating and negotiation.[101] It is the dependent status of women in the family that means that it is usually women who have the job of mediating and negotiating with the "human service agencies" charities or government bureaucracies when that mediation is from a position of powerlessnness.[102]

The nexus between caring and dependency as it is currently constituted means that becoming the outside carer of a prisoner has the potential for involving women in a complex set of dependent relationships with penal, welfare, housing and education bureaucracies. In this aspect of the intersection of domesticity and penality, women in the mid 1980s are continuing a tradition of active contestation with authorities that was also a significant part of the labour of wives of convicts in the earliest non-Koori settlement of New South Wales.[103]

The feminist analysis of bureaucracy emphasises that all clients, because they are in relatively powerless relationships with welfare bureaucracies, are disadvantaged by the way that bureaucratic discourses are constituted.[104] Information is controlled by the bureaucracy as a one way flow. The information is usually complex, hidden from the client and expressed through a maze of disparate and contradictory regulations.[105] This control over complex and contradictory information which is nevertheless crucial to the client is manifested, Piven and Cloward argue, as apparently arbitrary action.[106] Families of prisoners are involved as clients with both welfare and social control bureaucracies. The transactions between prison staff and women who are doing the work of caring for prisoners are translated into exactly these service provider-client forms in which women negotiate from a position of powerlessness. Twenty of the women had stories to tell about the work of negotiating with legal penal bureaucrats.

It is particularly the first period of arrest, sentencing and imprisonment prior to classification that consumes women's time in the labour of trying to work with the bureaucracies concerned with supporting the man but at the same time maintaining the family outside:

Julie: Husband arrested for the first time.
Two daughters — 13 and 5 years.

The first couple of weeks I was in shock. I know I had to keep on going because things had to be done, forms, a whole lot of things had to be done. And those first couple of weeks they were hell. My eyes were almost popping out of my head through not enough sleep. All the running around. I was doing it on public transport and trying to keep up with everything. Hell ... *what were the key things you had to do?* Get things organised ... the solicitors. The two weeks before he went in he was the most unstable. After he went in, running around organising the pension, the housing commission (for changes in the arrangements about paying the rent). It was a lot of running around. I didn't need it at the time and I was feeling I was working from one minute to the next.

The most severe criticisms of the unresponsiveness of bureaucracies, and their reluctance or inefficiency in giving out information essential for women to do the work of supporting the prisoner, were directed at the police in the initial periods of arrest and sentencing.

Julie

The night he was locked up I rang the police station wondering why he was still kept in the cells because I wasn't sure if he had been sent out to one of the gaols, because at least then he could move around and have a cigarette, and he hadn't been taken out. And some of the police in Penrith are smart. I asked how he was handling it (because he can't stand closed spaces) what was his mental attitude? And they said 'O he's very comfortable here, he's got a water bed, a colour television' and all I wanted to know was the man mentally handling it. Not to be played around — these are all the things you just don't need. You just don't need at all. I think Penrith especially for the women (wives of arrested men) must be the worst.

Lauren

I didn't know where to go, what to do, I was just lost ... They took him to the cells and I went round to the police station to see him. I still hadn't seen him for ten days. And they wouldn't let me. And I asked where he was going to be sent and they weren't quite sure. They phoned and they told me that he was sent to Long Bay Gaol and I rang there and they told me they didn't have him there. (laughing) So that was the start of that series of phone calls. Cause I was frightened that something was going to happen to him because of something that was said by the police, which I'd better not go into. And I was frightened that he'd be harmed. I rang Parramatta and they said they didn't have him. Then I rang Penrith police station, they said he was definitely sent to Long Bay and I found out in the end he was at Parramatta. I just kept going there and after about three quarters of an hour ... Terror is how I felt ... I was getting all worked up.

However, even during the more routine period of imprisonment women have to act as negotiators in order to maintain contact with the man inside prison:

Esther

They granted us a special visit and when I went on that special visit they said 'no' I couldn't visit ... He goes in for a liver biopsy, it's due this week I rang up this morning 'come up to see him now, he's in hospital' and they say I can't see him until next weekend ... so it's a big let down, I'm here all geed up for a visit and they won't let me see him ... it's this big anxiety to wait for the special day to get up and go to see them and then you have to sit down and wait and wait and wait and the waiting to see him and see that they're not hurt and see that they're surviving. Because nobody can survive prison.

Beth

Shipping happens to everybody. They don't like you to be in the same jail very long; I think their reasoning is that if you get to know the environment too well you might be able to plan an escape. But you can be shipped if you tell a screw to f— off, you can be shipped ... they don't tell me when he's going. I think they think you're going to land on the side of the road with a machine gun to break him out of the van you see. So they won't tell you when they're taking him somewhere. So its very frustrating ... Jim always gets a message out somehow, then it's up to me. In those circumstances I've had to do a lot of telephoning ... I have to ring up try to get it stopped or at least try to find out where he is. And that's where I've had to bring welfare officers, parole officers in, they don't want to tell you too much ... they don't want to tell you too much. They pretend they're interested but they never contact you back. They don't let you have too much information.

Because imprisonment is constituted as a career from segregation to correction to normalising women also have to become involved in the work of ensuring that the man's civil rights are defended during the various in-prison judicial procedures that determine his prisoner status —

the classification and the parole decisions. The work of negotiation and contestation can often seem fruitless:

Fay

Yes, I've had to get solicitors for him — probation reports going to classification board. I go in to see what's happening to him. He tells me one thing and I know he's not telling me the truth so I just follow it through, find out for myself. I feel that *I'm* being sentenced. All this running around I have to do everything.

The unequal balance of power between the legal penal administrators and the women outside is manifested in control over access to the physical resources of administration such as fax machines and telephones. To contest and negotiate with the powerful yet often inefficient legal-penal administration demands both skill and determination. It was notable that the three women who gave the most detailed accounts of the way they were able to fight what they saw as unfair decisions by the parole board were women who either had managerial experience themselves or whose partners had a reputation for political activism whilst in prison:

Claire: Retired Public Servant

(You have to do) lot of incidental legal work. The thing that causes the biggest problem of all is remissions — nobody seems to know what they are doing. Finally they get the thing (computer) working. There's an anniversary point (date of conviction) — But they got it wrong and everybody had to have their sheet altered. They must have been going crazy in the office. Len found out I had to go to Roden Cutler House, I took the forms to him — I explained I was in there because the computer had broken down — He would have had to stay in ... several men have served longer than they need. Having had 23 years experience in government departments I know there's a way through the red tape and at the same time filling in their proper forms — these places are very daunting. *There's this bureaucratic hand over you. It controls whether you have a man or you don't.*[107]

Cheryl: Partner a member of the Parramatta Resurgent Group

I went to the Parole Board and asked that his case be brought up that day. They refused. They said they didn't have his records. I said 'Please,' (I was crying) I said, 'send an officer down the road and pick his files up and bring them back,' you know, 'you can fax it through.' The gaol was waiting, they wanted him out too, because they really were good up at the gaol. They were going to get them to fax it through and Bernie could be released that day. The Parole board wouldn't do it. She just totally refused and I said 'You revoked his parole on the (basis that) he couldn't report, on the assumption of guilt.' She said 'I did not, there's more to it than that.' I said, 'there was not.' I said, 'I've got the paper.' It was because he was a 'troublemaker'. He was part of the Resurgence Group at Parramatta, and he'd spent so much time in the retractable section and so forth. I said, 'You're trying to justify something he done in 1969'. Now! We're talking about 15 years later. How long does he have to pay for his crime ... we just got into one hell of a slanging match. Bernie's family was there, and I ... was screaming at her. I just said, 'Look, you stink,' I said. 'You've got no bones in your body at all,'

I said, 'you just don't care about a solitary thing.' I just walked out and slammed the door. After I left they decided to hold a special meeting on the Monday, but that left him in gaol over the weekend ... He was released on the Monday and when he was released I was fuming.

However, although the inequalities of power between the penal and domestic spheres are so great it was not only the mature women who reported some success in their negotiations with prison administrators.

Karen

He's been in remand for 8 months. It's really inefficient. They put him in segregation three weeks ago. I went to the governor and said 'He shouldn't be in there. There's no way he could have done that' (been involved in setting off a bomb in one of the cells) ... they've let him out now and are all over him saying 'Sorry' and apologizing to me. But it was terrible for him that three weeks ... I broke down crying (when they apologised). I didn't mean to, but I couldn't help it ... then a few weeks ago when he went to court, they sent him to the wrong court. They couldn't get anything right.

Sally

Once, Peter's friend, a twenty seven year prisoner at Cessnock, his mother had a stroke, I phoned Akister, then I phoned the Governor, every 15 minutes I phoned him. He wasn't taking my calls, but I kept phoning him every fifteen minutes. In the end (laughing) I got through and he said 'don't bloody phone again, he can stay' (with his mother).

In some cases it is explicitly the moral basis of domesticity on which women base their mediations with or contestations of penal decisions:

Olive: Son has been in MRP and CIP

There were that many attempts to rape him. That's the most fear for the boys. I was always frightened. I turn on the news and hear someone escaped or murdered in gaols, they give their age but not their names. You sort of live in their fear and you're helpless. You can't do a thing ... (Once) there was two country boys got raped. I told him 'I'm going to see the Governor'. I demanded to see the Governor. He did see me I'll say that for him. He called the three boys together. He said 'you three boys stick together, don't let each other out of sight' and he called another chap who'd been there for 15 years and asked him to look after him ...

... I've rung her[108] (Superintendent of Metropolitan Reception Prison) up a couple of times and she's always had the time to talk. You ring up CIP and you'll always get their secretaries you won't get them. You'll never get the superintendent. If I went up there and he was a bit down, he's done something, I can ring her. The last time he didn't want to be sent to Cessnock. That was worrying him. She said she'd hold him here as long as she possibly could. I wrote her a letter and she wrote me back a lovely letter.

Graham uses "coping" as a central analytic term to make visible the masked and devalued political economic significance of the work of "caring" as well as to indicate the way in which that work becomes devalued. Coping as responsiveness to crises or problems created beyond the control of the worker has four characteristics: it involves *responsibility,* accepting the obligations and duties which go with the job of "being a mother"; *culpability* or willingness to take the responsibility for righting crises caused by others; *flexibility* or malleability, the ability to be adaptable to the diffuse and complex demands of the chronic crises of dependency; and *negation* or self-effacement, the denial that these skills are causing any problems for the carer herself. These aspects of coping coalesce into its fifth characteristic, *political quiescence.* In denying oneself a voice in responding competently and invisibly to the chronic and the acute, diffuse demands of dependency, coping provides a form of metaphorical shock absorber for the various crises created by the contradictions of the external social relations of productive life.

Nevertheless, there is an ambiguity about the relationship between domesticity and political order. Family life provides the basis for both control and contestation.[109] There are several historical accounts of the ways in which the obligation to care can lead to political action to defend the interests of family dependents, as well as political quiescence.[110] In the New South Wales prison system in the 1980s this ambiguity of caring has been manifested in political action by the carers as single individuals and through collective action. Families of prisoners directly confronted the Minister for Corrective Services to make public the damaging effects on prisoners of the prison officers' strike at Parramatta in 1983.[111]

This political aspect of the work of caring extends beyond mediating, negotiating and fighting with penal bureaucracies. Although several of the prisoners were not in waged work prior to imprisonment, the loss of freedom to exchange labour for waged income is a central part of the symbolism of punishment by confinement in Australia. Work, when it is available in prison, usually brings a wage of only $9 to $12 a week.[112] Work release schemes only apply to men in minimum security prisons at the normalising end of punishment. Five of the thirty women were directly affected by the loss of their husband's wage which had been the primary income in the household. Their dependency was then transferred to the State as social welfare clients which put them at risk of the humiliation of negotiating from a position of powerlessness.

The skill involved in being a client of a bureaucratic system includes having to learn a new language to comprehend the mass of bureaucratic regulations and to learn both those formal rules and the informal rules governing appropriate conduct.[113] This means having to acquire the skill of what Goffman called "impression management" to be able to "bow properly to immense institutional power, understand and flatter the bureaucratic personality and (to) otherwise legitimate herself before the officials." However, this skill imposes material costs on the "client". There is the strain inherent in "the disidentification between the individual and the manipulative role". But more fundamentally there is also stress in internalising and acting upon the bureaucratic definition of themselves. These accounts of bureaucratic power relations accord with the experiences of women with family obligations to prisoners in New South Wales:

Claire: 53 year old woman. Partner in CIP

Then there is the hassle of getting on to a benefit. Finally they put me on widows pension benefits. I was seven days down at the social security, they are so rude. They've stopped special benefit for prisoner wives — but my Social Security — couldn't have supplementary and I'm too young for oap at 53.

Many more women, eleven in all, were involved in changing accommodation either because their income had become insufficient or because the husband or son was sent to a prison too far away for visiting to be feasible. Four of the women who were also the outside carers of the prisoners' children spoke about mediations or negotiations they had had to make with their children's teachers as a result of the effects of imprisonment on either the child's own behaviour or school work, or because of the taunting of school friends. Imprisonment then impinges on women's lives by drawing them more tightly into the network of human service agencies, the welfare service-client relationships in which their work of caring has to be performed from the position of dependent and therefore relatively powerless negotiator.

The contradiction between domesticity and penality takes on a very material form when punishment extends to the loss of the family home. The caring work of families of prisoners comprises not only the reproduction of the personality of the prisoner and his children but also the reproduction of the conditions in which that work can be carried on, the material physical setting of the home. Maintaining the sense of "family" or "home" when the actual physical home is lost is especially onerous work.

Cheryl: Husband in Remand prison.
Two children — daughter 10 years, son 7 years

I was fortunate we did have that (lawn mowing) business because we had a two and a half ton truck and I'd never driven a truck in my entire life and I refused point blank to ask anyone (to help me move) because I was frightened that people would know where I lived. So I literally loaded the truck, brought everything downstairs. We took a railing off the stairs, put it back on, loaded everything onto the truck, brought everything down. It took four truckloads of furniture, and we moved. It just shows you what women can do. The most scariest part was driving the truck, just getting behind the wheel. It was so enormous, after driving a small car. It was like taking up the whole road ... my brother-in-law did help me carry the freezer and the washing machine, and the fridge, but I helped him carry it, I nearly broke my thumb doing it. I got it stuck on the trailer ... we managed the whole lot. I was really pleased.

Brenda: Two children

When he was arrested we were living at a flat $130 a fortnight. Then I only got $288 a fortnight income for me and the two children so we went to live in the hostel after he got arrested as it's only $70 a fortnight.

For women who are the outside carers of prisoners' children the range of mediation work can also include making special visits to the children's school:

Cheryl: Two children son aged 7 and daughter 10.
Husband falsely arrested for murder of a policeman.

Kelly, my daughter did get into a big argument with one of the girls there and she came home, she was really distressed. I went to the school and the girl was not put over the coals, so it would rebound back on Kelly, but she was just talked to.

This aspect of the caring work of families of prisoners, that of being the outside carer of the prisoners' children, locates women within a particularly complicated and contradictory set of prescriptive and proscriptive behaviours. The people living day-to-day with the family obligation to care for prisoners and for prisoners' children are in Gross's words, occupying an "impossible middle ground excluded by logic and reason in their present forms".

6 THE DOUBLE ROLE: CARING FOR CHILDREN OF IMPRISONED MEN

Although there have been several studies of the impact of imprisonment on children of prisoners, the work of the outside carers tends either to be a taken for granted, "natural" aspect of parenting,[114] or the problems that they face are interpreted, in part, as a consequence of their individual, social class, or family category, or pathology.[115] The literature focuses on either the needs or rights of the prisoner, on the penal system by constituting parenthood as a path to rehabilitation, on the general functioning of society when the "leader and breadwinner"[116] in the family is removed, or on the needs or rights of the child. It is only in the recent feminist descriptions that the domestic labour of caring for children of imprisoned parents is constituted as a problematic aspect of social life.[117]

If, as Garland argues, imprisonment condenses the social relations of inequality of outside life, then it is in the skilled labour of mothering, as it is worked out in the day to day job of being the outside carer of a prisoner's child, that this condensation of social relations operates in its most compressed form. It is a condensed form of mothering in that:

1   the skills involved are complex and diffuse;
2   the paradigms which constitute the constraints within which the work of caring is carried out are several and contradictory;
3   the time, labour and level of skill are virtually socially invisible;
4   the labour of caring has no economic reward but rather involves the worker in extra economic, physical and emotional costs;
5   it is one of the forms of "double caring" in which the organisational skills, of judging the balance of demands, being able to pace the work, and give priority to one or other of the

130

different individuals within the circle of dependants, are most exploited.[118]

The initial problem, the detention of the imprisoned parent, sets up a sequence of inter-reflexive crises of care and dependence that makes the work of the outside carer a singularly complex and demanding form of domestic labour.

Problems arise out of the reversals of age and gender boundaries in caring work, but this initial problem is masked when the state constitutes that work as unproblematic.[119] This marginalisation of the complexity of caring for adult dependants further compounds the problem by making the carers feel guilty about the extra problems they are facing. This complex aspect of caring work is even further compounded in the case of the outside carers of imprisoned men and their children by the condensed gender and class structures of inequality in the legal penal sphere: the heightened masculinity of prison culture, the contradictions of "keeping the father's place open"[120] in a culture that defines the role of father as the representative of law and order but subjects these specific fathers to manifest forms of penal control.

In the 1970s liberal-reformist period of penality, the rights of men and women prisoners to increased access to family life were played out differently. Chapter three indicates the way that, for men, these rights were more likely to be constituted in terms of access to sexuality and, for women prisoners, in terms of access to parenthood.[121] Although in this period there were two New South Wales policy documents[122] reviewing the situation of children of men in prison, few of their recommendations were implemented and neither document is commonly cited in the literature on imprisonment in New South Wales even in the liberal reformist or radical critiques of penality. Men's parenthood is not a very visible aspect of the relations of penal life even during the liberal swings in prison life. The authors of the Children of Imprisoned Parents document showed that the same situation occurred in New South Wales, as Jones had found in Victoria, with the father's role of prisoner not being taken into consideration by the prison system in either of the two states in the early 1970s to mid 1980s.[123] There was no routine access for the prisoner to his children unless an outside carer was willing to bring them.[124] There were no father-child visits as children always shared visits with the outside carers. Visiting conditions were generally inappropriate for children, with expectations that child visitors behave as adults, no provision was made for the lower attention span of children, nor for the special needs for the mundane tasks of bottle or breast feeding and nappy changing for small children. The worst aspects of taking children to visit their imprisoned parents were lessened to some extent in the normalising moment of imprisonment. However the dominant and official discourses in both states de-emphasised the significance of men prisoners' parenthood.[125]

Neverthless there is evidence that men, as prisoners, are able to maintain their identities as parents more easily than women. Koban's overview of the United States children of prisoner's literature indicates that imprisonment of men is less disruptive of family life than the incarceration of a woman.[126] Sixty-one per cent of male prisoners' children remained with the co-parent in contrast to only 26 per cent of children of women prisoners. Men's children are much more likely to remain in a stable household with a continuous primary caretaker. Men were more likely to report that their children were happy. Men were more likely to have telephone or mail contact with their children. Men were more likely to have children brought to visit them. Women's children were more likely to be with a fostering family. Women prisoners' children were more likely to be separated from their other brothers or sisters and cared for by different carers, and women were more likely, on release, to return to a splintered family than were men prisoners.

Overall, women are closer to their children prior to imprisonment but imprisonment is likely to be more disruptive for the above reasons for women and because women's prisons are likely to be further away from their family. Koban's article was directed towards the particular problems that women prisoners experience. However, it also points up the extent to which women as outside carers of male prisoners provide an infrastructure of domestic labour in the penal sphere. Dan Gowler and Karen Legge[127] introduced the concept of the hidden contracts that are made between employers and male management workers in the productive sphere: that the wife/mother will be responsible for maintaining the well ordered home that can be used by the employers in the entertainment of the husband's clients, that her own work will be drawn on in this aspect of managerial life, that she will take responsibility for all the chronic crises of child rearing — school holidays or children's illnesses, and that her time and lifestyle is centred around the variable and indeterminate demands of her husband's managerial career. Gowler and Legge's model of the hidden contract is valid for the condensed relationships of prison life; women will be available to:

1   maintain the home for the child and the "absent father" that is a necessary part of the prisoner's continuing sense of "self";
2   care for prisoners' children; and
3   ensure that the man's personality will be maintained through the material and emotional work that women do in maintaining contact between children and their fathers.

That the American evidence is parallelled in New South Wales is illustrated in the imbalance in the requests to the Children of Prisoner Support Group. The group established as a result of the 1982 FACSA report by Hounslow et al,[128] has, as one of its major tasks, the work of escorting children to prisons to visit the prisoner parents who were at risk of losing contact with their children because there was no outside carer able to do that work. The major part of the work of the group is to escort children to visit their mothers in prison.[129] Although there is escort work for children of fathers in gaol, it is predominantly women prisoners, in New South Wales, who lack family support in maintaining contact with their children and so have to draw on the support of outside agencies.

The 1982 New South Wales report estimated that one third of all prisoners, and one half of women prisoners are parents.[130] Thirteen[131] of the thirty women in the interviews for this study were caring for the children of prisoners and they talked of the double importance of the prisoner's parenthood — to the men inside and to the children. They saw the work they did in ensuring a continuing contact between the father inside, and the child or children outside, as an important part of the constitution of the personality of both the father and the child. Maintaining the sense of family between themselves, the prisoner and the prisoner's child was a central concern for them, but "the family" was something that they were all having to struggle to maintain:

Virginia: Son fifteen months old. Partner in CIP

It's a strain taking him but he's not going to know his father. Now he goes to him straight away, but if they move him down to Goulburn there's no way I can visit him down in Goulburn, because I've already been told by my doctor that because I'm seven months pregnant that it's risky for me to take him on any long visits.

Lauren: Partner in CIP. Two children

The kids idolise him. My son cries his eyes out. It just devastates them to bring them out here (but they do come). I thought it was better that they know.

Mary: Partner in CIP. Baby daughter

She's three now, I was pregnant when he first went in, so she only knows her Daddy as being in prison. I nearly always bring her with me when I visit. She loves seeing him. She can't wait to get to see him when we come.

Sack, Seidler and Thomas, talking to prisoners and their families in Oregon in 1976, found that the effect of children's visits on prisoners was uniformly positive: "it holds me together".[132] With the other positive aspects of life being denied by imprisonment, being a parent was an area of life that men were eager to discuss. It was the one area of life in which they struggled to see themselves most positively. For the outside carers of children of these prisoners, visiting was especially tension ridden work. It was stressful because children were irritable after visiting. However, the mothers also felt that it was good for children to visit to maintain contact.[133] The loss of the imprisoned parent, even of fathers not apparently close, was experienced as grief, and prisoner parents were seen in a positive light. However, this relationship was difficult, for social isolation was a common experience of both outside carers and children. Sack et al argue that "society offers the children no honourable way out" as does separation, for example, by death or divorce. Imprisonment is a double loss for children — of separation from the prisoner parent but also a loss of sociality. Isolation and stress from the deceptions they were forced into was a common feature of the experience of social life of the children.[134]

In these interviews in New South Wales only one of the thirteen mothers had not told her child about the other parent's imprisonment. Otherwise all twelve of the outside carers of the prisoner's children made efforts to keep the children in contact with the imprisoned parents.

MOTHERING AS "ATTENTIVE LOVE" AND THE MORAL CONTRADICTIONS OF OUTSIDE CARERS OF PRISONERS' CHILDREN

The work of being the outside carer of prisoners' children is a particularly condensed form of mothering, especially in terms of the moral contradictions through which the work of caring has to be implemented. Ruddick's description of the "attentive love" of mothering as a particular form of intellectual skill is very evident in the way that women as outside carers of prisoners' children negotiate the inherent contradictions of being the outside co-parent of a child whose father is being punished by the State. Clearly illustrated in the experiences here are the usual problems that all parents face in balancing the contradictions between the three major interests: preservation of life, creating the conditions for growth, and the development of social acceptability, that shape the development of the intellectual skills and cognitive abilities of "attentive love": resilience, realism, respect for persons, responsiveness to change, and tolerance for ambiguity. Ruddick's thesis is supported by the evidence from crisis management studies.[135] The literature identifies three essential features of the ability to cope: commitment, control and challenge. However the asocial, psychological emphasis in this interpretation of the intellectual skills of mothering means it does not face the central paradox of the work of coping as it is experienced in the unequal social relationships of patriarchal capitalist societies: that the people who are most at risk of having to do the work of coping are exactly those who are least likely to have control over the conditions that make that work necessary. It is precisely the lack of control over so many intersecting facets of life that constitute the everyday experiences of women who are carers of prisoners' children, yet they are the women who have to provide the most complex forms of caring labour.

Gwen: Husband in CIP. Daughter aged five

Once last year, my girlfriend's little boy, he went and told every one in the school that Nicol's father was in gaol ... and they gave my daughter hell about it, and that made her even more determined to fight with them. and I told her 'You don't have to' I sort of explained to her 'well you don't have to worry what they're saying. You just have to worry about how you feel, like, if you don't feel bad that Daddy's in gaol then you don't have to worry about it. It's not your fault'. I think that's what you mainly have to tell the kids, that it's not their fault that they're there, because I think kids tend to think that it's got a lot to do with them, that's why it's happening. I said to her 'It's not your fault, you don't have to be punished for it. He did it ... It's his problem. Me and you we're just here because we're with him and we just got stuck in it and ...' you know, that's all.

Mothers make a special kind of moral space for children of prisoners. As both the moral controllers and the emotional supporters of children of men undergoing State punishment, women draw heavily on the skills of empathy and sensitivity to achieve this space. Any separation from a person who is close is likely to lead children to blame themselves for the loss. This is not to make a universalistic statement about an essential characteristic of parenting in all societies. It is the specific form of parenting, as constituted within the close emotional ties of the family in contemporary social life, that places children at risk of this internalisation of guilt. Significantly, both Morris and Jones point to the wider network of supporting kin as helping to reduce the problems of caring for children of prisoners.[136] Nevertheless, the stigma of the separation by imprisonment means that self-blame or internalisation of guilt for children, is likely to be particularly acute. A common finding in the research into the impact of the parent's imprisonment on the day to day lives of their children is that the children are at greater risk of falling behind in their school work and of going through a "brief flurry of anti-social behaviour".[137] Sack et al and Fritsch and Burkhead found that children of men prisoners were more likely than children of imprisoned mothers to act out their distress in the forms of aggressive behaviour.[138] However, although problems with child management is one of the five problems cited in most "family of prisoners" studies, both Morris and Jones have argued that the majority of mothers are able to deal with the extra problems of child management that imprisonment creates.[139] Jones found that fathers were more likely to be missed as "child carers" rather than as controllers and that it was the practical problems resulting from having children "constantly underfoot" that was the major concern for most mothers.

That women *can* manage the crisis of the impact of imprisonment is perhaps associated with the fact that the work of mothering always contains components of balancing. Susan Hutson and Richard Jenkins have shown how this skill is especially an aspect of mother-child relations in working class families in insecure economies, as children are encouraged to maintain their self-respect but nevertheless not to opt out of a social, moral and economic order which constantly rejects them.[140] That skill becomes particularly finely honed in the work of carers of prisoners' children. The women in New South Wales in the mid 1980s, as in other studies of children of prisoners,[141] develop the skill of responding to the day to day traumas that their children face at school or in the street by constantly negotiating the fine line between not condoning but not condemning the father. They "keep his place open" morally at the same time as they protect the children as best they can from internalising the guilt on his behalf. They tell the children the truth but they have to try to protect them also from exposure to the stigma of that truth.

Gwen

She'll say to me like 'how come my dad's always naughty' ... I just try to explain to her that, you know, that he has been naughty and he has to pay for being naughty. That he has to go to gaol and that's the reason why ... but I try to explain that he's not been naughty to us. That he's not bad to me and her, not really.

Julie

I've always told them (13 & 5) the truth ... the only thing comical with the five year old — she was proud of the situation so she was telling the postman, and the milkman, every body where he was, where daddy was so I tried to change it to 'hospital' ... she's always been proud of what he's done so she just didn't think it was anything less. She didn't I suppose she didn't realise the seriousness, she still doesn't. But she knew what gaol was I think. I said you tell every body 'it's hospital' and she'd say to somebody 'daddy's in hospital — he's not really'.

Hilary: Husband in CIP. Daughter eight and son five

I tell my kids he's done something bad and if you do anything wrong, like steal or anything you come in here ... I think it's best if you do tell your kids what gaol's all about, and let them see, so when they do get older they know right from wrong ...

Lucy and Mike know that Long Bay Jail is a gaol. They know what it's all about. Most kids when they're 5 or 6, they think if they go in a shop and they pick up something and they get away with it and they think that's alright but telling my kids what gaol is, it's stopping them from stealing, and it's even stopped them from telling little lies.

Sack et al found that explanations to the child were usually the mother's job, whether they were the prisoner or the outside carer.[142] Although one option for resolving the contradiction is to keep the reason for the father's separation secret, most mothers decide that that is not a practicable solution for children.

Only one of the mothers who spoke with me had made the decision not to tell her son of his father's imprisonment. There is a tendency in the children of prisoners literature to categorise women who shield children from this knowledge as being irrational. However, in this situation it was a considered decision made in relation to the specific position of the child — the other children in the family did know about their father's imprisonment. Moreover shielding this 13 year old boy from the knowledge of his father's imprisonment involved the mother in considerable extra work and financial cost in negotiating visits and day leaves:

Audrey: Three teenage or adult sons. Husband at day leave period of imprisonment

... even day leave's an uncertainty. I was supposed to have it last week. But it was cancelled because the ... or something, I only know it was cancelled, that week. I had a lot of mucking around sort of organizing, sending Troy (son) off for the day, roller skating (and then they cancelled it)

Most of the women wanted to maintain the contact between the father and the child by taking the children to see their father in prison. Both jobs, letting the child know about the imprisonment and maintaining family contact with the imprisoned father, were important aspects of the work of continuing to provide the "conditions for growth". If the children were to be allowed to lead as normal a life as possible, and not be shielded from the wider society, that meant that the children were likely to be exposed to the risk of finding out about their father's imprisonment at school or in the streets if the mother did not talk about the imprisonment very soon after the arrest. Even so this did not protect the child completely from being exposed to the shared stigma of imprisonment. Half of the mothers spoke about their children being exposed to taunting or some form of social stigma.

Cheryl: Husband had been in several maximum security gaols. Two children, daughter ten and son seven

Anthony (the seven year old) was outside on his pushbike, and he kept saying 'what time will dad be home?' (this was the day after the arrest) This kid riding past on his bike kept singing out 'Murderer, Murderer' and then Anthony said 'What's he talking about', you know, seven years old, he didn't know what murderer was, not really and Anthony came inside and he was really, really crying.

Tricia: Husband in CIP. Son aged three

When he was out (the last time), the police would put their sirens on when they went by him on the road ... they called Anthony (the then two year old son) 'Killer', 'We'll be seeing him when he grows up, won't we Killer', they hassled us all the time. We went and lived right next to St Mary's cop shop. That was the worst mistake we ever made.

It is at the point of arrest and during the earliest part of imprisonment that the family is most at risk of stigmatisation even to the extent of being treated as sharing the criminality of the prisoner.

Jane

They picked him up at our place. The police weren't the best. All I got out of them: 'we should take you too for covering for him. If it wasn't for that baby we'd be taking you in too.'

Tricia

Wayne's (3 year old son) hyperactive now, it affected him a lot. You see when they arrested him, he saw them grab Richard and put the handcuffs on him, and they slapped Wayne. One of the police slapped Wayne when they arrested his Dad. He has nightmares now about that one particular officer. I'm going to the courts now to get him out of the force. He shouldn't be allowed to hit kids like that. Anthony's on medication now.

Arresting a suspect in the home makes explicit the tensions between domesticity and penality. Police, by the nature of the way that their work is presently constituted, adopt the most extreme forms of impersonality in their relations with suspects. Since the mid 1970s there has been a shift to an increasingly militaristic style of policing that includes violent "swoops" on houses of suspects by specially trained tactical police squads.[143] Within this setting the whole family is likely to be constituted as representing "the enemy within". The impact on children of being defined in these terms can be especially traumatic. Bernie Matthews was one of the active members of the political prisoner organisations in the pre and post Nagle era. After his release he was re-arrested on a charge of murder for which he was later found to be innocent. Nevertheless, the hostility that was manifested towards him in the police search in which he came to be represented as a particularly threatening "enemy within" was extended, too, to his family. This militarisation of relations between the State and ex-prisoners with a reputation for political action had especially traumatic consequences for his seven year old son. Cheryl Matthews points to the paradox of the relationship between the State, violence, civil status and the family in the parallels and contrasts between her experience and of violence as it was inversely experienced by the man responsible for the constitution of her family as enemies:

Cheryl

It was ironical. Not long after Bernie got pinched, I read where the head of the SWAT squad, his daughter, was a bank teller in a bank that was robbed. She was going for compensation for the trauma she went through with a gun held her up, and that man sent his men into my house and held guns on my seven year old boy in the middle of the night in their bedrooms ... Two thirty in the morning and held guns on my two children. They weren't even teenagers, they were only seven, and he talks about how his daughter should get compensation! I think that's a crime. I think my children are victims of crime. A crime's been committed against them!

In this case it was not only the style of policing that was militaristic. In a later conversation with the Detective Sergeant involved in the arrest, Cheryl Matthews found that the attitudes of the SWAT squad were oriented towards constituting the family as military enemies:

Cheryl

I questioned a Detective Sergeant of Homicide and said 'Please tell me why my kids had to be mentally hurt the way they were.' You know what his justification for it was? That the children in Vietnam were the children who held the guns and threw the grenades! And we're talking about Australia! ... we've got people with that sort of attitude running around with guns in their hands. Now what if one of those guns had gone off. I asked him what if one of those guns had gone off. He said "O, those men are fully trained." But they're so psyched up, they're like mental people. They're like people who have gone crazy. They just stormed through the house, they were running around on the roof. We have got a tin roof ... we've got a verandah part you can walk around on. They were running around there. They were on the roof. They were checking kitchen cupboards.

Few of the women had experiences as extremely traumatic as this and most of the arrests took place when the children were not around. Nevertheless, the symbolic importance of Cheryl Matthews' experience needs to be emphasised. Central to the way that the State and civil life are currently constituted is the possibility that once a person is imprisoned, unless they give up their civil rights to be humanely treated in prison and to be able to protest whilst in prison, they not only put themselves but also the individual women and children in their family at risk of being defined as "enemies within", and therefore legitimately subject to the extreme application of the physical violence of the State. Moreover the population at risk of undergoing the trauma of a militaristic police investigation is much wider than one comprising either politically active prisoners or of households in which men or women are suspects. One feature of police militarism is the "broad swoop" and, in both Sydney and London, households which have had no previous criminal connections but are located in the lower social economic areas of the inner city have been included in police invasions that have involved such militaristic aspects as doors being broken in at four in the morning, guns held at the head of residents, and children being held at rifle point.[144]

The trauma of separation is not always avoided by the child's absence at the time of arrest. The sudden absence of their parent can create anxieties and uncertainties for children that might not be evident until some time after the arrest:

Gwen: Daughter five

Nicol went round to sleep at her girlfriend's house and the funny thing was that she asked me for my bank-card. And I said to her 'what do you want my bank-card for' and she says to me 'to make sure that you come back' because when her Dad left, Dad left in the morning and said to her 'See you tonight, give us a kiss' and then she went to school and then Dad didn't come home again and I think she thinks in her mind that Mum's going to leave me too and I tried to explain that this would never happen yet. I nearly cried when she said that. I gave it to her but she just was funny.

Ruddick arguees that maternal practice involves a high level of self-reflection and internal monitoring to achieve a balance between control and permissiveness. The two principles of maternal practice — the preservation of life and the development of growth and individuality in the child — demands an ability to balance the contradictory processes of attachment and detachment. Ruddick's thesis takes on an especially condensed meaning in this example of the intersection between domesticity and penality. The conflict between the earlier and the later moments of penality, firstly as the site of punishment and control based on the legitimated violence of the state and then, as the man "progresses" through imprisonment, as the site of reformation and eventual release, contains an inherent and deep seated contradiction in the way that the "family of the prisoner" comes to be constituted. This in turn imposes major strains upon the labour of women as the outside carers of prisoner's children.

The complex layering of this contradiction needs to be spelt out:

1   prisoners are constituted as both "enemies within" and as men who will achieve an unthreatening civil status as free men in the outside world;
2   the constitution of families of prisoners develops along parallel lines. Their civil status changes from potential collaborators and invaders of the secure space of the prison to allies of the therapeutic controllers providing a positive self for the prisoner through which he achieves his civil status as a free man;
3   the prisoner's parenthood is either denied or defined as threatening but is eventually transformed into the aspect of his life that becomes the basis for his redemption and re-entry to civil life;
4   domesticity is alternately excluded from, then welcomed into the sphere of penality at different moments in the relations of reproduction of the social relations of production. *Inconsistency* is an inherent feature of the relationship between the two relations of reproduction;
5   parenthood however is achieved by continual and regular contact with children. Domesticity demands *consistency*;
6   in order to provide the appropriate form of domesticity that is allied *with* penality in the latter normalising stages of imprisonment women have to work *against* the way that domesticity is defined in the earlier segregating stages. To do the work that the State requires of them they are obliged to work against the way that the State defines them.

There is a further layer of discourses that makes this sequence even more contradictory. These are the writings that focus on the constitution of the personality of the child of the prisoner. All the authors in this field, irrespective of their discipline, advocate the full disclosure of the parent's imprisonment to the child and constant and consistent contact between the prisoner and the child.[145]

Nevertheless there are major problems, deriving directly from the way that prison life is constituted, that make this "ideal" response to children of prisoners extraordinarily difficult:

Virginia: Husband in CIP. Son aged five months

It's a strain taking him (five month old son) but he's not going to know his father. Now, he goes to him straight away, but if they move him down to Goulburn ...

Women who had experience of visiting the Central Industrial Prison shared a universal condemnation of its lack of facilities for children.

Claire

... there are children racing around. The atmosphere is total aggression in the CIP it's aggression.

Jane

At CIP you can't take nappies in for the baby, so the baby's got to stay in the one nappy for the visit. You can't take the bottles in or the dummies or anything. If he's wet you've got to cut the visit short or wait until the visit's over to change them. I've had times when I've checked Mark just before I went in there and he's been bone dry and then the next minute he's just piddled and piddled and piddled. He' s held it all the way from home to here then just let go.

This conflict between domesticity and penality, in the maximum security conditions in the early period of imprisonment, creates dual problems for the outside carers' work of visiting as maintaining contact between children and their prisoner fathers. The conditions undermine rather than enhance the prisoner's contact with the children. The labour of making the visit then is negated in terms of the constitution of the man inside as a parent. That this labour is a particularly arduous form of caring work is illustrated in the 1975 account by a British researcher who on one occasion did the work of taking a child to visit their father in a maximum security prison in the UK.

Anyone who had the experience of taking small children to visit their father in prison will know the impossibility of giving him attention, let alone discuss any difficult question, when an eye has to be kept on infants who get under the feet of officers (sometimes friendly, sometimes the reverse) or who disturb visitors at other tables. The mother's eyes must be all over the place all the time. The writer had this experience once, and *emerged a wreck after a visit of 40 minutes.*[146]

The accounts by the women in New South Wales in the late 1980s indicate that this condensed form of caring work retains all of these labour intensive, complex, contradictory and enervating characteristics.

In addition the visit in these conditions can also undermine the wellbeing of the child:

Jane

I don't like bringing the kids here. It's not the place itself ... but I think kids that are coming down here, it's really heartbreaking when they have to say goodbye to their father. I've seen some women walking out and they've had to, just sort of, calm the kids down. I've had to do that with Sherie and with Mark, when it's time for a visit to finish, Mark and he's only two, says 'Jock, no go'.

Julie: Husband in CIP. Two daughters aged thirteen and five

They take turns (coming with me) the first time I was very tense. My husband was very very tense and I looked at my little girl as I was walking through the gate and the tension must have gone to her something phenomenal, she looked as if she was going to pass out ... she just had a strange look all over. I thought 'My god, this poor kid's feeling the tension from him and me and she's just picking it up'. She was very strange then she started to relax for a couple of minutes, then the next visit wasn't so bad.

Visiting was severely punishing at first for Julie's five year old daughter but she became used to the conditions under which she was able to see her father. This resilience is one of the major findings in the literature on the impact of imprisonment on children of prisoners. Sack et al found that although most of the children in the Oregon interviews experienced stress and that this was manifested in some form such as "school phobia", this was usually only temporary.[147] This study marginalised the extensive domestic labour that contributed to the children's ability to survive the chronic crisis of their parent's imprisonment. Nevertheless, Judy Jones, working from a more feminist perspective, found similar evidence of resilience both in her review of literature on children of prisoners and in her own interviews with prisoner parents in Victoria.[148]

However, in the interviews by Sack et al, the one group of children who experienced more permanent and more extreme stress, manifested in "anti-social" behaviour, were the children between 10 and 15 who never visited their imprisoned parent. Jones, on the other hand, found that it was children between five and eight years old who were most distressed. Like Sack et al she found that it was those children who were least in contact with their father, particularly those who were not told that their father was in prison, who were most distressed. She argues that the children were not deceived but the attempt at deception increased their vulnerability. Having to aquiesce in their own deception was in itself stressful and, in not being told of the details of the imprisonment, the children lost all control in managing the conditions of the separation.[149] There were, however, two further factors in Jones' study, that increased children's vulnerability. The most vulnerable children, those who experienced severe physical ill health, were also those who had been close to their father prior to his imprisonment and whose mothers had been severely emotionally distressed by the imprisonment. Resilience in the mother is a condition of the material wellbeing of all children. However, for children of prisoners the mother's resilience becomes an even more important component of family life, at the same time as the conditions in which she has to work are manifestly constructed to undermine the "resilient good humor," that Ruddick describes as a condition of the "attentive love" of mothering. One of the major material costs to women, and to children of prisoners, are the risks to their health.

MATERIAL COSTS: HEALTH

A common finding in reports on families of prisoners over the thirty or so years that the literature has been published is that women are at risk of stress and physical illness when they have family responsibilities for men inside prison.[150] Responsibility without control is a particularly stressful combination of factors. It is a combination that is an inherent aspect of the powerless morality of family life. That combination, however, takes on a particularly condensed form in the case of partners and parents of prisoners.

There are further layers of punitive conditions that aggravate the stress created by this contradiction. First, the extension of punishment to the women outside through the immense financial problems, the loss of economic and personal resources that she experiences on the imprisonment of the other parent, are associated with ill health and "problems of adjustment" in both the mother and the child.[151] Secondly, social isolation means that the stresses are not likely to be diffused through family or neighbourhood supports. The pressure to alleviate the problems facing the man inside, by negating the day to day effects of the crisis of imprisonment on the family, blocks the possibility of sharing the stress with somebody who might well be the only other person who could understand the detailed implications of the various problems. Moreover, stress is inherent in the frustrations of visiting and of negotiating from a position of powerlessness with the range of bureaucratic officers on whom partners and parents of prisoners have to depend. If stress is particularly linked to uncertainty it becomes a routine aspect of the work of maintaining family contact as uncertainty is routine to the obligation to care for prisoners. It operates at several levels. Uncertainty characterises the state of knowledge about the prisoner's well being, the parent or partner's day to day expectations about visiting, the possibility of planning where to live in the next month or year, the classification or parole decisions that have a major impact on schooling, housing and income for the family outside. Unsurprisingly, the majority of women spoke of either lost sleep, a loss of appetite, "crankiness", taking medication or increased smoking as a direct result of their experiences of the penal system. It is in the social space between the prison and home that the skill of "being available", that is at the centre of all forms of caring work, makes the most severe demands on the organisational abilities, the material wellbeing and the physical strength of the women who do that work.

MATERIAL ASPECTS OF RESILIENCE

However, even in circumstances when domesticity and penality are most at odds, resilience characterises many women's experiences of visiting. Ruddick distinguishes between the blind resilience exemplified by Brecht's "Mother Courage" and the strength that, she argues, mothers exert in facing yet surviving the contradictions of child rearing. Ruddick's class neutral account does not take into account the added stress placed on women's resilience by the contradictions of the systematic economic and political inequalities produced in a class society. Women doing the solidary labour of maintaining family contact in the penal sphere experience the stress of working against the indifference and hostility of the penal bureaucracies in an especially condensed fashion. In the following story women are maintaining their right to reinforce family relations in the face of the contrary control of penality.

One of the major ways in which personalities are constituted within the family is the marking off of specific days as being the particular space in which the uniqueness of that person's self is celebrated. Exchanging presents on birthdays and special anniversaries is the usual way that this particularistic aspect of family life is reaffirmed. This very material form of signifying care is especially important in the exchanges between parents and children. In the impersonal universalism of prison life this aspect of particularism takes on even greater significance. However the significance of birthdays is alternatively ignored or recognised at the different moments of penality. In 1986, on the coach trip back from Berrima, a minimum security prison, the parents of one prisoner described to the other families who had been visiting under the maximum security conditions of Goulburn the birthday party that had been arranged for their prisoner-son that day. Nevertheless in the segregative moment of imprisonment, the constitution of the prisoner and his family as "enemies within" severely limits the ways that women can encourage this significant particularistic contact between prisoner fathers and their children.

Cheryl

one time I drove a young girl and her family over (to CIP) from Cabramatta. It was Father's Day and this young girl had made a Father's Day card. It was the first one she'd made with her own handwriting in it. She was about five years old. She wanted to give it to her dad herself, to be the one to give it to him, not to leave it with his property so he'd get it later that afternoon, and any other time, you were allowed to take cards in, give it to them but they'd have to give it back. Then it would go with their property. Now this particular day the Deputy Superintendent made the ruling 'No cards to be taken into the gaol' on *that* particular day, you weren't allowed to take anything in to them.

Being able to give presents as well as receive them is crucial to the way that family life is constantly negotiated in normal conditions of domesticity. It is particularly significant for children because it is a very concrete expression of particularism. Children are often even more excited about giving presents that they have made themselves than they are about receiving them. This aspect of domesticity is at odds with penality when the family is constituted as a threat rather than an ally. In the CIP prison, officers confiscated presents of fruit or chocolate being taken out of the prison. Resilience in the face of this humiliating process was expressed by defying penal authority rather than in submission to it:

Cheryl

One particular case a young lass was visiting her boyfriend and he bought her some chocolate. It was with her money. She was taking it home and at the gate they, the screws, made a comment about the chocolate and she burst out crying. I said, 'Eat it. Stand there in front of them and eat it.' She said, 'I couldn't eat it all.' I said, 'There's six kids, give each kid a piece.' So she stood there, defiant, which was really, really good, and just gave every kid a piece of chocolate. That's just the way, you know. We paid for it but they, the screws, would get it. You know I used to stick my fingers in oranges, you know. I was just as bad. I used to get really petty at times.

SUMMARY

Patricia O'Brien's history of the birth of the prison in France contests the Foucaultian version in demonstrating that the subjects of the penal technology of power were "not an inert mass passively accepting the dictates of the new mode of domination".[152] The history of penal life in New South Wales gaols similarly provides evidence of the resistances of men controlled in prison. However both accounts also demonstrate that in resisting, prisoners are nevertheless, of course, constructing that resistance within the terms constituted by the prison. Similarly the women locked into penal life through their family obligation to imprisoned men are engaged in a struggle to maintain their own worth as individuals within a set of singularly oppressive conditions, the contradictory moralities of penal and domestic life. The contradictions inherent in the family obligation to care for imprisoned men are made even more complex and convoluted when that obligation includes the duty to be the outside carer of the prisoner's child. The material and emotional dimensions of the work of maintaining contact with imprisoned men, and of maintaining contact between imprisoned men and their children, involves all the aspects of caring labour described in the literature on "labouring and loving". Moreover the women are working in a social space that is the focus of a range of contradictory discourses about the constitution of the personalities of the prisoner and of the prisoner's child. Imprisonment recreates a particularly condensed form of domesticity, if domesticity is taken to be the sphere of the constitution and the reconstitution of the personality.

The extensive labour of sustaining the self of the prisoner, and of the prisoner's child, which also imposes major costs on the women carers, then places them at risk of becoming locked into socially isolated lives. Moreover, their labour of caring in the penal sphere makes particular demands on the intellectual skills of empathy, malleability and resilience.

The experiences of this specific group of carers, alternately rendered invisible then significant in the penal discourses, make the point made by Seyla Benhabib, in her discussion of the Gilligan/Kuhlberg debate, particularly significant. She describes the world constituted in contemporary mainstream moral psychology, and in liberal political theory, as a "strange world" because it is one in which "mothers, sisters and wives do not exist".[153] It is rather the place where, in the imaginary psychological world drawn by the theorists of personality from Freud to Piaget, it is the relationship to "the brother" that is viewed as the humanising experience. The hold of this universalistic model of moral development and justice then means that the dominant taken for granted assumptions about the world define the public world of justice as the world in which men acquire their "self" through their relationships with the "generalised other" in the public institutional relations of formal equality and reciprocity. Men are regarded as having reached maturity once they are able to "take the viewpoint of others", but it is the abstract "generalised other" who is the hypothetical other in this social contract view of the world. It is in the penal sphere that this model of responsibility is both, realised in its most condensed form, and where the supposedly universalistic relations of the wider world are authorised. It was the falseness of this universalism that was exposed in the wave of prison riots in the 1970s. The realisation of the damage to a general concept of "civility", that arose out of the actual masculinities of prison life, brought about various attempts to domesticise "the prison". Nevertheless these did not replace the contractual relations, but were superimposed on the false universalism of prison life. In this especially contradictory and "overburdened" intersection of penality and domesticity, it was the people who provided the caring labour of maintaining family contact with prisoners who bore the major burdens of living day to day in this "impossible middle ground".

The ambivalence of domesticity — that it can become the basis for both resistance *and* quietism — is an intrinsic feature of the work of caring for imprisoned men. The next chapter details the way that this political strand of penal and domestic life is threaded into the material and emotional aspects of the labour of loving men inside gaol.

NOTES

1   Donzelot, J, *The Policing of Families: Welfare versus the State* (1979) at 150.

2   Zdenkowski, G and Brown D, *The Prison Struggle* (1982) at 65.

3   Vinson, T, *Wilful Obstruction* (1982); Findlay, M, *The State of The Prison: a Critique of Reform* (1982).

4   Vinson, above n3 at 22–24.

5   Id at 217.

6   Id at 65–66.

7   Findlay, above n3 at 77.

8   Nicholson, R, "Women's Function in New South Wales Male Prisons" in Hatty, S (ed), *Women in the Prison System* (1984) at 194.

9   Above n3 at 77.

10   Id at 76.

11   Vinson, above n3 at 217.

12   Id at 221. Here Tony Vinson was enthusiastically supporting ideas initially proposed by Gerry Hay, a senior prisoner executive at Bathurst.

13   New South Wales Department of Corrective Services, *Annual Report* (1983) at 15.

14   New South Wales Department of Corrective Services, *Annual Report* (1986) at 33.

15   Dobash, R, Dobash, R E and Gutteridge, S, *The Imprisonment of Women* (1986) at 41–56.

16   Anderson, T, *Inside Outlaws* (1989) at 36.

17   Above n13 at 27.

18   New South Wales Department of Corrective Services, *Annual Report* (1978–9) at 18.

19   New South Wales Department of Corrective Services, *Annual Report* (1981–2) at 81.

20   Id at 30.

21   Above n13 at 20.

22   Above n16.

23   New South Wales Department of Corrective Services, *Annual Report* (1986–7) at 13.

24   This inquiry was set up following the severe physical assault by a long time prisoner upon a man imprisoned for a few days for a fine default. The Corrective Services Teachers Association report was given legitimacy in the Muir Report by being printed in full and being described by Muir as 'a most helpful submission'.

25   Muir, A G, *Report of the Inquiry into the Central Industrial Prison August* (1988) at 437.

26   New South Wales Department of Corrective Services, *Annual Report* (1987–8) at 19.

27   Kemp, B, Cheron, M, McClelland M and Cooney, G, *The Effects of Separation on Marital Relationships of Prisoners and Their Wives*, Department of Corrective Services, Research and Statistics Division (Research Publication No 2), 1982.

28   However Kemp's preliminary paper, reviewing the literature on prisoner's families, indicates that this perspective was deliberately and pragmatically chosen as the one most likely to persuade the Department to fund the recommended services for prisoners' wives. In the earlier publication she gives priority to the social equity claim. (Kemp, B, *Imprisonment and Family Separation: a literature review,* New South Wales Department of Corrective Services, Research and Statistics Division (Research Digest No 2) 1980 at 1.

29   Above n27 at 17.

30   Id at 6.

31   Hounslow, B, Stephenson, A, Stewart, J and Crancher, J, *Children of Imprisoned Parents*, Family and Childrens's Service Agency, Ministry of Youth and Community Services, New South Wales, 1982.

32   This position was lost in the 1988–1990 period of economic rationalisation.

33   Above n13 at 38. These programmes are described in greater detail in chapter 7.

34   Wortley, R, "Mad, Bad or Normal: perceptions of prisoners by prisoners, prison officers, and prison specialist staff" (1987) 1/1 *J St Just* 11–16 at 12–13.

35   Vinson, above n3 at 60–67.

36   Willett, T, "Anomie, Ritualism and Inertia among Custodial Staff in Canadian Prisons: some implications for research and policy" in Gandy, J, Robertson, A and Sinclair, S (eds), *Improving Social Intervention* (1983).

37   Ibid.

38   Cited in Sandery, A, "Prison Officers and Their World, by Kelsey Kauffman" (1989) 22/4 *ANZ J Crim* 279–281.

39   Above n36 at 110.

40   Mathiesen, T, *The Defences of the Weak* (1962).

41   Grant, D, "Prison Security Issues", speech presented at the Australian Bicentennial International Congress on Corrective Services, Sydney, 24–28 January 1988.

42   Id at 28.

43   Id at 25.

44   Ibid.

45   Ibid.

46   Greenberg, D (ed), *Corrections and Punishment* (1977) at 9.

47   Above n2 at 318.

48   Above n16.

49   Nagle, J, *Report of the Royal Commission into New South Wales Prisons* (1978).

50   Brown, D, "What Truth? Sentencing Changes (New South Wales)" (1989) 14/4 *Leg Serv B* 161–164.

51   Grant, D, "A Reflection on Prison Crowding" in Vernon, J (ed), *Developments in Correctional Policy: More Prisons?* (1987) at 85.

52   Brown, D, "Returning to Sight: Contemporary Australian Penality" (1989) 16/3 *Soc Just* (Issue 37) at 147.

53   Calculated from data presented in Potas, I and Grant-Jones, D, *Australian Community Based Corrections Data*, No 90 (1986) at 1, and Biles, D and Johnson, M, *Australian Prison Trends*, No 117 (1986) at 1.

54   New South Wales Department of Corrective Services, *Annual Reports* 1984–1988.

55   Vinson, above n3; Brown and Zdenkowski, above n2; Findlay, above n3.

56   Martin, T, *The Martin Report: judicial inquiry into the New South Wales Department of Corrective Services prisoner classification procedures* (1987).

57   This delineation draws on studies of the unpaid care of children, the handicapped and the aged detailed in chapter one.

58   Graham, H, "Caring: a labour of love" ch 1 in Finch, J and Groves, D, *A Labour of Love: women, work and caring* (1983) at 25.

59   Finch, J and Groves, D (eds), *A Labour of Love: Women, Work and Caring* (1983); Ungerson, C, "Why do women care?" ch2 in Finch & Groves, ibid; Ungerson, C, *Policy is Personal: Sex, Gender and Informal Care* (1987).

60   Baldwin, S and Glendinning, C, "Employment, women and their disabled children", in Finch & Groves, ibid; Moroney, R M, *The Family and The State: Considerations for Social Policy* (1976); James, N, "Emotional labour: skill and work in the social regulation of feelings" (1990) 37/1 *Sociol R* 15–42; Watson, E and Mears, E, *Women in the Middle: care-givers with a double burden of care*, Canberra, 1988.

61   Ungerson, above n59 at 31.

62   Goffman, E, *Asylums* (1961).

63   Above n49; Vinson, above n3 at 42, 60–63, 165; above n2; Findlay, above n3.

64   Vinson, above n3 at 42.

65   Findlay, above n3 at 95.

66   Above n52 at 146.

67   Porritt, D, "Reasons For Escape: reported by recaptured escapees", Sydney: New South Wales Department of Correctives Services, Research and Statistics Division, 1987; Gorta, A and Nguyen, M, *An Analysis of Interviews with Recaptured Escapees: some suggestions of reasons for escape*, Sydney: Research and Statistics Division, New South Wales Department of Corrective Services, 1988.

68   Vinson, above n3 at 33.

69   Pseudonym used for this thesis.

70   Reported in Terry, P, "Official neglect 'led to black's suicide'" *The Australian* 2 Jan 1990 at 4.

71   Findlay, above n3 at 91.

72   Nagle, 1978 at 468 cited in Findlay, above n3 at 91.

73   Above n27 at 4.

74   Hatty, S and Walker, J, *Deaths in Australian Prisons* (1986) at 29.

75   Id at 28.

76   Jones, J, "Prisoners and their Families", unpublished PhD thesis, Melbourne: Monash University Department of Anthropology and Sociology, 1983 at 82–83.

77   Above n16 at ch8 & ch9.

78   Id at ch5.

79   Boyle, J, *The Pain of Confinement* (1984).

80   Above n76 at 82–83. Albert Cohen's paper on the sociology of prison violence makes the same point about the structural sources of impersonality: cf Cohen, A, *Prison Violence* (1975) at 15.

81   Ernie Hinton's article in *Contact* 1979 cited in Anderson (above n16 at 92).

82   Above n76 at 68–74.

83   Id at 72.

84   Lewis, J and Meredith, B, *Daughters Who Care* (1988) at 64; Finch, J, *Family Obligations and Social Change* (1989) at 209; Ungerson, C, *Policy is Personal: Sex, Gender and Informal Care* (1987) at 96.

85   Above n27 at 15.

86   Id at 17.

87   Hounslow, B, "Children & Families of Prisoners: convicted without a trial" (1984) 9/1 *Leg Serv B* 26–28 at 27.

88   Above n31 at 142.

89   Id at 150.

90   By late 1989 this transport service was no longer being provided.

91   New South Wales Department of Corrective Services, *Annual Report* (1987) at 23.

92   Vinson, above n3 at 155.

93   Above n16 at 37.

94   Corrigan, P, "Gender and the Gift: the case of the family clothing economy" (1989) 23/4 *Sociology* 513–534.

95   Id at 516.

96   Id at 517.

97   Above n16 at 42.

98   Ferguson, K, *The Feminist Case Against Bureaucracy* (1984) at 142.

99   Id at 140.

100   Anderson describes this as being moved suddenly and unexpectedly, often in the evening or at night and sometime as a move against prisoners who are organisers.

101   Graham, H, "Providers, Negotiators and Mediators: women as the hidden carers" ch 2 in Lewin, E and Olesen, V (eds) *Women, Health, and Healing* (1985); above n98.

102   Above n98 at ch4.

103   Robinson, P, *Women of Botany Bay: a reinterpretation of the role of women in the origins of Australian society* (1988) at 238.

104   Above n98 at ch4.

105   Id at 143.

106   Piven and Cloward, 1965 cited in Ferguson, above n98 at 145.

107   My emphasis.

108   At that time this Superintendent was the only female superintendent of a men's prison in Australia. It was notable that of all the references to contacts with superintendents it was only this woman who was spoken of with some warmth by the women doing the work of maintaining family contact. Three other women made similar points about the immediate, personal and sensitive help that either they or their imprisoned sons received from her.

109   Albury, R, "All Quiet on the Home Front? The Contradictions of Family Life" (1987) 99 *Aust Left R* 24–29.

110   Rowbotham, S, *Hidden from History* (1973) at 24–28; Stone, J, "Brazen Hussies and God's Police" (1982) 89/1 *Hecate* 6–23; Allen, M, Hutchinson, M and MacKinnon, A, *Fresh Evidence, New Witnesses: Finding Women's History* (1989) at 218–220.

111   Above n16 at 20.

112 Holcroft, C, "Wages and Conditions of Prisoners in New South Wales Gaols — a Brief Review" (1988) 88/1093 *Public Information Bulletin*, New South Wales Department of Corrective Services.

113 Above n98.

114 See Appendix I. The following works comprise the key texts in the psychological literature: Sack, W, "Children of Imprisoned Fathers" (1977) 40/2 *Psychiat* 163–174; Sack, W, Seidler, J and Thomas, S,"The Children of Imprisoned Parents: A Psychosocial Exploration" (1976) 46/4 *Amer J Orthopsychiat* 618–627; Fritsch, T and Burkhead, J, "Behavioural Reaction of Children to Parental Absence due to Imprisonment" (1981) 30/1 *Family Relations* 83–86; Garner, E, "Why Should Children Visit in Prison?" (1983) *Staying Together* (Winter).

115 See ch4. In Australia Nancy Anderson's 1965 report on prisoners' families in Victoria was the major text that adopted the family crisis framework (Anderson, N, *Prisoners' Families: Reports I & II*. Melbourne: Victorian Council of Social Services, 1965); Ariela Lowenstein ("Coping with Stress: The Case of Prisoners' Wives" (1984) 46/3 *J Marr & Fam* 699–706) is a recent USA reworking of the family pathology approach.

116 Williams, E, Elder, Z and Williams, S, "The Psychological Aspects of the Crimes of Imprisoned Husbands on their families" (1970) 62/3 *J NMA* 208–211 at 208.

117 Schwartz, M and Weintraub, J, "The Prisoners's Wife: a study in crisis" (1974) 38/4 *Federal Probation* 20–26; Jones, above n76; Hounslow, B, Stephenson, A, Stewart, J and Crancher, J, "Children of Imprisoned Parents", Ministry of Youth and Community Services, 1982; Smith, S, "Neglect as Control: prisoners' wives", paper presented to the XIVth Annual Conference of the European Group for the Study of Deviance and Social Control, September 1986; Smith, S, "House Arrest: the pain of prisoners' wives" (1986) 21 *New Society* 11–13; Bauhofer, V, "Prison Parenting: challenge for children's advocates" (1987) *Children Today* (Jan–Feb) 15–16; Light, R (ed), *Prisoners' Families* (1989); McDermott, K and King, R, "Prison Rule 102: Stand By Your Man", unpublished paper, Bangor Wales: Centre for Social Policy Research and Development [nd]; Shaw, R, *Children of Imprisoned Fathers* (1991).

118 These neglected skills have been delineated in the literature on the domestic labour of 'double caring', for example in Elizabeth Watson and Jane Mear's study, *Women in the Middle: Care-givers with a Double Burden of Care* funded by the Office of the Status of Women (1988).

119 Above n84.

120 Kemp et al (above n27) use this term to describe this particularly contradictory aspect of child-care.

121 See ch3 particularly in the discussion on co-ed prisons and conjugal visiting programmes.

122 Above n31; above n27.

123 Above n76 at 486.

124 Id at 486–7.

125 Bauhofer (above n117) in New York, and Smith (above n117) in England also indicate that male prisoners' parenthood is similarly invisible in the penal discourses in those administrations in the late 1980s.

126 Koban, L, "Parents in Prison" (1983) 5 *Res L Dev & Soc Cont* 171–183.

127 Gowler, D and Legge, K, "Hidden and Open Contracts in Work and Marriage" in Rapoport, R, Rapoport, R N and Bumstead, J (eds), *Working Couples* (1978).

128 Above n31.

129 Children of Prisoners Support Group, *Annual Report*, New South Wales (1988).

130 Above n31 at 7–9.

131 Nine were co-parents, one woman was a grandmother caring for her prisoner-son's daughter, three of the women had prisoner-partners who were effectively the stepfathers of the children.

132 Sack et al, above n114 at 624.

133 Ibid.

134 Id at 623–625.

135 Kobasa, S, "Stress Response and Personality" in Barnett, R, Biener, L and Baruch, G (eds), *Gender and Stress* (1987).

136 Morris, P, *Prisoners and their Families* (1965) at 130; above n76 at 438.

137 Friedman, S and Esselstyn, T, "The Adjustment of Children of Jail Inmates" (1965) 29 *Federal Probation* 55–59; Anderson, N, *Prisoners' Families* (1965); Morris, above n136; Sack et al, above n114; Newton, A, "The Effects of Imprisonment" (1980) 12/1 *Crim Just Abstr* 134–151; above n76.

138 Sack et al, above n114 at 626; Fritsch & Burkhead, above n114 at 86–88.

139 Morris, above n136 at 219–220; above n76 at 457–458.

140 Hutson, S and Jenkins, R, *Taking the Strain: Unemployment and the Transition to Adulthood* (1989).

141 Newton, above n137; Jones, J, "Prisoners and their Families", unpublished PhD thesis, Melbourne: Monash University Department of Anthropology and Sociology, 1983 at 445 & 457.

142 Sack et al, above n114 at 621.

143 Above n76 at 445.

144 Williams, F, *Social Policy: a Critical Introduction* (1989) at 216.

145 Among others Schwarz & Weintraub (above n117); Sack, and Sack et al (above n114); Bauhofer (above n117); Schiff, S, "The Preschool in Prison Project: OMEP Canada", unpublished paper, Canada, 1986. This is not to say that these writers directly influence any one woman who has the family obligation to provide this domestic labour. Nevertheless the universality of this position is likely to affect the woman through her contact with the various welfare workers with whom she has to work.

146 Crosthwaite, A, "Punishment for Whom? the Prisoner or his Wife?" (1975) 19/3 *Int J Offend Ther & Comp Crim* 275–284 at 283; my emphasis.

147 Sack et al, above n114 at 624.

148 Above n76 at 464–473.

149 Id at 472.

150 Among others: Morris, above n136 at 92; Kemp et al, above n27 at 15; Newton, above n137 at 147–149.

151 Lowenstein, A, "Coping with Stress: the case of prisoners' wives" (1984) 46/3 *J Marr & Fam* 699–706.

152 Poster, M, *Foucault, Marxism and History* (1984) at 111.

153 Benhabib, S, "The Generalized and the Concrete Other: the Kohlberg-Gilligan Controversy and Feminist Theory" at 56–76 in Benhabib, S and Cornwell, D (eds) *Feminism as Critique: on the politics of gender* (1987) at 90.

6

PENALITY, DOMESTICITY AND CONTROL

INTRODUCTION: THE HIERARCHY OF MORALITY

In the first three chapters it was argued that the work of the outside carers of imprisoned men is performed within sets of conditions whose essential contradictoriness stems from the basic structures of contemporary social life. In summary, with the development of liberal, industrial then corporate capitalism there develop three spheres in which power and morality intersect: the powerful amorality of the market in the economic sphere, the powerful morality of the State in the public sphere manifested in the formal, institutional, rational structures of the legal penal system and the powerless morality of the domestic sphere as it is experienced in the diffuse, particularistic, emotional relationships of family life. The two domains concerned with social control, the polity and the family, thus become constituted as two opposing and conflicting bases of morality. Values underpinning the morality of family life are in direct conflict with those that comprise morality in public life: the particularistic and volatile affectivity that underpins the intimacy of family life in the sphere of the reproduction of personality is in direct opposition to the universalism of the abstract impersonal realm of justice. Not only are the two spheres in conflict but, as was argued in chapter one, the morality of public life comes to be defined as the superior form. Gilligan[1] summarises this constitution of the inferiority of domestic morality in this way:

> Women's moral weakness, manifest in an apparent diffusion and confusion of judgment, is thus inseparable from women's moral strength, an overriding concern with relationships and responsibilities. The reluctance to judge may itself be indicative of the care and concern for others that infuse the psychology of women's development.

Although all women — who are defined primarily by their association with domesticity — experience the day to day stresses that result from living the concrete reality of being caught within the contradictions set up between these two co-existing but conflicting spheres of morality, it is the women who are constituted as "families of prisoners" who are likely to experience these stresses in their most condensed form. They are the personal representatives of the domain of powerless morality who nevertheless have to try to implement the devalued morality of the domestic sphere within the sphere of the State — the powerful domain whose morality is based on values in direct contradiction to those constituting the basic rules of family life.

This emphasis upon the two spheres as being centrally though contradictorily constituted to reproduce moral life in a political economy based upon the amorality of the free market, leads to the following propositions:

(1) that *control* is the central feature which dominates the working conditions of the caring labour of families of prisoners;
(2) that *control* is exercised in several complex and contradictory intersections between family and prison life.

The complexity of the way that *control* impinges on the lives of families of prisoners results from the historical construction of the two realms of morality. In Chapter two it was argued that a layering of punishment practices and policies presently constitute daily life in prison. As the boundaries between state, economy and family have shifted there have been several "deposits" of often conflicting ideologies and styles, and the prison system in New South Wales has become characterised (to shift metaphors mid-sentence) as a Byzantine maze of policies, practices and regulations.

FAMILY POLICY, PENAL POLICY AND THE STATE

Family policy in Australia operates not through a coherent and overt set of policies explicitly directed to the structuring of domesticity but through a diffuse set of policies and practices that nevertheless continually serves to constitute and reconstitute the asymmetric gendered relations of the nuclear family. This set of covert "family policies" should include penal policies: that the way that domesticity is incorporated into the legal-penal sphere serves both to reinforce the relationships of care and dependency that comprise family life and to draw on the infrastructure of hidden labour that those relationships create.

In the analysis in this chapter of the intersection of control, care and dependency, domesticity and penality are presented as being dialectically related, with the relationships of power, morality and rationality within each sphere being drawn on to reinforce the other.

From the conversations with the 38 women visiting prisoners in New South Wales in the years 1986 to 1988, domesticity is incorporated into legal-penal control in several forms. Although in the day to day work of caring for men in prison these controls are experienced as diffuse and contradictory constraints, they are delineated here as comprising:

1 Control as neglect and isolation of the family;
2 Control of the prisoner through the family: sexuality and humiliation;
3 Control of the prisoner: the constitution of the family as a "reward";
4 Control of the carers: the constitution of the family as "access-ories" and moral enemies;

5   Control of information: the "rule of anticipated reaction": the family as moral allies;
6   "Emphasised femininity" as control.

The first of the forms of control as it was experienced through the caring work of the women was:

CONTROL AS NEGLECT

It is important to disentangle the two strands of this basic form of control that is experienced by families of prisoners: it comprises both "neglect as control" and the "neglect of this neglect":

1   NEGLECT AS CONTROL

Chapter three cited Robinson's research which shows that for at least two of the children of convicts sent out in the First Fleet, their father's imprisonment and transportation led to their deaths through starvation.[2] The several texts on the living conditions of families of prisoners in the US and in Europe in the latter half of this century demonstrate that although this extreme form of neglect no longer operates as a control upon imprisoned men, the husband's imprisonment nevertheless usually results in considerable economic and material losses for the family outside.

Unsurprisingly in a society like Australia in which being a single-parent family puts that family at risk of being below the poverty line,[3] similar findings have been made about families of prisoners in Victoria[4] and in New South Wales.[5] This material cost to their families outside is a significant part of the punishment experienced by prisoner husbands and fathers.[6] The neglect of the family outside is one of the key intersections between home and prison outlined in Chapter Three. This policy of control by neglect is one of the basic "deposits" of penality still affecting families of prisoners in New South Wales. Family life as it is constituted as a set of relationships predicated on the economic dependence of women and children upon the primary bread-winning father, means that the state is manifestly responsible for the poverty of those women and children when punishment is the loss of freedom to exchange labour for wages.

2   THE NEGLECT OF NEGLECT AS CONTROL

The relative economic powerlessness of women and children within the family is continually reconstructed through the variety of social security, education, occupation and economic policies that comprise the unwritten "family policy" in the Australian familial-political economy.[7] This powerlessness as an essential element in the construction of family life means that the poverty of the women and children who are families of prisoners is central to the way that morality is constituted within the contemporary Australian familial-political economy. The home, as the site in which the morality underpinning the social relations of the wider society is reproduced, is centred on this principle of unequal relationships, the economic dependence of the caring mother and wife whose love is essentially expressive not instrumental. Women as mothers are constituted as people who are economically dependent upon men as breadwinners. Nevertheless the price that women pay for this dependence is the willingness to keep offering that love even when men are unable to provide economic support.

However this centrality of the punishment by neglect of women and children who comprise the population "families of prisoners" is masked and made invisible in the powerful morality of the political sphere. Because of the principle of specificity upon which the universalistic, legal authority of the penal system is based, the rational state is inherently unable to formally acknowledge the arationality of the centrality of the punishment of the family. To paraphrase Graham, caring, constituted as dependent love, is at the heart, not the periphery, of the political economic system.[8] But the false universalism of that system depends upon the masking of the significance of caring. This neglect of neglect then further punishes the population caught up in this contradiction at the heart of the legal-penal system. The vulnerability of children of prisoners to the punishment of poverty is a particularly contradictory aspect of the intersection between home and prison. Childhood has been constructed as "innocence" in the family relations of liberal capitalism.[9] To recognise the punishment of innocents then undermines the rationality of the legal-penal sphere. Moreover, as Susan Smith argues, even to recognise the parenthood of prisoners would be to undermine the image of prisoners as individualistic evil-doers. It is this image that pervades the law and order discourses of the current era. There are for example no official statistics on the numbers of children undergoing the hidden punishment of having a parent imprisoned.

There is then no base upon which to articulate the unfairness of that punishment. Moreover, the familial commitment to care "for better or for worse" conveniently shifts the responsibility for this central aspect of punishment — neglect — from the state to the family. It becomes the woman's responsibility to bear that punishment quietly in order to demonstrate the neo-feudal loyalty that characterises familial obligations.

This however describes an "ideal type" of neglect as punishment. The literature on families of prisoners indicates that the economic punishment of neglect imposed on families of prisoners is experienced in its extreme forms only in those families in which women are determined to obey the rules of domesticity. The enforced loss of the breadwinning father and husband among families of prisoners in the period of corporate consumer capitalism has different results for families depending, in part, on whether women respond by remaining committed to sustaining the man's role as major breadwinner even when he is unable to provide for the family. The families who experienced the most severe economic punishment among the women interviewed by Jones in Victoria in the early 1980s were those who made the deliberate decision not to find paid work for themselves. This decision was directly related to their commitment to care for the prisoner: "wives who suffered most hardship were previously happily married wives who wanted to keep marital roles unchanged ... in the hope the marriage would remain happy."[10]

Kemp et al also found that amongst wives of New South Wales long term prisoners in the early 1980s, there was a group of women whose attempts "to keep the marriage alive" involved them in building their lives around this closeness, as distinct from other wives who were more involved in what Kemp et al described as "personal development activities.[11]

Commitment to the "ideal type" of family relationship, and to her own emotional labour of keeping the husband/father's place open, thus inevitably also commits the woman to bearing the most extreme forms of impoverishment or punishment by neglect. It is, then, the women who are the most committed to the caring labour of providing support for the "self" of the prisoner, who bear the highest economic costs. To further unpeel the contradictions in the intersections of the two spheres of morality, it is important to emphasise here that it is precisely the women who are conforming to the ideal of domesticity that is appropriate to the latter normalising moment of imprisonment who are most at risk of punishment by neglect. Families of prisoners then exemplify in a most condensed form the paradox of gender inequality as it is defined by Graham, that it is those who do the work of providing caring labour who pay the costs: "for men economic dependency and poverty is the cost of being cared for: for women, economic dependency and poverty is the cost of caring."[12]

3   NEGLECT AND CONTROL AS MANIFESTED IN NEW SOUTH WALES
     IN 1986-88

For fifteen of the thirty people whose partners were prisoners, the imprisonment meant the loss of the prisoner's wage. For five more the loss of the partner's share of their combined social security income was also a penalty in that it meant that they had had to move out of their home. Three women said they were better off because they had more control over their income when their husband was inside gaol.

It was women with young children who lost most in financial terms. Women without children, or whose children were in secondary school, were more likely to be in paid work. Jones found that one of the effects of imprisonment on partners of prisoners in Victoria was that, for some women, their access to paid work was threatened because they lost their co-child carers.[13]

The way that the social space in which domesticity and penality has been constituted (particularly in the segregative end of prison life in New South Wales) reinforces this condensation of the relationship between care, dependency and control. The work of supporting prisoners, especially in maximum security gaols, by maintaining contact through visiting is feasible only if visits are made during the working week.[14] There are no visits after normal working hours during the week and there are so few resources of space and staff that weekend visiting does not enable women to have "a good visit".

Sally

Q: Would you be able to hold down a full time job and visit? No, no way. Not possible. I was doing barmaid and I was on nightwork then they put me on daywork. They put me from ten o'clock in the morning until seven o'clock at night. I said 'No'. I left the job because I was getting four visits a week ... There's no way, I would never have seen him, there's no way ...

Hilary

I've been looking for a job ... I'd go for part-time jobs so that doesn't muck up my visiting.

Ray

Well I lost a day's wages when I visit him. When I'm doing part time work because I visit him during the week, the weekend is hopeless.

Towards the normalising end of imprisonment the work of visiting can only be done at weekends for those prisoners who have been allocated to the various special programmes in the minimum security gaols, the external study, industrial training or work release schemes. So if women had managed to secure weekend work that had provided a sufficient income for independence in the earlier segregative moment of imprisonment, in order to maintain the work of caring for the prisoner in this latter moment of penality that access to independence would have to be surrendered or the weekly hours renegotiated to fit the changing demands of the penal sphere. It is the malleability of women's caring work that is being drawn on in the way that the legal penal sphere is constituted here. Punishment constituted initially as the loss of the freedom of the breadwinner to exchange his labour for a wage is then transformed into punishment as improving his access to the labour market. This progressive model however can operate only on the hidden infrastructure of either the impoverishment of the family outside or the willingness of the woman to "cope" by reshaping her life to fit the changing demands of the legal-penal sphere. The loss of the man's wage means that women have to make a choice between:

(1) a continued dependence on the state,
(2) dependence on a weekend wage that has to be renegotiated into dependence on the state with the transforming moments of penality, or
(3) a dependence on a wage based on the "normal" working week that then has to be constantly manipulated to allow for the occasional "free" day to visit during working hours.

Graham's argument that:

> through the concept of coping we can understand both the malleability and the invisibility of women within the family ... the concept sensitises us to the way women's lives can be radically restructured in response to changing socio-economic conditions without their role being formally redefined.[15]

is particularly apposite in relation to the impositions that the contradictions of penal life impose on those women, who, in attempting to adapt to the morality of the legal penal sphere, do the work of "keeping the father's place open".

These choices are made even less free when added to these constraints are the loss of the imprisoned parent as a potential co-child carer, the several geographical moves that constitute the individual prisoner's experience of punishment, and the difficulties that women in families of prisoners share with all other women in their gender, age and class groups in getting access to paid work in the segmented labour market as it operates in Australia.[16] Comparable figures for other societies with largely similar familial-political economies indicate that Australia is likely to be a particularly punitive country for women who are the outside carers of prisoners' children, for two reasons. Firstly because Australian women with domestic obligations have less access to paid work: 76 per cent of sole mothers in France, 60 per cent of sole mothers in the Federal Republic of Germany and 87 per cent of sole mothers in Sweden have access to independence through paid work. In the United States 56 per cent of sole mothers have full time paid employment.[17] The second reason that the people, women and children who comprise the population "family dependants", in Australia are more exposed to the hidden punishment of neglect than are people caught in this social space in some other western countries is because the Australian state has chosen the policy of equating State dependence with impoverishment. In Australia in the mid 1980s single parents not in the labour force received only 50 per cent of the net average production workers wage in contrast to 93.8 per cent of that wage received by single parents in Sweden.[18] Australia had the second highest percentage of children living in poverty in countries with comparable familial-political economies.[19]

NEGLECT AND HOUSING

The intersection of penal and housing policies in Australia creates a particularly contradictory hidden control on outside carers. The irrationality of juxtaposing the home successively as the object of control, then the object and the site of normalisation, operates in these stages:

1   the segregative moment of penality centres on the loss of freedom to exchange labour for income;

2   the loss of the breadwinner's income places the family outside at the risk of the loss of "the home" as a mortgaged or privately rented property. This parallel punishment constitutes part of the punishment of the prisoner inside gaol;

(3) the partner and co-parent of the prisoner's children works to re-establish "the home" as both a material and an emotional space for herself and the children to exist in for the duration of the period of segregation. Moreover this domestic labour is further extended as the work of home making is achieved with access only to the reduced resources extended to a sole parent dependent on state resources;

(4) the normalising moment of imprisonment reconstitutes "the home" as the site of the potential reintegration of the prisoner both as a physical resource protecting him from the necessity to steal to live and as a set of domestic relationships which will lock him into the socially controlling role of the primary breadwinner responsible once again for the rent/mortgage of himself and his dependent wife and children.

It was men who were able to join parents or partners in a relatively stable living arrangement who were less at risk of being returned to gaol.[20]

Australian housing policies play a particularly useful part in the construction of this elegant contradiction of penality. Australian housing policy is characterised by an emphasis on the constitution of "the home" as a commodity to be purchased on the free market either through mortgaged ownership or through private rentals, with only 5 per cent of housing stock available in the form of public rented housing.[21] Access to the subsidised public rental housing stock then is likely to be much more difficult for those made marginal to productive life. Women in particular have been excluded from home ownership through a complex set of familial-political economic discourses that have "marginalised women in housing terms."[22] Although the needs of several groups of women — the aged, young single women wage earners, single parents — have been omitted from orthodox housing discourses, women who occupy the complex social space "families of prisoners" are placed in a particularly contradictory situation in the intersection of housing and penal discourses.

The impact on families of prisoners in Australia is marked. Eleven of the 30 partners of prisoners in these interviews had to move house as a direct result of their partner's imprisonment. Although the methodology of the study means that it is not possible to generalise from these figures, other data on the impact of imprisonment indicates that 55 per cent – 70 per cent is a reasonable estimate of the risk of this form of dispossession.[23] As Jones points out, in contrast in England in the 1960s less than 30 per cent of families of prisoners had to move house as a consequence of the husband's imprisonment.[24]

The range of hidden "family policies" that include housing, child care, social security, training and education and industrial and immigration policies as they operate or fail to operate in Australia in contrast to those in other countries indicates that Australian women are particularly vulnerable to being caught up in the underside of penal control as neglect.[25]

VULNERABILITY TO CRIME

Poverty, enforced social mobility and poor housing are then linked to a further hidden punishment. Victimisation studies have indicated that it is just those geographic areas of city and suburban life in which people are most vulnerable to arrest in which they are also most vulnerable to assault. This dual vulnerability is much more likely to be part of the day to day experience of people in the low cost housing areas that comprise the everyday environment of people made marginal to productive life. The increased risk of impoverishment is also then likely to place the women impoverished by their partners' imprisonment at an increased risk of violence, either because they have to move to areas which places them at greater risk or because they continue to live in those areas in which to be a woman on her own increases their already considerable vulnerability or thirdly, because the exigencies of working and travelling to support men inside gaol place some women at greater risk of assault. Three women had experienced this added "punishment" of being at risk because of the loss of their partner:

Julie

In the area we're in it didn't take long to find out that he was inside. They just know I'm by myself and the two girls and the area (I live) there's quite a few of them on drugs and whatever so they get in to the house ... there was one crouched down by the light post, one beside the window and one at the back ... That wasn't the only time that was the night that I caught them.

Katherine

I was in a Housing Commission place that's in Sydney and I left that place because I used to have to travel backwards and forwards Sydney to Bathurst. I left that place because while I was down here visiting the house was broken into three times — the three times that I visited ... they knew.

To identify vulnerability to crime as being an uncomplicated consequence of "losing a man about the house" is to oversimplify the social processes impinging on the lives of people with family obligations to prisoners. It is social mobility and social isolation as much as separation from any other one member of the household, that places women at risk of this additional punishment of social defencelessness. John Minnery found that people who were living in rented households and who were more recent arrivals were at greater risk of being victims of crime.[26] These two factors most likely to be associated with becoming a victim in inner city suburbs, then, are both social conditions which characterise the experience of women in the population "families of prisoners".

SOCIAL ISOLATION

Being a partner or parent of a prisoner can be experienced as a punishment that is in some ways more difficult to bear than the imprisonment of the man inside gaol. Being with other prisoners means sharing an experience of deprivation, but being the partner or parent of a prisoner outside means living in but apart from the community around you and experiencing from day to day a singular form of isolation — the constant reflection from the generalised or significant others of being morally different and devalued:

Beth

I think the wife pays. She does time. She mightn't be locked up but she still does time. He thinks that she's got it OK because she's out. But you can be in prison in your own home and not go anywhere because your husband or your boyfriend's locked inside. You're just as much in gaol.

Dulcie

Now I'm ignored, even at work. It was in the newspapers. They don't talk to me anymore.

Tricia

I moved to get away (from people living next door) after the arrest so now I don't have anyone to talk to. I really need someone who's got kids too. That's who I'd like to talk to. They'd know more about it, but I don't have anyone.

The hidden punishment of social isolation is especially likely to reinforce the risks of the other hidden punishment — of impoverishment. An important factor influencing access to paid work for Australian women in this period was access to child care.[27] Sole parents in Australia were particularly likely to have difficulties entering the paid labour force because of child care problems.[28] For these single parents, lack of child care comprised the major obstacle to access to work skills and to the labour market.[29] The 1984 study of women's employment by the Institute of Family Studies found that Australian women were much more likely to depend upon informal than formal child care arrangements.[30] The added restrictions a partner's imprisonment imposed on access to informal networks of support then potentially imposed multiple stresses on women outside.

If social isolation is a condition of domesticity, then in that social space in which domesticity and penality coincide, women who do the caring work of supporting prisoners experience that isolation in a particularly condensed form.[31] Moreover this loneliness is derived from multiple sources. Sometimes it occurs because friends and neighbours shun families of prisoners or it occurs because wives, especially if they are the outside carers of prisoners' children, move away from established friendships to avoid the risk of stigma.

The sense of isolation is exacerbated for carers of imprisoned men when the social dynamics of imprisonment create a gulf between the prisoner and the outside carer. At various crisis points the experience of imprisonment can be so extreme that the "selfishness" of men inside dominates the visit. Sometimes this can be a reflection of specific injustices that the prisoner is undergoing:

Beth

It does boil down indirectly to affecting the visitors (and their families) because if your man's being degraded, if your man's being picked on or your man's coming out aggro because of some things that happened and you've gone all that way to see him and all you want is a nice visit and all he can talk about is how much he hates them and how stupid they are, it upsets you and you come back feeling 'O God', you know.

Rebecca

Sometimes it (visiting) is very difficult. Sometimes the tension in there sets me off — the general tension. He brings his own tension. I go back outside and feel so depressed.

However there is also a long period when the prison becomes the "real world" and visitors feel excluded by the processes of institutionalisation that are inherent in the way that penal life is constructed.

Olive

They do become accustomed to the gaol, life. My son said he could stay there another ten years. He's got his own cell, his video, his TV, his little Breville. He's paid for all that. He works. Now and again I'll put $10 in his property, or I'll take him in some socks and undies.

Ray

I feel bitter. After a while the man inside becomes more oriented to the people inside. After all the effort of visiting and contact I feel as if it's wasted. I feel bitter about that.

There has been an extensive literature on institutionalisation and imprisonment following on from Goffman's analysis of total institutions. Kemp, Cheron et al, summarising this literature in their report for the New South Wales Department of Corrective Services, reflected the reformist technological arguments current in North America and in Europe a decade earlier. They argued that institutionalisation results from the routinisation of prison life and from the pressures to conform to the prison system and to be "a good prisoner". Imprisonment then, paradoxically, leads to "regression" and undermines the prisoner's chances of "making it" once he is released. Their report argued that visiting was an antidote for this pathological aspect of imprisonment. However they also point to the evidence in the literature that there is a crisis point sometime between 18 months and two years when the prisoner becomes "emotionally inaccessible". Their concern was that this withdrawal "weakened the marital ties" and the loss of the family as a key element in the "re-integration" of the prisoner into normal social life.[32]

The introduction of less intimidating visiting conditions in the new maximum security prison at Parklea followed the publication of this report.[33] However there was little alteration to the punitive atmosphere of visiting at the older maximum security gaols. Moreover Parramatta, the gaol which was closed with the opening of the new more humane maximum security gaol at Parklea, was reopened after a short time, to soak up the increase in the prison population. This variation in visiting conditions then adds another layer of control into the relationship between domestic and penal life.

The social isolation of the carer also results from the way that control in prison life is constructed around gossip and sexuality. This aspect of control leads onto the second major category in this chapter — the control of the prisoner through his direct contact with the family.

CONTROL OF THE PRISONER THROUGH DOMESTICITY:
Gossip, Sexuality and Prison Life

The feminist deconstructions of the term "coping" indicates that caring work places carers at risk of internalising a sense of responsibility and culpability for crises not of their own making.[34] This socially contructed vulnerability of carers is particulary evident in the penal realm where partners and parents feel guilty for the punishment that their son or partner is experiencing. Jones found that even in marriages which had previously been based on a relatively companionable relationship, prisoners either directly or inadvertently exploited this characteristic of domestic life by transferring a sense of guilt onto their "free" partners.[35]

This particularly powerful dynamic of penal and domestic control impinged on the lives of women in New South Wales. Being "free" outside was experienced as an unfair condition when the partner was so manifestly "unfree".

Dulcie

Yes, we're in there with them. He said 'you can walk away from here'. I never turn around when that door slams.

Beth

You really do (feel guilty). You really want to take them with you ... you can walk away and (you feel guilty) and in a way even though they won't admit it they probably feel that too ... I could never turn around and watch him go back inside — especially Parklea because they're pretty strict with the searches there. You feel you can walk out and they can't. You really do (feel guilty).

Both prisoners and prison guards reinforce the self-imposed control over women's social behaviour. Fishman found that men in prison use telephone contacts to place restrictions on their wives and to maintain their authority and domination of the woman outside.[36] "Keeping the man's place open" means maintaining his right to define the limits over the extent of socialising that women can experience.

Audrey

the men expect you to really behave yourself when you're out there all the time, and they question you all the time.

165

Beth

You can't plan to go anywhere weekends because you're spending that time in gaol, visiting. You have to be there. He expects you to be there. You just have to be there ... I've seen it ... I've seen the fight because she's five minutes late and maybe it's because the screws were mucking around outside and wouldn't let her in straight away. He says 'it's about time you were here' ... She cops the lot!

Ray

because the person inside is deprived — it's a feeling I suppose of wanting to help that person who's in a rough situation ... knowing that you have freedom and they don't, and they do, they do make you feel that, even though they might not be conscious of it.

Sexuality and power intersect in several ways in the control of prisoners. Homosexual rape between prisoners is as much about the power hierarchies within prisons as it is about sexuality.[37] The institutionalised power of prison officers is manifested in their right to strip prisoners, even to the right to invade the body of prisoners for "ingenious hiding places". The autobiographical accounts of prison life indicate that this right is used to maintain the unequal power relations between officers and prisoners.[38]

The paradox, outlined in the previous chapter, that masculinity excludes dependence at the same time as it makes men vulnerable, becomes especially focused in that area of masculinity associated with sexuality. This contradiction, which operates in its most condensed form in the penal sphere, is central to the construction of the relationship between gender and class in the familial-political economy of liberal capitalism. This aspect of the specific dynamic between power, morality and rationality as it is expressed through sexuality in liberal capitalism is indicated in the definition of the term "domesticity" in chapter one but it needs to be elaborated in greater detail here.

Although the political relationships of sexuality underpin several forms of familial-political economies, it is sexuality as it is constituted within the historically specific dynamic of power, morality and rationality of liberalism that circumscribed the experiences of women partners of prisoners in New South Wales in 1986 to 1988. The free expression of sexual desire is proscribed behaviour in New South Wales maximum and medium security prisons, even when that freedom is expressed through the limited prescribed relationships of legalised sexuality as it is regulated within the domestic relations of the family. This form of punishment and discipline, the proscription of sexuality, is specific to "modern" liberal penality. The unfreedom of imprisonment is the unfreedom of this most central way in which masculinity, as self-determined will, is expressed in the possessive individualism of liberalism.[39] Civil society, the particular social invention and mainstay of liberalism, is predicated upon the very specifically defined notion of the individual: the individual as a possessor. The principle of possessive individualism is itself based on the central theme of the possession of free will. Civil society is the mutual recognition of the free will of the other, an inherently contradictory and unstable form of social relationship. Moreover the freedom (expressed as self-interest) of each individual is "bought at the price of its abstraction from any specific content" in the necessarily universalistic relationships of civil society.[40] This means that the principle of "individual as possessor "is predicated upon the family being bracketed out of the universal relations of social interaction in which the individual will is expressed in the relations of mutual indifference of the market place. However that mutual indifference, which is essential to the expression of the will, is also the basis for its erosion. Although liberal political philosophy has attempted to get to grips with this "problem of voluntarism" it is the feminist analysis of the contradictory interdependence between universalism and particularism that uncovers the actual mechanisms through which liberalism operates.

The primacy of the individual will is qualified in civil society. To assert itself, it requires another which accords it primacy by this other denying itself to be a separate and autonomous will.[41]

The recognition of the self of the individual depends upon "the other" itself possessing a will which it is nevertheless prepared to sacrifice. Women's sexuality in liberalism then is locked into a continuing cycle of will subsumed, then reasserted, to once again be subsumed. The masculine possession of a will that has been absolutely and perpetually subsumed, that is of women made into absolute slave-like sexual objects would mean that masculinity itself could not be regenerated through affirmation.

... the individuals of civil society require another order of persons, lying outside of civil society and within the family, and whose raison d'être is to affirm the existence of the former as wills. Love is the form this affirmation takes.[42]

Romantic love resolves this contradiction: love that freely chooses to be unfree. Love, in the sexual relationships of patriarchal liberalism, is a relationship between an autodetermined will and a will that is unobligated, always having the potential to realise itself in its own autodeterminism but freely and *willingly* choosing not to.

The interdependence between civil society and domesticity in patriarchal liberalism then has to be "bracketed out" of the liberal political analysis. The contradiction here is that this failure of self-reflexivity undermines the very rationality on which liberal thought is supposedly based. The contracts remain "hidden".

Mike Donaldson has shown how this contradiction operates in the 1990s. He recorded several accounts of the social construction of masculinity amongst labouring men. His interpretation of these accounts indicates that the unequal relationships of the familial-political economy serve to make the meanings that men bring to sexuality so contradictory as to be self defeating. In the exploitative relations of the labour market, in which constant humiliation and aggravation degrade labouring men's sense of self worth, men become "real" again only within the heterosexual relationships of family life.[43] In the domestic relations of family life as it is constituted as the economic dependence of women upon men, sexuality simultaneously becomes the basis for the regeneration of the sense of self and "freedom" for men, and part of the "production line" of caring work that is expected of women.[44] Moreover in the economically unequal relations of family life, if "sex is used to construct and sustain male identity" then men will "tend to react with pain, confusion and violence in the face of female sexual expression outside the relationship" because unfaithfulness exposes the vulnerability of masculinity.[45]

In the condensed exploitative relations of prison life where humiliation and authority become ends in themselves, rather than means to the ends of productivity, this dynamic of class and gender in the control over women's sexuality becomes even more significant. Jones describes prisons in Victoria as being hotbeds of gossip over all aspects of prisoners' lives including their family relations.[46] Women in New South Wales experienced the surveillance over their visits that this implies.

Claire

Visits are very important to them. (Prisoners are) very resentful if women are late, if they don't come. Those women who come regularly, the whole lot watch. The ones who don't get visits take most interest in those who do and the prison officers. I've been told 'you're late' by this prison officer. I realised the interest in me because I was regular.

The accounts of Sally, Phillip and Gwen give complementary support to the argument that control over the partner's sexuality is an intrinsic part of penal life.

Sally & Phillip

After his (Phillip's) sentence we began to get a few hassles. He was worried about me. **Phillip:** You get very jealous in there, you get that much time to think, things go round in your head and I was imagining things. Since I got out I found, I had no reason to be treating her like that ... it is because that's all you've got to hang on to ... you can't be out there with them. You worry that something might happen.

Gwen

At Cooma one night I was at the pub because there's nothing else to do at night time, and there was a prison officer there and he told Terry I'd been in the pub, and we were all really drunk and stuff. And it wasn't true. I said 'why do that, it's nothing to do with you, you're only here to supervise, not to tell him everything what's going on on the outside, you're just making it worse for him'. Terry was really upset about it thinking I was with all these guys at the pub. I said to him 'you've got no right to do that'. Other prison officers knew we went to the pub but it was just this one guy and Terry never got on with him. It was like the conflict between him and him got pushed off on me ... He said in the pub 'O you can tell where they come from'.

Whilst Gwen emphasised the singularity of this prison officer's control of both her and her partner through sexual gossip, her account also indicates that any prison officer *can* use his position to control the prisoner through sexual gossip and when the prison is located in a small country town, he can also use his knowledge to penalise the women by putting "the wives on show".

Rebecca

they (prison officers) say things about (the) wife. 'Your wife's really nice' and 'we're out and you're inside', 'we can get on with her and you can't', using her to make you or break you.

Teresa (married her husband in prison after he had already served five years of his sentence)

The officer's turned round, 'your wife is probably screwing around mate. It wouldn't matter to you, you're in here, it doesn't make any difference' and he's got rigged up and he's known for his bad temper ... He's confronted me paranoid sometimes ... The officers can't always help it, they're pressured, they're getting double shifts. It's not always the officers' fault. They get pressured. They get cranky.

The connection between domesticity, sexuality and power within the prison can operate at a more indirect level. Particularly within the discourses of drug control, domesticity is easily translated into moral inferiority. By constituting domestic life as threatening to the good order of the prison the state is able to reassert its "authoritative masculinity" over the body of the prisoner at precisely the time when domesticity seems to have returned to the prisoner a sense, however limited, of sexual assertion and masculinity. Women know that for the men they visit, visiting always carries with it the risk of degradation, even (or especially) after the relatively relaxed atmosphere of minimum security visiting:

Beth

and they have this search, when you come out to a visit — and it's not universal, it's not standard in any gaol in the state, it depends on the screw that's on, it depends on the time of day, if it's raining, how they search you. They singled out Jim one day and they all strip off down to nothing in front of all the other crims in front of these screws. They all do that. And this particular screw when I had visited, he (Jim) was coming back from a visit, he asked Jim to lift his balls and he said 'No', he wouldn't, 'You want to search, you lift them' and the screw said 'alright, I'll charge you, if you don't lift your balls'.

It is important to contrast this use of sexuality in the relations of control within the penal sphere with the contrasting and contradictory use of sexuality and control as it operates in the normalising moment of penality. It is specifically the prisoner whose sexuality is channelled into the appropriate domestic contours of family life who is most likely to achieve his freedom from institutional imprisonment. A variation on this dynamic of domesticity, penality and control is the way that prison officers set women up as "mirrors" reflecting and amplifying their partner's humiliation.

Teresa

They (prison officers) do their best, (but) they're just mongrels. You can see it in their mannerisms when they come up. They play the line of discipline a little bit in front of the wife. 'Right,' you know. (But) he's a man, he's got individuality, he doesn't need to lose any more face than he is ... At the training centre they come up and they say 'you can't sit on the grass, sit on the edge of the grass.' I haven't been talked to like that since I was 14. He was upset.

Hilary

... the CIP was the hardest bit I had ... some of (the guards) are nice and some are pretty awful ... the other day I was visiting when my husband started to have a joke with one of them and he put my husband on a charge, you know it just makes you feel ... I don't know ... just little, just awful.

CONTROL OF THE CARERS:
THE CONSTITUTION OF THE FAMILY AS "ACCESSORIES" AND MORAL ENEMIES

A common term recurring all the time in conversations with individual women and with groups of women visiting gaols is "a good visit". "Having a good visit" means that both prisoner and visitors feel that the visit has given them some support to survive another day of the imprisonment. Support is the epitome of what visiting is about, providing enough emotional support to each other to sustain the day to day degradation of imprisonment. There are several ways that visiting as this domestic labour of the reconstitution of the particular personality of the prisoner, can be undermined. The conditions of visiting, especially in the segregative end of penal life, can grossly interfere with this work. The grimness of visiting conditions in some of the maximum security prisons are the antithesis of domestic comfort. The socio-political relations of visiting are an even more important hindrance.

At the segregative end of imprisonment the constitution of the prisoner as an enemy extends to the constitution of the family as potential accessories. Surveillance over visiting can be so intrusive as to undermine the conditions of intimacy and relative freedom of expression that would constitute a "good visit":

Ray

At Goulburn the attitude is that you must be a piece of dirt if you are associated with a prisoner whereas here (at Long Bay) they're very direct with the rules, it's pretty civilised. MTC they actually give you a smile, CIP they're very direct with the rules, but they are not like the guards at the country gaols.

Hilary

The way they walk around and some of them just walk around and stop and stare at you for no reason. You feel like you're in gaol too, that you're one of the prisoners.

Olive

Parramatta, I don't like it at all. You don't feel ease there. They look at you as though you're the worst in the world. They have their eyes on you all the time. They're eyeing you all the time as much as to say 'well, you're the prisoner's mother so you must be bad' and I've never been in trouble in my life, ever!

The political relations of prison life can be manifestly extended to control over visitors. Women can be punished for attempting to do the work of defending the prisoners' rights:

Lauren

CIP isn't really good ... at the moment I'm having a lot of hassle with the officer there because I made a statement when he was first brought down here and ever since then I've had a real hard time. They were letting other people in before me, making me wait ... I'm just worried that if I do something they'll make it more difficult for him, which they do. The other day it was the same. They gave out table numbers, and what table number you are, goes before the next time and they let four people in before me. I was table no 5 ... and he kept the table for me so I'd have to leave first. He's been doing it for a while now. I left here crying my eyes out the other day because I had that much to say to my husband, you know, I couldn't believe how quick they cut the visits ... It takes me nearly two hours to come here ... a bus, a train, a bus, which really is time consuming.

Although control over individual visits is important, it is the sense that prison officers and administrators have an arbitrary and overarching control, that can be most debilitating for women whose experience of visiting covers several years.

Rebecca

the worst thing about visiting is the degradation, the way they put you down, playing different mind games, keeping you waiting, clearing around you unnecessarily. The box visits are dreadful. They play on that, they feel above you, not just prisoners but families as well. They want the person broken in spirit, to be seen as the people with the keys, the power, whether you get the visit or not, the letter or not, whether you get a box visit or not.

CONTROL OVER INFORMATION:
UNCERTAINTY, THE "RULE OF ANTICIPATED REACTION" AND THE CO-OPTATION OF CARERS INTO THE STRUCTURES OF POWER

Sue Smith has argued that whilst the prisoner has the rules and boundaries of prison life explained to him, women have to operate in situations characterised by uncertainty and a lack of information.[47] The mystification of the rules and regulations of prison life means that women visiting prison or maintaining contact by telephone or letters are vulnerable to transgressing unknown limitations.

171

Virginia

how come one gaol has one set of rules and another gaol has another set of rules ... because at Maitland I used to be allowed to take his (babies) bottle in but down here in the CIP section you're not allowed.

Elizabeth

I touched my man on the leg one day and I was told to get my hand away and I wasn't doing anything wrong, you know, it's just normal things that you do at home that you can't do here. It's totally depressing.

Beth

when they had a riot out at the Bay I didn't know if he was there because they were sending him up to Maitland and they don't let them tell you what is happening — you can't hear from them. Everything you hear is by hearsay. You don't understand the message. You ring round frantically, totally in the dark you are. It amazes me how people who can't speak English manage.

Control of information within penal bureaucracies is an important feature of the power to punish. Moreover it is especially likely to occur in the social space where penal and domestic life intersect. Firstly, the way that penality has developed historically, as an arena of contradictory policies and practices often implemented as a result of ad hoc decision making, means that the confusion of penal life affects even those people who are the administrators.[48]

Hilary

One day when they moved him down here they said it was an all day visit. So I came here at 8 o'clock in the morning thinking I can stay here all day with him and when I got here they said 'You can have only the afternoon visit or the morning visit'. So I said 'you should get your telephone calls straightened out', so he just walked away and ignored me. And I've spoken to a lot of people and it's happened to them.

Secondly, the particular power relations within prison means that the custodial officers, the workers with whom prison visitors are most likely to interact, are allowed a great deal of discretion. This arbitrary power of individual warders was a major feature in the descriptions of the uncertainties surrounding the work of visiting for all the women interviewed.

Beth

I used to think that the way crims react to screws was wrong, but they (prison officers) really do react to childish things, and they glorify in that, they really do ... — childish things, if you (the prisoner) wear a white tee shirt, you lose your television for three days, if you wear thongs — and they have this search, when you come out to a visit — and it's not universal it's not standard in any gaol in the state, it depends on the screw that's on, it depends on the time of day, if it's raining, or ...

However, control over information is set much deeper into the relationship between domesticity and penality as they are constituted as the two sites of morality based upon opposing sets of values. Even within the official class-blind paradigm of the nature of penality, domesticity is inherently threatening to the legal-penal sphere as the two sites are constructed within liberalism. The moral obligations of family life are intrinsically opposed to the impersonal demands of punishment predicated upon universalism. Denying information to partners or parents of prisoners, for example about prison transfers of officially defined "dangerous" men, inevitably results from this definition of the two spheres as mutually incompatible arenas of morality. When the power relations of class and gender are layered on to this liberal interpretation of social life, and the relationships between prisoners and custodians is interpreted as one reflecting and condensing the humiliating masculinities of political economic life then the control of domesticity becomes an even more embedded aspect of the power to punish. This includes control over information. The accounts, outlined in the previous chapter, of the problems surrounding the mediating and negotiating work of partners and parents of prisoners, demonstrate the practical difficulties that confront women battling a bureaucracy which has control over a one-way flow of information. The legal-penal bureaucratic control over information has a more diffuse and more powerful impact. When the uncertainty that characterises women's day to day experiences of supporting men in gaol inculcates a *diffuse* sense of fear of the penal bureaucracy, this fear of trangressing boundaries (which are themselves not clear) interacts with the other levels of control that are exerted on families of prisoners and "harnesses" the particular skills of malleability and culpability that underpin the domestic work of coping. The work of maintaining contact with imprisoned men then becomes an exercise in anticipating and avoiding prohibited behaviours, but in situations in which the exact nature of the regulations appears arbitrary. Women then become involved in controlling their own behaviour and the behaviour of their children and of the prisoners themselves, not only over specific incidents but through the more diffuse policy of "keeping your head down" and of not causing trouble. Jones has shown how, in Victoria, this controlling work of women was strongly associated with the career model of imprisonment.[49] When visiting conditions are made less stressful as part of the general improvement of penal conditions in the medium and minimum security prisons, women are at great risk of being controlled to be the controllers.

Cheryl

at Parklea they've got swings and grass. In fact if every prison in New South Wales was like Parklea, gaol visiting wouldn't be so bad ... whereas in the CIP it's like going back to the days of the penal colonies.

Sally

... I've told him not behave stupid otherwise we'll be back to those days again (when she was only allowed box visits) ... and he has listened to me, he has, because he doesn't want them either.

173

The "rule of anticipated reaction"[50] then becomes a significant aspect of the intersection between home and prison, but in a complex form. It is not only that the rules are unclear. It is rather the lack of coherence in the *rules about the rules* that makes visiting an intellectually demanding labour. It is the arbitrariness of the way that the regulations are imposed that is puzzling. It then becomes the work of those who are the subjects of bureaucratic power to impose meaning on the contradictory and incoherent messages about the nature of imprisonment. Moreover the more tightly the regulatory structures are drawn the more contradictory are the experiences of the people on whom the power is being imposed. It is in the maximum security prisons that women become the targets of the most confusing messages about their work of maintaining contact with imprisoned men. The accounts of confusion about times of visits, whether there can be a contact or a no contact visit, whether young children can have spare nappies or bottles during the visit, or whether cards or presents can be given directly to the prisoner, were much more likely to be told by women visiting men in the segregative moment of punishment. There is however another peak period of uncertainty. This occurs during the normalising end of penality when men are due for day leave.

Prison, the site of a range of abstract universalistic rationalities, legal-penal, scientific, economic, is at the same time the site of gross forms of irrationality. However, to be able to operate in this complex and contradictory sphere of power relations, women doing the work of maintaining contact with imprisoned men have to impose meaning on that incoherence and in doing this they are then at risk of being co-opted through the "rule of anticipated reaction" into the structures of power within the prison. However there are other ways in which women are drawn into the structures of discipline and control. They become constitued as "a reward" for good prison behaviour.

The prison as it is constituted as a series of "progressive" stages operates as a powerful form of control on men when they reach the medium security and minimum security prisons.[51] The segregative end of imprisonment is distinguished in many ways from the latter more open end of imprisonment. In improved contacts with the family outside in the exchange of gifts, the numbers of telephone calls, visiting hours and the conditions of visiting are all rewards for prisoner compliance. Women's domestic work of maintaining contact becomes intertwined within the penal sphere in the management of control and punishment in prison.

Jane

The last time I travelled to Goulburn I was about eight months pregnant ... travelling down there a few times, I've got down there and been told I can't see him, the superintendent's orders ... it just turns out it's something that one screw had against my husband and he sort of rang through and said that he can't have a visit because he's on, what do they call it, 'loss of privileges'.

Sally

Phillip was in maximum ... which affects the visits. I've travelled all the way from Minnamura to see him and get twenty minutes ... because minimum you can have two to three hour visits, couple of times a week, plus he can ring me two or three times a week. In maximum I'm allowed two visits a week, maybe between twenty minutes and forty minutes ... they're not very good visits, you can't even have a smoke there. Whereas at the MTC you can bring in food ... have a barbecue if you want to ... in low security gaols they like to play their little game more and more. They threaten to send you back to maximum if you don't do every little thing they want.

The ambiguity of family life is that it both supports and controls men in both economic and penal life. Mat King contrasts the relative power in the workplace of single and married labouring men:

I know people that have got young families and it's real tough on them, they have to do all the overtime they can ... when the boss comes around, you get up slow, but they jump, because they realise what their job means to them.[52]

Prison relationships parallel this control through domesticity as it is experienced in the work place. In the interview with Sally and Phillip, Phillip recounted the difference that his relationship with Sally made after going through ten years of prison life with no family.

Phillip

They couldn't hurt me any other way because before when I done gaol I had nobody outside. I'd been cut off from me family and everyone and I got through me gaol really easy because I didn't have no worries. All I worried about then was the screws and giving them heaps and then with Sally, they had it over you. 'You don't do this you lose visits'. I had a few box visits through the glass and used to go back to the gaols feeling even worse ...

Cheryl Matthews met her husband after he had spent several years in prison and had been a political activist. When he was sent to prison again after he had become a family man his experience of prison life changed:

Cheryl

He says now that sixteen months were harder than the eleven years he did and he'd spent eight years of that in the retractables section of the gaol. I think it's (partly) ... because he did have a family ...

Beth

I've heard Bernie say 'a cut across the head is better than not having visits'. They'll stop your visiting. They will do that. They put you on a box visit. They will do that which is a dreadful experience, to be sitting in a wire cage or a glass cage or a cardboard box type thing and talking to the man on the other side.

This form of control is intricately tied to the neglect and invisibility of the importance of domestic life. Even in a penal system which incorporates the several links to domestic life through day leave, parole, home leave, visiting is defined only in relation to the individuality of the prisoner and not in relation to the other basis of morality, the family relationship with

175

parents, partners or children outside. The moral claim based on domesticity, that children have a right to maintain contact with parents, is subordinated to the moral claim of penality, that the authority of the state over the prisoner be dominant. Contact with the family outside is defined as a privilege of the prisoner not as the right of the child or partner outside. The previous chapter indicated that in the powerful moral sphere of penality the right of children to give Fathers-day cards to prisoners was redefined as a privilege that could be taken away. There are other examples of the way in which domestic morality, based on particularism expressed through special days and gifts, can be incorporated into the structures of control in prison:

Beth

You can take in magazines and books, depending on how much of an activist you are (affects) whether you get them or not. I gave Jim a birthday present in Parklea and he wouldn't have got it only I told him I'd sent it and he fronted them and asked them where it was.

With visits defined as the prisoner's privilege, men's behaviour inside gaol can make major differences to the women's experience of visiting. Women then become coerced into becoming the co-controllers of the men, encouraging them to do their time as legally as possible.[53]

June

I told him, if he touched drugs I'd cut his frigging fingers off. *Why is that?* Well, first, I don't want to spend the next few years coming to this place and second we're planning to get married whilst he's inside and I don't want to give them anything so that they can stop that.

However the move to prisons with better visiting facilities can also be a contradictory experience. Jane's partner was about to be transferred to Silverwater, a minimum security gaol, which is one of the prisons placing most temptation on prisoners to escape (and the kind from which most escapes are made).

Jane

He wants to go to Silverwater but he's worried if he goes to Silverwater he might jump the gate. I've told him, I've said to him 'if you do take off, don't come back home'. He said 'What?' and I said 'because I don't want coppers knocking on the door'.

Women as co-controllers of men inside gaol also have to moderate their own behaviour. Concern about keeping prisoners out of trouble inside gaol means that visits sometimes get cut short:

June

Some of them (prison officers) are really nice but some of them are pigs. Most of them understand the situation but this guy's just been in too long. He came up to us four times on one visit and Wayne was getting that cranky I said I'd better go or he'll get to you and you'll have a go at him and get into trouble.

It also means that the work of visiting involves not disclosing the extent of the problems that imprisonment imposes on women outside. The Department of Corrective Services research into prison escapes shows that the prisoner's concern about problems that the family face outside is one of the major reason for escaping.[54] Concern about the impact of disclosure was a major feature of the women's descriptions of visiting. Coping work as negation is very evident in this downplaying of the parallel punishment that is extended to families of prisoners.

Olive

I can hide a lot. I never let my son know just how upset I can be. Because if I get upset, he gets upset and if he gets upset that's when he gets in trouble.

Most of the women said that they did not tell their partners or sons the problems they were experiencing on the outside in order to protect the prisoner either from getting upset or from getting into trouble as a result of getting upset. Prison control then extends outside into women's lives, preventing them from sharing the stress they experience with the one person who can understand the dimensions of the problems that cause that stress.

"EMPHASISED FEMININITY" AS CONTROL

The feminist materialist analyses of caring work emphasise that that work has to be understood in terms of the symbolic bonds that hold the caring relationship together.[55] "Women are controlled to be the social controllers" through their identification with the private sphere of reproductive life.

The segregation of private and public spheres brought about the social construction of what Connell calls an "emphasised femininity".[56] This was reworked in the cultural packages marketed in consumer capitalism. Although this reconstitution of femininity placed greater emphasis on receptive sexuality, compliance and caring remained basic themes around which femininity was constructed. However the structural changes of this era, particularly those which drew women into the paid work labour market, have also meant that some women have access to a wider range of choices in interpreting femininity. Nevertheless, it is "emphasised femininity" that can be exploited in the State's use of the caring work of women for those people made marginal to productive life. At the same time it is through the work of caring that women, otherwise isolated from social life, are able to achieve a sense of self-fulfilment. In Graham's influential 1983 article, she emphasised that the analysis of domestic labour has to bring together the economic and the psychological dimensions of caring: "caring is the constitutive activity through which women achieve their femininity and against which masculinity takes shape."[57]

In this conceptualisation of femininity, caring creates a sense of "meaning, value and significance" through the experience of feeling needed. However there is some question about how essential this is to women's experience of being a woman. Other studies of caring work indicate that femininity can be constituted in other ways that place women at less risk of exploitation. Ungerson found that it was largely the carers' greater economic and material powerlessness that placed them at risk of the obligation to care.[58] Moreover Briggs' work indicates that it is domesticity rather than gender that is significant in constituting caring work as "natural" labour, in both the external and internal control over those providing that work.[59] There seems to be a dynamic relationship between:

(1) economic powerlessness and/or domestic status;
(2) the commitment to unpaid nurturing work; and
(3) the exploitation by the state of that commitment, through a series of social policies that foster women's caring role at the same time as they restrict the carers' access to material resources.

Especially contradictory is the way in which this dynamic is worked out in the labour of caring for men made marginal to productive life through imprisonment. The loss of the "breadwinner" through imprisonment has parallels with other forms of separation through divorce or death that contrast with the position of women who have the obligation to do the day to day work of caring for invalid or aged adults. Nevertheless, the obligation to maintain contact with the man in gaol imposes restrictions on women's time and labour that are similar to the practical restraints experienced by carers of dependants in the home. Imprisonment then would seem to have an inbuilt complexity in the potential for increasing or decreasing women's dependence.

Four recent feminist studies of the impact of penality upon wives of prisoners have centred their focus on the extent to which imprisonment led to an inversion of these dependent relationships of family life.[60] Their findings indicate that there is no simple picture of an overall inversion of dependencies when women are caught between the two conflicting moralities of prison and home.

Geraldine Wilson talked to twelve wives of a specific group of prisoners in London — short term prisoners most of whose sentences had resulted from offences related to heavy drinking. Of these twelve women, seven had been battered by their husbands and for them prison meant primarily a "rest from battering".[61] The other five women found that imprisonment meant that they were able to gain more control over their own lives. This article emphasises the *a*sociological feminist concern with women's independence within the family relationship, but only within the micro relationships of the family. The work of Jones[62] and Smith[63] broadens the analysis and shows how gender and class are linked in the lives of women with obligations to care for men in prison.

Jones found that for some women imprisonment reversed aspects of dependence, especially in the emotional relationship between prisoners and their wives. The husbands' imprisonment increased their emotional dependence on their wives and this meant that the power to maintain or discontinue the marital relationship was shifted to the women who "exerted far more informed control over the decision about marital reunion than they had over the original decision to marry".[64]

A major overall conclusion in this Victorian study of wives of long term prisoners was that some women did come to control their own lives in a more independent fashion.[65] However, although fifteen of the 35 women in that Victorian study became the family "breadwinners" during the man's imprisonment, this did not lead to an uncomplicated reversal of the economic relationship of care and dependence. The women who had previously regarded themselves as "lucky" in having a companionate relationship made what Jones calls the "rational" decision to maintain their economic and emotional dependence on their husbands to keep his place open.[66] Jones makes the point that women's commitment to economic dependence was reinforced by the range of penal practices and practitioners as well as the practicalities of living in the welfare state as it was constituted in Victoria at that time.[67] The social policies, the social workers, the husbands and significant others all "... acted to maintain the wives' financial dependence even when the wives themselves questioned it". This meant that "the wives were still controlled by their financial dependence even after their husband's departure".[68]

Laura Fishman in her study of thirty US prisoners' partners indicates that a third of the women benefited from their partner's absence by an increased sense of personal autonomy and a greater sense of competence.[69] However, for the majority: "rather than feeling 'liberated' they were emotionally and socially isolated as well as overloaded with demands on their time and energy."[70]

Sue Smith's research originated from her own experience as a prisoner's wife. From her own standpoint of having gained some independence from this experience, she started out in her research to elaborate on this aspect of the dynamic of family and penal power. Nevertheless, in her conversations with 27 women with family obligations to men imprisoned in England, she found that there was little eagerness on their part to exchange their economic and emotional dependence on their husbands for greater independence.

Only 8 per cent of the women preferred their new independence and wished to maintain it even when their partner was released. The majority voiced an overwhelming longing to 'Let him take over everything again.'[71]

Smith shows how inequalities of gender and class are condensed as they are played out in the penal sphere and makes the point that even the women who are forceful and articulate feel powerless to challenge the limitations and responsibilities placed on them because of their political "invisibility" and social isolation.[72] Like Hounslow et al in New South Wales in 1982, she argues that in order to overcome the loss of confidence brought about by the gross material and social punishments of being a wife or parent of a prisoner, what is needed is a form of state intervention centred around a point of advice, support and information for prisoners' families. She found an overwhelming desire amongst the women she talked with for this form of State intervention.[73]

In the era of consumer capitalism, prior to the retreat from welfare, from the late 1960s to the early 1980s, when there was an expansion of political protests challenging a range of constraints and inequalities, there developed in London, Sydney and in all the "prison cities" in the Netherlands small groups of women with family obligations to prisoners, who attempted to provide this form of support for each other. In London the South London Wives Group was established in 1965.[74] In Sydney, Carole Johns was one of the founder members of the Families of Prisoners Associations in 1977.[75] The major material and social burdens that are imposed on partners of prisoners, and the very dynamics of prison life, however, mean that self-support groups depend on the energies of a small number of highly committed women unless there is some level of external support. In the words of the 1982 Children of Imprisoned Parents Report, "too often self-help groups are expected to be self-annihilation groups".[76] All of these accounts[77] emphasise the fragility and yet the resilience of the group-based resistances of women in the population "families of prisoners". One other form of resistance to the control of femininity is for the outside carer to give up the relationship with the prisoner, to reject the family obligation to care. Nancy Anderson found that the response to the imprisonment of their husbands for fourteen of the 55 women interviewed in Victoria in the mid 1960s was that they "were pleased to see his backside".[78] The loss of family relationships (ie, the loss of the unpaid work of the outside carer) is especially probable in the case of long term prisoners.[79] One argument has been that it is the institutionalisation of the prisoner and his emotional turning away from the partner or parent outside that leads to this break up.[80] However this is not necessarily an easy option for the women outside. Both the London and the Netherlands groups found that severing the relationship with the prisoner was one of the reasons that women needed support from the group.[81] Jones also found that it was women who had wider social support who were able to make this break.[82] In the 1986 New South Wales interviews one partner of a man constantly being arrested and reimprisoned found that the women's group in the women's refuge, together with Al Anon, gave her the support she needed to be able to redefine the caring and dependent relationship she was caught up in:

Katherine: Five children. Husband imprisoned several times in past fourteen years

My husband ... attended AA and I went along to a few meetings of Al Anon and one lady said 'you're not to blame and he's using you as an excuse', and I come to believe it because there were times when the kids weren't even around so he'd still use that excuse 'that I had to drink because I was thinking about you all the time' ... I was like a child ... spoke to and spoken to and do what I'm told. Now I can stand up and I can say 'No', you know, just through this friend's advice ... This time 12 months ago I'd have been too frightened to even mention not going up to the gaol and visit him ... while he's in gaol I was frightened, that he could do anything there, it was when he come home. There's always that threat that he was going to kill me if ever I left him ... It's hard to let go. Everyone said you know for the kids' sake. That's one of the reasons why I let go, for the kids' sake. I can't bear for them to see their father abuse me in front of them.

Because wives separate from men during imprisonment this does not necessarily mean that those men are doing their time with no caring support from women.

Firstly, one universal finding of the many reports of prison visiting is that it is the prisoner's mother who is the consistent carer. Mothering is the most powerful manifestation of femininity as uninterested love. Whereas both men who are caught up in the recidivist cycle of arrest and re-arrest and men doing long term sentences are likely to lose their original partner, it is the prisoner son/mother relationship which is "the most durable".[83]

Secondly, Ungerson describes the commitment to caring that femininity exposes women to, as then outlasting the love that originally sustained it.[84] She was talking about the tending work of caring for aged or invalid adults but this commitment is evidenced too in the work of caring for men in gaol. The 1982 Children of Prisoners Report records that women separated from men before imprisonment are among those who do the work of visiting and maintaining his contact with his children whilst he is in prison.[85]

Thirdly, some men are able to establish new family relationships with other partners. Six of the 38 women cited here had established their relationship with their partner only after he had been imprisoned.

The section on mediating and negotiating work in the previous chapter indicates that there is no simple relationship between the commitment to care and the broader political commitment to acqiescence or resistance. Whilst imprisonment can reverse some aspects of the caring-dependent relationship, Jones found that the injustices that men suffered, especially in the early period of arrest, sentencing and segregation, served to shake women's initial belief in the legal-penal system and in doing this reinforced the women's support for the man. They redefined their husbands as victims of an inhumane and overly harsh punishment.[86] This process emphasised the importance of the women's commitment to the work of caring.[87] Several of the women in New South Wales said that they had experienced this same reappraisal. They had usually condoned the general principle that their son or partner should be punished by the State.

Olive: Son in prison for second time

I think they should have to pay for what they do wrong. Even though it might hurt the family. If they didn't you wouldn't be safe to walk anywhere ... You've got to live by the rules and the world doesn't owe you a living so you've got to get out of that, and start thinking about it.

**Beth: Office supervisor, met her partner (a prison activist)
after his imprisonment**

I used to think that the way crims react to screws was wrong ... I'm still a
square head too.

However, the implementation of that punishment, particularly through the
earlier moments of arrest, sentencing, early imprisonment and classification, and in the later semi-judicial processes of applying for early release,
was so manifestly unjust in their eyes that they reassessed their own
position vis-à-vis the State.

Margery

He (the policeman) was going like this, like this ... with that look on his face
as though to say 'o what a lad, o fancy him getting away'. I said 'do you
know addiction's a disease? He said 'the only good junkie's a dead one, the
only one who won't use again is a dead one ... yes, and he was a lovely
handsome young policeman and I thought 'O, isn't it sad' and I said 'have
you ever been to a Narcotics Anonymous meeting?' and he said 'aagh, I've
got better things to do', I said 'why are you a policeman', he said 'lady, I'm
in it for the money'. O, it was just his whole attitude.

Femininity then has a double potential. It can commit women to
greater labours of nurturing work but it does not necessarily mean that
women do not act as agents making some attempts for control in their own
lives. The work of caring for the prisoner involves women in contesting, at
an individual level, the class inequalities that are mediated through the
control of the State. However even though their experience meant that they
re-identified the penal situation as one of unequal power, the sense of
injustice that this evoked usually meant that women became more
committed to the individual work of caring for, or acting as advocates for,
the man in gaol. However some women specifically identified collectivity
as a possible basis for change. It was Cheryl Matthews' experience of the
injustices meted out to Bernie Matthews that led to her commitment to the
Prisoners Action Group. Similarly Beth's experience of her partner's
unjust treatment drew her into greater contact with prisoner activism and
the need to defend the rights for greater prisoner-family contact that had
been fought for in the 1970s:

Beth

Box visits ... they're dreadful. That's a regular visit. They don't have to give
you a contact visit. People have fought to get that. And that's only recent. In
the last five years, I'd say.

Cheryl Matthews' experience of the injustices of policing in the period
of arrest was shared by other women and in Tricia's experience the
concern for her partner was so strong as to provoke a class response:

Tricia

... the police at Penrith ... what I'd like to do is to get a whole lot of women
who are in the same position as me, get them all together and picket Penrith
police station, just to bring it out into the open what goes on there ... there

are a lot of ... women who know, who've been through what I've been through. Penrith station is bad, Sergeant X ... there are a lot of women who know ...

However there are both pushes and pulls for collectivity and co-operation between women in the same situation. Having a partner inside gaol means people are especially likely to want to preserve a sense of being different to other wives:

Dulcie

But you have to be careful who you talk to — our husbands are white collar criminals — some of those women you wouldn't want to associate with.

Other women deliberately resist this initial feeling of being different and emphasise the bond that the situation creates:

Beth

When you visit the same gaol for a long period of time and you see the same faces, its quite easy to strike up a friendship, and part of me backs off, saying I don't want to, because something inside me keeps saying 'Leonard and I are different' and the other part of me — I've given lifts to people going to gaol and going back ... I think women in that situation do have a bond, it's an unspoken bond, they understand the situation where a normal square head (wouldn't) and I'm still a square head too ...

Maintaining support for the man inside can also mean isolation. The special emotional pressures on imprisoned men can mean that he demands an exclusive loyalty that excludes contact with other women:

Audrey

My husband doesn't want me to get too friendly with the other men's wives, but if I didn't come here to the Family Support Centre I wouldn't be able to manage. He doesn't realise ... it's only by talking to Elisabeth and the other women here that I get to know ... it's information that's important ...

Imprisonment intensifies the potential for emotional blackmail between carer and dependent that other carers of dependent relatives experience.[88] The extraordinary material and emotional pressures on women as well as the social isolation inherent in being a prisoner's partner can undermine attempts to act collectively. Betty Hounslow et al describe the pressures on the five women who started the Families Of Prisoners Association in the late 1970s:

(in all) self help groups ... individuals wear themselves out, sacrificing personal needs to the group cause. 'Burn out' rates are high. The usual problems of non-funded community organisations were compounded in FOPA by the continual emotional and material strain which, of necessity, characterised the lives of its members. As well, 'prison-wives' have more than the normal demand on their time and energy. Maintaining a relationship with a man inside is a time consuming business. Energy levels are quickly depleted.[89]

The material and economic burdens however can became the basis for the collective action. Esther was one of the women who had met her partner during his imprisonment. That is to say she was one of the women who had made a rational decision to provide the labour of caring for an imprisoned man. Her commitment to femininity in terms of a commitment to providing uninterested nurturing and care for a prisoner was clearly also associated with a sense of control and agency, not compliance:

Esther

Up at Cessnock I knew people that were going up there, I'd organise to meet them and we'd all jump in a cab and pay a certain amount each which cuts down the cost a lot. Then we'd all share a caravan which as pretty good. Then when I bought a house up there they moved in some of them with me so it was pretty good. Everybody always got somewhere to stay there even if they have to camp on the lounge room floor. At one stage we had 15 people there. We had air mattresses all over the kitchen floor all in the lounge room. The kids would come, run round, wake us up early in the morning ... and I had blokes at Cessnock write to me and say 'can you put my lady up' and we made a lot of friends, that way, we had a good time ... I love those people and they feel the same about me, they're like my own sisters and if I've got a problem I want to talk about all I've got to do is go to them.

Ten per cent of the long term prisoners in the Aitkin and Gartrell study had established their relationship with their partners whilst they were in prison.[90] Six of the women in these interviews had met the prisoner after he had gone to gaol. This commitment to take on the work of caring for someone even without any earlier non-imprisonment experience of being together and establishing a loving relationship indicates the strength of the force of femininity and domesticity on women. It is important to emphasise here that it was these six women who were among the most articulate and forceful in their work of supporting the man inside by mediating, negotiating and contesting the inequalities of penality. Femininity then is not necessarily constituted as compliance. The ambivalence of family life, that it can act as a source of control yet also be the basis for resistance is clearly demonstrated in the work of women like Beth and Sally and Esther, who took on the labour of loving *after* their partner had been imprisoned. Their particularly determined commitment to femininity then locked them into the contradictory position of being moral controllers but also their partners' primary advocates in contesting the injustices of penal life.

Feminist analysis has been described as confronting the false ordering of reality that is based on the dualisms of modernist social science: for example of individual/society, of agency/structure.[91] These dichotomies rest on the principle of a unitary standpoint of individual agency, whereas women's experiences, as are those of other minority groups, are embedded in more manifestly multiple and self contradictory identities. Agency in orthodox social science has been associated with the heroics of bourgeois individualism. However the moral hierarchies of Rawls, Maslow, and Kohlberg have little explanatory value in interpreting the contradictions of the complex moralities which women such as Esther, Katherine, Sally,

Cheryl or Beth experience in their day to day lives as individuals with family obligations to imprisoned men.

SUMMARY: THE COMPLEXITY OF CONTROL

Foucault's description of the prison as a configuration of the four elements: the punitive, the disciplinary, the network of knowledge and the reproduction of criminality is clearly applicable to the penal system as it operates in New South Wales. The complexity of the contradictions of control that develop out of this configuration becomes even more condensed in that social space in which domesticity and penality intersect.

Prisons are sites of institutionalised violence. They constitute the social space where ascendancy of one group of men[92] over the other is explicitly and legitimately based on brute power. Moreover in countries that are not at war the legal-penal sphere is the only site in which rational morality can be legitimately expressed as the physical coercion of one group of men over another. In Genevieve Lloyd's examination of the connections between the masculinity of war and the masculinity of the ideals of citizenship in the Western philosophical tradition she describes "the state's capacity to wage war as the ultimate source of the self conscious individuality of its citizen ..." because to be ready to die in war is to achieve the final victory of rationality as domination over nature.[93]

It is not surprising then that the era of Australian history following the withdrawal of troops from Vietnam was also the era of an increasing militarisation of police and prison life. This reconfiguration of power, morality and rationality coincided too with the reshaping of the familial political economy both in Australia and in the UK when the restructuring of the labour market increased the proportion of workers marginal to productive life. Moreover this period was also the era of an increasing commodification of daily life with its parallel emphases upon the values of consumerism and impetuous desire. In chapter two the argument was made from the review of the literatures on domesticity and penality, that this restructuring of the wider familial-political economy was associated with the reshaping of penality as a complex combination of "soft" community controls, and "hard" militarised imprisonment.

Lloyd emphasises the way in which domesticity, in the intertwining themes of ethical self-consciousness, death and gender in Western liberal thought, becomes both "what is left behind" and "what is drawn in". These contradictory processes are very evident in the way in which domesticity is incorporated into the penal sphere. Control by neglect, control by coercion and control by "soft" promises of finely measured out increases of family contact are the conditions that circumscribe the work of labouring and loving in the penal sphere in New South Wales.

The discourse of prison life as the sphere of courage and physicality coexists — and very uneasily — with the alternative interpretation of penality as the site of the scientific management of reformation. Nevertheless the post-Nagle confrontations between the representatives of the two schools in the New South Wales penal system indicate that the introduction of a separate set of specialist experts in the field of human management has paradoxically reinforced rather than undermined the relationship between prisoners and prison officers as that of soldiers and enemies.

In this increaingly condensed contradiction between the two moralities (domestic and legal-penal) the experiences of women who do the work of reproducing the "self" of men degraded by the punishment of imprisonment becomes an extraordinarily condensed version of the duality of social control that impinges on the day to day lives of all women: that they are socially controlled to be the controllers.

The prison, as the site of the contradictory discourses of segregation, correction and normalisation, is part of the wider network of penal control comprising a range of forms of surveillance and "care" operating out in the community. The way that the contradictory experiences of penality and domesticity are reworked when punishment is extended to men outside of the institutional prison is examined in the following chapter.

NOTES

1   Cited in Ungerson, C, *Policy is Personal: Sex, Gender and Informal Care* (1987) at 147.

2   Robinson, P, *Women of Botany Bay: a reinterpretation of the role of women in the origins of Australian society* (1988) at 127–8.

3   Raymond, J, "Bringing Up Children Alone: Policies for Sole Parents", Social Security Review Issues Paper No 3, Woden: Department of Social Security, 1987 at 77.

4   Anderson, N, *Prisoners' Families: Reports I & II* (1965); Jones, J, "Prisoners and their Families", unpublished PhD thesis, Melbourne: Monash University Department of Anthropology and Sociology, (1983).

5   Kemp, B, Cheron, M, McClelland M and Cooney, G, *The Effects of Separation on Marital Relationships of Prisoners and Their Wives*, Research and Statistics Division, Research Publication No 2. Sydney: Department of Corrective Services, 1982.

6   Morris, P, Prisoners and their Families (1965); Jones, above n4 at 30.

7   Bryson, L, "Welfare Issues of the Eighties" ch 16 in Najman, J and Western, J, *A Sociology of Australian Society: Introductory Readings* (1988) at 489–509.

8   Graham, H, "Caring: a labour of love" ch 1 in Finch, J and Groves, D, *A Labour of Love: women, work and caring* (1983) at 30.

9   Gittings, D, *The Family in Question* (1993) at 47.

10   Jones, above n4 at vi.

11   Above n5 at 7.

12   Above n8 at 24–25.

13   Jones, above n4 at 223.

14 Visits to minimum security are more likely to be weekend visits only.

15 Graham, H, "Coping: or how mothers are seen and not heard" in Friedman, S and Sarah, E (eds) *On the Problem of Men* (1982) at 105.

16 Jordan, A, "Lone Parent — and Wage-Earner? Employment Prospects of Sole-parent Pensioners", Discussion Paper No 31, Social Security Review Series, Woden: Department of Social Security, 1989 at 114.

17 Id at 11.

18 Cass, B and O'Loughlin, M, "The Needs of Single Parents" (1984) *Australian Society* 1 Jan 1984 at 20–22.

19 Saunders, P and Whiteford, P, "Pricing the poverty pledge" *Australian Society* Sep 1987 at 23.

20 Dewdney, M, Swarris, K and Miner, M, "The History and Administration of the New South Wales Work Release Scheme — 1969-1977" (Publication No 16), Sydney: New South Wales Department of Corrective Services, 1978 at 13, 14, 25, 43; Gorta, A and Cooney, G, "What makes a good parolee?" (1983) 16 *ANZ J Crim* 106–118.

21 Kemeney, J, "The Political Economy of Housing" in Wheelwright, E and Buckley, K (eds), *Essays in the Political Economy of Australian Capitalism* (vol 4, 1980) at 175; Milligan, V, "The State and Housing: Questions of Social Policy and Social Change" in Graycar, A (ed), *Retreat from the Welfare State* (1983); Harman, E, "Capitalism, Patriarchy and the City" ch5 in Baldock, C and Cass, B (eds) *Women, Social Welfare and the State* (1983).

22 Watson, S, *Accommodating Inequality: Gender and Housing* (1988).

23 Hounslow, B, Stephenson, A, Stewart, J and Crancher, J, *Children of Imprisoned Parents*, Sydney: Family and Childrens's Service Agency (Social Research and Evaluation Ltd), Ministry of Youth and Community Services, 1982 at 7 in Appendix; Jones, above n4 at 227.

24 Morris, above n6 at 74–80; Jones, above n4 at 227.

25 The family policies that affected women in the period 1986–1988 are described here. The 1988–1990 changes to those policies are briefly covered in the epilogue in chapter nine.

26 Kinsey, R, Lea, J and Young, J, *Losing the Fight against Crime* (1986) at 47; Minnery, J, *Crime Perception and Victimisation of Inner City Residents* (1986).

27 Glezer, H, "Mothers in the Workforce" (1988) 21 *Family Matters* at 30–34.

28 Frey, D, "Survey of Sole Parent Pensioners' Workforce Barriers" Social Security Review Discussion Paper No 12, Woden: Department of Social Security, 1986 at 1–2.

29 Ibid

30 Above n27 at 31.

31 These experiences of women in New South Wales reinforce the evidence from virtually all other reports of families of prisoners that social isolation is one of the major "hidden punishments" that they experience.

32 Above n5.

33 It would be wrong to imply that the report caused the changes, it is more probable that the report and the improved visiting conditions were both facets of a more general diffuse reorientation to the relationship between domestic and penal life, with New South Wales lagging a decade behind the USA in this reformist stance.

34 Above n15.

35 Ibid.

36 Fishman, S, *Women at the Wall* (1991) at 272.

37 Lockwood, D, "Maintaining Manhood. Prison violence precipitated by aggressive sexual overtures", paper presented at the annual meetings of the Academy of Criminal Justice Sciences, New Orleans, March 1978; Lockwood, D, *Prison Sexual Violence* (1980).

38 Anderson, T, *Inside Outlaws* (1989) at 122.

39 Yeatman, A, "Despotism and Civil Society: the limits of patriarchal citizenship" paper presented to the XIIth world congress, International Political Science Association, Rio de Janeiro, Brazil: 9–14 August 1982.

40 Id at 3.

41 Id at 2.

42 Id at 6.

43 Donaldson, M, "Labouring Men: Love, Sex and Strife" (1987) 23/2 *ANZ J Sociol* 165–184, at 172.

44 Id at 173. Whether this is the way that women experience that relationship is not a part of that research. Both Donaldson's research and the analysis of sexuality in this thesis are focusing on the social construction of the relationship of sexuality.

45 Ibid.

46 Jones, above n4 at 399.

47 Smith, S, "Neglect as Control: prisoners' wives", paper presented to the XIVth Annual Conference of the European Group for the Study of Deviance and Social Control, September 1986.

48 Weatherburn, D, "Reducing the New South Wales Prison Population: sentencing reform and early release" (1986) 10 *Crim LJ* 121–138, at 137.

49 Jones, above n4 at 348–353.

50 Bell, R, Edwards, D and Wagner, H, *Political Power: a reader in theory and research* (1969) at v.

51 Or the more rewarding maximum security prisons such as Parklea.

52 King, cited in Donaldson, above n43 at 177.

53 This is a common finding in the theses of Smith (above n47) and Jones (above n4).

54 Porritt, D, "Reasons For Escape: reported by recaptured escapees", Sydney: New South Wales Department of Correctives Services, Research and Statistics Division, 1987; Gorta, A and Nguyen, M, *An Analysis of Interviews with Recaptured Escapees: some suggestions of reasons for escape*, Sydney: Research and Statistics Division, New South Wales Department of Corrective Services, 1988.

55   Above n8 at 29.

56   Connell, R W, *Gender and Power: Society, the Person and Sexual Politics* (1987) at 183–188.

57   Above n8 at 17.

58   Ungerson, above n1 at 142–143.

59   Cited in Arbler, S and Gilbert, N, "Men: the forgotten carers" (1989) 23/1 *Sociology* 111–119 at 116–117.

60   Jones, above n4; Wilson, G, "I Know While He is in Prison He's Safe" (1984) *New Society* 1 Nov 1984 at 172–4; Smith, above n47.

61   Wilson, id at 172–175.

62   Jones, above n4.

63   Smith, above n47.

64   Jones, above n4 at 522.

65   Id at 200.

66   Id at 201.

67   Ibid.

68   Ibid.

69   Above n36 at 204–205.

70   Id at 273.

71   Smith, above n47.

72   Id at 13.

73   Id at 8-9.

74   Crosthwaite, A, "Punishment for Whom? the Prisoner or his Wife?" (1975) 19/3 *Int J Offend Ther & Comp Crim* 275–284 at 275.

75   Hounslow et al, above n23 at 7.

76   Id at 149. Nevertheless in Britain in the late 1980s and early 1990s there has been a proliferation of non-funded family support groups resulting in the establishment of a Federation of Prisoners' Families Support Groups in 1991. This parallels a similar awakening consciousness and development of groups around Australia in the 1990s although there is no parallel federal body to act as a network of support and information.

77   This is not a necessarily definitive account of all "family of prisoners" groups. The very characteristics of the groups that make them fragile also means that they are relatively invisible.

78   Anderson, above n4 at 19.

79   Aitkin, J and Gartrell, G, *Sentenced to Life: Management of Life Sentence Prisoners in New South Wales Gaols*, Sydney: Criminology Research Council, 1981–1982.

80   Ibid; Merriman, P, "The Families of Long-term Prisoners" (1979) 26 *Probation Journal* 114–119.

81   In personal conversation (1986).

82   Jones, above n4 at 433.

83   Lovejoy, F and Barbaroza, E, "Gender Issues in Prison Visiting", unpublished paper presented at the Australian and New Zealand Society

of Criminology Third Annual Conference, 24–26 August 1987, in their review of the 'families of prisoners' literature.

84   Ungerson, above n1 at 144–146 & ch5.

85   Hounslow et al, above n23 at 26–27.

86   Jones, above n4 at 285–297.

87   Id at 300.

88   Finch, J, *Family Obligations and Social Change* (1989).

89   Hounslow et al, above n23 at 149.

90   Above n79 at 6.

91   Yeatman, A, "Feminism, Postmodernism and Sociology: versions II & I" unpublished paper (1990), ver 1 in Nicholson, L (ed), *Feminism/Post-modernism* (1990) at 15.

92   Although the domestication of New South Wales prisons has led to the employment of some women in custodial, corrective and administrative positions, masculinity is the continuing dominant characteristic of prison life in New South Wales.

93   Lloyd, G, "Selfhood, War and Masculinity" in Pateman, C and Gross, E (eds) *Feminist Challenges: Social and Political Theory* (1986).

7

DOMESTICITY AND
COMMUNITY CONTROL

Marriage and family are the most effective correctional institutions we have.[1]

THE EXPANSION OF COMMUNITY BASED CONTROLS IN
NEW SOUTH WALES

Increasingly, over the period from 1960 to the late 1980s the moral sphere of domesticity was becoming incorporated into the moral sphere of penality in New South Wales in more manifest forms. The site of social control in New South Wales was more and more likely to be the home in terms of both the numbers and of the relative rates of people under some form of penal control and surveillance.

There are two models of the relationship between the prison and the home that form the different frameworks for describing the dynamics of this new partnership between the two incompatible spheres of morality — penality and domesticity:

1   The techno-reformist linear model constitutes the prison and the home as the two end points in the career of the sentenced offender as he travels from the Segregative though the Corrective to the Normalising sequences of his time under penal control.

2   The radical critique of penality posits the relationship between the two spheres as having a cyclical component: an "iatrogenic feedback loop" between prison and home.[2]

Chapter two referred to Cohen's introduction of the term "feedback loop" to describe the relationship between control in the community and imprisonment. He describes the increase in the use of community based controls through a fishing net analogy. However a more useful metaphor in the case of families of men on parole, probation or other forms of home based surveillance in New South Wales might be to describe the home as a "fishing pond", with homes and local neighbourhoods of ex-prisoners making particularly useful catchment areas for the fishing expeditions of policemen. The relative merits of the two models are examined through the accounts of the twenty-seven women who have had some experience of living with men on conditional liberty. However, prior to investigating the impact of the expansion of penality into the home as it affected the day to day lives of women as partners or parents of sentenced men, this chapter outlines the various forms of extensions of penal control as they have occurred in New South Wales in the past three decades.

THE EXTENSION OF PENAL CONTROL OUTSIDE PRISON WALLS IN NEW SOUTH WALES (1950s to 1980s)

The unlinear model is the dominant paradigm framing the official discourses of penal control in New South Wales. There were several ways in which penality extended outside of prison walls in New South Wales by the early 1980s. These included:

Back End Programmes

> Day Leave
> Work Release I
> Work Release II (Home Release)
> Parole
> Release on Licence
> After Care Probation

Front End Programmes or Alternatives to Imprisonment

> Probation
> Community Service Orders
> Day Attendance Centres
> Periodic Detention
> Bail

The various programmes were introduced with varying degrees of contestation. Their introduction or remodification represent a series of victories or failures in the battles between the liberal reformists of the rational scientific management school of penal control and the less cohesive group of politicians, judiciary, penal administrators, or energetic pressure groups who loosely comprise the "law and order" school in the State.[3] Very often the key decisions about their introduction or modification were made not on the basis of clearly spelt out ideological positions but as a result of ad hoc decision-making as responses to specific political crises. It is in the debates over the introduction or modifications of these programmes that the assumptions about the contradictoriness or the complementarity of domestic and penal life as the two spheres of social control can be disentangled.

GENERAL

There were two key eras in the construction of the new partnership between prison and home as the two sites of punitive surveillance in New South Wales. The first from the 1950s to the mid 1960s reflected the optimistic positivism and the importance of the scientific rationalists. The significant term characterising the ideology underpinning this era was "rehabilitation". Through the promise of a reduction in recidivism by a focus on the individual psychological characteristics of the offender the "human scientists" made a major influence on penal policies that increasingly linked the prison and the home, firstly through the corrective and particularly the normalising moments within prison and then through the extension of penal surveillance out in "the community" which in the majority of cases meant the prisoner's day to day life at work and in the home. "Rehabilitative" principles of the normalising processes within prison, and the extension of control after prison, were linked explicitly by the Superintendent of Berrima Training Centre in 1949:

> To release these prisoners without some form of further guidance is like pruning and cultivating a tree until it promises to bear fruit and then neglecting it.[4]

The network of knowledges and psychologically oriented practices comprising the "rehabilitative" discourses were designed to extend from pre-sentence, through imprisonment and into the "after-care" of people defined as offenders. Initially in this period it was assumed that there would be perfect accord between the legal rational authority of the judicidary and the scientific rational control of the executive. The New South Wales Attorney General expressed this optimistic belief in 1950:

> ... judges feel deeply the responsibility of sentencing men and women without adequate information as to the background, the upbringing, the education and the mental condition of such persons. All these data will be available to judges before the sentencing of convicted persons, but more than that, the scheme will embrace after-care and supervision of persons on probation for any period.[5]

The period 1950–1951 was a key one in the establishment of this orientation. In that year prisoner after-care, adult probation and the Parole Board were all established.[6] Frank Hayes'[7] sensitive reflections on the initial introduction of parole in 1951 convey the atmosphere of the discourses surrounding the beginnings of the scheme: a belief that Australia was lagging behind the more "progressive" penal systems of America, a commitment to case work based on a cloudily defined professionalism,[8] a belief in rehabilitation through individual effort,[9] the justification for building up dossiers of information on the positivistic basis of the promise of the potential moral redemption of the offender,[10] the constitution of the main structure of the service as the mobilisation of voluntary community based resources,[11] and an acute sense of the practical limitations of working within a penal authority oriented to segregation.

This autobiographical account emphasises the liberal individualism in this remedial approach and from this period on there was a sense of parole as representing a liberalism embattled within an antagonistic conservative and punitive organisation, that continued into the 1970s naming of the welfare space in Long Bay as *Camelot*.

By the late 1960s and early 1970s however the promise but not the authority of the scientific managers was being undermined as the academic and administrative debates about penal control in New South Wales reflected the impact of the American and European discourses exemplified by the powerful two words of Martinson's critique of penal positivism: "nothing works". The New South Wales experience also parallelled the dynamics of the overseas prison experiences as, in Zimring's words, the prisoner struggles within the gaols "blew the cover on the "rehabilitative ideal".[12]

However in the second era, from the late 1960s on, the scientific managers were able to retain their claims to authority within the legal penal sphere by reworking the debates about recidivism and rehabilitation away from control over the individual in terms of his earlier psychological predisposition to criminality to the revised claim that they were able to provide programmes of control over the offender that would ameliorate the criminogenic effect of prison itself. It is notable that the major expansion of penal control in New South Wales occurred after this redefinition of scientific rationality. Thus the New South Wales experience neatly reinforced Foucault's account of the way that knowledge and power intersect in penal life with the very failure of imprisonment reproducing the conditions through which the experts are able to reassert their claims to authority.

WORK RELEASE, DAY LEAVE, WEEKEND LEAVE

The work release programme inroduced in New South Wales in 1969 was heavily influenced by the schemes introduced twenty or thirty years earlier in the United States and Northern Europe.[13] By the late sixties however home leave and work release programmes were specifically introduced as "normalising" programmes to counteract the criminogenic and the infantilising aspects of imprisonment. In their report on life sentence prisoners two members of the Indeterminate Sentence Committee[14] cite the views of one gaol superintendent that to manage to exist in prison these prisoners have to

> learn to manipulate both fellow inmates and the gaol system. In short they have to learn a fair amount of criminal behaviour — manipulating people, cheating, lying, standing over others, etc.[15]

The same issue of the tension between segregation and reintegration is represented, although from a slightly different perspective, by one prisoner talking to Hounslow et al in the 1982 study of children of imprisoned parents: "They belt you for nine years and rehabilitate you for the tenth."[16]

The normalising process is presented as a calculated and scientifically produced programme necessitating two years of gradual and measured re-entry into "the community".

> From trials and past experience it has been found that gradual re-entry into the community should be spread over approximately two years (that is from the first day leave until full time work release). If it is any shorter inmates suffer too much shock at the sudden changes in their lives. If it is any longer

194

than two years then the pressure of being neither free nor imprisoned becomes too great.[17]

Although the graduated releases through day leave and weekend leave were introduced within the treatment paradigm promoting "reintegration", they were also quite explicitly legitimated within the discourses of punitive control. In the 1976 interstate conference on penal philosophies and practices that had been organised in response to the prison crises of the early 1970s, the "home leave" schemes in New Zealand were recommended to Australian penal administrators because

... home leave has turned out, as we expected, to have a strong controlling effect on the institutional conduct of inmates.[18]

The work release programme explicitly links the spheres of domesticity and penality. It is specifically domesticity in terms of the man's role as income earner providing for his dependents that is central to the discourse here:

(the) advantages (of the scheme) are best realized when men on work release are placed in jobs carefully suited to their abilities and interests, *when provision is made for home visits*, when the offender contributes towards his board at the institution and *sends money to his dependents thereby defraying some of the costs of prison administration, of social services to his family* and contributing to revenue in the form of income.[19]

The first three prisoners on whom the programme was initially based were all "married with dependents"[20] and even after the selection criteria were widened and the number of prisoners in the programme had grown to over 20, the prisoner described as being the ideal candidate for entry into the work release programme was still defined as "a stable family man with dependents ..."[21]

As in all other forms of works release programmes re-entering the community in the New South Wales scheme specifically excluded re-entering one of the most normal sites of communal life. Jimmy Boyle describes the risks of humiliation for the prisoner and his family when prisoners celebrate their conditional release back into the community by behaving normally in this "normalising" phase of penality. On his entry to the Edinburgh work release prison one of his fellow prisoners

... describes this particular part of the sentence as 'running the gauntlet'. He expands on this saying that if a few minutes late on returning, or smelling of drink, you get thrown in the punishment cells. He described one occasion when it happened to him. He arrived back after a couple of pints but took some mints to cover the smell ... they took him to the punishment cells and kept him there overnight ... on occasions they've been in a pub and a prison officer has walked in and they've all ducked under the table ... if any of them are with their girlfriends. It is embarrassing.[22]

What seems clear then is that the "normal" domestic life as it is constituted within the programme does not mean "normal" life as the prisoner and the woman who is the partner or parent of the prisoner might interpret it. In the New South Wales scheme in 1981 church going was allowed but "community" otherwise extended only to the home, the work place or these specifically defined forms of recreation and leisure that reflect a very specific construction of "normality":

> extensive community involvement was encouraged through provision of weekend leave to be earned by participating in community service projects, organisation of sporting teams, encouragement of evening education, attendance at local technical colleges, local church services or district meetings of Alcoholics Anonymous.

Unsurprisingly then it is a shift to middle class values that is used as the criteria for success in one of the evaluative studies that the New South Wales report on work release approvingly cites

> two well controlled research studies provide some preliminary data on the effectiveness of particular work release schemes in changing inmate attitudes and behaviour ... in Florida in 1973 Waldo, Chiricos and Dobring concluded that work release participants do not have significantly better attitudes ... the attitudes that were studied comprised ... achievement motivation ... self esteem and a shift from 'lower class' to 'middle class' orientations.[23]

The narrow interpretation of "normality" as the change of prisoners' attitudes to a set of values fitting to a "middle class" life style means that the focus of the evaluation of work release glosses over the extensive practical problems that partners or parents of prisoners can face in this manifest intersection between penal and domestic life. Whilst the report on the New South Wales Work Release Scheme emphasised that half of the prisoners "were favourably disposed" towards making payments to dependents, in the appendices of the report (but included without any further comment or analysis) is the concern, expressed in a comment by the Superintendent of the scheme, that the income of the partner of the prisoner can be in jeopardy as a result of the complex intersection between prison, social security and domestic life brought about by this normalising moment of penality. Penality — comprising segregation, correction then normalisation — draws the prisoner into a cycle of restriction from, access to, then restriction from, waged work. The income of the family outside then follows a parallel cycle but in this case the cycle is one of dependence on social security, restriction on access to that form of material support when the man's income from the work release scheme is supposed once again to become the family's support, then once the period of imprisonment is at an end, and his wage from the work release scheme is lost,[24] the partner outside has to re-apply once more for full support from social security. In some cases this led to a lengthy period without resources:

> Superintendent's evaluation of the (past) scheme — problems for prisoner: on removal, the wife waits for six weeks for social security payments.[25]

PAROLE AND AFTER CARE PROBATION

Release on licence under the control of parole supervision constituted as professional care was introduced in 1951 in New South Wales but it was with the *Parole of Prisoners Act* in 1966 that prisoners were released as parolees. The concomitant statutory obligation that was placed on parole officers to maintain supervision of parolees and to prepare pre-release reports entrenched parole as an intrinsic element in the disciplinary and knowledge network of the penal sphere. The department's annual reports throughout the 1970s and 1980s detail the contradictions experienced by the new professionals because of the competing claims of record keeping and "caring".

The claims to scientific rationalist authority that underpinned the introduction of the parole service meant that there was a strong emphasis on tertiary qualifications and professionalism. From the beginning this reworking of penal control as early release in "the community" under penal surveillance was closely associated with the growth of social welfare as a form of less obviously overt control in the community:

> The growth of the parole service as an integral part of the Prison Department and later the Deparment of Corrective Services has facilitated the growth of institutional social work (in the state).[26]

The development of the schools of social work in the two universities closely parallelled the growth of professionalism through parole officers' claims to control rehabilitation within the penal sphere. By the late 1960s, however, the major ideology of rehabilitation upon which the introduction of the system of parole had been legitimated had been undermined.[27] In addition in 1978 the Nagle Report condemned several aspects of the way that Parole was operating in the State.[28]

PAROLE IN THE LATE 1970s

Although the positivistic promise of "rehabilitation" was diminished by this time, back end forms of community control became increasingly popular in New South Wales, as in all Western penal systems, as politicians faced the common problem of prison overcrowding in an era characterised by the socially explosive mixture of a consumerist culture, a restructured labour market that dispossessed signicant sections of the paid work force and a familial-political economy in which increasing claims were being made on the welfare and penal budgets of the state. The 1970s saw an escalation in imprisonment costs per prisoner. Between 1970 to 1979 the increase in costs of incarceration per prisoner was 500 per cent over the increase in the preceding decade.[29] Moreover this increase was occurring during a period of fiscal crisis.[30] The concern about the exponential increase in the costs of imprisonment led to an interstate meeting of Correctional Ministers in 1987 at which it was predicted that there was likely to be a 50 per cent increase in the national prison population in the period 1987–1997 which would result in "at least a $750

197

million capital expenditure programme with a subsequent increase of $300 million in recurrent expenditure".[31]

Weatherburn details the several New South Wales legislative attempts to reduce prison overcrowding by various forms of back end schemes, from the *Parole of Prisoners Act* in 1966 to the *Probation and Parole Act* in 1983.[32]

In 1973 there were 11,190 people under penal control in New South Wales who comprised prisoners in gaols, on periodic detention, on probation and on parole. By 1987 after an initial decline in prison numbers in the early 1970s, the total had increased to 16,734 and the range of forms of control had extended to include Community Service Orders and After Care Probation.[33] Most significantly however, the prison population increased in spite of the legislative attempts to reduce prison numbers.[34] In New South Wales, as in other States, the penal debates in this period were over the relative ideological merits of rehabilitation and reintegration, the clash between the legal rational power of the judiciary and the scientific rationality of prison administrators, and the pragmatic concerns about imprisonment costs. However added to these contestations was the specific circumstance of bribery and corruption over prison releases.

The Jackson Release on Licence Scheme was introduced in 1982. Under this programme over 1,000 prisoners were released on licence in the fifteen months of the scheme's run. The corruption surrounding the programme severely affected the implementation of parole. In the media scandals and hyperbole about "dangerous prisoners" that followed the scheme, the Parole Board reduced the rate of prisoners granted release on parole from 90 per cent to 30 per cent and this reduction was largely unrelated to either the seriousness of the offence or the prior criminal record of the offender.[35]

The relative benefits of parole over the Jackson release programme, in terms of the recidividism rates[36] of the two forms of conditional liberty, were the subject of a Department of Corrective Services study in the mid 1980s.[37] The research showed that parole supervision was itself criminogenic. In the contrast between the data for prisoners released without and with parole supervision, the recidivism figure for the former was 30.5 per cent and for the latter, 46 per cent.[38] Moreover the figure for return to prison because of further crimes committed after release, for both groups, was the same: 30 per cent. The difference between the two was mainly attributable to the 10.4 per cent of parolees who were reimprisoned for violations of the conditions of their parole. Interestingly the Department reports this study as indicating the success of their parole programme.[39] This is in marked contrast to Weatherburn's description of the Jackson Release on License Scheme as comparatively "spectacularly successful in reducing prison populations."[40]

If the release on licence scheme was measurably more successful than release on parole why did the parole system regain its place as the major form of release from prison? One answer lies in the level of corruption surrounding the Jackson Early Release on Licence Scheme that eventuated in the imprisonment of the Minister responsible for its introduction and administration and made both the penal legislative and executive bodies wary of future accusations of "leniency", a term that by then was conflated in the media discourse with "scandal". However Weatherburn and Janet Chan, in separate papers, indicate that there were other reasons associated more with the tensions inherent in any penal system comprising contradictory sets of discourses.[41] In this then the battles within the New South Wales system closely parallel the more general tensions between the judiciary and the executive branches of the penal sphere. O'Malley describes how, in the corporate era of capitalism in the late nineteenth century, the moral authority of legal rationality was reinforced by the scientific rationality of the human managers. However, the two coexisted in uneasy coalition throughout the twentieth century. There was bitter resentment amongst the New South Wales judiciary over the encroaching power of the executive especially as it was manifested in its power to usurp the legal rational authority of the courts through both the remissions and the release on licence scheme.[42] This bitterness was manifested in closely calculated political attacks on remission provisions by the judiciary in the courts to what Brown describes as "a pre-alerted press".[43]

Chan points out that in this battle over indeterminacy or determinacy in sentencing, as it was played out in the 1970s and 1980s, there were three major groups of contestants.[44] The prison administrators in their control over release dates sought in part to balance biases in judicial sentencing as well as to implement their scientific rational authority as human managers. The judiciary were opposed to this executive control over their power to punish. Parole could be reconstituted as it had been in Victoria to return power back to the bench. The third group of power holders in these decisions about the legitimate basis of the power to punish were the politicians. The pressures on politicians are complex. Their own power is mitigated by the broader political economic climate in which they operate, the bureaucratic systems they inherit in which various factions have an already established authority, as well as the specific exigencies of media sensationalism. The major force behind the media presentation of penal issues was the drive for high viewer or readership ratings which meant that prison stories emphasised the frightening or the lurid aspect of crime and imprisonment.[45] In New South Wales in the mid 1980s politicians responded in an ad hoc fashion to these various and contradictory pressures by taking "a strong line on law and order" at the same time as they attempted to keep control over the resulting increase in the costs of penal control. Politicians then interpreted parole in quite a different light than did either the liberal rationalists of the judiciary or the scientific rationalists, the managers of human behaviour within the prison administration. Releasing prisoners out into the community at the relatively invisible back end of imprisonment enabled politicians to emphasise their commitment to controlling crime in the streets whilst having the short-term effect of

199

keeping prison population rates down to manageable levels. The possibility that the longer term consequences of these back end solutions was an *increase* in imprisonment rates was put to one side in the pragmatic push to be seen to be able to control the law and order portfolio.[46]

By the early 1980s, New South Wales was facing the dilemma outlined by Joan Petersilia in her influential paper on the contradictions of community corrections in the United States.[47] The dilemma resulted from the volatile combination of three factors: increasing numbers of people coming before the courts, increasing pressures on state budgets which reduced the comparative rate of spending on both prison and "community" forms of control, and public concern, fed and politicised by the media, about the perceived ineffectiveness of non-imprisonment penalities. In addition, the prison administrators were interpreting the deinstitution-alisation of psychiatric control through the Richmond Report as adding to the problems of prison overcrowding.[48]

The solution was the design and implementation of penal programmes that promised to "reduce prison populations without serious hazards to the general public".[49] These schemes were the Intensive Surveillance Programmes (ISP) that were designed to:

> fulfil the public's expectations for harsh and punitive sentencing, but do so less expensively, and without jeopardizing the public's safety.[50]

The 1983 *Probation and Parole Act* was an attempt to relieve the crisis of prison overcrowding in New South Wales after the rise and fall of the notorious release on licence scheme. However the judiciary readjusted their sentencing practices in resistance to what they saw as an attempt to reduce the length of effective sentences.[51] This obduracy of the sentencers exacerbated the growth in prison numbers in the 1980s. The other elements adding to the pressures on imprisonment were the increased investments in policing and the creation of new offences.[52] So by 1986, prisoners were sleeping three to a cell in the one man cells at the Central Industrial Prison, and overcrowding was becoming the basis for increasing tensions within the prisons with for example the principal grievance of the prisoner "disturbance" in the CIP in September that year listed as overcrowding.[53] Moreover the parole professionals were arguing that the ad hoc nature of the Act and its implementation were creating greater confusions for them. In addition, they were having to face increased prisoner hostility as a result of the increased uncertainties that the Act created.[54] In the face of these increasing tensions by the late 1980s both the New South Wales Minister, senior members of the parole service and the prison administration, and some members of the judiciary were indicating that an intensive surveillance scheme, home imprisonment, would shortly be added to the forms of penal control available to the sentencing authorities.[55] The universality of the attraction of intensive surveillance and home detention for the three otherwise contending authorities lay in its many-sided appeal. For the legal rational authorities, the magistrates, Home Detention controlled not only the prisoner but also the parole officers who were being defined as too oriented to being "advocates" rather than controllers of prisoners on conditional liberty.[56] The probation and parole authorities saw in home detentention a chance to revive their case work skills through a revival of the promise of rehabilitation and reintegregation,[57] as well as the possibility that the surveillance and care aspects of community control could be separated with private security firms taking on the "punitive" aspects of control as surveillance of specific groups of home detainees such as fine defaulters, thus leaving the professionals free to focus on the human management aspects of those needing more personal care.[58] For the political and economic rationalists within the prison bureaucracy intensive surveillance offered the chance to extend early release to increasingly "hard" line prisoners, taking the pressure off the increasing crisis of prison overcrowding without having to choose between what Weatherburn describes as the Scylla and Charybdis of the two political risky choices of increasing legislative control over sentencing or of building new prisons.

The electronically monitored form of home detention was introduced by the Liberal administration in 1992. However, a form of home detention had already been in operation in New South Wales in the form of one of the "releases under community control" schemes. This was the Work Release II (home release) programme.

HOME IMPRISONMENT

The Work Release II (home release) programme operated from 1976 until its decline as a result of the notorious 1982 Early Release Scheme. Prisoners controlled in this programme worked at the Parramatta Linen Service during the day but were allowed to return to their own homes under conditions that virtually constituted the home as a place of detention in the evening and at night.[59] The intersection of penality and domesticity as sites of morality and control was carefully constructed in this programme with very specific criteria being laid down restricting access to the programme to those prisoners who were

> serving a first prison sentence for a non violent offence and had a *viable family unit with dependent children or parents*.[60]

The singular conditions under which the programme was introduced are worth detailing here as they indicate the way that the boundaries between the two spheres of morality were explictly renegotiated as a response to the specific political economy of the locality in which the programme was set. Fiori Rinaldi has pointed out that this first reintroduction (since the early forms of home based control under colonisation) of constituting the home as the site of control occurred without any claims by the government that the programme was an "enlightened penological advance.[61] It was rather the result of a very pragmatic compromise between the Government that had spent $10 million dollars on a new prison laundry at Parramatta and a union movement that was strongly resisting the introduction of cheap prison labour in an area particularly hard hit by unemployment. One alternative was to employ all prisoners at award wages but this costly move was avoided by allowing twenty prisoners release from prison to live with their families during the day whilst working for award wages during the "peak crime period" shift of 3pm to 11pm. The new home release prisoners were a trade-off in the agreement between the unions and the prison authorities that then allowed most of the work to be done by conventional prison labour at rates of $14 a week.[62]

It was this programme that fell into decline as a result of the introduction and subsequent collapse of the early release scheme in 1982–83. By the late 1980s however, the ground was set for its reintroduction. The penal administrators under the Labour administration had plans to reintroduce Home Detention as a back end programme to reduce prison overcrowding whilst assuaging judicial and public fears about "leniency". However before the programme could be implemented the Labour government lost office and it was another four years before home imprisonment was reintroduced into the penal sytem in New South Wales.

In summary, in New South Wales the period 1986 to 1988 was one in which the number of people under penal surveillance was increasing, whilst there was increasing tension between the various actors within the legal-penal sphere, that reflected and amplified the stresses deriving from the structural crises of the wider familial-political economy. As a consequence, the number of people in prison was accelerating but prison was increasingly becoming the site for the "hard cases" as a range of non-institutional forms of control in the form of both back and front end alternatives to imprisonment were impinging on the lives of a wider range of "offenders". Moreover, these non-institutional controls were feeding back into the prison a significant proportion of people further criminalised by the very processes that were nominally aimed at "normalisation".

Markedly omitted from the discourses constituting this expansion of penality was the extent to which these programmes further exploited the labour of women who were providing the infrastructure of domesticity on which this widening network of penal surveillance was based. This omission is despite the extensive literature on the range of "community controls" and their effectiveness. The "family" is included as a factor in the vast array of evaluations of recidividism.[63] However the "cognitive passion" of the professional programme evaluators fits neatly into Yeatman's description of the social sciences as blinded by a dual conflation with "familism" masking the work of individual women within the family through the constitution of the home as the site of a division of labour centred on the "natural" dispositions of women to love and care and "community control" masking significance of the home as the social space within which prisoners come to be reconstituted as citizens. Chapter three details the way that the reformist technologists conflate the terms community, family and women in their investigations of families of prisoners as community resources for the prison service. One of the most recent Australian texts on punishment and control reflects this process of invisibilising through conflation. John Braithwaite's 1989 sociological discussion of the possibility of reducing crime rates by refocusing punishment away from imprisonment through programmes of "reintegrative shaming" describes the relationship between the home and the legal-penal sphere as complementary sites of moral control because in Silberman's words,

> the most compelling reason for going straight is that young men fall in love and want to marry and have children. Marriage and the family are the most effective correctional institutions we have.[64]

However he gives no details about the import of this relationship for the women who are part of this useful compact between penal and domestic control in the community.

Nevertheless the women who talked about their experiences of being caught up into the system of "community controls" in New South Wales in the early and mid 1980s indicate that the unpaid work of the labour of loving in this intersection of prison and home is extensive.

Twenty-seven of the women visiting men in gaol in these interviews had had some earlier experience of their partner or son being controlled under one or more forms of these non-institutionally based punishments. The work of caring in each of its three aspects, as material, emotional and political labour, was in several ways amplified for these women when the prisoner was under these alternative forms of surveillance.

LABOURING, LOVING AND CONTROLLING UNDER CONDITIONS OF COMMUNITY BASED PENALITY

Both the malleability and invisibility of domestic labour becomes even more evident when punishment by institutionalised imprisonment merges through the normalising processes of penality into punishment in the "community".

The material, emotional and political aspects of the work of caring become even more densely interwoven when prisoners are controlled from home. In the minute to minute life of family interaction there are significant stresses of caring and controlling when partners or parents and prisoners experience the tensions of the contradictions between domestic and penal control. Although it is the density of this singular form of caring work that must be emphasised the different aspects of the work of caring that women do under these circumstances is separated out here as:

- culpability as a central aspect of the work of caring for prisoners on conditional liberty;

- emotional work and social control;

- mediating and negotiating work; and

- material costs to women when home is the site of "resource and resolve".

1 CULPABILITY AS A CENTRAL ASPECT OF CARING WORK OF PARTNERS OR PARENTS IN COMMUNITY BASED CONTROL

The Chairman of the New South Wales Department of Corrective Services argued in 1984 that the prisoners released under some form of conditional liberty were always controlled in the end because there are "powerful sanctions under existing legislation for people who are on conditional liberty to be easily returned to gaol".[65]

The release into the care of the partner or parent is always underwritten by this fear of return to prison. This form of penal control then incorporates the exploitation of that aspect of caring labour identified by Hilary Graham as being a significant part of coping work: culpability. The element of culpability that distinguishes caring work means that parents and partners of prisoners on parole are exposed to special stresses:

> **Olive: Son now in prison after previous period of imprisonment followed by parole**
>
> I think (the tension) is worse than in gaol. *Why?* If he goes out he might forget, go to the pictures or something, he might forget, then they can pull his parole. His life isn't his own. The last parole officer was really good, but there were a couple if he was ten minutes late they were willing to pull his parole. I worry if he doesn't get there on time. There's more tension at home than when he's in here. It's really not my responsibility but he's still my child. I've still got to stick with him. I want to see him come good. I say to him — he's got to do it.

This experience exemplifies not only the intensification of the hidden punishment that is extended to families of men on parole but the particular skill of sensitivity demanded of the controlling work of parents and partners. Penality is constituted as a sequence of different moments parallel to the stages of family life. Both are constituted as a series of different stages in the development of the personality of the individual. In this paradigm of penality as a progression to "maturity", parole parallels the period described by Donzelot as being the time when parenthood becomes the difficult balancing act of control — the period of adolescence in which the parents have to weigh the contradictory demands of "freedom" and "containment" to secure the individuality of the maturing child. The prisoner has to be contained but at the same time has to be allowed to make his own decisions. Moreover the penalties for getting the balance wrong are severe: the prisoner can be returned back to the brutal and infantilising moment of penality as segregation.

This specific form of tension was evident in most of the replies about control outside prison. Day leaves and weekend leaves, for example impose particular responsibilities on women.

> **Audrey: Husband in day leave period of pre-release**
>
> ... you're responsible for them, you've got to sign papers (but) the men have their own ideas, as far as they're concerned they've got (free) time. I'd be worried if John wanted to drive but I'm lucky John doesn't drink or smoke.

These periods of "freedom" are strictly policed and to make the most of the short periods allowed it is useful to be able to ferry the prisoner by car rather than public transport. As men are not allowed to drive when they are on this form of release it is specifically the woman's responsibility to ensure that he conforms to the rules about getting back in time. This sense of responsibility is reinforced by stories women tell about other prisoners' families who have failed to beat the deadline.

Claire: Husband about to be given day leave

Girls don't realise the seriouness of it, but the men are released into our custody, we are responsible for them. If we don't get them back on time we can be arrested for aiding an escape. One lady with four children and a car accident blocked the traffic, they phoned the gate house, 'we will be late', they said 'that's OK'. When he got in he was confined to his cell: day leave for the next month was cancelled.

Audrey: Three children, husband in day leave period of pre-release programme

but it isn't day leave, they're not to do this, they're not allowed to do that, they're not allowed to go here, they're not allowed to go there. Not allowed to drive, so virtually you've got to get yourself around and back again on the dot of five and you're responsible for them. If they go down and get in trouble. You're responsible. You've got to sign papers.

The pre-release period comprising the finely graded programmes of day and weekend leave prior to parole is one of the high points of the surveillance procedures of penal control when minute details of the individuals' lives are processed and subjected to judgement. Time as lateness, driving as a proscribed activity are made the object of penal surveillance. Success or failure in conforming to the finely defined regulations becomes the responsibility of both the prisoner and his sponsor.

An acute understanding of the delicacy of the situation of being the person nominally responsible for an adult partner who has just been released from prison was a common feature of the descriptions of people who had previously experienced that situation as well as of the women who were about to undergo it:

Ray: Partner has been in and out of prison twice before

There's a feeling that you're the prison warder now but yet not necessarily, you can't tell them what to do — when they come out they want total control. It messes up your own life.

Teresa: Partner about to be released on parole after several years in gaol

He'll be facing an extra 15 years if he breaks parole. It wouldn't take much for anything to go wrong then — WANG he' got 15 years to worry about. *How are you going to manage that?* It's his responsibility and its my responsibility to keep him clear. What worries me is the time he's spent in there and the extent he's going to break loose. That's what worries me ... I just wish there was something I could do.

Caring for men on conditional liberty however can also mean resisting exhausting emotional pressures:

Kay: Nephew on weekend detention

He is always asking for money to pay for his methadone treatment, or his rent, and then coming home and telling me he has been robbed so he needs more money ... the other day in the car, he was screaming at me 'you don't understand, you don't understand' and saying 'if you don't give me the money I'll go and do a robbery'. I said 'go ahead, go ahead then, and rob somebody, look there's a little old lady over there, she looks as though she could be knocked over easily, why don't you go and rob her and knock her out. I'm not going to give you any more money'.

2 EMOTIONAL WORK AND SOCIAL CONTROL

Graham argues that the caring work of women looking after aged or invalid adults is negated by the language of normalisation. The constitution of family life as natural means that the work of caring can be marginalised by defining it as normal and unproblematic even when care is for aged or invalid adults and the usual dependent relationships of family life are inverted. These processes of negation are especially relevant to the work of women whose husbands are either about to enter gaol or who have just been released from gaol. In both cases there are major stresses deriving from the injustices and uncertainties of penal life. There is major emotional work for women who have to attempt to manage the households when men are living through these stressful periods of penality. The next accounts indicate that both the period prior to imprisonment as well as the time immediately following release on parole can make major demands on the emotional skills involved in the work of caring:

Julie: Two children and a husband who had been out on bail

He was on $2,000 bail because it was his first offence and I had to scrape together $2,000. I did it and then when he was out and it got adjourned it was just the pressure of the court case. Just what was going to happen, what type of judge we were going to get, all those things ... he was working slowly trying to pull us out of debt and I was mainly more or less sort of keeping him stable. That was the most important thing ... and the last week was the worst. He was very tense and It was just like waiting for somebody to ... and the kids suffered once again because at that stage it was very irrational, and he was the most important then so the kids sort of got side tracked for that time.

Cheryl: Husband had been released on parole, arrested, wrongly accused, imprisoned for sixteen months and acquitted of murder. He is[66] serving an extra penalty of control under conditional liberty as a consequence of the false imprisonment which had forced him to breach the conditions of his previous parole

Bernie had just totally cut off (whilst he was in prison). It really scared me because I had this guy when he went to gaol who was really soft and gentle and considerate to me and all of a sudden he just wasn't there. I couldn't understand it. I visited him 16 months and we used to talk about everything and then ... he came out of gaol and he was just filthy on the world. Here he was — he'd just spent sixteen months in gaol for a crime he didn't commit and everything he'd worked hard for when he first came out of gaol in 1980 ... he was dirty on the government (because his lawn mowing business had run down). He was incarcerated for the revoking of his parole, and adding an extra three and a half years to his parole because his time didn't count, and in that anger, we got lost, the kids and I just didn't exist. He lost his cool. He's never hit me I must admit. And he'd go really, really cranky and just screamed and crashed things, but he came back. The guy I knew came back. It was a month period we went through. I wanted him to go. I wanted to finish with him. It was over because I couldn't take the person he'd become, because I'd never been through it. I didn't understand. In this crack up of his he let all his anger and frustrations out. So I think it's important that families of prisoners realise that the guy comes out of gaol they have to give them a little bit of, not breathing space, but a little bit of letting them have their selfish ways and being angry with everyone, and just cope with it because eventually you'll get that guy back ... their emotions do eventually get turned back on. It just depends on how much they had (frustration) when they went to gaol. How much emotion they had inside them.

Although the injustices of Bernie Matthews' imprisonment exacerbated the stress of parole, the tensions that Cheryl Matthews had to counter were also due to the dynamics of prison life. The pressures on men to contain their emotions when they are doing time in prison have repercussions that go beyond imprisonment. Haege's investigation in New South Wales in 1989 into the health of people released from prison into some form of community based control, found that the death rate of people under community supervision is six times that of people in a comparable age group.[67] The most common cause of death is suicide, and the most common period in which deaths occur is in the first few weeks after release from prison. One of the few accounts of this particular intersection between the home and the prison in which the people in the prisoners family are allotted any substance as individuals is the research by William Wardell.[68] His overtly phenomenological account accords with Cheryl Matthews' experience that, in this period, there are strong emotional reactions that all the people in the family work through.[69] Cheryl Matthews' own experience of working with other families when men had been freed, had been that most prisoners were at risk of needing to "be selfish" and that they imposed major demands on the supportive labour of caring of their partners or parents, in the period immediately after release. Her account is supported by other people's experiences of the early weeks after release on parole.

Hilary

I've just adjusted to not having him back home with me, so now I've got to adjust back to having someone there ... (when he came out last time) the first few weeks was the hardest because there was times to do this times to do that and it was hard in those weeks. The first day he gets out we don't ever go out where its crowded until he's adjusted ... and then when he's adjusted to that he can do whatever he wants to. We sort of take it slowly and not rush into things. That sort of helps him.

Ray: Partner in prison after earlier period of imprisonment and parole

when they come out they expect you to be the prison system almost. There's always a transition of about four weeks — a pattern of quietness, the hostility and it's towards you, for having ... you're the person who's been the closest and you're the person who's been free whilst they've been inside.

Jimmy Boyle described the difficulties that weekend leaves imposed on him as a long-term prisoner in Scotland:

Weekend leaves are atrocious that after such a long period of confinement the simple example of getting used to sharing a bed with someone is in itself a traumatic experience. That once every three weeks is disruptive ...[70]

An almost parallel account of the impact of release as an experience of physical readjustment was made about weekend release in New South Wales:

Esther: Partner is a long term prisoner on weekend release

The first weekend release, he could stay overnight and all next day until 5 o'clock, they were the hardest. At night time, the first time, he woke up and he thought someone was strangling him.

Particular tensions derive too from the normalising moment of imprisonment constituted as a cycle of freedom and imprisonment. These occasional releases into conditional liberty were described by one partner as:

Ray

... it's (day leave) like dangling a carrot, they all go through trauma — both the prisoner and the person on the outside. For a week after they're severely depressed. It takes a week to get over it. It's like dangling a carrot.

To these tensions there can be an added stress from the seemingly arbitrary changes to the programme of normalisation:

Audrey: One teenage son who believes his father is in New Zealand. Partner in day leave programme

even day leave's an uncertainty. I was supposed to have it (day leave) last week. But it was cancelled because the ... um ... or something I only know it was cancelled, that week. I had a lot of mucking around sort of, organising, sending Troy (son) off for the day, roller skating. It's supposed to be tomorrow but the way I feel I could tell him to stay in there (in gaol) (laughing) it's horrible, but, you know, it's too much organising at home just for a few hours for him to go out and come back in again. I don't think I could stand putting him back in again. That's the worst thing you know, and he's got to understand that ...

These were accounts of release on day or weekend leave and parole but it is important to set these experiences against the proposals for home detention. The tensions that are clearly outlined in these accounts of release into conditional liberty could be expected to be far more volatile when the prisoner is literally imprisoned in the emotional sphere of the home.[71] Moreover the tensions of living in close confinement would be exacerbated by the stress engendered by the uncertainty inherent in the new panopticism of control. Surveillance by random telephone calls in the home as "the tiny theatre of punishment" is the electronic replacement for the moral architecture of Bentham's panopticon penitentiary. It is the randomness of the telephone call from the prison officer that endows it with panopticonism. If the prisoner does not know when the call will come he has to expect it at any time. One American designer of home detention schemes said that the stress of waiting for such a call is so difficult that prisoners reverse the surveillance relationship and initiate the contact with the monitoring officer if there is no call for 24 hours.[72] Although this new panopticism parallels the earlier architecturally based surveillance in that it directly depends upon the stress of uncertainty, it has the added refinement of potentially extending that stress to everyone in the home. The partner or parents of the prisoner come under the control of the penal "gaze" of the tantalising telephone call in this new technology of control. This intensification of surveillance then is a qualitatively different form of control than those experienced at present in New South Wales. None of the women in these accounts spoke about the parole officers' surveillance as a punitive invasion of their privacy. Most women regarded their contact with the parole officer as either insignificant or as a benefit.

Beth

You get home visits when they come out and check on you but it doesn't worry me ... they're only here for 10 minutes or so. It's all just rubbish.

Rebecca

I end up talking to her (parole officer) about things I can't cope with — money problems, work problems. I go to work just to get out of the house because the tension of, the insecurity of it.

Hilary

It's more easier (than gaol). His parole officer if he couldn't make it out to the office he used to come out to the house and talk to us in the house ... He asked us how do they look on life and how are finances going ... sometimes it's helpful because things he doesn't talk to you about it comes out in that conversation. So that sort of helps you too because you know what he's going through that he just doesn't want to talk to a woman ... Sometimes it feels like when they come they're invading your privacy but if it's going to help him in the long run it's better.

Graham has made the point that professional workers in health and education do not take away the work of caring from families or from women. Rather the "professionals listen and advise: it is left to mothers to put their advice into practice".[73] Although the enforced partnership between women carers and penal professionals has more manifest controlling characteristics for some carers of men on parole the same division of labour occurs:

Gwen: Partner now in prison again after an earlier period of imprisonment and parole

... they all (parole system) used to say to me 'well you're there, you can help him' but I used to say 'How can I help him, you know, I don't know anything about it. I know of it and know all the after effects of it because I'm the one that sits there and cops it all' I said, 'but, I don't know anything about what it's like to be on drugs or anything'. I said 'how can I help him?' he's saying 'help me, help me' and I try but it's always more stronger than what I was. It was just hopeless. It is really.

Although the arbitrary power of parole officers over revocation decisions was experienced as potentially stressful, it related to decisions about determinate times and conditions. The controlling gaze upon which the proposed intensive surveillance of home detention depends is based on indeterminacy. The control of home detention would then be an experience of a particularly severe "micro physics of power", a minute by minute invasion of the home.

Although parole officers visits were not regarded as punitive, surveillance by the police *was* stressful for women caring for men on conditional liberty:

3   MEDIATING AND NEGOTIATING WORK

A major factor increasing the stress on women caring for men on conditional release is the fear that they will be falsely arrested. The way that police work is constituted increases the chances that men released from gaol will be prime suspects for crimes committed in their neigbourhoods. Moreover the poverty induced by imprisonment as it is presently constituted means that the conditionally released prisoner is more likely to live in an area with high crime rates.[74] Three women gave accounts of the punishment and work of women and children in families of men on restricted freedom, when the home is the "fishing pond" for police needing to improve their arrest rates. The account by Cheryl Matthews of her partner's arrest when he was on parole for a murder he had not committed is outlined in chapter five. This was the most extreme example of the constitution of the home as a "fishing pond" but it was not the only one:

Laurel

he was in Redfern — they got him — two other fellows did it but they picked him up for — he'd just got out — on parole.

Olive

Anything that happens in our area they're first to our place, the police. The garage just up the street from us got robbed. It was lucky we seen them straight from the garage to our place, fortunately he was up at his, my, sister's ... We saw them, they came straight from the garage to our place. Once he had a gun put to his head when he was on parole ... I asked him to run down to the bank for me ... as he was running past the back doors of the bank (and his sister was there with a little baby) two detectives jumped out of a car, threw him up against the wall put a gun to his head and said 'go on run, we'd like nothing better than to do you' but his sister, was there with a little baby, saw them go over and pick up a bit of silver cigarette paper say 'look what I found in your pocket' and he didn't have it on him. She seen the detectives pick it up when they threw him up against the wall ... to try to get him for doping, heroin. They arrested him. My daughter ran back to me terrified. I dropped everything and ran to the police station ... they told me they'd let him go. As I was walked out, I glanced up.There was my son trying to attract my attention up the stairs ... I went back in, I said 'I've seen him. I want to see him and I want to see what he's been charged with'. So they brought me down this sheet and say he's been charged with heroin I said 'that's a lie. He didn't have nothing. He went to the bank for me. My daughter's seen you pick up something on the street and put it on him'. He had to go to court. He went to court and there wasn't even a writ ... he got let free but I had to go through all this for nothing. That's what really gets me. That no kid can go straight if they're going to hound him.

The constant cycle of arrest, release, revocation and re-arrest can be particularly punitive for the children of prisoners and their outside carers:

Dorothy: One son. Partner now in Bathurst after a series of periods of imprisonment and release

He's been in and out. Fourteen years ... sometimes he's been out a week, sometimes a month, sometimes just a day ... I've got a boy of seven, my son was terrified of the police.

The experience of being at constant risk of police harassment both when the man is on conditional liberty and during his imprisonment has been documented by the South London Wives Group in England in the 1970s.[75]

Because of Mr Y's criminal record, the family have suffered much from the attentions of the police. After her husband had been sent down on one occasion, the home was regularly visited by the CID, sometimes as often as twice a week, and everything in it turned over.

As was the case with the women in Sydney this harassment led to tough negotiations with the police:

Mrs Y's protestations that she was honest, that there were no stolen goods there, that she would not allow these in the house anyway, went unheeded. This persecution, as she considered it, became too much for her, and when her patience was finally exhausted, she went to the nearest public phone box, telephoned the Home Office, and demanded to be put through to the 'head man'. She seems to have managed to get through to a senior official, who listened courteously to her tale. She was successful; from that time on, she was left in peace and her possessions undisturbed.[76]

Possibly the most condensed contradiction between domestic and penal moralities occurs for women whose partners or sons have breached the conditions of their early release. Somewhere between 30 per cent and 46 per cent of prisoners on conditional release end up back in prison either for committing new crimes or for breaching the conditions of their release.[77] Whether prisoners are returned to gaol or not is decided by the arbitrary judgement of the police or parole officer depending on the form of conditional release the prisoner is undergoing. The work of managing the contradictions of domestic and penal obligations in this situation is perhaps one of the stressful and at the same time most skilful forms of the domestic labour of caring that women have to provide. The work can comprise having to balance the contradictory demands of the two moralities as well as mediating and negotiating to keep the man out of gaol.

Pauline: son had been on a bond prior to imprisonment

He had to report three times a week between April and September. One night it was raining and his bike had broken down. He rang, 'can you pick me up'. I rang the police station and they said OK as long as he's here before midnight. The next time they were not so helpful — I had to plead with them.

Sally

He's got to report between 6 pm and 9 pm. If he's not there by nine o'clock they'll put him back in gaol. One night it was pouring with rain and he had to get over to Mascot (from Glebe) ... He had a doctor's certificate too ... I phoned them and they said 'Bad luck, if you don't come there's going to be an instant warrant on him tonight' so I rang up called them all the bitches under the sun and hung up on her, then rang back and said 'Look I'm coming in now.' I rang my Mum up and they said 'come around and we'll give you $20 to get a taxi.' So I rang her back and said 'I hope you're happy, I've been able to get some money, I'm on my way in' and she said 'O, I've been a bit harsh. Make sure he reports tomorrow' ... they've got the power to do anything, them bastards, I hate them.

Rebecca

I do a lot of explaining to the parole officer to get Owen out of it. Emotionally and physically it's just exhausting. (I go) between the welfare worker and priest and police sometimes when he's had to sign on report every day to the police and sometimes he's been too drunk, I've had to go to them and talk to them or get a medical certificate. Sometimes with the parole officer, he just doesn't want to talk to her. He says you'll just have to talk to her for me.

One of the major criticisms of parole is that for the 40 per cent or so prisoners whose parole is revoked, their time under punitive control outside of prison walls, or their "clean street time" is not counted.[78] Parole then for a significant proportion of prisoners extends their total period of imprisonment. This is one of the most keenly felt injustices of the parole system.[79] However if men are falsely arrested the injustice of this extension of control is compounded and the stress of experiencing that injustice is keenly felt by the partner of the prisoner:

Cheryl: Partner arrested on a false charge whilst on parole

... when he was released I was fuming. I wanted to go back and physically strangle every member of the Parole Board. Because the three and a half years he done on the outside (between the two periods of imprisonment) they

212

said they didn't count. He's back doing five and a half, six years (on parole) he still owes them now.

Other forms of back end release can also extend the period of punishment. Day leave at the normalising end of imprisonment can impose major stresses on men who are faced in an immediate way with the responsibilities of family but who are nevertheless still constituted as "adolescents" needing to be confined to inside the walls of the prison:

Esther

He got in a bit of trouble at Silverwater. He was on a works release for three weeks. He was on day leave, about 8 day leaves over about six months. I got pregnant then I miscarried while he was still on the day release programme. That's why he did what he done (escape while on day leave). He got three months for that.

One of the commonest reasons for escapes from penal control in New South Wales is concern about family problems.[80] The normalising moment of penality constituted as a reintegrative programme of control imposes major tension on both the prisoner and the outside carer. In Esther's situation it was her partner who was caught in the double bind imposed by the contradictory moralities of home and prison. It seems likely that this tension is an inherent aspect of day leave as, in the period 1971–1983, 5.5 per cent of all prison escapes occurred during day or weekend leave. However this masks the increasing pressure on prisoners on this form of conditional liberty, as there was a steady increase in the rate from 2.2 per cent in 1975 to 10.1 per cent in 1982.[81]

One further basis of tension for women in this situation is the complexity of the reponsibilities they carry for different dependents in the family. Although the prisoner makes major demands on the labour of the outside carers, there may be other family demands that have priority. The hidden punishment of being an outside carer in this more complicated family pattern can be severe:

Kay: Nephew in CIP after breaching the conditions of a warrant

When he was out on a warrant he escaped to Adelaide. His mother told the police his address in Adelaide, now he won't talk to her. He is very angry with her. But she only told them because the police were coming around to our home to my mother (his grandmother) who is 82 and not well. She only told them to stop my mother being harassed and bothered by it all.

The re-arrest of the man when he breaches the conditions of parole can result in gross illegal physical punishment that then commits women to stressful frustrating contestations:

June

when he got into a fight (outside the pub) and the coppers held him down and when they got him back to the police station, they give him an hiding. His head, cut open twice He had 37 baton marks on his body. Then I went in and I wanted to, I went off me head and I said 'I want to put a charge against police officers' and I said 'O, he done it by himself in the back of the van, did he, really cut his head open did he?' and the sergeant turned around and he said 'look, I've go a lot coming up around this area soon' he said and 'I don't want any more trouble, see you later'. *What did he mean 'a lot coming up'?* Well it was over at Glebe so he said, he's got enough on his plate and he needs all the men he's got, without me charging any and getting them suspended. So in other words he wasn't going to do a bloody thing.

MATERIAL COSTS TO WOMEN WHEN THE HOME IS CONSTITUTED AS THE SITE OF "RESOURCE AND RESOLVE"

The most visible cost is related to the women's responsibility, outlined above, to collect and deliver the prisoner in the day and weekend leave programmes of release in the normalising phase of imprisonment. In the early 1980s day leave was extended to prisoners in some country goals and the geographical limits for prisoners from these gaols extend to over 100 kms. These liberal extensions of the programmes of controlled release then increase the demands on women's resources.

Release on parole however, can also involve women in major losses of income. The loss of income of the families of prisoners that is an inherent part of imprisonment as segregation is not inevitably reversed in the later stages of penal control. The work release programme is extended to only a minority of prisoners and not all prisoners on that programme are able to keep their jobs once they are on parole.[82] Braithwaite found that in 1979 only 26.9 per cent of prisoners released from gaol in New South Wales found jobs in the four to six months subsequent to their release.[83] Indeed, it is because the family is constituted as a resource providing material support for the prisoner that parole can be incorporated into the penal programme. Releasing prisoners without family support can involve the state in the additional costs of halfway houses.[84] About 10 per cent of long term prisoners, and an unknown proportion of other prisoners marry, or begin new de facto relationships, whilst they are in prison.[85] Aitkin and Gartrell suggest that this is because single prisoners in New South Wales interpret penal administrators' perceptions of the home as the most promising site of "resource and resolve". In these cross-currents of prison speculation it is specifically the home defined as the site of "normal" heterosexual relationships that prisoners aim for in their bid to influence parole decisions.[86]

The impact on women of this incorporation of the home as a material resource is rarely investigated. There are only two studies in the literature that have addressed the issue. Liker's study (described more fully in chapter three) indicates that the man's freedom placed severe financial burdens on scarce household resources.[87] Similarly, Fishman found that the problem of poverty was exacerbated by the prisoner's release even in those instances when men were able to get jobs.[88]

In the New South Wales accounts of the intersection of prison and home it was particularly the partners and parents of men locked into a

214

cycle of recidivism who described the material costs imposed on them through their family obligations to men on conditional liberty.

Katherine: Four children. Partner imprisoned 'several times'

(we were better off) financially while he was in gaol, because (for example) one Christmas all he wanted to do was buy the grog for a Christmas party and I had toys for the kids on lay-by. He couldn't understand they had to come out first.

Ray: Partner to be released in nine days after his third period of imprisonment

If he doesn't get a job straight away I have to feed him, pay his fares everywhere and so on. You know when they come out they should have some money, maybe they should save up through the year or work for it.

Aitkin and Gartrell pointed out in 1983 that the conditions of early release could impose costly restraints on both the parolee and his family, citing the example of one elderly man whose return to the home of his older sisters had meant that all three were prevented from entering a home for the elderly because of the licencees' reporting obligations.[89]

The alternative of imposing fines rather than imprisonment can make a direct impact on the economic resources of women in the family of the prisoner. Two of the women spoke about paying fines for their sons or nephews to make sure he was not imprisoned for fine default.

Kay: One nephew on weekend detention, one nephew in CIP

He (nephew on weekend detention) is always asking for money to pay for his methadone treatment, or his rent, and then coming home and telling me he has been robbed so he needs more money ... They come to me to pay their fines and their warrants because I'm the single aunt whose got a good job and no family of my own — I'm supposed to be the wealthy one. But I tell them they can't rely on me any more, now I've retired and living on my annuity. But I still paid $200, 4 weeks ago to pay off Edward's warrant. He still ended up in Long Bay though over another incident so I didn't get my money back this time either.

Pauline: Son, a truck driver, had a series of fines for traffic offences, was initially held for fine default, later imprisoned

He was to go to Silverwater but they were short of staff. So they kept him at Castle Hall police station. I rang and rang Silverwater. They didn't know anything. I said if I pay the rest of the fine can I get him out? I paid $80. He had had next to nothing to eat. He was there 8 pm Wednesday to midnight Thursday.

One study of fine defaulters in Britain in 1978 found that the majority of individuals who do not pay fines are people who have no family support.[90] The current discourse on how to keep fine defaulters out of prison draws directly on the help that relatives and friends can give.[91] It would not be far-fetched then to suppose that the classical liberal image of a penal economic contract being negotiated between the individual and the state in fact masks a redistribution of resources within households and that

215

that redistribution for at least some, if not most, families involves a shift of resources from women to men. The Softley study found that fine payers reduced their spending on food, clothing or shoes to pay the fine but did not indicate *who* in the family went without food, clothes or shoes in this renegotiation of the household budget.[92] This then is also likely to mean that it is a redistribution of resources from the pockets of individual women to the state as long as the constitution of penality as a career of increasing penality means that a fine default ends in other, more costly forms of penal control.

All of these examples indicate that the sources of the extra costs to women lay in either the individual responses of the released prisoner or in the *legitimate* but penalising structure of penal control as it is presently constituted. The final example indicates that the *illegal* activities of the legal-penal controllers might be a factor in putting women at risk of material losses in this moment of penality:

> **Sally and Phillip: Phillip had been imprisoned a number of times before he and Sally met. He had been sentenced both in prison and outside of prison for a series of small scale acts of aggression**
>
> He got picked up the other night, just look at his face. They (the police) bashed him up and took all our money. $210 of our money. Bashed him up again. I got Internal Affairs onto them again. Now he has to go to court. All he was doing was standing outside a shop and they reckoned he was trying to break into it, and they've charged him with a Breaking and Enter. They give him a hiding, took all his money. Now I've got to go through it all again now. They just took it, pocketed it, kept it for themselves. **Phillip:** I know how they go and I hid the money down me sock, I've had it taken before. They stripped me down. I had a pair of socks on. I didn't even get me socks back.

SUMMARY

The feminist materialist analyses interpret the domestic labour of caring as the work of reproduction. The work of caring for men on conditional liberty is doubly caught up into the relationship between productive and reproductive life. Penality has been constituted in a variety of forms from segregative imprisonment as the dominant form, to imprisonment as an end point in an increasingly wide smorgasbord of controls to "fit the punishment". This multiplicity of forms of punishment and control is intrinsic to the reproduction of the social relations of industrial then welfare then corporate consumer capitalism. The extension of penality, however hidden, to the carers of men under punitive control is part of this broader aspect of reproductive life. The home as the site of "resource and resolve" provides: the material infrastructure upon which contemporary penality rests, the potential psychological control upon the prisoner about to be reintegrated into the "normal" family relationships of care and dependency and, according to the penological theory of deterrence, the sufficient threat to the man who does not commit the offence for fear of sacrificing this relationship. In this the home is a significant element of the reproduction of the conditions of social life.

Secondly, the work of caring is constituted within present penal discourses as being about the reproduction of the individual personalities of each specific offender within the "haven" of the particularistic relationships of family love.

Presently authority in the penal sphere comprises the three powerful and often contesting rationalities: the judicial, the scientific and the economic. The moral powers deriving from these three spheres of rationality and from the debates between their particular representatives are currently constituting penality as a broad social net that will increasingly exploit the powerless, arational morality of the home as a source of control.

The home is both a physical space providing material resources and a set of relationships specifically constituted as a nexus of caring and dependence.

The two models of the relationship between prison and home posited at the beginning of this chapter are *both* relevant to the experiences of women caught in the singular social space where penality and domesticity intersect.

In the current reconstitution of penal life those men who are able to demonstrate their attachment to social life through their ability to fit the category of provident wage earner and/or through the evidence of having access to a home comprising sufficient material resources to enable him to cross the "bridge" back into normal life, are likely to experience punishment as a one way process through the "progressive" moments of penality. However having a "home" is not always a sufficient safeguard against entering and reentering the reprocessing cycle of punitive segregation and correction and conditional liberty.

The contradictions of the current dynamic of a familial-political economy characterised by the contradictory processes of consumerism and neo-classical deregulation is likely to place further stresses on the tensions between desire and control. These historically specific stresses are increasingly leading to an exploitation of the powerless arational morality of domestic life operating through the extensive and intensive labour of women in the home. The central characteristic of this labour, and of the material costs and extension of control to the women in the home of men under community surveillance, is its invisibility. It is the hidden labour, hidden costs and hidden control of women that underpins this moment of penality.

Penal and "family" policies are jointly constructing the dilemmas of "care as control" for larger numbers of women in the tensions of this current familial-political economy. The actual character of this current complex form of exploitation of caring work is not immutable. Within Australia there are significant differences in imprisonment rates reflecting both differences in sentencing practices as well as differences in the ways that laws are interpreted.[93] Moreover within OECD countries "family" policies are currently constructing the nexus between care and dependency in significantly different forms.[94] New South Wales in the period 1986–1988 was moving to the more punitive combination of increasing prison populations, widening "community" networks of penal control, but restricting public provision of resources for families without male breadwinners.[95]

NOTES

1   Braithwaite, J, *Crime, Shame and Reintegration* (1989) at 91. Braithwaite here is citing Bayley, D, *Social Control and Political Change* (1985) Research Monograph 49, Woodrow Wilson School of Public and International Affairs, Princeton University. Bayley in turn was citing Silberman, C, *Criminal Violence, Criminal Justice* (1978), NY: Random House. This dense layering of citations indicates the significance of the relationship between 'the home' and corrrectional control in this section of criminological discourses.

2   Cohen, S, *Visions of Social Control* (1985) at 55–56.

3   There was a third, more radical group of protagonists in this era comprising prisoner action groups and their outside supporters. However their impact was felt mainly in terms of the way the more powerful scientific or legalistic authorities responded to them rather than in their direct control over penal policies and practices. Janet Chan cites Zimring's comment that 'penal reform was dramatically demon-strated by prisoners, intellectually strengthened by liberal academics, and opportunistically exploited by law and order politicians' Chan, J, "The Limits of Sentencing Reform" in Potas, I (ed), *Sentencing in Australia* (1986) 445–484 at 446.

4   Cited in Hayes, F, "In Search of a Correctional Camelot: the idealism and reality of the first twenty five years of probation and parole in New South Wales: Part One" (1987) 7/2 *Welfare in Australia* at 19.

5   Id at 20–21, citing the response made by the current Attorney General, 27th September, 1950.

6   Id at 18.

7   Frank Hayes was one of the first two parole officers in New South Wales.

8   Id at 20 & 23.

9   Id at 22.

10   Id at 21.

11   Id at 23.

12   Cited in Chan, above n3 at 446.

13   Dewdney, M, Swarris, K and Miner, M, "The History and Administration of the New South Wales Work Release Scheme — 1969–1977", New South Wales Department of Corrective Services, 1978 at 2.

14   Both were former members at the time of the report.

15 Aitkin, J and Gartrell, G, *Sentenced to Life: Management of Life Sentence Prisoners in New South Wales Gaols*, Sydney: Criminology Research Council, 1985.

16 Hounslow, B, Stephenson, A, Stewart, J and Crancher, J, *Children of Imprisoned Parents*. Sydney: Family and Childrens's Service Agency (Social Research and Evaluation Ltd), Ministry of Youth and Community Services, 1982, at 65.

17 Above n15 at 136.

18 Garrett, W, "Penal Philosphies and Practices in the 1970s in New Zealand" in *Penal Philosophies and Practice in the 1970s*, Proceedings: Training Project No 24. Canberra: Australian Institute of Criminology, 1976 at 60.

19 Above n13 at 19, citing the initial objectives of the scheme set out in the 1966 legislation (my emphasis).

20 Ibid.

21 Ibid.

22 Boyle, J, *The Pain of Confinement* (1984) at 273.

23 Above n19 at 13.

24 Prisoners were often not able to keep the jobs after release "for geographic reasons". New South Wales Department of Corrective Services, *Annual Report* (1985) at 38.

25 Above n19 at 127. There was no indication in the subsequent reports on the scheme whether this problem was resolved or whether it continued into the later stages of the programme. (Turnbull, J Porritt, D and Coney, G, *Performance on Work Release and After*, Research Publication No 4 (August), Sydney: Research & Statistics Division, New South Wales Department of Corrective Services, 1982.)

26 Bradwell, L, "Parole in New South Wales" (1972) 19 *Int J Offend Ther & Comp Crim* at 78.

27 Rinaldi, F, *Australian Prisons* (1977) at 154; Chan, above n3. Nevertheless, 'rehabilitation' was still a central theme in the description of Parole by its senior officer in the professional journals. Bradwell, above n26.

28 Findlay, M, *The State of The Prison: a Critique of Reform* (1982) at ch8.

29 Weatherburn, D, "Reducing the New South Wales Prison Population: sentencing reform and early release" (1986) 10 *Crim LJ* at 124.

30 Ibid.

31 Australian Law Reform Commission, "Sentencing: Penalties", Discussion Paper 30, Sydney, 1987 at 202.

32 Above n29 at 122–125.

33 New South Wales Department of Corrective Services, *Annual Report*, 1987 at 85.

34 Above n29 at 122–125.

35 Brown, D, "Preconditions for Sentencing and Penal Reform in New South Wales: Some Suggestions Towards a Strategy for Contesting an

Emerging Law and Order Climate", in Potas, I (ed) *Sentencing in Australia* (1986) at 344.

36   Defined as reimprisonment two years after release.

37   Above n33 at 33.

38   Ibid.

39   Id at 34.

40   Above n29 at 10.

41   Chan, above n3 at 464–6; Chan, J, *Doing Less Time* (1992); above n29.

42   Chan, above n3; above n29; above n35.

43   Above n35 at 344.

44   Chan, above n3 at 460–75.

45   Brown, D and Zdenkowski, G, *The Prison Struggle* (1975) at ch3.

46   The party in opposition, as it was not having to face the contradictions of being in power, was able to afford the luxury of an almost wholesale condemnation of the 'soft' option of early release.

47   Petersilia, J, "Community Supervision: Trends and Critical Issues" (1985) 31/3 *Crime & Delinq* 339–347. Joan Petersilia's recommendation for 'a spectrum of punishments to match the spectrum of crimes' became a penological shibboleth.

48   Grant, D, "A Reflection on Prison Crowding" in Vernon, J (ed), *Developments in Correctional Policy: More Prisons?* (1987) at 85.

49   Above n47 at 345.

50   Id at 341.

51   Above n29 at 121.

52   Id at 127.

53   Id at 119.

54   Stoneman, N, "Probation and Parole Australian Capital Territory, New South Wales More Problems than Prospects" in Potas, I (ed), *Sentencing in Australia* (1986).

55   Above n48 at 86; Briese, C, "A Magistrate's View", in Vernon, J (ed) *Developments in Correctional Policy: More Prisons?* (1987 at 65; Robertson, M, "Expanding the Scope of Community Corrections to Meet Prison Population Pressures" in *Diversionary Programmes Workshop: Proceedings 10–11 September, Alice Springs.* Darwin: Northern Territory Department of Health and Community Services, 1986.

56   Briese, above n55.

57   Lay, R, "Home Detention: grounded in the community" paper presented at the Australian Bicentennial International Congress on Corrective Services, Sydney, 24–28 January 1988; Dorey, T, "Home Detention Program (Design and Implementation)", paper presented to the Diversionary Programmes Workshop, Alice Springs, 4 August 1986 at 12–15.

58   Robertson, above n55 at 2–3.

59   New South Wales Department of Corrective Services, *Annual Report* (1979) at 23; *Annual Report* (1985) at 38.

60   New South Wales Department of Corrective Services, *Annual Report* (1978) at 25.

61   Rinaldi, above n27 at 182.

62   Id at 181–3.

63   Above n2 at ch2.

64   Silberman, cited in Braithwaite, above n1 at 91. This citation was taken in turn from a further penological text. This layering of citations indicates the density of this discourse and thus the continuing power of the theory of the family, constituted as the site of *a*rationality and romantic love, as the basic building block of morality.

65   Dalton, V, in discussion in "Offender Management in the Eighties", 60 *Proc Inst Crim* (1984) at 34.

66   At the time of this account.

67   Haege, cited in Brown, D, "Returning to Sight: Contemporary Australian Penality" (1989) 16/3 *Soc Just* (Issue 37) at 150.

68   Wardell, W, "The Reunion of the Male Prison Inmate with his Family: a Humanistic Exploratory Study (Phenomenological)", unpublished PhD thesis, Clinical Psychology Department, The Fielding Institute, USA, 1983.

69   Wardell's work however is *a*political in both feminist and materialist terms. He does not indicate whether there are any problems associated with inequalities of power within the family nor does set up as theoretically problematic the work that women do in this period.

70   Above n22 at 298.

71   The evaluation of the New Jersey scheme indicates that these tensions are criminogenic — of the 29 'failures' in that programme 28 (95 per cent) were due to breaches of the conditions of the scheme (above n47 at 344.)

72   Ted Nissan in private conversation (1988).

73   Graham, H, "Surveying through stories" in Bell, C and Roberts, H (eds), *Social Researching: politics, problems, practice* (1984) at 7; Pascal, G, *Social Policy: a Feminist Analysis* (1986) at 72.

74   Minnery, J, *Crime Perception and Victimisation of Inner City Residents*, Brisbane: Queensland Institute of Technology, 1986; Kinsey, R, Lea, J and Young, J, *Losing the Fight against Crime* (1986).

75   Crosthwaite, A, "Punishment for Whom? the Prisoner or his Wife?" (1975) 19/3 *Int J Offend Ther & Comp Crim* 275–284 at 281).

76   Ibid.

77   Dewdney, M and Miner, M, "Parole Trends and Revocations" (Publication No 10), Sydney: New South Wales Department of Corrective Services, 1976 at 68; above n37 at 33–34.

78   Findlay, M, The State of the Prison: a critique of reform (1982) at 146; above n31 at 133.

79   Findlay, id at ch8.

80   Porritt, D, *Reasons For Escape: reported by recaptured escapees*, Sydney: New South Wales Department of Correctives Services, Research and Statistics Division, 1987; Gorta, A and Nguyen, M, *An*

Analysis of Interviews with Recaptured Escapees: some suggestions of reasons for escape, Research and Statistics Division, New South Wales Department of Corrective Services, 1988.

81   New South Wales Department of Corrective Services, *Annual Report* (1983) at App II table 6.

82   Above n77 at 146.

83   Braithwaite, J, "The Political Economy of Punishment" in Buckley, K and Wheelwright, E (eds) *Political Economy of Australian Capitalism* (vol 4; 1980).

84   The long term programmes of using halfway houses for men on parole were specifically introduced as 'family surrogate' schemes to compensate for 'deficient nuclear families' (Handler, E, "Family Surrogates as Correctional Strategy" (1974) 48/4 *Soc Serv R* 539–549). By the late 1980s the New South Wales Department of Corrective Services was contributing $500,000 per annum to the costs of their halfway houses.

85   Above n15 at 9; above n16 at 62.

86   Above n15.

87   Liker, J, "Economic Pressures on the Families of Released Prisoners: evidence from the TARP experiment" (1981) 16/1 *Cornell J Soc Rel* 11–27 at 16.

88   Fishman, S, *Women at the Wall* (1991) at 237.

89   Above n15 at 26.

90   Sinclair, P, "Alternatives to Gaol: solving some problems, creating some new ones" (1974) 15/2 *Health in NSW*.

91   Challenger, D, "Payment of Fines" (1985) 18/2 *ANZ J Crim* at 102.

92   Cited in Challenger, id at 106.

93   Walker, J, *Adults under Detention and Supervision Orders*, Canberra: Australian Institute of Criminology, 1988.

94   Bradley, R, Walters, C, Cooper, S, Kisch, J, Yeoman, P and Dapre, B, "Overseas Countries' Assistance to Sole Parents: Social Security Review", Background/Discussion Paper No 14, Woden: Department of Social Security, 1986; Oxley, C, "The Structure of General Family Provision in Australia and Overseas: a Comparative Study", (1987) Social Security Review Background/Discussion Paper No 17, Woden: Department of Social Security, 1987.

95   This latter aspect of the welfare/punishment package is a complex one. Whilst the Child Support Scheme places greater emphasis on the economic responsibility of the non custodial parent (Department of Social Security *Annual Report* (1988) at 9, 10), the Family Allowance element of the Social Security programme has helped to increase the level of income of sole parents. These programmes are discussed in greater detail in the next chapter.

8

FURTHER LAYERS OF THE CONTRADICTION: CHANGES SINCE 1988

In the four years since the collection of the material for this study there have been two major changes in policies that constitute domesticity and penality in New South Wales: changes in family policies and in the penal sphere.

In 1988 the Liberal party was elected to power in New South Wales following a campaign explictly articulating the political philosophy of the New Right.[1] This comprised the contradictory mixture of neo-liberal policies in the economic sphere and neo-conservatism in those areas of life concerning law and morality. This contradictory, yet complementary, combination of laissez-faire philosophies and social authoritarianism was most evident in the promises and the actual policies and practices that were enforced in the first three years of the Liberal administration of the Corrective Services Department.

Several feminist writers have delineated the consequences for the constitution of domesticity in the volatile mixture of neo-liberalism and neo-conservatism in the political philosophy of the New Right.[2] Briefly these are: women become invisible in the "free" market relationships of the economic sphere, with the principles of universalism and individuality being extended only to those people with no family obligations to provide the domestic work of caring. At the same time, the patriarchal family, constructed within the classically unequal relations of the economic dependence of the caring wife and mother on the breadwinning father, is constituted as the "natural" site for the transmission of values essential to "law and order". In the language of the contemporary New Right philosopher John Rawls, the home (as the site of the inferior morality of association) and the state (as the site of the superior morality of principles) are reconstituted as junior and senior members in a partnership of control to impose the sense of justice and balance upon the behaviour of men working in the economic sphere, the domain of self interest. Although the unequal relationships within the family are legitimated by their "naturalness", because "the family" is so crucial to the New Right's model of discipline and morality, they also become the legitimate object of state intervention.

The tensions which accrue from these contradictions within the invisible yet significant domestic sphere have been most clearly illustrated in the policies and practices of the Liberal administration of the Corrective Services department. The penal sphere is, at the same time, the area of social life in which economic rationalism is sanctioned through the constitution of law breakers as rational individuals who have chosen to break the rules, and the sphere in which the strong state and the family coexist as senior and junior purveyors of law and morality.

It is important to emphasise that this Liberal New Right management of prison life is not always clearly distinguishable from the administrative practices and public statements of the previous Labour government. The prison population was increasing to the point of overcrowding before 1988. Both parties foregrounded "Law and Order" as an election issue and promised to build new prisons, crack down on street crimes and drug offenders, and review sentencing policies.[3] Both parties were planning to introduce more intensive forms of community controls and "home detention" programmes. In general terms, the swing to the New Right initially led to a de-domestication of prison life, at the same time as it increased the stresses within prisons that placed greater demands on those people who constitute the population "families of prisoners". By 1991 the punitive rhetoric of the Liberal adminstration became more muted with the appointment of a Minister who was more inclined to the discourses of reform and rehabilitation.

The reconfiguration of the intersection of domesticity and penality occurred in three main areas: in policing, in the courts, and in imprisonment. In brief, the changes in the criminal justice system in New South Wales developed in the first three years of the Liberal administration were:

Social Authoritarianism

1   an increase in the range and militarisation of policing;
2   an increased militarisation of prison life;
3   an increase in the rate of imprisonment, prison overcrowding and an expansionist prison building programme.

Economic rationality

4   "Truth in Sentencing" and "back to justice" policies;
5   privatisation as the transfer of state responsibility for some of the unprofitable provision of penal services to the "private sphere" of the family and the voluntary sector;
6   corporatisation of several parts of the remaining state sector provision of penal services;
7   privatisation as the commoditisation of imprisonment.

The 1991–1992 period saw a resuscitation of 1950s style rehabilitative discourses. This most recent layering of penal discourses emphasises reform through industry and discipline.

SOCIAL AUTHORITARIANISM, PENALITY AND DOMESTICITY

There have been several changes in penal discourses influenced by this social authoritarian strand of New Right thought: an increase in policing in terms of numbers of policemen on the streets, an increase in the arbitrary power of the police to define behaviour as criminal with the reintroduction of the *Summary Offences Act*, and a "get tough" policy inside the gaols. This latter stance led to a variety of manifestly militaristic and punitive practices inside the prisons including an intensification of militaristic drug searches, greater restrictions on visiting rights of prisoners' legal advisers, greater access given to the police to interview prisoners, restrictions on prisoners' access to the Ombudsman, the suppression of prisoner produced magazines, abolition of the right of appeal against decisions by magistrates in prison disciplinary hearings, harsher penalties for escape, and the creation of a new set of in-prison offences. The costs of this re-masculinisation of prison life, to the people providing the infrastructure of family care, have been largely invisible in the commentaries surrounding their introduction.

POLICING AND THE *SUMMARY OFFENCES ACT*

One of the first changes made by the Liberal government in the area of crime and punishment was the reintroduction of the *Summary Offences Act*. This extended the arbitrary power of the police to define aspects of everyday behaviour in public places as criminal. The Act brought larger numbers of people into the sphere of control and punishment. It was especially those people most likely to be spending "unorganised" free time in public spaces who came to be at increased risk of criminalisation: the homeless, the young from lower socio-economic areas but particularly Koori people who were most at risk of being affected by this change.[4] Describing the effect of a parallel intensity of social control deriving from New Right policies in Britain four years earlier, Bryan et al describe how these "Law and Order" policies intensified the work and punishment of Koori women as:

> ... mothers and as workers we came into contact with institutions that daily compounded our experience of racism. We were the ones who rushed to the police station when members of our families got arrested ... We were the ones who had to clear up the debris when police entered our homes uninvited to harass and intimidate us.[5]

Although the militarisation of policing had already begun in New South Wales during the Labour government's period in power,[6] the continuing militarisation of everyday life for women in families on the margins of productive life was extended with the widening of police powers under the *Summary Offences Act*.[7] In a survey of the impact of the *Summary Offences Act* on arrest rates in three country towns, there was an increase of almost 300 per cent in the rate of arrests of people charged with offensive behaviour, following the introduction of the Act in 1988.[8]

The Human Rights Commission's National Inquiry into Racist Violence heard submissions from a number of different ethnic groups that of all forms of racist violence "police violence based on race came through as the most serious area of concern".[9] Three incidents in New South Wales have particular resonance with the experiences of the Black women in London: first, the armed invasion by police of a Koori sports day and carnival,[10] and secondly, the armed invasion of a number of homes by New South Wales police, in their search for a man suspected of killing a policeman. In one home, this eventuated in their killing a man — David Gundy — who was unconnected with the crime they were investigating. That shooting left a woman widowed and her son with the loss of his father.[11] In the same para-military operation, New South Wales detectives threw five stun grenades "to neutralise" the residents of another home in Queensland. The media also successfully "neutralised" the impact of the report of that raid in using the term "occupants" to mask the ages, gender and family relationships of the people stunned by the grenade.[12] Thirdly, in February 1990, in a strategically planned armed invasion, Operation Sue, several homes were broken into in one Koori area of Sydney. This was an early morning raid involving 135 police, in which doors were broken down, guns held to the heads of the children and adult residents and belongings ransacked.

The increased militarisation of policing, the push to "active policing", the introduction of the *Summary Offences Act* were all changes that served to increase the numbers of people imprisoned[13] in the state. Another was the increase in the numbers of police. The combined effect of these factors is illustrated in the increase in the overall arrest rate for New South Wales which was estimated by the director of the Bureau of Crime Statistics and Research to have risen by 17 per cent in 1989.[14]

One other major factor is the introduction of "Truth in Sentencing" legislation.

"TRUTH IN SENTENCING" LEGISLATION

The neo-liberalism and neo-conservatism of the New Right come together in the legal-penal sphere in its reconstitution of punishment as "a precise determinate quantity of pain inflicted on the wrongdoer in exchange for the offense (of infringeing) legally prescribed rules".[15]

The ideological emphasis upon individualism underpins the move to "Truth in Sentencing". The "Truth in Sentencing" legislation which came into force in 1989 abolished automatic remissions. The prisoner's non-parole period as it is handed down by the courts thus becomes the sentence that the individual actually serves in prison. The president of the Criminal Lawyers Association estimated that the legislation would mean that sentences would "effectively increase by 300 per cent".[16] By March 1990, the then Minister had acknowledged that

226

the rapid growth in the State's prison population was a direct result of the Greiner government's tougher sentencing policies as well as a more stringent approach to policing ... (and) the *Truth in Sentencing Act* ... appeared to be a major contributing factor to the increase in prisoners.[17]

By July 1990, the Department of Corrective Services itself reported that the legislation had resulted in prisoners serving an average of an extra 50 days. This translated into an increase of an extra 525 prisoners being in gaol at ay one time, with a prediction that that figure would increase to 830 as the full effect of the legislation flowed through.[18]

This central feature of Liberal penal policy is a promise to allocate only a determinate, and therefore calculable, amount of pain on individual rule breakers. However, as Russell Hogg points out, the calculability extends only to the amount of time served, not to the extent of brutality experienced within that time.[19] Thus "Truth in Sentencing", he argues, is ideological sloganising rather than a political principle underpinning a detailed and coherent penal policy. Indeed, as Hogg goes on to suggest, the "Truth in Sentencing" principle, as it is manifested in current penal discourses, has resulted in greater uncertainty within prison. This increase in indeterminacy derives from the juxtaposition of the "Truth in Sentencing" practices with the other major ideological principle of the current Liberal administration, "economic rationality".

ECONOMIC RATIONALITY, PRISON LIFE AND DOMESTICITY

The Corrective Services budget is one of the few areas of State expenditure that has expanded during the Liberal administration. Nevertheless, the principle of economic rationality has been applied to prison administration. There have been cut-backs in prison spending on prison officer staff, on welfare and education staff and programmes.[20]

There have been other transfers of the costs of imprisonment from the state to the people in the population "families of prisoners". The cutting back of public sector spending results in prison practices that are in manifest contradiction to the principle of determinacy in the "back to justice" and "Truth in Sentencing" features of Liberal ideology. Even by 1987, the cut-backs on prison resources were creating uncertainty, stress, and increased violence in the CIP.[21] Thus the principle of legal rationality as it was being introduced through the social authoritarianism of the Liberal administration, whilst promising to offer greater determinancy of punishment, was operating in direct conflict with its other central priority, economic rationalism, which constantly undermines the conditions on which that determinacy should be based.[22]

PRISON OVERCROWDING, "GETTING TOUGH" AND PRIVATISATION WITH THE TRANSFER OF COSTS TO THE DOMESTIC SPHERE

Prison overcrowding resulted in a rolling back of several of the reformist shifts that incorporated domesticity into prison life in the post-Nagle era. The unit system of prison management at Bathurst and at Parklea prisons was undermined by the increase in the numbers of prisoners and the reduction in prisoner-prison staff ratios. In the Central Industrial Prison, where overcrowding and stress were already high prior to 1988,[23] the numbers had increased to their highest level of 600 by October 1989, 296 more than its usual capacity. By that month, prisoners were staying up to seven weeks in police lock-ups that were designed only for overnight accommodation.[24] The Corrective Services recognition of the change in the use of police cells from overnight accommodation to longer term imprisonment was acknowledged in the transfer of a prison officer to administer the prisoners detained there, a move that prompted the president of the New South Wales Police Association to respond.

> ... we would like to find out whether it is the intention of this Government to use the SPC as a prison and if it is well and good but we'll get our police officers out of there.[25]

In chapter five it was argued that it was the visits to partners or sons in detainment in police cells that created most problems for the outside carers. The risk of death in custody is highest in this phase of imprisonment.[26] The work of maintaining family contact is at the same time most essential in this initial traumatic period of imprisonment yet it is conducted under the most difficult conditions.

The Liberal government's response to the issue of court delays and the misuse of police cells was to fund a $300,000 study by Coopers & Lybrand, a firm of private consultants, to report on the New South Wales court system. The major conclusion of the report, published in 1989, was that too many accused people plead "not guilty" and that more procedures to increase the guilty plea rate should be introduced into the court system, including the abolition of legal aid for habitual offenders.[27] In taking this approach to remedying the injustices created by the delays in the court system, which in turn are created in part by the increases in policing, the New Right is, at the same time, supporting a shift in the criminal justice system that (contradictorily) fits more with the scientific managerialism of corporatism than with the classic liberal principles of justice centred on individualism.

The term "prison overcrowding" focuses attention on the issue of restricted space within prison. However there were several other reductions of resources to prisoners in the current rise in prison populations. There were also shortages of mattresses, prison clothes and shoes as well as extra restrictions on education, welfare and health services. The decreased ratios of prison officers to prisoners meant that there were restrictions on a range of services within the prison. Two of the restrictions in particular, those on the processing of prisoners mail and on the supervision of visiting, made the work of maintaining family contact more difficult and time consuming. The relative invisibility of the family status of prisoners in the New Right "tough" discourses of prison life meant that the extra demands placed on the resources necessary for visiting, of time, of space and of supervisory labour, were not being met by an extra supply of those resources. Indeed the levels of prison staffing have been cut rather than increased.[28]

The denial of the family status of prisoners who were constituted in the "tough" New Right discourses as violent and threatening individuals then became a denial too of the extent to which the penal administration drew on the provision, by the outside carers, of extra material resources for men in overcrowded prisons. In addition to having to bear all the financial expenses of visiting, with the funding cuts to the community groups which provide free transport and family support services, women visiting the Long Bay prison complex in the winter of 1989 reported that prisoners were needing pyjamas, shoes and jumpers.[29] Their reports were supported by the complaints made to and by the Inmates Support Group in the Central Industrial Prison in their negotiations with prison administrators, in the winter of 1989, about the insuffecent supply of tracksuits, jumpers and tee shirts.[30]

> It's bloody cold lately and I want to know what a bloke has to do to get some warm clothing? I try to get across to Reception every day but keep getting told that Reception hasn't got any jumpers.[31]

In response to these negotiations, the Support Group reported that "track suits, shorts and tee shirts can now be sent in via the post".[32]

The cost to the actual people who provide these resources is not only invisible to the prison administrators. This report from the Inmates Support Group indicates the difficulty that men in prison have in accepting that this provision is likely to be made by drawing on the scarce resources of their children, parents or partners outside, a difficulty resolved by the use of the passive voice in this report — that these clothes "can now be sent". Nevertheless it is in the official discourses on penality that the invisibility of the material and emotional support provided by people with the family obligation to care for prisoners was most marked.

MILITARISATION OF PRISON LIFE

The freedom to escape the prison experience through drink and drugs was in 1989 constitituted as a particularly proscribed form of behaviour. This led to the restriction of fruit and vegetables in the prison diet, an increased use of militaristic drug searches, and a ban on the use of Milton disinfectant in prisons on the grounds that its use in sterilising needles would encourage drug taking.[33] All these actions and policies went against the findings of the Muir Report in placing the blame for prison violence and disorder on the prisoners.

A particularly concrete expression of the way that people in the population "families of prisoners" were constituted as enemies in this revival of militarism in prison life was the loss of contact visits at Parramatta prison. The individual tables and chairs in the visiting section of that prison were replaced by long tables at which prisoners and visitors faced each other separated by a transparent plastic barrier that extended the length of the table. The powerful rhetoric of drug control meant that handing babies over the barrier for a cuddle by their fathers brings immediate reprimands even though the babies have been strip searched prior to the visit.[34]

In a reinforcement of the constititution of the domestic labour of visiting as a threat to the state, the Minister asserted that it was mainly women making family visits to gaols who were responsible for drugs entering prisons: "Mr Yabsley said yesterday that most drugs entering jails were concealed in the vaginas of visitors".[35]

The Special Response Unit was given specialised training in visitor interception and visitor interviewing.[36] There was an increase in the numbers of visitors being searched by this unit.[37] By mid 1990, the New South Wales Council for Civil Liberties reported receiving several complaints by partners and other relatives of men in prison, especially those visiting men in Maitland and Bathurst prisons, about "unjustified and undignified body searches".[38] The labour of maintaining family contact under these conditions exemplifies the point that the work of caring for adults is not a normal extension of family relations but can involve reversals of relationships and breaching of sexual taboos that can be particularly stressful for those providing the labour, and for the people receiving it. In constituting partners or parents of prisoners as potential threats to prison security in this way, the state increases the appropriation of women's energy and women's bodies. Moreover the conflicting moralities of domesticity and penality placed women at greater risk of imprisonment themselves, in the militarisitic interpretation of drugs in prison. In February 1989 the Minister for Corrective Services reported that as a result of his increased monitoring of visitors several grandmothers were amongst those arrested for smuggling drugs to their relatives inside prison.[39]

However, one other Liberal administration response to the Muir Report was to end imprisonment as an option for fine defaulters. Traffic offenders, who comprise the larger proportion of people imprisoned for fine default are now liable to loss of their licence, not imprisonment, as a punishment for failure to pay traffic fines — a penalty that fits the economic rationality of "a utilitarian calculus of suffering" for this more "tolerated illegality".[40] Nevertheless, for those prisoners whose crimes did not fit this tolerated category, the move to a "just deserts" policy of punishment meant that there was a general re-masculinisation of prison life which had major consequences for domesticity and for the labour of people in the population "families of prisoners": parents, friends and partners of prisoners become constituted as potential accessories to crime in the drugs in prisons discourses, and the work of maintaining family contact became less visible in the general swing towards the brutalising and segregative policies that increased the level of stress in prisons.

As part of his campaign to present a public image as a minister who would "show who was in control of the prison",[41] the Minister for Corrective Services imposed restrictions on prisoners with an escape record. Prisoners with a record of escape were restricted from spending any part of their imprisonment in minimum security gaols. Invisible in this decision were the problems for the people who do the work of maintaining family contact and maintaining men's morale during their imprisonment. Moreover the introduction of this policy was infused with the symbolism of a "tough" minister getting to grips with hardened criminals using force to escape by "breaking out". Prisoners captured after an escape were to be moved to a high security prison, Tamworth, hundreds of kilometres from Sydney. The Minister declared that this new prison, which will house 150 prisoners, will be made as "spartan" as possible.[42] This policy was in contrast with the Department's own research which, as the discussion in chapter six indicates, shows that a significant number of escapes are by men who overstay their day or work leave, or who do not break out, but walk out of prisons because they have family problems they feel they can only resolve by being at home.[43] This plan was revised by the more reformist Liberal prison adminstration of 1991. However in this latest rehabilitative set of layering of penal discourses that centre around reform through industry, Tamworth — the punishment prison — is to become the home for those prisoners who refuse to work in prison industries. The emphasis on "reform through industry" in this revised form of rehabilitation then creates a population of family carers who will bear the hidden punishment and costs of caring for "the recalcitrants". It will be the outside carers of these prison "strikers" who will do the work of maintaining family contact by travelling the twelve hour return journey from the metropolitan areas of the state to this remote prison. However Tamworth symbolises the ambivalence of a reform adminstration as this country prison will also be used to reduce the travel costs for those people in the Tamworth region whose sons or partners were previously held on remand in a prison a three hour journey away.

Although it is at the remand stage of the penal process that the tension of prison overcrowding was felt most keenly in the 1988–1991 period, the stress of visiting prisoners in the Long Bay complex and at other maximum security prisons increased. With increased pressure on resources resulting from prison overcrowding, visiting times were cut and the period of waiting at the gaols for a visit extended. Prisoners caught with drugs were refused contact visits or telephone calls for five years as a penalty for drug taking.[44]

The greater difficulties of prison visiting occurred at just the time when there were greater pressures on parents and partners of prisoners to maintain family contact. The move to a militarisation of prison life produces a major point of tension in the intersection of prison and home as the two major sites of morality. The combination of prison overcrowding, the extended use of police cells for holding remand prisoners, and the increasingly militaristic constitution of prison life led to reports of increasingly higher levels of negativism and stress inside gaol.[45] One of the most telling indicators of this tension is the increase in prison suicides in the 1989–1990 period. By May 1990, although the administrative year was only three quarters of the way through, there had been fourteen deaths by suicide. Eileen Baldry pointed out that "this compares with an average of four to five over the previous 12 years".[46]

Chapter four of this study showed that concern for the material wellbeing of their partners or sons was one of the principal reasons that people perform the arduous and stressful labour of visiting prison. Whilst women are at risk of being made responsible for these deaths, both by themselves and by the judiciary,[47] the labour of maintaining family contact became more difficult, more hazardous and more costly in the reconstitution of penality in the 1988–1991 period.

PRIVATISATION OF PENAL CONTROL

Chapter two outlined the materialist argument that one of the major transformations of the legal-penal sphere was the transfer of the power to impose coercive force from the private sphere to the state. Both private policing and privately controlled prisons, in their various mercenary forms, became redundant, even threatening, to the imperative to maintain widespread control of the domestic population in the new more volatile class relations of a market society. The move to allocate to the state monopoly control over the power to use deadly force was part of the rationalisation of social control that "inserted the power to punish more deeply into social life" [48] whilst securing the appearance of the separation of that power from the dominant economic class. By these last decades of the twentieth century, the extensive range of goods and services that come under the umbrella of penal-welfare provision has meant that the economic role of the state has expanded to such an extent that the state controls a budget equal to one third or more of that of the entire private sector. The dominance of the economic rationalist imperative of the New Right gives greater priority to the policy that economic control in the penal sphere should be transferred away from the state back to the private sector, over the importance of securing the appearance of the disinterested admin-istration of moral force. This policy then makes more manifest the connection between the exploitation of labour and the control of the population. The boundaries between the economic and the political spheres become even more permeable.

The New Right governments in the United States of America, in the United Kingdom and in New South Wales have included commodification of punishment as part of their programme of economic rationalisation. Twelve states in the USA have implemented some form of private enterprise prisons. In Australia the "old right" in the form of the Nationalist Party administration in Queensland introduced a privately run prison in 1989 and in that year in New South Wales the Minister for Corrective Services commissioned a merchant banking firm, Kleinwort Bensom Australia Limited, to report into private sector involvement in the management of the prison system. The Minister endorsed the eventual report by these princes of private enterprise that did indeed recommend the introduction of privately managed prisons. in New South Wales. In New South Wales the first private prison will be a medium/minimum security gaol at Junee.

The commodification and marketing of prison life has several aspects. First, that the government pays a firm in the private sector for the provision of management and administrative services involved in either running a prison, or in providing perimeter controls, prisoner escorts or prison catering. Secondly, that in the privately run prison, prisoners' labour is tendered out to other firms for the production of commodities. Thirdly, that prison officers lose their security of tenure and have to compete for their jobs in the privately run prisons in a competitive system of regular contract renewal. The emphasis in this set of discourses of economic rationality is on the increased cost-effectiveness and administrative efficiency that market based competitiveness would bestow on the sphere of punishment and control.

The more overt fusion of capitalist interests with social control has led to several debates about the ethics of mixing profitability with imprisonment. The criticisms have included the arguments:

1   that the cost effectiveness is based on a false accounting that ignores the hidden costs of state infrastructural support;[49]
2   that cost effectiveness depends upon clauses in the contract guaranteeing a minimum bed occupancy rate. This then undermines community debate about reducing the rate of imprisonment;
3   that the priority given to cost effectiveness undermines the wages, security and job conditions of prison officers working in the private system;
4   that the priority given to cost effectiveness leads to greater dependence on capital intensive forms of surveillance that parallel the forms of containment condemned in the Nagle Report as an "electronic zoo" and thus a cruel and unusual form of punishment;
5   that the insertion of profitability into the sphere of punishment and control leads to the development of a new and powerful lobby group whose interests are to maintain and extend imprisonment as a form of punishment;

6   that the transfer of responsibility for the day to day running of prison life enables the state to distance itself from accountability for the crises that result from the complex contradictions of imprisonment as a form of control;

7   that one especially significant aspect of (6) above is that the transfer of responsibility for penal control also involves the delegation of the right to use deadly force to an agency that is not directly accountable to the electorate. Moreover, given the complex interconnectedness of corporate capital, it is possible that the firm that employs the labour of the prisoner is closely associated with the firm that has the constitutional right to kill the prisoner. This then not only reconstructs the relative power between capital and labour within the prison but has wider implications for the redistribution of surplus value in the production of commodities in the wider labour market. The pressure on productivity within the prison has the potential to undermine the bargaining power of labour in the outside economy;

8   that the civil rights of prisoners in privately run prisons would be at greater risk. The current scrutiny of state prisons by community civil rights representatives would be replaced by the state scrutiny of private prisons. Community surveillance then would be placed at one remove from its current position, being able only to monitor the monitoring of the state. Moreover the current (although relatively powerless) scrutiny of families of prisoners in state prisons could well become diffused in the duality of accountability involved in the system of private imprisonment. The mediating and negotiating labour of concerned parents or partners would become even more complicated with the risk that their complaint would be passed from one bureaucracy to another when the state is responsible for long term policy, and the private sector for the day to day administration of punishment and control.

The implications of the shift in penal policy for the people providing the labour of family support for prisoners has been generally invisible in the debate surrounding its introduction. However, because the current form of commodification of the penal sphere is focused on the medium security prison in the corrective and normalising moment of imprisonment, the Queensland profit making prison has been organised around a unit system of management, as this more domestic form of control is expected to be more cost-effective in reducing tension and thus making fewer demands on staff.[50] This prison also includes family counselling as part of its rehabilitative programme.

Borallon, the Queensland profit-making prison, has a special significance in the current negotiations between the State and the private sector in Australia. As the first prison run by a profit-making enterprise whose long term policy is to become a widespread and intrinsic part of the penal system in Australia, it has become a showpiece. The administrators, taking account of all the above criticisms, have taken care to demonstrate the superiority of private enterprise over state run prisons. The prison administrators emphasise its openness to community representatives as well as to the monitoring agencies of the State. The current financial arrangements are not based on per capita payments. The public discourse of both owners and supervisors emphasise the correctional rather than the punitive aspects of privatised imprisonment.[51] This image, however, is belied by the tensions that accrue when a profit-making enterprise becomes more deeply embedded in a penal system. The question arises as to whether this firm, or any private firm, will be as open as the State system, to criticisms of cost cutting, inhumane conditions, and an emphasis on brutality rather than reformation, if it takes on the management of an increased number and wider range of penal institutions.

HOME DETENTION

The Minister, when in opposition, criticised the Labour administration's plans for a Home Detention scheme as a penal programme that demonstrated that government's "softness" on criminals. However, in the first two years of his administration he indicated a more ambivalent attitude to the programme. By mid 1990, the minister had reaffirmed his unwillingness to go ahead with home imprisonment, indicating that periodic detention, that is weekend or midweek imprisonment, was the more favoured option for "intermediate" punishment.[52] There were however several public commitments to the programme of home based imprisonment by members of the judiciary and by senior members of his probation and parole policy administrative staff.[53] It was through the most recent layering of rehabilitative penal discourses that home imprisonment was eventually introduced in New South Wales. The scheme introduced in 1992 planned for 80 homes to be constituted as prisons by the end of that year.

Penality in New South Wales in the first three years of the Liberal administration was reconstructed as three more clearly demarcated sites of control, with the prison, in the segregative moment of control, becoming the site of more punitive and militaristic relations in which there was a negation of the prisoner as a man with a family life. In this moment of penality, economic rationality took the form of pressures to decrease resources and staff-prisoner ratios. Secondly, the corrective phase of imprisonment in the medium security prisons became defined as the province of a mixture of public and private sector interests in which economic rationality legitimated increasingly capital intensive forms of control and surveillance mediated by a more domesticated form of management. Labour costs are reduced in this phase by transferring responsibility for control to a non-unionised and thus a cheaper labour force. Thirdly in the normalising moment of imprisonment the boundaries between home and prison become far more permeable, firstly with the increasing use of periodic detention and secondly with the introduction of intensive surveillance in the form of home detention.

In chapter six it was argued that the tensions of prison did not end once a man had left gaol but that the frustrations experienced in prison were likely to be manifested in major emotional or physical tensions in the home. In the majority of the most visible current penal discourses in New South Wales, the negation of prisoners as men with a family life is in direct contrast with the emphasis placed on the family in other aspects of Liberal policy. At the same time that the state government is attempting to reconstitute family life as the site of unequal relationships between men and women and children it is creating a situation in which more men will leave prison having had months or years of experiencing the frustrations of imprisonment. The shift, then, towards an increasing invisibility of the family in the present discourses of penality seems likely to be the basis for major dangers to the people who constitute the population "families of prisoners". The nexus between caring and dependency is being realigned but at potentially major costs to the people providing that care.[54]

It is important, however, to interpret the changes in the penal sphere, and their impact on the population "families of prisoners", in a broader framework than that of penality alone. The changes are occurring in an era in which, in Australia, there has also been a change in the constitution of domesticity with the restructuring of the federal government's social welfare policies.

THE FEDERAL LABOUR ADMINISTRATION'S SOCIAL SECURITY REVIEW: INCREASING THE VISIBILITY OF THE LABOUR AND THE COSTS OF DOMESTICITY

Running parallel with the State-based changes to prison life outlined above are the Federal government's attempts to redistribute resources to *all* people performing the caring work of looking after children. This brief includes, as a particular goal, an attempt to improve the position of sole parents, and of children, in families on low incomes.[55] A general theme of the Social Security Review is to increase participation in the paid work force by those people who have also to do the work of caring for children. This includes carers in sole parent families. The implementation of the recommendations has improved the financial position of people doing the work of child care at the same time as it has enabled those carers to enter the paid work force without bearing exorbitant "tax cuts" in the form of an outright loss of their "carer's pension".

For people living in the complex social space "families of prisoners" the impact of these changes varies according to whether it rebounds:

1   on those people who are made "sole parents" by the imprisonment of the offender;

2   on those people who are either the partners or parents of a
prisoner but who do not have the added responsibility of caring
for the prisoner's child.

In the first case, the position of the outside carers of prisoners'
children who opt to do the triple work of child care, care for the prisoner
and paid work would be improved by the two aspects of the scheme that
make entry in the labour force less punitive: the proposals to increase the
numbers of child care places for those at work or undergoing some form of
training, and the proposals not to impose a 100 per cent "tax" on the sole
parents pension.

That group of carers who opt to conform to the "ideal" of total carer
by not taking up paid work benefit, in part, from the increase in family
allowances and from the schemes to supplement the rental allowances for
sole parents. To this extent then, imprisonment of the father becomes less
of a punishment to the family outside.

However, what is omitted from these "family packages" is the
acknowledgement that one particularly symbolic group of sole-parent
unpaid carers have a double and contradictory burden to bear: the loss by
"civil death" of the earning co-parent and the costs of supporting that
"civilly dead" man. The penal policies implemented at state level are
making it more difficult for people in the population "families of
prisoners" to negotiate the double roles of paid workers and "prisoner's
visitors" at the same time as the family policies, implemented at federal
level, are encouraging sole parents and other categories of working age
women to re-enter the paid work force.

This particular population of people in New South Wales then are
bearing the burden of the way that social life is split and divided between
the various administrative levels of government. The costs of caring for
prisoners are the responsibility of state governments whilst the costs of
caring for the children of prisoners largely come under the umbrella of
Federal responsibility. Between these two areas of responsibility, the
specific interests of the outside carers of prisoners and prisoners' children
disappear. The benefits that have accrued from the Federal government's
redistribution of resources could be seen to be simply contributing to the
expenses created by the State policies that have transferred part of the costs
of imprisonment to the carers of imprisoned men: a hidden and regressive
transfer incorporating, as it does, a shift of costs both from women to men
and from the lowest income groups to the general population.

A longer term consequence of the federally based redistribution of
costs could be an increased disillusionment with imprisonment as a
punishment. If the sole parents of prisoners' children are less likely than
other sole parents to take up the options of paid work, it is possible that
they will become an increasingly visible group of carers, whose economic
dependence on the state then could be at risk of becoming increasingly
defined as "deviant". The principle of "less eligibility" becomes

increasingly undermined as a *raison d'être* of institutional imprisonment when at the federal level the penality of being a sole parent is lessened, when at the same time at the level of state politics, the penal discourses become increasingly centred on economic rationality, which incorporates that same principle.

There is a further reason to be aware of this potential shift in the definition of the population "families of prisoners". The other strand of the Federal government's "family package" that is, in part, both financing and legitimating the redistribution of resources to families with children, is the relatively successful attempt to shift the costs of the maintenance of children to the non-custodial parent.[56] Prisoners are one group who are manifestly excluded from this responsibility. Those sole parents who are the outside carers of the children of the "civil dead" then are likely to be defined as even less "normal" in this reconstitution of domesticity. The actual intersection between "family policies" and penal policies could become a much more visible aspect of public discourses of punishment and control if the maintenance of families of prisoners becomes a more obviously costly aspect of imprisonment.

The extent to which these family policies *will* have an impact on penal policy in an era in which economic and social uncertainty engenders a hard line "law and order" atmosphere is unclear. Economic rationalism might well give way to social authoritarianism at just this boundary between prison and home, however visible it becomes with the implementation of the federal goverment's "family package". Nevertheless there is reason to expect a very heightened sense of volatility in this current constitution of "the home and the prison".

NOTES

1   Outlined in chapter two.

2   Williams, F, *Social Policy: a Critical Introduction* (1989) at 118–122; Sawer, M (ed), *Australia and the New Right* (1982).

3   Hogg, in Findlay, M and Hogg, R, *Understanding Crime and Criminal Justice* (1988) at 2–4.

4   Clark, P, "Arrests for Swearing Up 300pc under New Laws" *Sydney Morning Herald* 31 Aug 1989 at 2. Brown summarises recent studies indicating that a central aspect of contemporary penality is the imprisonment of Koori people for social behaviour that, in other groups, is not penalised (Brown, D, "Returning to Sight: Contemporary Australian Penality" (1989) 16/3 *Soc Just* (Issue 37) at 144–146).

5   Cited in Williams, above n2 at 216.

6   Davies, D, "From Dogberry to Cop Shop: the Police as the Arm of the Modern State" (1982) 79 *Aust Left R* 20–27; Rice, S, "Police may use

banned ammunition" *National Times* 3 Sept 1982 at 4198; Sturgess, G, "Drug Squad terror tactics cause alarm" *Bulletin* 29 July 1980 at 28–29; Cunneen, C, "The Policing of Public Order: Some Thoughts on Culture, Space and Political Economy", in Findlay and Hogg, above n3.

7   Evidence presented to the Royal Commission into Black Deaths in Custody sitting in Sydney on 6th February, 1990, demonstrated that both the *Summary Offences Act* and section 249 of the *Local Government Act* were being used by the police to imprison Koori people for consuming alcohol on public streets. Moreover, a number of youths have also been charged under the Act for wearing T-shirts with a pro-Treaty political message. See: Kennedy, A and Libesman, T, "Summary Offences, Australian Capital Territory (1988)" (1989) 2/37 *Abor LB* at 2.

8   However Bonney points out that the Act was one of a number of factors contributing to this increase.

9   Migliorini, P, *Report to the Human Rights Commissions's National Inquiry into Racist Violence*, Sydney: Office of Multicultural Affairs, 1989.

10   *Sydney Morning Herald* 17 July 1989 at 2; 18 July 1989 at 3; 21 July 1989 at 11.

11   In April 1989.

12   *Sydney Morning Herald* 29 Apr 1989 at 1.

13   When this term covers the range of forms of imprisonment including being held in police cells on arrest. In the six month period to the end of December 1988, only four people had been sentenced to imprisonment for offensive behaviour. See Bonney, R, *New South Wales Summary Offences Act*, Sydney: New South Wales Bureau of Crime Statistics and Research, 1989 at 30.

14   Cited in Harvey, S, "Prisons Bursting At Seams", *Sydney Morning Herald* 18 May 1989 at 4.

15   Above n3 at 7.

16   In a press interview on the 19th June 1989: McKnight, D, "Barristers Warned on New Sentencing Laws" *Sydney Morning Herald* 19 June 1989 at 3.

17   Michael Yabsley in a press interview: see Cornwall, D, "New South Wales has a record 5,200 people in jail" *Sydney Morning Herald* 12 Mar 1990 at 4.

18   Moore, M, "Government Blunders on Prison Sentences" *Sydney Morning Herald* 25 July 1990 at 3.

19   Above n3 at 8.

20   Harvey, S, "More Inmates, Fewer Staff in Gaol", *Sydney Morning Herald* 7 Oct 1989 at 9; Williams, above n2 at 7.

21   From evidence to the Muir Report on conditions in the CIP. Muir, A G, *Report of the Inquiry into the Central Industrial Prison*, Sydney: Government Printer, 1988 at 416–419.

22   Brown, above n4.

23   Muir, above n21.

24   Harvey, S, above n20 at 9.

25 Taylor, cited in Harvey, S, "Prison Crowding Angers Unions", *Sydney Morning Herald* 24 July 1989 at 5.

26 Hatty, S and Walker, J, *Deaths in Australian Prisons* (1986) at 29.

27 Coopers & Lybrand, *Report on the New South Wales Court System*, Sydney: Coopers & Lybrand, 1989.

28 Harvey, above n25 at 5 and above n20 at 9.

29 In personal conversation with women visiting imprisoned men at the Long Bay prison complex and with prison welfare officers in the winter of 1989.

30 *Rogues* (1989) 1/1 at 9 & 34.

31 Letter signed 'Frigid' in *Rogues* (1989) 1/1.

32 Id at 34.

33 Although this ban was subsequently revised after confrontations between Yabsley and the Liberal Minister for Health. Moore, M, "Hard Cell" *Sydney Morning Herald* 16 Dec 1989 at 42.

34 From personal accounts by women visiting Parramatta prison in February 1990. By May 1990, Parramatta had become the site of a number of prisoner political activities including the destruction of some sections of the prison by fire. Restricted visiting was one of the factors cited by prison officers as creating the tension in the prison prior to the demonstrations.

35 Aubin, T, "Ultrasound for Jail Visitors" *Sydney Morning Herald* 24 Feb 1989 at 5.

36 New South Wales Department of Corrective Services, *Annual Report* (1987–8) at 20.

37 Id at 100.

38 Ken Horler QC, President of the NSW Council for Civil Liberties cited by Luis Garcia ("Jail visitors must endure body search, Yabsley says", *Sydney Morning Herald* 1 June 1990 at 7).

39 In a media interview with Tracey Aubin (*Sydney Morning Herald* 24 Feb 1989).

40 Hirst, P, "The Concept of Punishment" in Hirst, P (ed), *Law, Socialism and Democracy* (1986).

41 This is a phrase that the Minister for Corrective Services has used in several of his interviews with the media.

42 In media interviews on 14th April 1990.

43 Gorta, A and Nguyen, M, *An Analysis of Interviews with Recaptured Escapees: some suggestions of reasons for escape*, Sydney: Research and Statistics Division, New South Wales Department of Corrective Services, 1988.

44 Above n35.

45 Harvey, S, "Prison Bursting at Seams", *Sydney Morning Herald* 18 May 1989 at 4; Moore, M, "Longer Terms for Youths After New Laws" *Sydney Morning Herald* 10 Sept 1989 at 2; Moore, above n33.

46 Baldry, E, "Death Behind Bars: the suicide crisis in New South Wales" *Sydney Morning Herald* 7 May 1990 at 17.

47   Chapter five cites the case of a magistrate who laid the responsibility for a prison suicide partly upon the prisoner's wife, for her refusal to take the prisoner's child to visit him in prison. Terry, P, "Official Neglect 'Led to Black's Suicide'" *The Australian* 2 Jan 1990 at 4.

48   Foucault, M, *Discipline And Punish* (1977).

49   These points have been made in a range of texts that include Krajck, K, "Punishment for Profit" (1984) 21/3 *Across the Board* 20–27; Zdenkowski, G, "The Private Life of the Prisoner" *Sydney Morning Herald* 22 Dec 1988 at 5; George, A, "The State Tries an Escape" (1989) 14/2 *Leg Serv B* 53–54

50   Hutto, D, from speech given on television program *The 7:30 Report*: "Prisons for Profit" 14 Feb 1989.

51   Roberts, G, "The Prison Where Privilege Beats Punishment" *Sydney Morning Herald* 16 Apr 1990 at 3.

52   In a press release on 24th April 1990.

53   Recorded for example in *Proceedings of the Institute of Criminology* No 77: "Punishment Outside Gaol" (1988).

54   And the specific population "families of Australian Capital Territory offenders" seem to be particularly at risk of experiencing the condensed contradictions of home imprisonment in the recommendation, cited in chapter four, that 80 per cent of its present prisoners be controlled under a home imprisonment programme.

55   Raymond, J, "Bringing Up Children Alone: Policies for Sole Parents", Social Security Review Issues Paper No 3, Woden: Department of Social Security, 1987; Department of Social Security, *Annual Report (1988–89)*, Canberra, 1989 at ch2.

56   Id at 98.

9

CONCLUSION:
THEORETICAL SIGNIFICANCE OF THE
PRISON AND THE HOME

The home and the prison are defined in this study as two of the major spheres of social control in a political economy in which the contradictions of freedom and inequality are played out. A basic argument that has been presented is that, as liberal capitalism becomes overlaid by its successive forms — industrial capitalism, welfare capitalism, and advanced corporate consumer capitalism — different rationalities have been brought into play so that the intersection of home and prison has become a maze of contradictory interdependencies.

Underlying this relationship between the prison and the home is a complex and often contradictory mass of ideas, philosophies, moralities, religious edicts and economic "laws". Sometimes aspects of this confusion of abstract but powerful ideas are explicitly stated. Sometimes they are presented as a seemingly coherent, consciously worked out statement of social order. However, more often than not the contradictions and complexities of the dual moralities surrounding the construction of penality and domesticity in liberal capitalism remain a confused, largely unspoken, yet influential set of social rules.

The femininist challenge to the social sciences centres on the significance of the relationship between the domestic, private and public spheres and on the way in which that relationship is made invisible in the dominant discourse. This argument, that the analysis of the construction of domesticity is essential to an understanding of power and inequality, centres on the basic contradiction of universalism. That is, that universalism is like being pregnant: it is not possible to be a little bit non-universal. If universalism does not hold for *all* citizens then, logically, it cannot hold for *any* citizen. Individualism can then not be the entitlement of only a section of the citizenry. Because of this basic character of the principle of universalism upon which liberal democratic capitalism is based, domesticity is far more central to our understanding of the embeddedness of inequality in social relationships than are race, ethnicity or gender. Although inequalities centred upon race, ethnicity and gender remain as contradictory aspects of the supposed universalism of liberal democratic capitalist relations, it is possible (even if it is not probable) to envisage that each of the inequalities based on these three social categories could eventually be dissolved through appeals to universalism. People whose inequality is centred upon domesticity, however, cannot make use of this appeal. The public/private duality of civil life is interdependent yet incompatible with domesticity. "The family" is necessary to civil life yet is constituted as a constant threat to the criteria on which civil life is based.

A key aspect of the embeddedness of this form of inequality is the relative invisibility of this interdependence between these apparently incompatible values of social life. It is in the lives of people in the population "families of prisoners" that this central contradiction is manifested in one of its most condensed forms. "Why" and "how" we persuade ourselves that the interdependence of domestic and public life does not exist are particularly significant questions when we pose them in the intersection of the two domains as it occurs in the legal-penal sphere. This is because it is in this area of public life that the powerful signifiers "power", "morality" and "rationality" (around which the contradiction between familism and individualism revolve) are most clearly articulated. This potential for clarity, that is a special characteristic of the legal-penal sphere, then makes more urgent, for the defence of the principle of universalism, the necessity to mask or marginalise the contradiction of the interdependence and incompatibility between domestic and public life.

It is from the perspective of the recent feminist materialist studies of the economy and welfare state that the contradictions and complexities of the often invisible social laws which construct this relationship have been most elegantly dissected. Over the past fifteen years this approach has delineated several aspects of the way that the state, through a variety of social policies, mediates family relations in a class society. The key concept in these analyses, of the significance of "caring" in the construction of inequality in class society, has been taken as the central tool of analysis of the way that the family is incorporated into the penal sphere. Social policy analysis indicates that it is *the nexus between caring and dependence* that is at the centre of the way that the relations of production and reproduction in a class society intersect. The evidence from the analysis of penal policies and practices and from the personal experiences recounted in chapters five to eight, indicate that this nexus, as it operates in the social space between the home and the prison, results in particularly condensed experiences of economic exploitation, political oppression and cultural domination. Hidden labour, hidden costs, and the hidden incorporation into the field of punishment and control, are the risks inherent in the caring relationships of the domestic sphere, when a partner, son or brother is sentenced to the "rational" punishment of imprisonment.[1]

When the outside carer of the prisoner also has the family obligation to care for the prisoner's child, the experience of living day to day between the two spheres of morality becomes particularly exploitative. The experiences of the women who took on this double load of caring in New South Wales in the late 1980s demonstrate the contradictions, and consequent burdens of caring, that occur when "the prison" reflects in a condensed form the gendered division of labour of parenting as it occurs in wider society. The evidence from this study[2] indicates that, in New South

243

Wales in the late 1980s, the parenthood of male prisoners is concurrently crucial to the sense of self of prisoner parents, yet is virtually invisible in the official penal discourses. It is the work of the outside carers of prisoners' children that provides the infrastructure of unpaid, yet costly, domestic labour that bridges the gap between these two incompatible aspects of punishment and control — the significance yet the negation of prisoner parenthood. The work of caring that is involved in this particularly condensed contradiction of social life also includes the extensive skills of managing the tensions and stresses experienced by the children. The principle of the innocence of children, which is one of the basic values of civil society in this moment of the familial-political economy, is at odds with the punishment that the children of prisoners experience. This punishment is manifested in several ways: in poverty, in the separation from the parent, in the particularly painful experience of separation because of the imprisonment of the parent, in the knowledge that ones father is being punished and the risk of stigma which that experience brings, as well as in the specific tensions that can be part of the experience of visiting prison. The work then, of caring for children of prisoners, ameliorating as it does some of the hidden punishments that the children experience, plays a particularly significant part in maintaining the "civility" of civil society. However, although this is an especially onerous form of domestic labour that draws on especially skilful aspects of the ability to care, there is little acknowledgement of its significance, either in official discourses of penality or in government, orthodox academic, or even feminist analyses of family life. Without that skilled labour however, the punishment of imprisonment would impose costs on both the prisoner and the child that would seriously undermine the legitimacy of the state as a body that has the right to impose just and universalistic punishment. The concept of the deprivation of liberty of prisoners does not extend to the notion that they should be forced, too, to lose for all time their civil status as parents. Given the current constitution of parenthood that emphasises "quality time", and bonding for both men and women as parents, the lack of all contact with their children would effectively cut prisoners off from their status as parents in contemporary society. Without the domestic labour of maintaining family contact, that consequence of imprisonment would became a more manifest aspect of penality. The material in this study, both from the review of the history of penality in the state, and from the accounts of the carers, indicates that the costs to the state, were that particularly significant form of domestic labour to be withheld, would be high. This is because that specific form of the work of caring has implications for the costs of the health of the children, of the wellbeing of the prisoners, and for the costs of imprisonment, as it is the loss of visits that plays such a large part in the pre-conditions of prison revolts and even in the destruction of prisons. The carers' work provides a bridge between domesticity and penality in this specific case, of the parenthood of prisoners, that is then extraordinarily theoretically problematic in its invisibility.

The extent to which the parallel punishment, and work, of the population constituted as "families of prisoners" is hidden varies with the different forms of rationality at different moments of penality. The shifts in the discursive practices of penality have a dual significance for those people who comprise the population "families of prisoners". The prison crises of the 1970s, coinciding with the "retreat from welfare" discourses in the social policy sphere, framed the immediate historical setting that constructed the complex and contradictory social space of the thirty-eight people whose experiences, of having a family obligation to care for prisoners in New South Wales gaols, form the basis of the study.

The "prison crisis" has been interpreted in part as a crisis of masculinity. The false universalism that disguised the masculinity of prison life became increasingly exposed throughout the 1960s and 1970s. The liberal response to that crisis was an attempt to reinsert domesticity into the penal sphere. This more manifest co-optation of domesticity into the sphere of punishment took a number of forms and the role played by the social sciences in this intersection of penal and domestic life was significant. What was also signifcant was that certain domesticities were bracketed out in this attempt to balance the stresses between segregation, correction and normalisation.

The introduction of these liberal reforms that were layered onto the more conservative, masculinist segregative and punitive penal policies, has brought some benefits to the people in the population "families of prisoners". The increased recognition of the importance of the intersection of domesticity and penality in the liberal reformist phases has alleviated some of the economic and personal costs of the work of maintaining family contact for some partners and parents of prisoners. However the accounts of the thirty-eight "carers" indicate, too, that the shift from the relative "invisibility" of family life in the classical liberal period to a greater recognition of the importance of "the family" in penal control in the reformist eras has also resulted in increased costs as their labour, and their family commitment to provide, is more manifestly incorporated into penal life. Moreover, during the 1980s, as domesticity was more openly inserted into penal life, the tensions that occurred between the co-existing sets of discursive practices — the segregative, correctional and normalising moments of imprisonment — also had punitive consequences for the people who were members of the population "families outside". It is particularly the concept of "coping" as it has been deconstructed within the feminist materialist analyses of social policy which provides a framework for interpreting the extensive skills and labour and costs to the outside carers of prisoners in their response to the complexities of current penal discourses.

The evidence from the carers of prisoners supports the arguments, from the feminist analyses of domesticity, that rationality is not exclusive to non-domestic areas of social life. The liberal discourses which construct the segregation of domestic and non-domestic life around the distinction between rationality and emotionality depend upon a very narrow definition of rationality, one that countenances only its abstract, intellectual components.

The socialist critique of this "abstracted" rationality deplores the false segregation of the senses and abstract thought in this liberal capitalist version of "intelligence". This differentiation between intellectual and manual skills, growing out of the productive system of industrial capitalism and compounded in the increasingly capital intensive forms of production in the early twentieth century, legitimated the devaluation of manual labour. The feminist materialist criticism goes further and focuses on the social construction of the segregation of the intellectual, sensual *and emotional* components of intellectual life, and the way in which the construction of false boundaries between those three components reinforces the devaluation of domesticity. The experiences of people with family obligations to prisoners add substantial weight to the feminist argument for a broader definition of rationality, one that reaffirms the holistic character of intellectual ability. This understanding of intellectual ability goes beyond the narrow definitions of either economic, legal-penal or scientific rationality that authorise our day to day experiences in the non-domestic spheres of contemporary social life. It is in the condensed experiences of people in the population "families of prisoners" that the compound skills of "caring" are set in clearest relief against the narrower rationalities of the public sphere. Nevertheless, although the sets of "knowledges" that are based on caring-for-the-prisoner are used and exploited in several ways throughout the experience of imprisonment (and of release on parole) it is through the narrower "rationalities" of the economic, scientific or legal-penal worlds that the power to prescribe and proscribe behaviours continues to be authorised. In this particularly unequal imbalance between power, morality and rationality, caring skills are translated into "coping behaviours" in an intensive way in the social space between prison and home. As in the other examples of the construction of family life as the long-time care of dependants, the state is able to draw on and exploit the complex skills of "coping" in the chronic crisis of imprisonment. However, although the penal discourses exploit the malleability, negation, and accountability inherent in "coping" and thus lead in many cases to political quietism, caring for prisoners can also involve the people who are the "outside carers" in both individual and collective political action. Family obligations to imprisoned men have contradictory capacities: to control carers into political quietism as well as to galvanise partners and parents into fierce and sustained opposition to the injustices experienced by the men inside.

There are four major ways in which boundaries are constructed between prison and home as the two moral sites of the reproduction of the social relations of capitalism: the home within the prison, the home clearly separated from the prison, the boundaries between home and prison becoming more permeable and fourthly, the prison within the home. Although it is possible to see an historical pattern in this model these patterns of intersection between home and prison also coexist and it is this coexistence that makes day to day life so contradictory for people with family obligations to prisoners. This model of the diverse relationship between the prison and the home indicates that there is likely to be an increasing exploitation of the domestic labour of the people who comprise the population "families of prisoners". The "rationalities" that legitimate the powerful morality of penal life seem to be reconstructing the boundaries between home and prison in the form of increasingly complex and contradictory methods of social control that alternatively constitute the family as the site of "resource and resolve" and as the site of a range of new criminalities.

The current restructuring of the social space between prison and family life makes more urgent the task of clarifying the complex and contradictory ways in which "home" and "prison" are constituted. Through constituting both family and punishment as unproblematic, the simplistic symbolisations of social relationships of New Right administrations that legitimate their attempt to reimpose classic liberal patterns of power, morality and rationality upon the already complex contradictory layers of penal control, seem likely to lock people with a family obligation to care for prisoners in even more exploitative forms of hidden labour, hidden punishment and control. Although the corrective and normalising moments of penality remain as important elements in the sphere of punishment and control there is a much greater emphasis upon the more punitive and segregative aspects of prison life. The tensions created in the contradiction between legal and economic rationalities in the New Right programme of control seem likely to result in an extension of the hidden costs, hidden labour and hidden punishment of parents and partners of prisoners.

It has been argued that the feminist challenge to sociology has a singular characteristic in being the first theoretical perspective created by those who are directly exploited and disempowered by the relationships they are analysing.[3] The energy resulting from that first-hand involvement has been manifested in an increasing number of empirical investigations of masculinist forms of control and exploitation and an explosion of theoretical debates about the specific patterns of class, ethnic and gender power relations in which women (and men who resist masculinist power relationships) are enmeshed.

Throughout this monograph, it has been argued that one of the most significant forms of exploitation, oppression and domination is the one experienced by those who have a family obligation to care for prisoners. Moreover, this argument emphasises that an inherent aspect of that experience is its opaqueness. The material, emotional and social deprivation of the people who comprise that population makes the labour of theorising, and the costs of making the theoretical implications part of a public discourse, a particularly difficult task. Nevertheless, the most recent literature about the family obligation to care for prisoners comprises a series of papers and texts which have made more transparent the exploitation (and the reason for that exploitation) of this singular form of caring labour. It is notable that several of these authors have had the practical experience of living in the social space between family and prison, and of providing family care for imprisoned men and women.

In these writings they have also contributed to the feminist challenge to the social sciences. Any theoretical discipline that attempts both to understand and to change the intricate pattern of power, morality and rationality that circumscribes the lives of all people caught up in the exploitative relationships of class, ethnicity and gender has also to grasp the special significance of the experience of people living the complex and contradictory social space in which "prison" and "home" intersect. Their experience is not marginal to, but centrally implicated in, the ways in which productive and reproductive life has been, and is being, renegotiated. The current opaque but powerful reinterpretation of social life being imposed by New Right governments in familial-political economies characterised by a global restructuring of capital/labour relations and the particular tensions of an advanced corporate consumer economy, makes the task of exposing that complex and contradictory relationship the more urgent. From the review of the penal discourses outlined in chapters two to eight, it is argued that more people are likely to be caught up in the networks of control. There are likely to be an increasing number of bifurcatory systems of classification that end in more people being sent to prisons in the "hard" end of the penal system and of those prisons becoming the site of more and more brutal and exploitative forms of containment. The home, constituted as the site of unequal relationships between men and women is also likely, for people still attached to productive relations in the economic sphere, to become the site of more criminogenic forms of community based control in the normalising moment of penal control. Meanwhile, in the increasing ten- sions at the "hard end" of imprisonment, the "home", for those made marginal to productive life, is likely to play an increasingly significant, but officially invisible part in providing an infrastructure of financial support and source of unpaid physical and emotional labour, legitimated by, but going far beyond, the appeal of the "natural work of family caring".

The consequences of the restructring of government provision of services in the New Right agendas of "neo-liberalism" have been outlined in several of the socialist feminist analyses of the care of people made unproductive in the current form of capital labour relations. It seems likely that it is in the condensed relations of power, morality and rationality as they are played out in the intersection between home and prison that this restructuring of social life is likely to involve the most complex and contradictory forms of exploitation and domination. It is important that the implications of these changes for the people in the population "families of prisoners" should be made a continually visible part of the discourses of punishment and control.

Yeatman's three questions about the relationship between domestic and non-domestic life have formed the major framework for this study. Yeatman's position includes the argument that the feminist "promise" to sociology should included the agenda of "disestablishing the 'other' as a permissible term".[4] This argument has particular relevance for critical criminology. The condensed constitution of people in the population "families of prisoners" as "others" should be the privileged not the marginalised problematic of the discipline. It is because these "carers" live and work in one of the most densely layered of all the spheres of social life that the accounts of their experience bear the greatest promise for an understanding of the complexity of the social construction of inequality.

In a familial-political economy characterised by the contradictory combination of an increasingly deregulated financial and employment market, an emphasis upon the constitution of the individuality of the citizen as a consumer, and a "retreat from welfare" in the field of social policy, social control is increasingly comprising a more punitive state at the "hard end" of prison life, together with an expansion of the state in the fusion of punishment and welfare systems at the "normalising" end of the control continuum. It is against this specific historical setting that the study concludes with the argument that the focus upon the construction of domesticity should become a central aspect of both feminist and criminological investigations and, with the argument that is the corollary of that position, that these analyses should cut across the so far relatively rigid boundaries between the disciplines of feminist criminology, social policy analysis, and the radical critique of penality.

NOTES

1 The study has not recorded the parallel accounts of the people in New South Wales who care for women in prison. However the overview of the literature by Koban (see Koban, L, "Parents in Prison" (1983) 5 *Res L, Dev & Soc Cont* 171–183), cited in chapter five, indicates that these hidden costs are especially compounded in the case of carers of women prisoners.

2 From the texts cited in chapter six that refer both to New South Wales and to other states and countries.

3 Yeatman, A, "Feminism, Postmodernism and Sociology: versions II & I" unpublished paper, 1990: ver 1 in Nicholson, L (ed), *Feminism/ Post-modernism* (1990) at 27, citing MacKinnon, 1982.

4 Yeatman, id at 20.

APPENDIX A

RESEARCH DESIGN

INTRODUCTION

The research design is based on two broad approaches: an analysis of penal policies and discourses with a particular focus on the way in which those discourses have constituted the population "families of prisoners", and a review of the impact of those policies and practices as they operated in New South Wales in 1987–1988. This latter part of the research draws on:

1   the specific penal policies, practices and debates that operated in New South Wales in the period 1960–1988, and

2   the accounts of 38 people who were in the population "families of prisoners" in the eighteen month period May 1987 to November 1988.

METHODOLOGICAL THEORY AND DISCUSSION

The feminist challenge to the social sciences intersects with the question of whether there is a unique feminist method of inquiry. Epistemological questions of the impact of feminist inquiry on sociological theory have generated vigorous discussion within feminism about the appropriate methods or techniques for gathering material as well as the broader issues about theories of how research should proceed.[1] These three levels of debate, of *knowledge*, *method*, and of *methodology* have been infused with the ontological question of what it is to be a woman: whether forms of being and forms of knowing are so intertwined as to be inseparable issues, and what the implications of this conflation might be for research design and choice of research technique in feminist inquiry.

The debate over whether and how a feminist sociological research is possible raises issues about the viability of disciplinary boundaries, the way that taken for granted aspects of social life can be made problematic, what questions can be asked, the concepts and language in which those questions can be formulated, the methods of collecting data, the relationship between research and women as the subjects or objects of knowledge. In short what Sandra Harding has summarised as "who can be the knower?", "what test beliefs must pass to be claimed as knowledge?" and "what kinds of things can be known?"[2]

These methodological, political and epistemological issues however, are not unique to feminist research. All these aspects of sociological investigation have been raised in recurring Marxist and phenomenological challenges to the mainstream social sciences, notably in the "value free debates" of the 1960s.[3] It is rather in the feminist *use* of the techniques developed by the earlier challenges to orthodox social science that feminist research can make claims to uniqueness. There is a particular resonance between the epistemology of feminism and the methodologies appropriate to "the central project of making known the voice of silence, ... the centrality of marginality and exclusion, the public nature of privacy and the presence of absence."[4]

This point is reinforced by the project that Grosz outlines as Irigaray's challenge to prevailing models of power and knowledge:

> ... to speak to evoke rather than designate, to signify rather than refer, to overburden oppositional dichotomous categories by refusing their boundaries or borders is to occupy the impossible 'middle ground' excluded by logic and reason in their present forms. This is not to create a discourse without meaning but rather to proliferate many meanings none of which could hierarchically unify the others.[5]

This text is centred on the sociological task of questioning the differentiation of social life. However, that questioning involves the further project of bringing together material from two clearly differentiated disciplines: criminology and social policy analysis. The way that this is done has been influenced by what Sandra Harding[6] has described as one of the basic features of a feminist methodology — "studying up".

STUDYING UP

This approach rests on the argument that the diffuse, contradictory and invisible nature of domesticity and of women's experiences within the domestic sphere means that women should not be the objects but the subjects of research. Because the collective basis of domestic life is so alien to the "agency-oriented" construction of human experience inherent in quantitative social investigations of the public sphere, the project of making visible the intersections between public and domestic life has to be organised around the principle of "studying up".

This has two major consequences for research design. First, any understanding of the detailed complexity of the contradictory inter-dependence between domestic and public spheres has to rely on the less interventionist, phenomenological methods of unstructured or semi-structured interviews, in which women control their own narratives and impose their own definitions on what is to be told. Secondly, "studying up" also means that it is the discourses of the powerful that need to be treated as "bizarre" and as appropriate objects of critical examination.[7] Para-doxically this means that the research design should incorporate both phenomenological and positivist strands. The specific intersection of state and economy in the public sphere, whether in the field of mental health, social services, child care provision, women's paid employment, or in any one of the several sites of exploitation, should be analysed as a case study of potentially self-interested discourses. The critical perspective of feminist research constructs the policies and practices of the powerful as

251

perpetually likely to be conveying half truths, masking poorly understood ideologies, and to be transferring the stresses brought about by the contradictions created by their own interpretations of social life to the least powerful. "Studying up" also means that because women — especially working class women — are the (often literal) embodiment of the condensed contradictions of the policies and practices, it is through their experiences that the investigations of the powerful are most effectively analysed. The focus of these feminist investigations is on both those who have control over material and cultural power — the political, scientific, academic, administrative and economic groups — as well as the debates between and within these groups.

Nevertheless there are major ethical problems in adopting a methodology that focuses on the insights of the powerless to investigate the discourses of the powerful.

TRUST AND EXPLOITATION IN THE RESEARCH PROCESS

Although unstructured interviews can in part redefine the power relationships between researchers and the women whose experiences provide the body of the analysis, they are also potentially exploitative. Janet Finch,[8] reflecting on her own experience as a researcher, argues that just "being a woman" has been a sufficient basis for establishing relations of trust in the relative intimacy of unstructured interviewing.[9] She points out that social isolation which characterises women's experience of domesticity, and which is part of the experience being recounted, can mean that women in powerless situations are often generous in giving extensive information about their lives. The standard attempt to allay the possibilities of betrayal in this relationship are those of orthodox social science research: strategies to guarantee anonymity and confidentiality. However, Finch argues that verbal guarantees of confidentiality, although often sufficient to establish a relationship of trust in the interview, are not really a sufficient safeguard for the women who provide that information. The very intimacy of qualitative research undermines the possibility for absolute anonymity.

Finch[10] also highlights the potential for the other more general form of betrayal inherent in this form of research. The detail and the complexity of material gathered in the "collaborative" atmosphere of the unstructured interview means that selective use of that material could be used to undermine the interests of women in general, reinforcing, for example, naturalistic or voluntaristic paradigms of gender inequality. Her resolution of this "moral dilemma" is to draw on what has by now become the major alternative to the orthodox tradition in the social sciences.[11] That is, to make quite clear "whose side we are on" both in the collection, analysis and reporting of the research. This argument then, whilst acknowledging the importance of transferring some control over the research process from the researcher to the people whose knowledge is being incorporated into the analysis, is also much more realistic about the practicalities of that position. The way that research can be done, given the pressures to individualism inherent in the way that knowledge and power are currently constituted, places major limits on the possibilities for women who are more powerless than the researcher in being able to have any effective control over the data. Finch's work shows that the issue of trust remains as a dilemma that has constantly to be addressed rather than an area of research design that can be easily resolved by reference to a clearly designed set of rules for an alternative sociology.

In summary, the research design comprises an investigation of the penal discourses that impinged on the lives of people in the population "families of prisoners" in New South Wales in the period 1986–1989. This specific analysis is set within an investigation of the broader criminological and penal debates within which the New South Wales policies, practices and debates operated. The greater part of the analysis of the intersection of penality and domesticity as it operated in New South Wales in the late 1980s is made through the insights provided by the 38 people who had family obligations to care for men imprisoned in the state during that period.

THE RESEARCH: INTERVIEWS WITH 38 CARERS

CONTACTING THE PEOPLE IN THE POPULATION "FAMILIES OF PRISONERS"

Before constructing the research design I had done some volunteer work with the Children of Prisoners Support Group and with the Civil Rehabilitation Committee (CRC), two community groups providing services and support for prisoners and for families of prisoners in New South Wales. One of the members of the executive of the CRC suggested I make contact with partners and parents of prisoners through the Family Support Centre at the Long Bay complex of prisons and the CRC bus that provided transport for families visiting men in country prisons. I made two bus journeys and visited the Centre over a period of eighteen months. The visits covered each day of the week including weekends. Four women, who had moved to Bathurst to be able to visit their husbands in prison there, agreed to talk with me at the women's centre. These interviews were arranged for me by the women organisers of the Bathurst women's centre. Cheryl Matthews, who was then working with people released from prison at Glebe House, a halfway house in Sydney, gave me a great deal of her time both in narrating her own experiences of being a partner of an imprisoned man and in contacting three other women whose partners were imprisoned or on parole.

There was a gap of about six months during this period when I made a preliminary analysis and skeleton paper centred on the first six interviews. During this time I restructured the general organisation of the thesis in light of the broader and more detailed picture that those six people had provided. In this time I was able to return the transcripts to three of these six women for their review and comments. The transcripts did accord with their general interpretation of their experiences, although in this second visit the women also gave me more information as the account in transcript form revived further memories.

Nearly all other published accounts of research with families of prisoners have involved contacting husbands in prison and asking his permission to interview the wives. I made a deliberate decision to avoid this method because I wanted to emphasise the centrality of the women's own situation and their interpretation of the work they were doing, rather than approach them as women controlled through their partner's decision. The disadvantages of this approach were:

1   that the men in prison for whom the women were caring were a heterogeneous group of prisoners. Their sentences ranged from a few months to life and the prisons they were in varied from minimum to maximum security;

2   that the women were those who had sufficient knowledge of the CRC to be using the Centre or the coach. Information about services was one of the aspects of the work of caring that was under investigation. In this then there was a significant bias in the set of answers about the difficulties of visiting.

In summary, four women agreed to talk to me in their own homes or work places, eight were interviewed in groups of two or three at the Family Support Centre at the Long Bay complex, fifteen women and one man were interviewed singly at the Family Support Centre at the Long Bay complex, four women came to the Women's Centre in Bathurst to describe their experiences as wives of prisoners and six women spoke with me on the CRC bus journeys to Goulburn and Cessnock:

Summary: Place of interview with people who spoke about their experiences as "outside carers of imprisoned men"

In their own home or workplace	4
In group interview at FSC	8
In individual interviews at FSC	16
At Bathurst Women's Centre	4
On CRC bus to Goulburn/Cessnock	6
TOTAL	38

RECORDING THE INTERVIEWS

After the first two or three approaches when I had described the paper as a thesis, I told all the women that I was preparing a paper for a university course. About six of the 38 women were interested in the research and those six interviews included a more detailed exchange of information about the research and my own political and instrumental interest in the topic. In several other interviews the accounts were also interspersed with exchanges of practical information or of some minor form of practical help such as giving lifts in cars or looking after babies or young children whilst the mother visited the man in prison. This came about as an obviously sensible practical response to the exigencies of the situation rather than as a planned philosophical attempt at "reciprocity" that had been manifestly incorporated into the research design. The idea that there could be "reciprocity" in research for a PhD thesis into the experiences of families of prisoners is manifestly hypocritical. I was obviously asking and receiving far more from the women than I could give back to them.

Finch's warning about trust and betrayal has particular relevance for research based on talks with women whose sons or partners are in prison. There was no attempt to find out the names of either the women or the prisoner, nor the offence for which the man had been imprisoned. This was to ensure both that the anonymity of the answers was protected and to reassure the women that that anonymity was secure. There was one exception to this. One woman, Cheryl Matthews, has made a central part of her political position as a prisoner's wife the stance that stigma can be better fought openly rather than through anonymity. Her account was one of the most detailed and insightful as was her review of the transcript of her narrative.

All interviews, except four, were recorded with the women's permission, on a tape recorder. Two exceptions were because the women preferred to talk without being recorded on tape, one because I forgot to switch the recorder on and the fourth because the two year old son kept banging the microphone and the eventual recording was too painful to transcribe.

THE INTERVIEW SCHEDULE

The interview was based on a conversation centering around a set of topics presented as open ended questions, the form of interview described by Margaret Stacey as a "focused interview".[12] The interview sheet (included as Appendix B) began with a few easy to answer closed ended questions about some impersonal and unthreatening aspects of the woman's situation. After these questions had established the direction of the topics I was interested in, the interviews were closer to open ended conversations with the women about their experiences. Because even basic questions often provoked women's memories about specific aspects of their experiences with the legal-penal bureaucracies the interviews rarely followed a set pattern. The interview sheet was used then as a list to check that any topic was not omitted rather than a guide imposed on the women.

The recorded interviews were transcribed by hand on the day of the interview or the following day. The transcriptions were then typed onto a Macintosh Word 3.1 programme which has a SORT mechanism which separated out the aspects of women's experiences into the areas covered in chapters five to seven after the comments had been catalogued. The cataloguing was based on the issues that developed out of the theoretical model of "care and dependence" and out of the revisions to that framework that were made after the initial six interviews.

THE RESEARCH: PENAL DISCOURSES

The material was collected from several sources:

1   seminars on penal policies at the Australian Institute of Criminology, the Institute of Criminology at Sydney University and other criminological and legal penal conferences and the formal and the informal material presented there;
2   New South Wales Department of Corrective Services annual reports and research reports;
3   review of literature based on criminological data bank searches and following through the footnote references from that literature;
4   newspaper and journal articles on prison policies and ministerial responses;
5   basic texts on penality, especially on the prison experience in New South Wales;
6   Royal Commissions and Inquiries into aspects of the New South Wales penal system in the period 1960–1988;
7   visits to families of prisoner centres in London and Amsterdam and personal contact through letters with individual researchers investigating aspects of penal policy that affect families of prisoners, in London, Edinburgh, Sweden and the United States;
8   informal interviews with New South Wales welfare officers, parole and probation officers, policemen, Department of Corrective Services Research Branch researchers, and with people working in the semi-autonomous field of community service provision at Glebe House and Station House in Sydney.

No material was taken directly from any of these interviews with the people in the population of paid workers in the penal sphere in New South Wales. They provided background information for checking several of the points raised in the study and were used particularly to map out the contrast between the visible official discourses on what should happen, and what does happen in the state's prisons.

NOTES

1   Among others Oakley, A, *Subject Women* (1981); Finch, J, "It's Good to have Someone to Talk to" in Bell, C and Roberts, H (eds), *Doing Feminist Research* (1984); Harding, S, *Feminism and Methodology: Social Science Issues* (1987).

2   Harding, above n1 at 1.

3   Edel, E, "Social Science and Value: a study in interrelationship" in Horowitz, I (ed), *The New Sociology: essays in social science and social theory in honour of C W Mills* (1964); Gouldner, A, "Anti-Minotaur: The Myth of a Value Free Sociology" (1962) *Social Problems* (Winter) 199–213; Dahrendorf, R, "Values and Social Science" ch 1, in *Essays in the Theory of Society* (1967).

4   MacKinnon, C, "Feminism, Marxism, Method and the State" in Harding, S (ed), *Feminism and Methodology: Social Science Issues* (1987).

5   Grosz, E, "Philosopohy, Subjectivity and the Body: Kristeva and Irigaray" in Pateman, C and Grosz, E (eds), *Feminist Challenges* (1986) at 138.

6   Above n2.

7   Harding, above n1.

8   Finch, above n1.

9   Watson and Mears rework these ideas in their discussion of research in the area of "care" in Australia (Watson, E and Mears, E, "Political and Moral dilemmas in Research Related to Women and Social Policy" paper presented at the Social Research and Policy Conference University of Queensland, August 1988.

10 Above n8 at 85.

11 The "committed" approach could, by the late 1980s, be called the alternative orthodoxy. The false universalism of apolitical sociological research was exposed in the value free debates of the late 1960s.

12 Stacey, M, *Methods of Social Research* (1969) at 75–76.

APPENDIX B

LIST OF TOPICS DISCUSSED WITH CARERS IN THE INTERVIEW

Basic

1 Relationship with prisoner
2 Caring for child of prisoner
3 Experience of visiting which prisons?
4 Visiting one or more prisoners?
5 Any experience of living with prisoner when he has been on some form of community based control

Travelling

1 Distance
2 Time
3 Preparation
4 Cost: economic/other

Visiting: general

1 "Would you take me through your day when you visit: your experiences of getting there, then having the visit and so on."

Reasons

1 Why visit?
2 Why bring children to visit?

Impact of imprisonment on you and other people in the family

1 — at arrest
2 — on bail/waiting for sentence
3 — early imprisonment
4 — classification
5 — day leave/parole

Work involved in being "outsider carer" in addition to visiting?

1 Mediating/negotiating
2 Caring for children

General impact

1 Economic costs to you of imprisonment
2 Housing changes as a result of imprisonment
3 Personal (health/other) costs to you/children: parallel punishment?

Managing

1 Any help from relatives/friends/government departments/other
2 Any benefits from whole experience
3 What you would like to see changed

BIBLIOGRAPHY

A: FAMILIES OF PRISONERS LITERATURE

Aitkin, J and Gartrell, G
   Sentenced to Life: Management of Life Sentence Prisoners in New South Wales Gaols, Sydney: Criminology Research Council, 1985.
Altaahr-Cederberg, B
   "Current Course for Inmates and their Families at Gruvberget" a personal account sent in a private letter through the Information Office, Kriminal Vaardsstyrelsen, National Prison and Probation Adminstration, Norrkoping, Sweden, 1986.
Anderson, N
   Prisoners' Families: Reports I & II. Melbourne: Victorian Council of Social Services, 1965.
Bauhofer, V
   "Prison Parenting: challenge for children's advocates" (Jan–Feb 1987) *Children Today* 15–16.
Baunach, P
   Mothers in Prison. New Brunswick: Transaction Books, 1985.
Boudoris, J
   Prisons and Kids. New York: American Correctional Association, 1985.
Brodsky, S
   Families and Friends of Men in Prison. Lexington: DC Heath & Co, 1975.
Burnstein, J
   Conjugal Visits in Prison. Lexington: DC Heath & Co, 1977.
Cavans, R and Semands, E
   "Marital Relationships of Prisoners in 28 countries" (1958) 49 *Journal of Criminal Law, Criminology and Police Science* 133–139.
Cobean, S and Power, P
   "The Role of the Family in the Rehabilitation of the Offender" (1978) 22 *International Journal of Offender Therapy and Comparative Criminology* 29–37.
Crosthwaite, A
   "Voluntary Work with Families of Prisoners" (1972) 16/3 *International Journal Offender Therapy and Comparative Criminology* 253–259.

Crosthwaite, A
   "Punishment for Whom? the Prisoner or his Wife?" (1975) 19/3
   *International Journal of Offender Therapy and Comparative
   Criminology* 275–284.
Daniels, S W
   "The Needs of Prisoners Wives: a challenge for the Mental Health
   Profession" (1981) 17/4 *Community Mental Health Journal*
   310–322.
De Conninck, G
   "Actualities bibliographiques: La families de detenu: de la
   suspicion de la idealization" (1982) 6/1 *Deviance et Societé*.
Deane, H
   *The Social Effects of Imprisonment on Male Prisoners and their
   Families*. Wellington: Study Series 2, Institute of Criminology,
   Victoria University of Wellington, 1988.
Dickinson, G
   "Changes in Communication Policies" (1984) 46/2 *Corrections
   Today* 58–59.
Elkland-Olson, S, Supancic, M, Campbell, J and Lenehan, K
   "Post release depression and the importance of familial support"
   (1983) 21 *Criminology* 253–275
Fenton, N
   The Prisoner's Family. Palo Alto: Pacific, 1959.
Fishman, S
   Women at the Wall. New York, SUNY Press, 1991.
Fishman, S and Alissi, A
   "Strengthening Families as Natural Support Systems for
   Offenders" (1979) 43/3 *Federal Probation* 16–21.
Friedman, S and Essellyn, T
   "The Adjustment of Children of Jail Inmates" (1965) 29 *Federal
   Probation* 55–59.
Fritsch, T and Burkhead, J
   "Behavioural Reaction of Children to Parental Absence due to
   Imprisonment" (1981) 30/1 *Family Relations* 83–86.
Garner, E
   "Why Should Children Visit in Prison?" (1983, Winter) *Staying
   Together*.
Gaudin, J
   "Social Work Roles and Tasks with Incarcerated Mothers" in
   Social Casework 12 Nov 1984 279–286.
Goetting, A
   "Conjugal Association in Prison: A World View" (1982) 14/3
   Criminal Justice Abstracts 406-416.
Goetting, A
   "Conjugal Association in Prison: Issues and Perspectives" (1982)
   28/1 *Crime and Delinquency* 52–71.

261

Goetting, A
"Conjugal Association Practices in Prisons of the American Nations" (1984) 6/3 *Alternative Lifestyles* 155–175.

Guss, S, Goodwin, D and Game, B
"Psychiatric Study of Wives of Convicted Felons: an example of Assortative Mating" (1970) 126 *American Journal of Psychiatry* 115–118.

Handler, E
"Family Surrogates as Correctional Strategy" (1974) 48/4 *Social Service Review* 539–549.

Hatty, S
"Maternal Infant Incarceration: sociological and psychological perspectives", in Hatty, S (ed) *Women in the Prison System*, Canberra: Australian Institute of Criminology, 1984 at 115–162.

Holt, N and Miller, D
Explorations in Inmate-Family Relationships, California Department of Corrections Research Report 46, Sacramento, California, 1972.

Hopper, C
Sex in Prison: the Mississippi Experiment with Conjugal Visiting, Baton Rouge: Louisiana State Press, 1969.

Hounslow, B, Stephenson, A, Stewart, J and Crancher, J
Children of Imprisoned Parents, Sydney: Family and Childrens's Service Agency (Social Research and Evaluation Ltd), Ministry of Youth and Community Services, 1982.

Hounslow, B
"Children & Families of Prisoners: convicted without a trial" (1984) 9/1 *Legal Services Bulletin* 26–28.

Howser, J, Grossman, J and MacDonald, D
"The Impact of Family Reunion Program on Institutional Discipline" (1983) 8/1–2 *Journal of Offender Counseling, Services & Rehabilitation* 27–37.

Johns, C
"The Hidden Costs of the Personal and Emotional Deprivation of Prisoners and Their Families", paper presented at The Resurgents Group Seminar, Parramatta Gaol, 14 November 1979.

Jones, J
"Prisoners and their Families", unpublished PhD thesis, Melbourne: Monash University Department of Anthropology and Sociology, 1983.

Kaslow, F
"Marital or Family Therapy for Prisoners and their Spouses or Families" (1978) 58/1 *Prison Journal* 53–59.

Kemp, B

Imprisonment and Family Separation: a literature review. Research and Statistics Division, Research Digest No 2, Sydney: New South Wales Department of Corrective Services, 1980.

Kemp, B

The Impact of Enforced Separation on Prisoners' Wives, Research and Statistics Division, Research Bulletin No 4. Sydney: New South Wales Department of Corrective Services, 1981.

Kemp, B, Cheron, M, McClelland M and Cooney, G

The Effects of Separation on Marital Relationships of Prisoners and Their Wives, Research and Statistics Division, Research Publication No 2. Sydney: New South Wales Department of Corrective Services, 1982.

Koban, L

"Parents in Prison" (1983) 5 *Research in Law, Deviance and Social Control* 171–183.

Light, R

(ed), *Prisoners' Families,* Bristol: Bristol and Bath Centre for Criminal Justice, 1989.

Liker, J

"Economic Pressures on the Families of Released Prisoners: evidence from the TARP experiment" (1981) 16/1 *Cornell Journal of Social Relations* 11–27.

Light, R

Prisoners' Families, Bristol & Bath Centre for Criminal Justice, 1991.

Lovejoy, F and Barbaroza, E

"Gender Issues in Prison Visiting", unpublished paper presented at the Australian and New Zealand Society of Criminology Third Annual Conference, 24–26 August 1987.

Lowenstein, A

"Coping with Stress: The Case of Prisoners' Wives" (1984) 46/3 *Journal of Marriage and the Family* 699–706.

Lowenstein, A

"Temporary Single Parenthood — The Case of Prisoners' Families" (1986) 35/1 *Family Relations* 79–85.

Marsh, R

"Services for Families: a Model Project to Provide Services for Families of Prisoners" (1983) 27/2 *International Journal of Offender Therapy and Comparative Criminology* 156–162.

McDermott, K and King, R

"Prison Rule 102: Stand By Your Man", unpublished paper, Bangor Wales: Centre for Social Policy Research and Development [nd].

McGowan, B and Blumenthal, K
Why Punish the Children? A Study of Children of Women Prisoners, New Jersey: NCCD, 1978.
Merriman, P
"The Families of Long-term Prisoners" (1979) 26 *Probation Journal* 114–119.
Moller, K and Gosden, S
"Recidivists, Their Past and Families compared with First Time Only Prisoners" (1983) 13 *Australian & New Zealand Journal of Criminology* 117–123.
Morris, P
Prisoners and their Families, London: George Allen & Unwin, 1965.
Nagle, J F
Report of the Royal Commission into New South Wales Prisons, Sydney: New South Wales Government Printer, 1978.
Newton, A
"The Effects of Imprisonment" (1980) 12/1 *Criminal Justice Abstracts* 134–151.
New South Wales Task Force on Women in Prison
Report on Women in Prison, Sydney: New South Wales Government Printer, 1985.
Perry, W
"Marital Relations of Prison Parolees", PhD thesis, School of Human Behavior, United States International University, San Diego, 1974.
Relaties van Gedetineerden
"Vereniging Relaties van Gedetineerden en Ex Gedetineerden", Sekretariaat, Kleine Gartmanplantaoen 22–11 1017 RR Amsterdam, 1986.
Sack, W
"Children of Imprisoned Fathers" (1977) 40/2 *Psychiatry* 163–174.
Sack, W, Seidler, J and Thomas, S
"The Children of Imprisoned Parents: A Psychosocial Exploration" (1976) 46/4 *American Journal of Orthopsychiatry* 618–627.
Schaffer, N E
"Descriptive Study of Policies and Practices Related to the Visiting of Prisoners in Correctional Institutions", Doctoral thesis, University of Michigan, 1977.
Schiff, S
"The Preschool in Prison Project: OMEP Canada" (1986) unpublished paper by S Schiff, 12111 39a Avenue, Edmonton, Alberta, Canada.

Schneller, D

The Prisoner's Family: a Study of the Effects of Imprisonment on the Families of Prisoners, San Francisco, California: R & E Research Associates, 1978.

Schneller, D

"Prisoners' Families: a study of some social and psychological effects of incarceration on the families of Negro prisoners" (1975) 12/4 Criminology 402–412.

Schwartz, M and Weintraub, J

"The Prisoners's Wife: a study in crisis" (1974) 38/4 Federal Probation 20–26

Shaw, R

Children of Imprisoned Fathers, London: Hodder & Stoughton, 1987.

Showalter, D and Jones, C W

"Marital and Family Counselling in Prisons" (1980) 25 Social Work 224–228.

Smith, S

"Neglect as Control: prisoners' wives", paper presented to the XIVth Annual Conference of the European Group for the Study of Deviance and Social Control, September 1986.

Smith, S

"House Arrest: the pain of prisoners' wives" (1986) 21 New Society 11–13.

Struckhoff, D

"Adjustment of Prisoners' Wives to Separation", PhD thesis, S Illinois University, 1977.

Struckhoff, D

"Toward a model of involuntary separation of families" (1979) 3 Offender Rehabilitation 289–297.

Wardell, W

"The Reunion of the Male Prison Inmate with his Family: a Humanistic Exploratory Study (Phenomenological)", unpublished PhD thesis, Clinical Psychology Department, The Fielding Institute, USA, 1983.

Williams, E, Elder, Z and Williams, S

"The Psychological Aspects of the Crimes of Imprisoned Husbands on their families" (1970) 62/3 Journal of the National Medical Association 208–211.

Wilmer, H, Marks, I and Pogue, E

"Group Treatment of Prisoners and their Families" (1966) 50 Mental Hygiene 380–389.

Wilson, G

"I Know While He is in Prison He's Safe" (1984) New Society 1 Nov 1984 at 172–174.

Zemons, E and Cavan, R
"Marital Relationships of Prisoners" (1958) 47/1 *Journal of Criminal Law, Criminology and Police Science* 133–139.
(anon)
"On Prisoners and Parenting: Preserving the Tie that binds" (1978) 87/7 *Yale Law Journal* 1408–1429.

B   GENERAL BIBLIOGRAPHY

Albury, R
"All Quiet on the Home Front? The Contradictions of Family Life" (1987) 99 *Australian Left Review* 24–29.
Alford, K
Production or Reproduction? An Economic History of Women in Australia, 1788–1850, Melbourne: Oxford University Press, 1984.
Allen, J
Sex & Secrets: Crimes Involving Australian Women since 1880, Melbourne: Oxford University Press, 1990.
Allen, M
"Domestic Ideology and Maude Jeanne Franc", paper presented at the Third Women and Labour Conference, Adelaide, 1982.
Allen, M, Hutchinson, M and MacKinnon, A
Fresh Evidence, New Witnesses: Finding Women's History, Adelaide: South Australian Government Printer, 1989.
Amilaon, C
"The Lessons to be Learned from the Scandinavian Experience in Penal Reform", in *Penal Philosophies and Practice in the 1970's Proceedings–Training Project No 24*, Canberra: Australian Institute of Criminology, 1975.
Anderson, T
Inside Outlaws, Sydney: Redfern Legal Centre Publishing, 1989.
Annette, J
"Bentham's Fear of Hobgoblins: law, political economy and social discipline" in Fine, B, Kinsey, R, Lea, J, Picciotto, S and Young, J (eds), *Capitalism and the Rule of Law: From deviancy theory to Marxism*, London: Hutchinson, 1979.
Arbler, S and Gilbert, N
"Men: the forgotten carers" (1989) 23/1 *Sociology* 111–119.
Aries, P
Centuries of Childhood, Harmondsworth: Penguin, 1973.
Aubin, T
"Ultrasound for Jail Visitors" *Sydney Morning Herald* 24 Feb 1989 at 5.

Aungles, A
"Family Economies in Transition: Adelaide Women in the Depression", unpublished MA thesis, Flinders University, Adelaide, 1982.

Aungles, A
"Illawarra Women in the 1930s Depression", unpublished thesis for MSoc, University of Wollongong, New South Wales, 1984.

BI Inc
"Backgrounder On BI's Home Escort-System: The electronic monitoring system of house arrest as a reliable and cost-effective alternative to incarceration" (sales pamphlet), Boulder: BI Incorporated [nd].

Baldry, E
"Death behind bars: the suicide crisis in New South Wales" *Sydney Morning Herald* 7 May 1990 at 17.

Baldwin, S and Glendinning, C
"Employment, women and their disabled children" in Finch J & Groves D (eds), *A Labour of Love: Women, Work and Caring*, London: Routledge & Kegan Paul, 1983.

Baldock, C and Cass, B
(eds), *Women, Social Welfare and the State*, Sydney: George Allen & Unwin, 1983.

Banfield, E
The Moral Basis of a Backward Society, New York: Free Press, 1958.

Barbalet, M
Far from a Low Gutter Girl. The Forgotten World of State Wards: South Australia 1887–1940, Melbourne: Oxford University Press, 1983.

Barnett, R, Biener, L and Baruch, G
(eds), *Gender and Stress*, New York: The Free Press [nd].

Barrett, M and McIntosh, M
The Anti-Social Family, London: Verso, 1982.

Beechey, V
"Women and Production: a critical analysis of some sociological theories of women's work" in Kuhn, A and Wolpe, A (eds), *Feminism & Materialism*, London: Routledge & Kegan Paul, 1978.

Bell, R, Edwards, D and Wagner, H
Political Power: A reader in theory and research, New York: Free Press, 1969.

Benhabib, S
"The Generalized and the Concrete Other: the Kohlberg-Gilligan Controversy and Feminist Theory" at 56–76 in Benhabib, S and Cornwell, D (eds) *Feminism as Critique: on the politics of gender*, Minneapolis: University of Minnesota Press, 1987.

Bennett, N, Coward, R and Heys, R
"The Limits to Financial and Legal Independence: a Socialist Feminist Perspective on Taxation and Social Security", in *Politics and Power I: New Perspectives on Socialist Politics*, London: Routledge & Kegan Paul, 1980, at 185–202.

Biles, D and Johnson, M
Australian Prison Trends, No 117, Canberra: Australian Institute of Criminology, 1986.

Blumberg, H
Industrial Democracy: the Sociology of Participation, London: Constable, 1968.

Bonney, R
New South Wales Summary Offences Act, Sydney: New South Wales Bureau of Crime Statistics and Research, 1989.

Box, S
Power, Crime and Mystification, London: Tavistock, 1983.

Boyle, J
The Pain of Confinement, London: Pan, 1984.

Bradley, R, Walters, C, Cooper, S, Kisch, J, Yeoman, P and Dapre, B
"Overseas Countries' Assistance to Sole Parents: Social Security Review", Background Discussion Paper No 14, Woden: Department of Social Security, 1986.

Bradwell, L
"Parole in New South Wales" (1972) 19 *International Journal of Offender Therapy and Comparative Criminology* 77–82.

Braithwaite, J
"The Political Economy of Punishment" in Buckley, K and Wheelwright, E (eds), *Political Economy of Australian Capitalism* (vol 4), Sydney: ANZ Books, 1980.

Braithwaite, J
Crime, Shame and Reintegration, Cambridge: Cambridge University Press, 1989.

Briese, C
"A Magistrate's View", in Vernon, J (ed), *Developments in Correctional Policy: More Prisons?*, Seminar Proceedings No 22, Canberra: Australian Institute of Criminology, 1987.

Broverman, I, Broverman, D, Clarkson, F, Rosenkrantz, P and Vogel, S
"Sex Role Stereotypes and Clinical Judgements of Mental Health" (1970) 34 *Journal of Consulting and Clinical Psychology* 1–7.

Brown, D
"Preconditions for Sentencing and Penal Reform in New South Wales: some suggestions towards a strategy for contesting an emerging Law and Order climate", at 341–362, in Potas, I (ed), *Sentencing in Australia*, Canberra: Australian Institute of Criminology, 1986.

Brown, D
"What Truth? Sentencing changes (New South Wales)" (1989) 14/4 *Legal Services Bulletin* 161–164.

Brown, D
"Returning to Sight: contemporary Australian penality" (1989) 16/3 *Social Justice* (Issue 37) at 141–157.

Brown, D and Zdenkowski, G
The Prison Struggle, Sydney: Penguin, 1975.

Brown, W
"Black Gangs as Family Extensions" (1978) 22 *International Journal of Offender Therapy and Comparative Criminology* 39–46.

Bryson, L
"Welfare Issues of the Eighties" ch 16 in Najman, J and Western, J, *A Sociology of Australian Society: Introductory Readings*, Melbourne: Macmillan, 1988.

Bryson, L, Mugford, J, Mugford, S and Weiser Easteal, P
"Social Justice, Public Perceptions and Spouse Assault in Australia" (1989) 16/3 *Social Justice* (Issue 37) 103–124.

Burman, S
(ed), *Fit Work for Women*, London: Croom Helm, 1979.

Bythell, D
Sweated Labour: Outwork in Nineteenth Century Britain, London: Batsford Press, 1978.

Cancian, F
"The Feminization of Love" (1986) 13/4 *Signs* 702–709.

Cass, B
"Redistribution to children and to mothers; a history of child endowment and family allowances" in Baldock, C and Cass, B (eds), *Women, Social Welfare and the State*, Sydney: Allen & Unwin, 1983.

Cass, B
"Population Policies and Family Policies: State Construction of Domestic Life" in Baldock, C and Cass, B (eds), *Women, Social Welfare and the State*, Sydney: Allen & Unwin, 1983.

Cass, B and O'Loughlin, M
"The Needs of Single Parents" (1984) *Australian Society* 1 Jan 1984 at 20–22.

Cass, B and Radi, H
"Family Fertility and the Labour Market" in Grieve, N and Grimshaw, P (eds), *Australian Women: Feminist Perspectives*, Melbourne: Oxford University Press, 1981.

Cassidy, F J
"What is the Role of the Prison Officer?" in *The Conflict of Security and Rehabilitation of the 1970s* (Training Project No 5), Canberra: Australian Institute of Criminology, 1975, at 11–22.

Cavior, H E
"Ethnographic Evidence for Three Positive Aspects of Co-corrections: normalization, inmate sexuality, and inmate violence", paper presented at Bureau of Prisons Conference on Confinement of Females, Washington, March 1978.

Challenger, D
"Payment of Fines" (1985) 18/2 *Australian and New Zealand Journal of Criminology* 95–109.

Challenger, D
"Front End or Back End. There's no place like Home" (1989) Sept/Oct *Criminology Australia* 18-23.

Chan, J
"The Limits of Sentencing Reform", in Potas, I (ed) *Sentencing in Australia*, Canberra: Australian Institute of Criminology, 1986 at 445–484.

Chan, J
Doing Less Time, Sydney: Insitute of Criminology, University of Sydney, 1992.

Chan, J and Zdenkowski, G
"Just Alternatives — Parts I & II" (1986) 19/2–3 *Australian and New Zealand Journal of Criminology* 67–90 & 131–54.

Chappell, D and Norberry, J
AIDS in Prison, Canberra: Australian Institute of Criminology, 1990.

Children of Prisoners Support Group
Annual Report, Sydney: CPSG, 1988.

Clark, P
"Arrests for Swearing Up 300pc under New Laws" *Sydney Morning Herald* 31 Aug 1989 at 2.

Cohen, A
Deviance and Control, New Jersey: Prentice Hall, 1966.

Cohen, A
Prison Violence, Lexington, Massachusetts: DC Heath Pub Co, 1975.

Cohen, S
Visions of Social Control, Cambridge: Polity Press, 1985.

Connell, R and Irving, T
Class Structure in Australian History: Documents, Narrative and Argument, Sydney: Longman Cheshire, 1980.

Connell, R W
Gender and Power: Society, the Person and Sexual Politics, Sydney: Allen & Unwin, 1987.

Cooper, H
"Punishment Outside Gaol: a Court Perspective", No 77, *Proceedings of the Institute of Criminology,* Sydney: Institute of Criminology, University of Sydney, 1988 at 11–26.

Coopers & Lybrand
  Report on the New South Wales Court System, Sydney: Coopers
  & Lybrand, 1989.
Cornwall, D
  "Police raid: 'They were real animals'" *Sydney Morning Herald*
  16 Feb 1990 at 1.
Cornwall, D
  "New South Wales has a record 5,200 people in jail" *Sydney
  Morning Herald* 12 Mar 1990 at 4.
Corrigan, P
  "Gender and the Gift: the case of the family clothing economy"
  (1989) 23/4 *Sociology* 513–534.
Cott, N
  Bonds of Womanhood. Yale University Press, 1977.
Crowe, A
  Why Can't a Woman? London: Women's Action Alliance, 1987.
Crowley, F
  *A Documentary History of Australia, Volume 2: Colonial
  Australia 1841–1874*, West Melbourne: Thomas Nelson, 1977.
Cunneen, C
  "The Policing of Public Order: some thoughts on culture, space
  and political economy", in Findlay, M and Hogg, R, *Under-
  standing Crime and Criminal Justice*, Sydney: Law Book Co,
  1988 at 189–208.
Dahrendorf, R
  "Values and Social Science", ch1 in *Essays in the Theory of
  Society*, London: Routledge & Kegan Paul, 1967.
Dalton, V
  in discussion in "Offender Management in the Eighties", 60
  Proceedings of the Institute of Criminology, Sydney: Institute of
  Criminology, University of Sydney, 1984.
Daniels, K
  (ed), *So Much Hard Work: Women and Prostitution in Australian
  History*, Sydney: Fontana, 1984.
Daniels, K, Murnane, M and Picot, A
  Women in Australia: an Annotated Guide to Records, Canberra:
  Australian Government Publishing Service, 1977.
Darlington, C D
  The Little Universe of Man, London: George Allen & Unwin,
  1978.
Davies, D
  "From Dogberry to Cop Shop: the police as the arm of the modern
  state" (1982) 79 *Australian Left Review* 20–27.

Deacon, D
"The employment of women in the Commonwealth Public Service: the creation and reproduction of a dual labour market" (1982) 41/3 *Australian Journal of Public Administration* 232–250.
Department of Social Security
Annual Report 1988–89, Canberra: Australian Government Publishing Service, 1989.
Dewdney, M and Miner, M
"Parole Trends and Revocations" (Publication No 10), Sydney: New South Wales Department of Corrective Services, 1976.
Dewdney, M, Swarris, K and Miner, M
"The History and Administration of the New South Wales Work Release Scheme — 1969–1977" (Publication No 16), Sydney: New South Wales Department of Corrective Services, 1978.
Dewdney, M, Swarris, K, Miner, M and Crossing, B
"The Performance of Work Releasees on Parole" (Publication No 19), Sydney: New South Wales Department of Corrective Services, 1978.
Dobash, R, Dobash, R E and Gutteridge, S
The Imprisonment of Women, Oxford: Basil Blackwell, 1986.
Donaldson, M
"Labouring Men: Love, Sex and Strife" (1987) 23/2 *Australian & New Zealand Journal of Sociology* 165–184.
Donzelot, J
The Policing of Families: Welfare versus the State, London: Hutchinson, 1979.
Dorey, T
"Home Detention Program (Design and Implementation)", paper presented to the Diversionary Programmes Workshop, Alice Springs, 4 August 1986.
Dorey, T
"Queensland Home Detention Program", unpublished paper presented to the Australian Bicentennial International Congress on Corrective Services, Sydney, 1988.
Duffecy, J
"Home Detention as an Alternative to Imprisonment", paper prepared for the Policy Planning and Review Unit, Department of Corrective Services, Perth, 1986.
Durkheim, E
The Division of Labour in Society, New York: Free Press, 1893, transl 1960.
Eaton, M
Justice for Women? Family, Court and Social Control, Milton Keynes: Open University Press, 1986.

272

Edel, E

"Social Science and Value: a study in interrelationship" in Horowitz, I (ed), *The New Sociology: essays in social science and social theory in honour of C W Mills*, New York : Oxford University Press, 1964 at 218–238.

Edwards, A

Regulation and Repression. Sydney: Allen & Unwin, 1988.

Ellickson, L

"South Australian Home Detention" (1989) 1/2 *Criminology Australia* 21–22.

Ellis, D Grasnick and Gilman, B

"Violence in Prisons: a sociological analysis" (1974) 80/1 *American Journal of Sociology* 16–43.

Elshtain, J

"Moral Woman and Immoral Man: a consideration of the public-private split and its political ramifications" (1974) *Politics and Society* 453–461.

Eysenck, H and Gudjonsson, G

The Causes and Cures of Criminality, Plenum: DA, 1989.

Feiner, M

"Home Detention: a summary paper" issued by Victorian Office of Corrections, Melbourne, 1987.

Ferguson, K

The Feminist Case Against Bureaucracy, Philadelphia: Temple University Press, 1984.

Finch, J

" It's Good to Have Someone to Talk To: the ethics and politics of interviewing women", in Bell, C and Roberts, H (eds), *Doing Feminist Research*, Routledge and Kegan Paul, 1984.

Finch, J

Family Obligations and Social Change, Cambridge: Polity Press, 1989.

Finch, J and Groves, D

"Community Care and the Family: A Case for Equal Opportunities" (1980) 9/4 *Journal of Social Policy* 487–511, reproduced in Ungerson, C (ed) *Women and Social Policy: a Reader*, London: Macmillan, 1985 at 218–242.

Finch, J and Groves, D

"By Women for Women: caring for the frail elderly" (1982) 5/5 *Women's Studies International Forum* 427–438.

Finch, J and Groves, D

(eds), *A Labour of Love: Women, Work and Caring*, London: Routledge & Kegan Paul, 1983.

Findlay, M

The State of The Prison: a Critique of Reform, Bathurst: Mitchell-search Ltd, 1982.

Fine, B, Kinsey, R, Lea, J, Picciotto, S and Young, J
(eds), *Capitalism and the Rule of Law: from deviancy theory to Marxism*, London: Hutchinson, 1979.

Fischer, E
Marx in His Own Words, Harmondsworth: Penguin, 1973.

Fisher, S
"An Accumulation of Misery?" ch 2 in Kennedy, R (ed), *Australian Welfare History: Critical Essays*, Melbourne: MacMillan, 1982.

Ford, D and Schmidt, A
"Electronically Monitored Home Confinement" (1985) 194 *National Institute of Justice Reports* 2–6.

Foucault, M
Discipline And Punish, London: Allen Lane, 1977.

Fox, R
"Dr Schwizgebel's Machine Revisited: Electronic Monitoring of Offenders" (1987) 20 *Australian & New Zealand Journal of Criminology* 132–147.

Frey, D
"Survey of Sole Parent Pensioners' Workforce Barriers" Social Security Review Discussion Paper No 12, Woden: Department of Social Security, 1986.

Garcia, L
"Jail visitors must endure body search, Yabsley says", *Sydney Morning Herald* 1 June 1990 at 7.

Garland, D and Young, P
(eds), *The Power to Punish*, London: Heinemann, 1983.

Garland, D
Punishment and Welfare, Aldershot: Gower, 1985.

Garrett, W
"Penal Philosophies and Practices in the 1970s in New Zealand" in *Penal Philosophies and Practice in the 1970s, Proceedings — Training Project No 24*. Canberra: Australian Institute of Criminology, 1976.

Garton, S
"The Melancholy Years: Psychiatry in New South Wales, 1900–1940" in Kennedy, R (ed), *Australian Welfare History*, Sydney: Macmillan, 1982.

Garton, S
" 'Bad or Mad': developments in incarceration in New South Wales 1900–40", Sydney Labour History Group (ed), *What Rough Beast? The State and Social Order in Australian History*, Sydney: Allen & Unwin, 1983 at 89–110.

Garton, S
"The State, Labour Markets and Incarceration: a critique" in Findlay, M and Hogg, R (eds), *Understanding Crime and Criminology*, Sydney: Law Book Co, 1988.

Gattis, L
> *Prison Survival*, Altamonte Springs, Florida: Cheetah, 1986.

George, A
> "Privatising Prisons" (1988) *Australian Society* (Sept) at 32–33.

George, A
> "The State tries an escape" (1989) 14/2 *Legal Services Bulletin* 53–54.

Gilding, M
> *The Making and Breaking of the Australian Family*, Sydney: Allen & Unwin, 1991.

Gilligan, C
> *In a Different Voice: psychological theory and women's development*, Cambridge, Massachusetts: Harvard University Press, 1982.

Gittings, D
> *The Family in Question*, London: MacMillan, 1993.

Glaser, D
> *The Effectiveness of a Prison and Parole System*, New York: Merrill, 1969.

Glezer, H
> "Mothers in the Workforce" (1988) 21 *Family Matters*, newsletter of the Australian Institute of Family Studies, at 30–34.

Goffman, E
> *Asylums*, Harmondsworth: Penguin, 1961.

Goode, W
> *The Family*, New Jersey: Prentice Hall, 1964.

Gorta, A and Cooney, G
> "What makes a good parolee?" (1983) 16 *Australian & New Zealand Journal of Criminology* 106–118.

Gorta, A and Nguyen, M
> *An Analysis of Interviews with Recaptured Escapees: some suggestions of reasons for escape*, Sydney: Research and Statistics Division, New South Wales Department of Corrective Services, 1988.

Goss, M
> Commentary given at the seminar "Home Detention and Intensive Supervison Programmes" at the Australian Bicentennial International Congress on Corrective Services, Sydney 24–28 January 1988.

Gough, I
> *The Political Economy of the Welfare State*, London: Macmillan, 1979.

Gouldner, A
> "Anti-Minotaur: The Myth of a Value Free Sociology" (1962) *Social Problems* (Winter) 199–213.

Gouldner, A
"The Sociologist as Partisan — Sociology and the Welfare State" in Gouldner, A (ed) *For Sociology*, London: Heinemann, 1968.

Gowler, D and Legge, K
"Hidden and Open Contracts in Work and Marriage" in Rapoport, R, Rapoport, R N and Bumstead, J (eds), *Working Couples*, London: Routledge & Kegan Paul, 1978.

Grabosky, P
Sydney in Ferment: Dissent and Official Reaction 1788–1973, Canberra: ANU Press, 1977.

Graham, H
"Coping: or how mothers are seen and not heard" in Friedman, S and Sarah, E (eds), *On the Problem of Men*, London: Womens' Press, 1982.

Graham, H
"Caring: a labour of love" ch 1 in Finch, J and Groves, D, *A Labour of Love: women, work and caring*, London: Routledge & Kegan Paul, 1983.

Graham, H
"Surveying through stories" in Bell, C and Roberts, H (eds), *Social Researching: politics, problems, practice*, London: Routledge & Kegan Paul, 1984.

Graham, H
"Providers, Negotiators and Mediators: women as the hidden carers" ch2 in Lewin, E and Olesen, V (eds) *Women, Health, and Healing*, London: Tavistock, 1985.

Grant, D
"A Reflection on Prison Crowding" in Vernon, J (ed), *Developments in Correctional Policy: More Prisons?* Seminar Proceedings No 22, Canberra: Australian Institute of Criminology, 1987.

Grant, D
"Prison Security Issues", speech presented at The Australian Bicentennial International Congress on Corrective Services, Sydney, 24–28 January 1988.

Graycar, A
(ed), *Retreat from the Welfare State: Australian Social Policy in the 1980s*, Sydney: George Allen & Unwin, 1983.

Greenberg, D
(ed), *Corrections and Punishment*, Beverley Hills: Sage, 1977.

Grimshaw, P and Willett, G
"Women's History and Family History: an Exploration of Colonial Family Structure" in Grieve, N and Grimshaw, P (eds), *Australian Women: Feminist perspectives*, Melbourne: Oxford University Press, 1981 at 134–155.

Grosz, E
"Philosophy, subjectivity and the body: Kristeva and Irigaray" in Pateman, C and Grosz, E (eds), *Feminist Challenges*, Sydney: Allen & Unwin, 1986.

Grossman, B
"Warden's Summary" paper presented at the Bureau of Prisons Conference on Confinement of Female Offenders, New South Wales, March 1978.

Hamilton, R
The Liberation of Women, London: Allen & Unwin, 1978.

Harding, S
(ed), *Feminism and Methodology: Social Science Issues*, Milton Keynes: Indiana University Press and Open University, 1987.

Harman, E
"Capitalism, Patriarchy and the City" ch 5 in Baldock, C and Cass, B (eds) *Women, Social Welfare and the State*, Sydney: George Allen & Unwin, 1983.

Hartmann, H
"The Family as the Locus of Gender, Class, and Political Struggle: the example of housework" (1981) 6/2 *Signs* 366–394.

Hartmann, H and Banner, L
(eds), *Clio's Consciousness Raised*, New York: Harper Row, 1974.

Hartsock, N
"The Feminist Standpoint: developing the ground for a specifically feminist historical materialism" in Harding, S (ed), *Feminism and Methodology: Social Science Issues*, Milton Keynes: Open University Press, 1987.

Harvey, S
"Prisons Bursting at Seams", *Sydney Morning Herald* 18 May 1989 at 4.

Harvey, S
"Prison Crowding Angers Unions" in *Sydney Morning Herald* 24 July 1989 at 5.

Harvey, S
"More Inmates, Fewer Staff in Goal", *Sydney Morning Herald* 7 Oct 1989 at 9.

Hatty, S and Walker, J
Deaths in Australian Prisons, Canberra: Australian Institute of Criminlogy, 1986.

Hayes, F
"In Search of a Correctional Camelot: the idealism and reality of the first twenty five years of probation and parole in New South Wales: Part One" (1987) 7/2 *Welfare in Australia* 18–24.

277

Hayes, R and Hayes, S
"Criminal Justice and Public Health" (1988) 10/2 *Australian Crime Prevention Council Journal* 7–17.

Hearn, J
"Patriarchy, Professionalisation and the Semi-Professions" in Ungerson, C (ed), *Women and Social Policy*, London: MacMillan, 1985 at 190–208.

Heidensohn, F
Women and Crime, London: Macmillan, 1985.

Hill, R
Families Under Stress, New York: Harper, 1949.

Hindess, B
Freedom, Equality, and the Market: Arguments on Social Policy, London: Tavistock Publications, 1987.

Hirst, P
"The concept of punishment" in Hirst, P (ed), *Law, Socialism and Democracy*, London: Allen & Unwin, 1986.

Hofrin, A
"The Sole Parents who Work and Save Taxpayers Money" *Sydney Morning Herald* 14/3/90 at 2.

Hogg, R
"Sentencing and Penal Politics: current developments in New South Wales" paper presented to a seminar on Sentencing at the Institute of Criminology, Sydney University Law School, 28 November 1988.

Holcroft, C
"Wages and Conditions of Prisoners in New South Wales Gaols — a Brief Review" (1988) 88/1093 *Public Information Bulletin*, Sydney: New South Wales Department of Corrective Services.

Holley, J
"The Two Family Economies of Industrialism: factory workers in Victorian Scotland" (1981) 6/1 *Journal of Family History* 57–69.

Horowitz, L
The New Sociology, New York: Oxford University Press, 1964.

Hutto, D,
from speech given on television program *The 7:30 Report*: "Prisons for Profit" 14 Feb 1989.

Hudson, B
"The Rising Use of Imprisonment: the impact of decarceration policies" (1984) *Critical Social Policy* No 2 (Winter) 46–58.

Hutson, S and Jenkins, R
Taking the Strain: Unemployment and the Transition to Adulthood, London: Open University Press, 1989.

Ignatieff, M

"State, Civil Society and Total Institutions: a critique of recent social histories of punishment" in Cohen, S and Scull, A (eds), *Social Control and the State*, Oxford: Basil Blackwell, 1983.

Irwin, J

The Felon, Englewood Cliffs: Prentice Hall, 1970.

Irwin, J

The Jail: Managing the Underclass in American Society, Berkeley: University of California Press, 1985.

James, N

"Emotional labour: skill and work in the social regulation of feelings" (1990) 37/1 *The Sociological Review* 15–42.

Jankovic, I

"Labour Market and Imprisonment" (1977) 8 *Crime and Social Justice* 17–33.

Johnson, R

Hard Time: Understanding and Reforming the Prison, New York: Brooks/Cole, 1986.

Jordan, A

"Lone Parent — and Wage-Earner? Employment Prospects of Sole-parent Pensioners", Discussion Paper No 31, Social Security Review Series, Woden: Department of Social Security, 1989.

Kamerman, S and Kahn, A

(eds), *Family Policy: Government and Families in Fourteen Countries*, New York: Columbia University Press, 1978.

Karier, C

"Testing for Order and Control in the Corporate Liberal State" in Dale, R, Esland, G and MacDonald, M (eds), *Schooling and Capitalism: a Sociological Reader*, Open University London: Routledge & Kegan Paul, 1976.

Kearns, D

"A Theory of Justice — and Love: Rawls on the family" ch 14 in Simms, M (ed), *Australian Women and the Political System*, Melbourne: Longman Cheshire, 1989.

Kelly-Gadol, J

"The Social Relation of the Sexes: methodological implications of women's history", ch2 in Harding, S, *Feminism and Methodology: Social Science Issues*, Milton Keynes: Open University Press, 1987.

Kemeney, J

"The Political Economy of Housing" in Wheelwright, E and Buckley, K (eds), *Essays in the Political Economy of Australian Capitalism*, vol 4, Sydney: Australian and New Zealand Book Co, 1980.

Kennedy, A

"Playing Tough" *Sydney Morning Herald* 22 Sept 1989 at 21.

Kennedy, A and Libesman, T
"Summary Offences, Australian Capital Territory (1988)" (1989) 2/37 *Aboriginal Law Bulletin* 2.

Kidson, B
"Controlling Prison crowding — the Victorian Approach: practical aspects of Victorian approach" in Vernon, J (ed), *Developments in Correctional Policy: More Prisons?* Seminar Proceedings No 22, Canberra: Australian Institute of Criminology, 1987.

Kingston, B
My Wife, Daughter and Poor Mary Ann, Melbourne: Nelson, 1975.

Kinsey, R, Lea, J and Young, J
Losing the Fight against Crime, London: Blackwell, 1986.

Kobasa, S
"Stress Responses and Personality" in Barnett, R, Biener, L and Baruch, G (eds), *Gender and Stress*, New York: The Free Press, 1987.

Krajick, K
"Punishment for Profit" (1984) 21/3 *Across the Board* 20–27.

Kruttschnitt, C
"Women, Crime and Dependency" (1982) 9/2 *Criminology* 495–513.

Lagan, B
"Electronics May Allow Prisoners to Live at Home" *Sydney Morning Herald* 15 Aug 1988 at 6.

Lagan, B
"Government Plans Home Detention for Prisoners" *Sydney Morning Herald* 11 Jan 1989 at 7.

Lambiotte, J
"Sex Role Differentiation in a Co-correctional Setting" in Smykla, J (ed), *CoEd Prison*, New York: Human Sciences Press, 1980, 221–247.

Land, H
"Who Cares for the Family?" (1978) 7/3 *Journal of Social Policy* 257–283.

Law Reform Commission
"Sentencing: Penalties", Discussion Paper 30, Sydney: Australian Law Reform Commission, 1987.

Lay, R
"Home Detention: grounded in the community" paper presented at the Australian Bicentennial International Congress on Corrective Services, Sydney, 24–28 January 1988.

Lea, J

"Discipline and capitalist development" in Fine, B et al (eds), *Capitalism and the Rule of Law: from Deviancy Theory to Marxism*, London: Hutchinson, 1979.

Levi-Strauss, C
Introduction to a Science of Mythology, London: Cape, 1964.
Lewis, J and Meredith, B
Daughters Who Care, London: Routledge, 1988.
Lloyd, G
"Selfhood, war and masculinity" in Pateman, C and Gross, E (eds), *Feminist Challenges: Social and Political Theory*, Sydney: Allen & Unwin, 1986.
Lobban, A
"Whose Gaols? Whose Goals?" in Vernon, J (ed), *Developments in Correctional Policy: More Prisons?* Seminar Proceedings No 22, Canberra: Australian Institute of Criminology, 1987.
Lockwood, D,
"Maintaining Manhood. Prison violence precipitated by aggressive sexual overtures" paper presented at the annual meetings of the Academy of Criminal Justice Sciences, New Orleans, March 1978.
Lockwood, D
Prison Sexual Violence, New York: Elsevier, 1980.
Lockwood, D
"The Contribution of Sexual Harassment to Stress and Coping in Confinement" in Parisi N (ed), *Coping with Imprisonment*, Beverley Hills: Sage, 1982.
Lynch, C
"Solidary Labour: its nature and marginalisation" (1989) 37/1 *The Sociological Review* 1–14.
Macartney, W
Walls Have Mouths, London: Victor Gollancz, 1936.
MacKinnon, C
"Feminism, Marxism, Method and the State" in Harding, S (ed), *Feminism and Methodology: Social Science Issues*, Milton Keynes: Indiana University Press and Open University, 1987.
McKnight, D
"Barristers Warned on New Sentencing Laws" *Sydney Morning Herald* 19 June 1989 at 3.
Malos, E
(ed), *The Politics of Housework*, London: Allison & Busby, 1980.
Marglin, S
"What do the bosses do?" in Gorz, A (ed), *The Division of Labour: the labour process and class struggle in modern capitalism*, Sussex: Harvester Press, 1976.

Martin, T
> The Martin Report: judicial inquiry into the New South Walees Department of Corrective Services prisoner classification procedures, Sydney: Australian Government Publishing Service, 1987.

Martinson, R
> "What Works? Questions and Answers about Prison Reform" (1974) 35 Public Interest 22–54.

Marx, K
> Capital (vol 1), Moscow: Progress, 1887 repr 1974.

Mathiesen, T
> The Defences of the Weak, London: Tavistock, 1962.

Matthews, J
> Good and Mad Women, Sydney: Allen and Unwin, 1984.

Mednick, A, Gabrielli, W and Hutchings, B
> "Genetic Influences in Criminal Convictions: Evidence from an Adoption Cohort" (1984) Science 25 May 1984 at 891–894.

Melossi, D and Pavarini, M
> The Prison and the Factory System: Origins of the Penitentiary System, London: Macmillan, 1981.

Melossi, D
> "Institutions of social control and capitalist organisation of work", ch6 in Fine, B et al (eds), Capitalism and the Rule of Law: from Deviancy Theory to Marxism, London: Hutchinson, 1979.

Merquior, J
> Foucault, London: Fontana, 1985.

Migliorini, P
> Report to the Human Rights Commissions's National Inquiry into Racist Violence, Sydney: Office of Multicultural Affairs, 1989.

Miller, W
> "Lower class culture as a generating milieu of gang delinquency" (1958) 14/3 Journal of Social Issues 5–19.

Milligan, V
> "The State and Housing: questions of social policy and social change" in Graycar, A (ed), Retreat from the Welfare State, Sydney: Allen & Unwin, 1983.

Minnery, J
> Crime Perception and Victimisation of Inner City Residents, Brisbane: Queensland Institute of Technology, 1986.

Moller Okin, S
> Women in Western Political Thought, London: Virago, 1980.

Moore, M
> "Longer Terms for Youths After New Laws" Sydney Morning Herald 10 Sept 1989 at 2.

Moore, M
> "Hard Cell" Sydney Morning Herald 16 Dec 1989.

Moore, M
"Government Decides Prisoners Don't Need Condoms" *Sydney Morning Herald* 8 May 1990 at 8.

Moore, M
"Government Blunders on Prison Sentences" *Sydney Morning Herald* 25 July 1990 at 3.

Morgan, F
"Parole and Recidivism in South Australia", ch12 in Biles, D (ed), *Current Australian Trends in Corrections*, Annandale: Federation Press, 1988.

Moroney, R M
The Family and the State: Considerations for Social Policy, London: Longman, 1976.

Morris, J
"New Jail Replaces 'Unfit' Quamby" *Canberra Times* 14 Apr 1990 at 1.

Morris, M and Patton, P
Michel Foucault: Power, Truth and Strategy, Sydney: Feral Publications, 1979.

Mott, J
"Social Research on Adult Prisons and Prisoners in England and Wales" (1984) *Research Bulletin No 18*, London: Home Office Research and Planning Unit, at 31–33.

Muir, A G
Report of the Inquiry into the Central Industrial Prison, Sydney: Government Printer, 1988.

Mukherjee, S
Crime Trends in Twentieth-Century Australia, Sydney: George Allen & Unwin, 1981.

Murton, T
"The Penal Colony: Relic or Reform" (1984) 12/1 *Free Inquiry in Creative Sociology* 20–24.

New South Wales Department of Corrective Services
Annual Reports for the years ending 1973 to 1988. Sydney: Government Printer.

Nacci, P and Kane, T
"Inmate Sexual Aggression: some evolving propositions, empirical findings and mitigating counter forces" (1984) 9/1–2 *Journal of Offender Counselling, Services and Rehabilitation* 1–20.

Naffine, N
Female Crime: the Construction of Women in Criminology, Sydney: Allen & Unwin, 1987.

283

Nassi, A and Abramowitz, S

"From Phrenology to Psychosurgery and Back Again: Biological Studies of Criminality" (1976) 46/4 *American Journal of Orthopsychiatry* 591–607.

National Conference on AIDS

Report on the 3rd National Conference on AIDS, report of conference held in Hobart, 4–6 August 1988, Canberra: Australia Government Publishing Service, 1988.

Nettler, G

Explaining Crime, New York: McGraw-Hill, 1974.

Nicholson, R

"Women's Function in New South Wales Male Prisons" in Hatty, S (ed), *Women in the Prison System*, Canberra: Australian Institute of Criminology, 1984.

Norton, W

"Developments in the Study of Power" in Norton, W (ed), *Concepts and Controversy in Organizational Behaviour*, California: Goodyear Publishing Co, 1976, at 437–450.

Oakley, A

Housewife, London: Allen Lane, 1974.

Oakley, A

The Sociology of Housework, London.: Martin Robertson, 1974.

Oakley, A

Subject Women, New York: Pantheon Books, 1981.

O'Malley, P

Law, Capitalism and Democracy, Sydney: Allen & Unwin, 1983.

Oxley, C

"The Structure of General Family Provision in Australia and Overseas: a Comparative Study", Social Security Review Background Discussion Paper No 17, Woden: Department of Social Security, 1987.

Oren, L

"The Welfare of Women in Labouring Families 1860–1950" (1974) 1/3–4 *Feminist Studies* 107–25.

Pahl, J

"Patterns of Money Management with Marriage" (1980) 9/3 *Journal of Social Policy* 313–335.

Parsons, T and Bales, R

Family Socialization and Interaction Processes, London: Routledge & Kegan Paul, 1955.

Parsons, T

"The Law and Social Control" in Evans, W (ed), *Law and Society*, Free Press of Glencoe, 1962 at 56–72.

Parsons, T

Societies: Evolutionary and Comparative Perspectives, New Jersey: Prentice Hall, 1966.

Pascal, G
   Social Policy: a Feminist Analysis, London: Tavistock, 1986.
Petersilia, J
   "Community Supervision: Trends and Critical Issues" (1985) 31/3 *Crime & Delinquency* 339–347
Petersilia, J
   "Exploring the Option of House Arrest" (1986) 50/2 *Federal Probation* 50–56.
Peterson, C
   "Siege at Parramatta Jail" *Direct Action* ll Mar 1987 at 803.
Peattie, L and Rein, M
   Women's Claims: a Study in Political Economy, Oxford: Oxford University Press, 1983.
Picciotto, S
   "The theory of the state, class struggle and the rule of law" in Fine, B et al (eds), *Capitalism and the Rule of Law: from Deviancy Theory to Marxism*, London: Hutchinson, 1979.
Pierson, C
   "New Theories of the State and Civil Society" (1984) 18/4 *Sociology* 562–571.
Porritt, D
   "Reasons For Escape: reported by recaptured escapees", Sydney: New South Wales Department of Correctives Services, Research and Statistics Division, 1987.
Poster, M
   Foucault, Marxism and History, London: Polity Press, 1984.
Potas, I
   "Statistics' Reporter" (1986) 7/3–4 *Australian Institute of Criminology Quarterly* 18–19.
Potas, I and Grant-Jones, D
   Australian Community Based Corrections Data (No 90) Canberra: Australian Institute of Criminology, 1986.
Quinney, R
   Class, State and Crime: on the theory and practice of criminal justice, New York: David McKay, 1977.
Quinney, R
   "Crime and the Development of Capitalism" in Quinney, R (ed), *Capitalist Society: Readings for a Critical Sociology*, Homewood, Illinois: Dorsey, 1979.
Raymond, J
   "Bringing Up Children Alone: Policies for Sole Parents", Social Security Review Issues Paper No 3, Woden: Department of Social Security, 1987.
Rice, S
   "Police May Use Banned Ammunition" *National Times* 3 Sept 1982 at 4.

Rimmer, L
"The economics of work and caring" ch 7 in Finch, J and Groves, D (eds), *A Labour of Love: Women, Work and Caring*, London: Routledge & Kegan Paul, 1983.

Rinaldi, F
Australian Prisons, Canberra: F and M Publishers, 1977.

Roberts, G
"The Prison Where Privilege Beats Punishment" *Sydney Morning Herald* 16 Apr 1990 at 3.

Robertson, M
"Expanding the Scope of Community Corrections to Meet Prison Population Pressures" in *Diversionary Programmes Workshop: Proceedings* 10–11 September, Alice Springs. Darwin: Northern Territory Department of Health and Community Services, 1986.

Robinson, P
The Hatch and Brood of Time: a study of the first generation of native born white Australians 1788–1828, Melbourne: Oxford University Press, 1985.

Robinson, P
Women of Botany Bay: a reinterpretation of the role of women in the origins of Australian society, Sydney: Macquarie Library, 1988.

Rosalda, M
"Women, Culture and Society: a Theoretical Overview" in Lamphere, L and Rosalda, M (eds), *Women, Culture and Society*, Stanford, California: Stanford University Press, 1974.

Rothman, D
The Discovery of the Asylum: social order and disorder in the New Republic, Boston: Little, Brown and Co, 1971.

Rowbotham, S
Hidden from History, London: Pluto Press, 1973.

Ruback, B
"The Sexually Integrated Prison" in Smykla, J (ed), *CoEd Prison*, New York: Human Sciences Press, 1980 at 33–60.

Ruddick, S
"Maternal Thinking" (1980) 6/2 *Feminist Studies* 343–367.

Rusche, G and Kirchheimer, O
Punishment and Social Structure, New York: Columbia University Free Press, 1939.

Sandery, A
"Prison Officers and Their World, by Kelsey Kauffman" (1989) 22/4 *Australian and New Zealand Journal of Criminology* 279–281 (book review).

Saunders, P and Whiteford, P
"Pricing the poverty pledge" *Australian Society* Sept 1987 at 22–24.

Sawer, M
> (ed), *Australia and the New Right*, Sydney: George Allen & Unwin, 1982.

Schmidt, A
> "Electronic Monitoring: Who uses it? How much does it cost? Does it work?" (1987) 49 *Corrections Today* 28–34.

Schocet, G
> *Patriarchialism and Political Thought*, Oxford: Basil Blackwell, 1975.

Scull, A
> *Decarceration: Community Treatment and the Deviant — a Radical View*, Englewood Cliffs, New Jersey: Prentice Hall, 1977.

Scull, A
> "Community Corrections: panacea, progress, or pretense?" in Garland, D and Young, P (eds), *The Power to Punish*, London: Heinemann, 1983 at 146–65.

Sinclair, P
> "Alternatives to Gaol: solving some problems, creating some new ones" (1974) 15/2 *Health in New South Wales*.

Sinclair, W
> "Women at work in Melbourne and Adelaide since 1871" (1981) *Economic Record* (December) 344–353

Smart, B
> *Michel Foucault*, London: Tavistock, 1985.

Smith, D
> "Women's Perspective as a Radical Critique of Sociology" in Harding, S (ed), *Feminism and Methodology: Social Science Issues*, Milton Keynes: Indiana University Press and Open University, 1987.

Smykla, J
> *CoEd Prison*, New York: Human Sciences Press, 1980.

Spitzer, S
> "The Rationalization of Crime Control in Capitalist Society" (1979)3 *Contemporary Crises* 187–206.

Spitzer, S and Scull, A
> "Social Control in Historical Perspective: from private to public responses to crime" in Greenberg, D (ed), *Corrections and Punishment*, Beverly Hills: Sage, 1977.

Stacey, M and Price, M
> *Women, Power, and Politics*, London: Tavistock, 1979.

Stacey, M
> *Methods of Social Research*, Oxford: Pergamon, 1969.

Stapleton, J
> "AIDS tests stall, but life goes on in 'Death Row'" *Sydney Morning Herald* 4 Feb 1989 at 6–7.

Stone, J
"Brazen Hussies and God's Police" (1982) 89/1 *Hecate* 6–23.

Stone, L
The Family, Sex and Marriage in England, 1500–1800, Harmonsworth: Penguin, 1979.

Stone, M
"The housing crisis, mortgage lending and the class struggle" (1975) 7 *Antipode* 22–37.

Stoneman, N
"Probation and Parole Australian Capital Territory, New South Wales More Problems than Prospects" in Potas, I (ed), *Sentencing in Australia*, Australian Institute of Criminology Seminar Proceedings No 13, Canberra: Australian Institute of Criminology, 1986.

Sturgess, G
"Drug Squad Terror Tactics Cause Alarm" *Bulletin* 29 Jul 1980 at 28–29.

Summers, A
Damned Whores and God's Police, Ringwood: Penguin, 1985.

Sutherland, E and Cressey, D
Criminology, Lippincott: Philadelphia, 1966.

Swain, M
"Mrs Hughes and the deserving poor" in Lake, M and Kelly, F (eds), *Double Time*, Victoria: Penguin, 1985.

Swinnen, E
"Sexuality and Imprisonment: forced celibacy in prison" ("Sexualiteit in de Gevangenis. Het celibaatsregime in de gevangenis") (1983) 28/1 *Tijdschrift-voor-Sociale-Wetenschappen* 36–57.

Taperell, K, Fox, C and Roberts, M
Sexism in the Public Service: The Employment of Women in the Australian Government Administration, Sydney: Australian Government Publications, 1975.

Terry, P
"Official Neglect 'Led to Black's Suicide'" *The Australian* 2 Jan 1990 at 4.

Thatcher, M
"Facing the Challenge" in Ungerson, C (ed), *Women and Social Policy*, London: MacMillan, 1981 at 213–217.

Tilly, L and Scott, J
Women, Work and Family, New York: Holt, Rinehart & Winston, 1978.

Turnbull, J Porritt, D and Coney, G
Performance on Work Release and After, Research Publication No 4 (August), Sydney: Research & Statistics Division, New South Wales Department of Corrective Services, 1982.

Ungerson, C
"Why do women care?" ch2 in Finch J and Groves, D (eds), *A Labour of Love: Women, Work and Caring*, London: Routledge & Kegan Paul, 1983.

Ungerson, C
(ed), *Women and Social Policy*, London: MacMillan, 1985.

Ungerson, C
Policy is Personal: Sex, Gender and Informal Care, London: Tavistock Publications, 1987.

Vernon, J
(ed), *Developments in Correctional Policy: More Prisons?* Seminar Proceedings No 22, Canberra: Australian Institute of Criminology, 1987.

Vinson, T
Wilful Obstruction, Sydney: Methuen, 1982.

Vodanovich, I
"The Future of Parole — A West Australian Overview" paper presented at The Australian Bicentennial International Congress on Corrective Services, Sydney: 24–28 January 1988.

Waldgrave, K
"Kevin Swann, with daughter Hayley, tests an electronic bracelet and receiver" captioned photograph (1988) for Jones, B, "The Electronic Ball and Chain" *The Mail on Sunday* (London) 19 June 1989 at 15.

Walker, J
Adults under Detention and Supervision Orders, Canberra: Australian Institute of Criminology, 1988.

Watson, S
Accommodating Inequality: Gender and Housing, Sydney: Allen & Unwin, 1988.

Watson, E and Mears, E
Women in the Middle: care-givers with a double burden of care, School of Community and Welfare Studies, MacArthur Institute of Higher Education, Campbelltown, and the Office of the Status of Women, Canberra, 1988.

Watson, E and Mears, E
"Political and Moral dilemmas in Research Related to Women and Social Policy" paper presented at the Social Research and Policy Conference, University of Queensland, August 1988.

Wearing, B
The Ideology of Motherhood, Sydney: George Allen & Unwin, 1984.

Weatherburn, D
"Reducing the New South Wales Prison Population: sentencing reform and early release" (1986) 10 *Criminal Law Journal* 121–138.

Willett, T

"Anomie, Ritualism and Inertia among Custodial Staff in Canadian Prisons: some implications for research and policy" in Gandy, J, Robertson, A and Sinclair, S (eds), *Improving Social Intervention*, London: Croom Helm, 1983.

Williams, F

Social Policy: a Critical Introduction, Cambridge: Polity Press, 1989.

Williams, G

"Shake up to Gaol Education Programmes" *Sydney Morning Herald* 19 July 1989 at 7.

Wilson, E

Women and the Welfare State, London: Tavistock Press, 1977.

Wilson, J Q and Herrnstein, R

Crime and Human Nature, New York: Simon & Schuster, 1988.

Windschuttle, E

"Women and the origins of Colonial Philanthropy" in Kennedy, R (ed), *Australian Welfare History*, Sydney: MacMillan, 1982.

Worral, J

"ACA Study Team Visits Unique Mexican Penal Colony" (1982) 44/6 *Corrections Today* 73–75.

Wortley, R

"Mad, Bad or Normal: perceptions of prisoners by prisoners, prison officers, and prison specialist staff" (1987) 1/1 *Journal of Studies in Justice* 11–16.

Wright, F

"Single Carers: employment, housework and caring", ch5 in Finch, J and Groves, D (eds), *A Labour of Love: Women, Work and Caring*, London: Routledge & Kegan Paul, 1983.

Yeatman, A

"Despotism and Civil Society: the limits of patriarchal citizenship" paper presented to the XIIth world congress, International Political Science Association, Rio de Janeiro, Brazil: 9–14 August 1982.

Yeatman, A

"Women, domestic life and sociology" in Pateman, C and Grosz, E (eds), *Feminist Challenges: Social and Political Theory*, Sydney: Allen & Unwin, 1986.

Yeatman, A

"Feminism, Postmodernism and Sociology: versions II & I " unpublished paper, 1990, ver 1 in: Nicholson, L (ed), *Feminism/Post-modernism*, New York: Routledge, 1990.

Zdenkowski, G

Introduction, in Anderson, T, *Inside Outlaws*, Sydney: Redfern Legal Centre Publishing, 1989.

Zdenkowski, G
> "Problems in Yabsley's Plan to Dangle Prisoners at End of Line" *Sydney Morning Herald* 10 Feb 1989 at 11.

Zdenkowski, G
> "The Private Life of the Prisoner" *Sydney Morning Herald* 22 Dec 1988 at 5.

Zdenkowski, G and Brown D
> *The Prison Struggle*, Melbourne: Penguin, 1982.

Zedlewski, E
> "Making Confinement Decisions" National Institute of Justice: Research in Brief, Washington: US Department of Justice, July 1987.

Index

INDEX

293